Talk in Action

Language in Society

GENERAL EDITOR
Peter Trudgill, Chair of English Linguistics,
University of Fribourg

ADVISORY EDITORS
J. K. Chambers, Professor of Linguistics,
University of Toronto

Ralph Fasold, Professor of Linguistics,
Georgetown University

William Labov, Professor of Linguistics,
University of Pennsylvania

Lesley Milroy, Professor of Linguistics,
University of Michigan, Ann Arbor

1 Language and Social Psychology, *edited by
Howard Giles and Robert N. St Clair*

2 Language and Social Networks (2nd edn.),
Lesley Milroy

3 The Ethnography of Communication
(3rd edn.), *Muriel Saville-Troike*

4 Discourse Analysis, *Michael Stubbs*

5 The Sociolinguistics of Society:
Introduction to Sociolinguistics, Vol. I,
Ralph Fasold

6 The Sociolinguistics of Language:
Introduction to Sociolinguistics, Vol. II,
Ralph Fasold

7 The Language of Children and Adolescents:
Suzanne Romaine

8 Language, the Sexes and Society,
Philip M. Smith

9 The Language of Advertising, *Torben
Vestergaard and Kim Schrøder*

10 Dialects in Contact, *Peter Trudgill*

11 Pidgin and Creole Linguistics, *Peter
Mühlhäusler*

12 Observing and Analysing Natural Language:
A Critical Account of Sociolinguistic
Method, *Lesley Milroy*

13 Bilingualism (2nd edn.), *Suzanne Romaine*

14 Sociolinguistics and Second Language
Acquisition, *Dennis R. Preston*

15 Pronouns and People, *Peter Mühlhäusler
and Rom Harré*

16 Politically Speaking, *John Wilson*

17 The Language of the News Media,
Allan Bell

18 Language, Society and the Elderly,
*Nikolas Coupland, Justine Coupland,
and Howard Giles*

19 Linguistic Variation and Change, *James
Milroy*

20 Principles of Linguistic Change, Vol. I:
Internal Factors, *William Labov*

21 Intercultural Communication (2nd edn.),
Ron Scollon and Suzanne Wong Scollon

22 Sociolinguistic Theory (2nd edn.),
J. K. Chambers

23 Text and Corpus Analysis, *Michael Stubbs*

24 Anthropological Linguistics, *William Foley*

25 American English: Dialects and Variation
(2nd edn.), *Walt Wolfram and Natalie
Schilling-Estes*

26 African American Vernacular English,
John R. Rickford

27 Linguistic Variation as Social Practice,
Penelope Eckert

28 The English History of African American
English, *edited by Shana Poplack*

29 Principles of Linguistic Change, Vol. II:
Social Factors, *William Labov*

30 African American English in the Diaspora,
Shana Poplack and Sali Tagliamonte

31 The Development of African American
English, *Walt Wolfram and Erik R. Thomas*

32 Forensic Linguistics, *John Gibbons*

33 An Introduction to Contact Linguistics,
Donald Winford

34 Sociolinguistics: Method and Interpretation,
Lesley Milroy and Matthew Gordon

35 Text, Context, Pretext: Critical Issues in
Discourse Analysis, *H. G. Widdowson*

36 Clinical Sociolinguistics, *Martin J. Ball*

37 Conversation Analysis: An Introduction,
Jack Sidnell

38 Talk in Action: Interactions, Identities,
and Institutions, *John Heritage and
Steven Clayman*

Talk in Action

INTERACTIONS, IDENTITIES, AND INSTITUTIONS

John Heritage
and
Steven Clayman

WILEY-BLACKWELL

A John Wiley & Sons, Ltd., Publication

This edition first published 2010
© 2010 John Heritage and Steven Clayman

Blackwell Publishing was acquired by John Wiley & Sons in February 2007.
Blackwell's publishing program has been merged with Wiley's global Scientific,
Technical, and Medical business to form Wiley-Blackwell.

Registered Office
John Wiley & Sons Ltd, The Atrium, Southern Gate, Chichester,
West Sussex, PO19 8SQ, United Kingdom

Editorial Offices
350 Main Street, Malden, MA 02148-5020, USA
9600 Garsington Road, Oxford, OX4 2DQ, UK
The Atrium, Southern Gate, Chichester, West Sussex, PO19 8SQ, UK

For details of our global editorial offices, for customer services, and for information
about how to apply for permission to reuse the copyright material in this book
please see our website at www.wiley.com / wiley-blackwell.

Library of Congress Cataloging-in-Publication Data

Heritage, John.
Talk in action : interactions, identities, and institutions /
John Heritage and Steven Clayman.
p. cm. — (Language in society)
Includes bibliographical references and index.
ISBN 978-1-4051-8550-9 (hardcover : alk. paper) —
ISBN 978-1-4051-8549-3 (pbk. : alk. paper)
1. Conversation analysis.   2. Dialogue analysis.
I. Clayman, Steven.   II. Title.
P95.45.H47 2010
302.3′46—dc22
2009033119

A catalogue record for this book is available from the British Library.

Set in 10/12pt Erhardt by Graphicraft Limited, Hong Kong
Printed and bound in Malaysia by Vivar Printing Sdn Bhd

1   2010

Contents

1   Introduction   1

Part 1   Conversation Analysis and Social Institutions   5

2   Conversation Analysis: Some Theoretical Background   7
3   Talking Social Institutions into Being   20
4   Dimensions of Institutional Talk   34

Part 2   Calls for Emergency Service   51

5   Emergency Calls as Institutional Talk   53
6   Gatekeeping and Entitlement to Emergency Service   69
7   Emergency Calls under Stress   87

Part 3   Doctor–Patient Interaction   101

8   Patients' Presentations of Medical Issues: The Doctor's Problem   103
9   Patients' Presentations of Medical Issues: The Patient's Problem   119
10 History Taking in Medicine: Questions and Answers   135
11 Diagnosis and Treatment: Medical Authority and Its Limits   154

Part 4   Trials, Juries, and Dispute Resolution   171

12 Trial Examinations   173
13 Jury Deliberations   186
14 Informal Modes of Dispute Resolution   200

Part 5   News and Political Communication   213

15   News Interview Turn Taking   215
16   Question Design in the News Interview and Beyond   227
17   Answers and Evasions   245
18   Interaction en Masse: Audiences and Speeches   263

19   Conclusion   280

Transcript Symbols   283
References   288
Index of Names   304
Index of Subjects   309

Acknowledgments

The contents of this book have been repeatedly tested in the laboratory of our UCLA class on "Talk and Social Institutions". We have benefited immensely from the experience of presenting the material in many forms and incarnations over the years. We are grateful to the undergraduate and graduate students in our course, and to our conscientious teaching assistants, who were a critical audience for the material and who provided us with clues and advice on how to improve it.

Paul Drew and two external reviewers read through the entire manuscript, and Doug Maynard and Don Zimmerman gave a close read to individual chapters. We are deeply grateful for their efforts and for the critical feedback they provided. Danielle Descoteaux, Julia Kirk, and Glynis Baguley at Wiley-Blackwell gave much valuable editorial guidance and support, together with essential jolts of enthusiasm to galvanize our efforts when we flagged. We thank them for this, and for making the production of this book such a happy experience.

This book is dedicated to our students.

1

Introduction

This book is about the workings of language and interaction in the everyday life of institutions. It arose from our long-standing conviction that, while it was all but ignored in conventional analyses of occupational worlds, professions, and organizational environments, the study of interaction had much to offer to the analysis of these domains of social life. Accordingly, in the early 1990s we decided to start a seminar that applied the emerging findings of conversation analysis to occupational environments of various kinds. At that time, studies of this sort were few and far between, and concentrated in a limited range of domains, notably courtroom interaction, 911 emergency, and mass communication. Our seminar was correspondingly small, attracting perhaps a dozen intrepid participants.

Since that time, the field has expanded dramatically. Conversation analytic (CA) research, once all but absent from the doctor's office, has now become an established presence in the field of medicine, where it is used to examine everything from genetic counseling to surgery. It has also colonized the world of business, from business meetings and decision making to, perhaps especially, the examination of technology-in-use. In education, CA has advanced from classroom lessons to embrace more far-flung enterprises such as one-on-one pedagogy, disciplinary hearings, and parent–teacher conferences. In the socio-legal area, a focus on formal trials has given way to a more differentiated range of studies encompassing the more informal legal proceedings such as mediation, arbitration, and plea bargaining. The study of 911 emergency has broadened to embrace an ever-widening array of help lines and support services. Mass media research has exhibited a similar diversification, with the initial news interview research joined by studies of campaign debates, radio call-in shows, and talk shows of various stripes. This growth and diversification is not confined to the English-speaking world; it is a world-wide phenomenon embracing many languages and diverse cultures.

In the meantime, our small seminar expanded to a large-scale lecture course that has been taken by students who now number in the thousands. Naturally there are limits to what can be covered within the confines of a 10-week course and, rather than spread ourselves too thinly, we chose to cover a smaller range of environments in a sustained way. Accordingly, while our teaching registered the many advances of an evolving field, three main criteria determined our selection of topics. We focused on domains of interaction that, first, have intrinsic interest as specimens of the everyday world; second, have significant outcomes for individuals and the society of which they are a part; and third, have an exemplary status within a continuum of social contexts: private versus public, formal versus informal, and professional versus bureaucratic. This book is based on those choices.

It is important to emphasize that our aim is not to draw a dividing line between ordinary conversation and interaction that is professional, task-focused, or "institutional". This is because we do not believe that a clear dividing line can be drawn. Most important in this regard is the fact that practices of interaction in the everyday world are unavoidably drawn on in every kind of institutional interaction. For example, a witness in court may be confined by a variety of rules of legal process, but she will still deploy her ordinary conversational competences in constructing the details of her testimony. By the same token, the kind of rhetorical formulations used to persuade others in political speeches are also to be found in argumentative conversations over the dinner table and at the office water cooler. For this reason, we do not propose any hard-and-fast distinction between "ordinary conversation" on the one hand and "institutional talk" on the other. Rather, we investigate the ways in which ordinary conversational practices are brought to bear in task-focused interactions. Because the tasks of these interactions are recurrent, so too are the specific practices that they frequently engage. For this reason, we can fairly readily observe systematic relationships between practices of interaction on the one hand, and institutional tasks and identities on the other. It is the intersections between interactional practices, social identities, and institutional tasks that lie at the heart of this book.

These intersections take many forms. To prepare for their analysis, we begin with a theoretical and methodological overview of conversation analysis and its application to occupations and institutions. These chapters (2–4) provide an account of the theoretical origins of CA in the work of Erving Goffman and Harold Garfinkel, and explicate the methodology of CA and how it can be applied to institutional settings. We then offer an overview of different levels of analysis of institutional interaction that will be in evidence throughout the book.

The body of the book centers on four main institutional domains: calls to 911 emergency (chapters 5–7), doctor–patient interaction (chapters 8–11), courtroom trials (chapters 12–14), and mass communication (chapters 15–18). The pioneering work of Don Zimmerman and his colleagues established 911 calls as one of the first applications of CA to an institutional task. The domain is a useful starting point both because of its intrinsic interest and also because the overwhelming task focus of these calls starkly exemplifies the extent to which a task's organizational imperatives can shape multiple aspects of interactional organization and practice. 911 calls also highlight the extent to which the personal circumstances and emotional states of participants are enmeshed with, and become adjusted to, the demands of the business at hand.

In our second domain, doctor–patient interaction, we focus on primary care, in part because it is the largest part of the health care system, and also because of its clear exemplification of professionalism in action. Here we focus on the twin themes of professional authority and personal accountability in medical decision making by both doctors and their patients, and also on ways in which authority and accountability are challenged and contested.

For the third domain, we focus on one of the earliest applications of conversation analysis to a social institution: formal trial proceedings. In contrast to our first two domains, which essentially involve private interactions, trials are public events and are regulated by public and highly codified rules of conduct. Here we address the bookends of the trial process: examination of witnesses, and jury deliberations. In both areas, our analysis concerns how legal codes, rules of procedure, and the "facts of the case" are selectively deployed and creatively articulated in the give and take of often contentious interactional processes. We also examine processes of informal dispute resolution, which have assumed an ever-increasing role in the legal system.

Our final domain, mass communication in the form of broadcast news interviews, news conferences, and political speeches, is also highly public in character. Our primary focus is on how the competing journalistic norms of objectivity and adversarialness are reconciled and implemented in practice, and how interviewees strive to stay on message in an environment of interrogation. We also consider political speeches, which are of course a context in which it is relatively easy to stay on message. However, in this form of interaction en masse, public speakers face the task of keeping audiences attentive and mobilizing their support. We examine the rhetorical resources that speakers deploy to this end, and show some ways in which these resources can, outlasting the speech itself, pass from utterance to history.

In our class at UCLA, we found that we were not only examining particular institutional domains, but also introducing our students to the methodology of conversation analysis. Studying institutions, we found, was a motivation for our students to learn the techniques of interactional analysis necessary to get at the workings of human organizations. Our class necessarily had a kind of double curriculum, which is carried over into this book. Accordingly, our aim is to be exemplary rather than encyclopedic in the hope that we will attract interest in both the institutions and the interactional practices through which they are talked into being.

I

Conversation Analysis and Social Institutions

2

Conversation Analysis: Some Theoretical Background

Social interaction is the very bedrock of social life. It is the primary medium through which cultures are transmitted, relationships are sustained, identities are affirmed, and social structures of all sorts are reproduced (Goodwin & Heritage 1990). It is, in Schegloff's (1996) phrase, "the primordial site of human sociality". In almost every imaginable particular, our ability to grasp the nature of the social world and to participate in it is dependant on our capacities and resourcefulness as social interactants (Enfield & Levinson 2006).

In the past, as Goffman (1964) noted, social scientists have had little to say about how interaction works, treating it as an inscrutable black box that is beyond coherent description. In particular, it was believed that individual episodes of interaction are fundamentally disorderly, and that attempts at their systematic analysis would only be a waste of time (Sacks 1984a). Lacking systematic knowledge of how interaction works, social scientists had even less to say about the relationship between interactions and institutions. Yet it is through interaction that institutions are brought to life and made actionable in the everyday world.

Consider the following segment of talk from a medical consultation. The patient is a divorced, middle-aged woman who lives alone and works a sixty-hour week in a restaurant she owns and manages. At line 4, the doctor asks a lifestyle question. Though compactly phrased, the question clearly raises the issue of her alcohol consumption. She responds with an apparently bona fide effort to estimate it as "moderate" (line 6). Pressed further, she elaborates this in a turn that conveys, without directly stating, that her drinking is social and infrequent (lines 9–10). The doctor is not satisfied with this, and pursues a more objective numerically specified estimate (lines 11–12). After a brief struggle, a compromise quasi-numerical estimate is reached (lines 15–16) and accepted (line 18):

```
(1)
 1  Doc:    tch D'you smoke?, h
 2  Pat:    Hm mm.
 3          (5.0)
 4  Doc:    Alcohol use?
 5          (1.0)
 6  Pat:    Hm:: moderate I'd say.
 7          (0.2)
 8  Doc:    Can you define that, hhhehh ((laughing outbreath))
```

```
 9 Pat:    Uh huh hah .hh I don't get off my- (0.2) outta
10          thuh restaurant very much but [(awh:)
11 Doc:                                    [Daily do you use
12          alcohol or:=h
13 Pat:    Pardon?
14 Doc:    Daily? or[:
15 Pat:             [Oh: huh uh. .hh No: uhm (3.0) probably::
16          I usually go out like once uh week.
17          (1.0)
18 Doc:    °Kay.°
```

Consider some questions which are absolutely central to understanding this sequence of interaction. What considerations led the patient to evaluate her drinking as "moderate" (line 6) and, when challenged, to frame her response in terms of not "going out" very much? Why did the doctor ask "Daily do you use alcohol or:=h" with the "Daily" at the beginning of the sentence and the "or:" at the end of it? Why did the patient say "Pardon?" at line 13 when she plainly heard the question? Why, after all this, did the patient still end up talking about how much she "goes out" (lines 15–16)? And how are all these details about the actions and reasoning of the participants connected to the roles of doctor and patient?

If you had been presented with this segment in 1960, you would have found few systematic resources with which to answer these questions, and none that could offer any significant clues as to the details of the actions the participants are engaged in. The dominant systems of analysis involved standard categories (e.g., "shows solidarity", "gives suggestion", "asks for opinion", "shows tension" [Bales 1950]) which were simply imposed on the data even though, as in our example, they frequently had little or nothing to do with what participants were actually doing in their interactions.

The advent of conversation analysis in the 1960s changed all this. Today, the details of this segment can be specified with a high degree of resolution. This is possible because we now recognize not only that there is a "world" of everyday life that is available to systematic study, but also that it is orderly to a degree that was hitherto unimaginable. Our aim in this chapter is to introduce you to the basic ideas that underlie this revolution in thought.

Two great American social scientists – Erving Goffman and Harold Garfinkel – laid the groundwork for this conversation analytic revolution. Both of them dissented from the view that the details of everyday life are an inherently disorderly and unresearchable mess, so we begin with them.

Origins: Erving Goffman

Erving Goffman's fundamental achievement, developed over a lifetime of writing (see Goffman 1955, 1983), was to establish that social interaction is a form of social organization in its own right. Interaction, he argued, embodies a distinct moral and institutional order that can be treated like other social institutions, such as the family, education, or religion. Goffman came to term this the *interaction order* (Goffman 1983) and, he argued, it comprises a complex set of interactional rights and obligations which are linked both to "face" (a person's immediate claims about "who s/he is" in an interaction), more enduring features of personal identity, and also to large-scale macro social institutions. Goffman further argued that the institutional order of interaction has a particular social significance. It underlies the operations of all the other institutions in society, and it mediates the business that they transact. The work of political, economic, educational, legal and other social institutions is in large part discharged by means of the practices comprising the interaction order.

Goffman's central insight was that the institution of interaction has an underlying structural organization: what he called a "syntax". In the Introduction to *Interaction Ritual* (Goffman 1967) he observes: "I assume that the proper study of interaction is not the individual and his psychology, but rather the syntactical relations among the acts of different persons mutually present to one another" (Goffman 1967: 2). The participants use this syntax – which provides for the sequential ordering of actions (see Goffman 1971: 171–202) – to analyze one another's conduct. By looking at the choices people make within this structure, persons can arrive at judgments about personal motivations and identities. The syntax of interaction, Goffman argued, is a core part of the moral order. It is the place where face, self, and identity are expressed, and where they are also ratified or undermined by the conduct of others.

Thus, in contrast to his predecessors, Goffman viewed the normative organization of practices and processes that makes up the interaction order as a domain to be studied in its own right. He repeatedly rejected the view that interaction is a colorless, odorless, frictionless substrate through which social processes operate (Goffman 1964, Kendon 1987), and asserted instead that the interaction order is an autonomous site of authentic social processes that inform social action and interaction. With this framework, Goffman carved out a new conceptual space, and with it a new territory for systematic analysis: the interaction order as a social institution.

Goffman's inspired conceptualization, while influential, also presented limitations. He was interested in how face and identity are associated with action, and how moral inferences about them can *motivate* interactional conduct. However, he was much less interested in, and did not pursue, a second equally fundamental issue concerning how participants *understand* one another in interaction. How does this process of understanding work? And, just as important, how do persons know that they share the *same* understandings within interaction? Without this crucial component it is not obvious how the interaction order could operate as a working institution. Largely for this reason, Goffman's approach – brilliant though it was – failed to stabilize as a systematic approach to the analysis of interaction. There is no "Goffman School" of interaction analysis, and his seminal insights might have been stillborn but for their intersection with a quite separate emergence of interest in cognition and meaning in the social sciences during the 1960s.

Origins: Harold Garfinkel

This emergence can be traced, above all, to the extraordinary researches of Harold Garfinkel (1967). Garfinkel argued that all human action and human institutions, including Goffman's interaction order, rest on the primordial fact that persons are able to *make shared sense* of their circumstances and act on the shared sense they make. He further argued that coordinated and meaningful actions, regardless of whether they involve cooperation or conflict, are impossible without these shared understandings. Garfinkel wanted to know how this is possible, and he hit on the notion that persons use *shared methods of practical reasoning* (or "ethno-methods") to build this shared sense of their common context of action, and of the social world more generally. Thus any analysis of social action is incomplete without an analysis of how social actors use shared commonsense knowledge and shared methods of reasoning in the conduct of their joint affairs. It is these shared methods that enable our doctor and patient to build and navigate their sequence of interaction knowing, for example, that issues are not quite resolved until the doctor says "Kay" at line 18. Thus Garfinkel insisted that shared sense-making is a primordial feature of the social world. Nothing can happen in the social world without it. His project – ethnomethodology – was to study how socially shared methods of practical reasoning are used to analyze, understand, and act in the commonsense world of everyday life.

To demonstrate the significance of these ideas, Garfinkel used a series of quasi-experimental procedures (known as "breaching experiments") to create basic departures from taken-for-granted social expectations. For example, using the game of tic-tac-toe (British "noughts and crosses"), Garfinkel (1963) had experimenters invite the subjects to make the first move, where-upon the experimenters erased the subject's mark, moved it to a new cell, and then made their own mark while acting as if nothing out of the ordinary was happening. These exper-imental departures engendered deep confusion and moral indignation in their subjects but, Garfinkel found, the deepest anger and indignation was engendered in those who *could not make sense of the situation*. From this Garfinkel concluded that the rules of tic-tac-toe are not only regulative rules that define how one should act within the game, they are also con-stitutive rules: resources for *making sense* of moves, and of the state of play more generally. It is the rules of tic-tac-toe that allow the one playing "O", who has the next turn to play, to see that the situation in figure 2.1 is hopeless. Similarly, they can be used by the "O" player to see (figure 2.2) that "X" has two in a row and is threatening to win. They can also be used to see that if you miss seeing that "two in a row" situation, you're being inattentive. And other understandings can be laminated onto this one. If the "O" player in figure 2.2 is an adult, and the "X" player is a child, missing "two in a row" by putting the next "O" in other than the bottom right square can leave the adult open to the accusation that "it's no fun because you're letting me win."

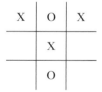

Figure 2.1

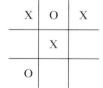

Figure 2.2

From quasi-experimental procedures like this, Garfinkel concluded that shared methods of practical reasoning inform both the *production* of action, and the *recognition* of action and its meanings. In fact, he argued, we produce action methodically to be recognized for what it is, and we recognize action because it is produced methodically in this way. As he put it: "the activities whereby members produce and manage the settings of organized everyday affairs are identical with members' procedures for making these settings account-able" (Garfinkel 1967: 1). In other words, the *same methods* organize both action and the understanding of action. We can unpack this complex sentence with the rules of tic-tac-toe. These rules are resources for analyzing and understanding what has happened in the game so far, and for deciding what to do next. Looking backwards in time they are resources for making sense of actions, and looking forwards in time they are resources for methodically producing next actions:

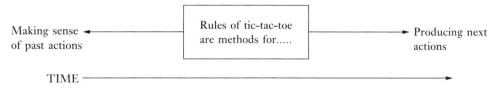

Figure 2.3   Rules of tic-tac-toe as methods

Most of social life is a great deal more complicated than games. And Garfinkel used other breaching experiments to demonstrate practical reasoning in these more complicated social situations. These experiments clearly indicated that social actions, shared understandings, and ultimately social institutions are underpinned by a complex body of presuppositions, tacit assumptions, and methods of inference – in short, a body of methods or methodology. This body of methods informs the production of culturally meaningful actions and objects, and it also is equally and profoundly involved in our recognition and understanding of them.

Methods of commonsense reasoning are fundamentally adapted to the recognition and understanding of events-in-context. Garfinkel epitomized the operation of these methods as "the documentary method of interpretation". Social interaction is a prime site for its implementation. Garfinkel argued that it involves assembling linkages between an action and its physical and social context by using a wide array of presuppositions and inferential procedures. This process involves the property of reflexivity: an action will be understood by reference to the context in which it occurs, but it will also, in turn, initiate changes in a person's understanding of the context itself. For example, a second person's greeting will be understood in context as a "return", but its occurrence will also transform the context from one in which engagement is unilaterally proposed to one in which it is mutually ratified (Heritage 1984b). When it is employed in a temporally dynamic context, which is a characteristic of all situations of human interaction, the documentary method forms the basis for temporally updated shared understandings of actions and events among the participants.

The upshot of Garfinkel's researches was that every aspect of shared understandings of the social world depends on a multiplicity of tacit *methods of reasoning*. These methods are socially shared and they are ceaselessly used during every waking moment to recognize ordinary social objects and events. These methods also function as a resource for the production of actions. Actors tacitly draw on them so as to produce actions that will be *accountable* – that is, recognizable and describable – in context. Thus, shared methods of reasoning are publicly available on the surface of social life because the results of their application are inscribed in social action and interaction.

Conversation Analysis

Conversation analysis (CA) was developed by Harvey Sacks (1992) in association with Emanuel Schegloff and Gail Jefferson, and emerged in the late 1960s. Sacks and Schegloff were students of Goffman at the University of California at Berkeley and were also in close touch with Harold Garfinkel at UCLA (Schegloff 1992a). The program of research they developed together stood at the intersection of the perspectives developed by Goffman and Garfinkel. From Goffman, they took the notion that talk-in-interaction is a fundamental social domain that can be studied as an institutional entity in its own right. From Garfinkel came the notion that shared methods of reasoning are implicated in the production and recognition of contributions to interaction, and that these contributions advance the situation of interaction in an incremental, step-by-step fashion.

In the early CA publications (e.g. Schegloff & Sacks 1973) these two perspectives were melded into a new methodology. Integral to the methodology was a reversal of the old social science perspective that individual actions are inherently disorderly, and that their patterns can only be approximated using statistics. Instead Sacks and Schegloff insisted that social interaction is *orderly* on an individual level, action by action, move by move. If it were not so, how could interaction be reliable and meaningful in the ways that common experience tells us it is?

As CA developed during the 1970s a number of basic assumptions that now underlie the field began to crystallize.

The primacy of ordinary conversation

A basic CA assumption is that ordinary conversation between peers represents a fundamental domain for analysis, and that the analysis of ordinary conversation represents a basic resource for the extension of CA into other, "non-conversational" domains. This assumption was not a guiding principle of CA research from the outset. Indeed in his lectures, Sacks (1984a) did not portray the decision to study conversation in these terms. However, by the time that the work on turn taking (Sacks, Schegloff, & Jefferson 1974) was completed, it had become apparent that ordinary conversation differs in systematic ways from, for example, interaction in the law courts or news interviews; the conceptualization of these differences has developed substantially in recent years (Drew & Heritage 1992).

There is every reason to view ordinary conversation as the fundamental, in fact primordial, domain of social interaction. It is the predominant form of human interaction in the social world, and the primary medium of communication to which the child is exposed and through which socialization proceeds. It thus antedates the development of other, more specialized, forms of institutional interaction both in the life of society and in the life of the individual person. Moreover the practices of ordinary conversation appear to have a bedrock or default status. They are not conventional nor subject to rapid historical change, nor generally subject to discursive justification (by reference, for example, to equity or efficiency) in ways that practices of communication in legal, medical, pedagogical, and other institutions manifestly are. As we shall see in this book, research is increasingly showing that communicative conduct in more specialized social institutions embodies task- or role-oriented specializations that generally involve a narrowing of the range of conduct that is generically found in ordinary conversation. The latter thus embodies a diversity and range of combinations of interactional practices that is unmatched elsewhere in the social world. Communicative conduct in institutional environments, by contrast, involves socially imposed and often uncomfortable departures from that range (Atkinson 1982).

The use of naturally occurring recorded data in CA

CA is completely insistent on the use of recordings of naturally occurring data as the empirical basis for analysis. This outlook was first articulated in Sacks' lectures (Sacks 1984a, 1992) where he stressed the value of recordings as a resource that could be analyzed and reanalyzed. Moreover, Sacks argued, naturally occurring data represent an infinitely richer resource for analysis than what can be invented or imagined. And invented data have another disadvantage: others may deny that they represent possible events in the real world. This is a problem not faced by empirical data (ibid.)!

These comments made their appearance in an intellectual context in which invented data were the stock in trade of linguistics and the philosophy of speech acts (Searle 1969, 1979). CA continues to stress that the use of recorded data is central to recovering the detail of interactional organization, and that all forms of non-recorded data – from memorized observations to all forms of on-the-spot coding – are inadequate and inappropriate substitutes. These substitutes inevitably compromise the linguistic and contextual detail that is essential for successful analysis. As these remarks suggest, recorded interaction is a fundamental constraint that disciplines conclusions by making them answerable to what real people actually do, rather than what an armchair theorist – no matter how talented – might imagine they do. The empirical advances that CA has made rest squarely on the use of recorded data that, together with data transcripts, permit others to check the validity of the claims being made.

The parallel insistence on naturally occurring data is similarly motivated. While experimental situations and role-play data can be recorded, there are reasons for regarding each of them as less than fully desirable. Experimental and related circumstances in which the participants are "set up" for some activity often yield data that are only partially usable. Often the limitations of the experimental situation narrow the relevance of the data and the applicability of findings (Schegloff 1987, 1991). Similarly role-plays, as those who have compared them with "real-life" interactions will know, are often compromised in terms of the range and authenticity of the conduct that emerges within them, not least because the empirical consequentiality and moral accountability that are associated with "real" interactions are attenuated in the role-play context.

Given these considerations, CA has approached the world of social interaction in the same spirit as the naturalist. The aim has been, as far as possible, to obtain recorded data of interactional practices in the natural contexts in which those practices occur. Once obtained, the data can be analyzed and reanalyzed in the context of new research questions and of growing knowledge and can be employed as cumulative data corpora in processes of comparison that accumulate over time.

The structural analysis of conversational practices

Fundamental to the inception of CA is the idea, inherited from Goffman, that social interaction is informed by institutionalized structural organizations of practices to which participants are normatively oriented. This assumption, perhaps more than any other, reflects the sociological origins of the field. Associated with this assumption is the notion that these organizations of practices – as the conditions on which the achievement of mutually intelligible and concerted interaction depends – are fundamentally independent of the motivational, psychological or sociological characteristics of the participants. Indeed conversational practices are the medium through which these sociological and psychological characteristics manifest themselves.

It is this structural assumption which informs, in fact mandates, the basic CA imperative to isolate organizations of practices in talk without reference to the sociological or psychological characteristics of the participants. For example, a structured set of turn-taking procedures is presupposed in the recognition of an "interruption". Moreover, both these turn-taking procedures and the associated recognizability of interruptive departures from them are anterior to, and independent of, empirical distributions of interruptions as between males and females or between powerful and powerless individuals (Zimmerman & West 1975, West & Zimmerman 1983, Kollock, Blumstein, & Schwartz 1985). It is thus only *after* the structural features of, for example, turn taking and interruption have been determined that it is meaningful to search for the ways in which sociological factors such as gender, class, and ethnicity, or psychological dispositions such as extroversion or a disposition to passive-aggressive conduct, may be manifested in interactional conduct.

CA searches for structural organizations of interactional practices in a particular way. Rather than starting with a set of theoretical specifications of "structure" or "action" (cf. Parsons 1937), with an *a priori* theoretical specification of particular actions (for example, Searle's [1969] speech act specifications), or with a theory of the motivation of action such as the theory of "face" (Goffman 1955, 1959, 1971, Brown & Levinson 1987), CA has worked to avoid premature and idealized theory construction in favor of the empirical identification of diverse structures of practices. The shift is one from an idealized and conceptually simplified model – "the structure" of social action (Parsons 1937) to a particularized and multiplex one – "structures" of social action (Atkinson & Heritage 1984). It is the accumulation of empirical findings about the multiplex practices organizing social action that forms an ever-expanding background against which further empirical advances have been made.

The Sequential Structure of Interaction

When it comes to actual analysis, the basic idea of CA "is so simple that it is difficult to grasp" (Arminen 2005: 2). CA consistently and insistently asks a single question about any action (or indeed any component of any action): *why that now?* And in response to this question CA examines what the action does in relation to the preceding action(s), and what it projects about the succeeding action(s).

From its inception, CA has been occupied with the analysis of the sequential organization of interaction. Underlying this notion are a number of fundamental ideas. First, turns at talk are context-shaped: they are overwhelmingly produced with an orientation to preceding talk, most commonly the immediately preceding talk (Sacks 1987, 1992, Schegloff & Sacks 1973). Speakers design their talk in ways that exploit this basic positioning, thereby exposing the fundamental role of sequential positioning as a resource for the production and understanding of their utterances (Schegloff 1984). Second, turns at talk are context-renewing: They ordinarily project the relevance of a particular "next" action, or range of next actions, to be done by a subsequent speaker (Schegloff 1972). Finally, turns at talk are the building blocks of intersubjectivity: By the production of next actions, speakers show an understanding of a prior action and do so at a multiplicity of levels: for example, by an "acceptance", an actor can show an understanding that the prior turn was possibly complete, that it was addressed to them, that it was an action of a particular type (e.g., an invitation) and so on (Schegloff 1992c). CA methodology is premised on the notion that all three of these features – the grasp of a next action that a current one projects, the production of that next action, and its interpretation by the previous speaker – are methodically achieved by means of a set of socially shared procedures. CA analyses are thus analyses simultaneously of action, context management, and intersubjectivity, because all three of these features are simultaneously, if tacitly, the objects of the actors' actions.

Finally, the procedures that inform these activities are normative in that actors can be held morally accountable both for departures from their use and for the inferences which their use, or departures from their use, may engender. It was in the integration of these three themes that the separate ideas of Goffman and Garfinkel became fused into a single, powerful research program that crystallized into a clear set of empirical working practices which were applied, without exception, to tape recordings of naturally occurring interactions.

Conversation Analysis: Two Research Traditions

Most of the early work in conversation analysis focused on "ordinary conversation" – a term that has come to denote forms of interaction which are not confined to specialized settings or to the execution of particular tasks. Ordinary conversation is often defined negatively: wedding ceremonies are not ordinary conversation, legal proceedings in court are not ordinary conversation, though both adapt practices of talk and action from ordinary conversation and press them into service in these more specialized and restricted speech settings (Schegloff 1999). In contrast, the studies of "institutional talk" which began to emerge in the late 1970s focused on more restricted environments in which the goals of the participants are more limited and institution-specific, there are often restrictions on the nature of interactional contributions, and talk is understood in terms of institution- and activity-specific inferential frameworks (Drew & Heritage 1992).

Two general lines of research have developed from this starting point. The first, and original, research line developed by Sacks, Schegloff and Jefferson studies everyday conversational interaction as an institution in its own right. This research process involves identifying particular conversational practices; for example:

(2) Examples of Conversational Practices
Turn-initial address terms
(a) A: Mary, do you want another piece of cake?

Oh-prefaced responses to questions
(b) A: How are you feeling Joyce.
    B: Oh fi:ne.
    A: 'Cause- I think Doreen mentioned that you weren't so well?

Polarity in question design
(c) Doc: Are there any other concerns you want to discuss?

To be identified as a practice, a feature of talk must (1) be recurrent, (2) be specifically positioned within a turn or sequence (or both), and (3) have some specific interpretation, consequence or set of consequences. For example, turn-initial address terms are a basic means of selecting a next speaker to respond (Lerner 2003). Oh-prefacing responses to questions is a means of conveying that the question was inappropriate (Heritage 1998); note that in (b) the questioner reacts by *defending* the relevance of her question in the third turn. Polarity items like "some" or "any" in questions are elements of design that favor positive (some) and negative (any) responses relative to one another (Heritage, Robinson, Elliott, et al. 2007).

Practices like these are, in turn, involved in larger-scale elements of conversational organization. Turn-initial address terms are one of a set of ways in which a current speaker can select another to talk next (Lerner 2003). This set, in turn, is part of the turn-allocational arrangements which are a part of the turn-taking system for conversation (Sacks, Schegloff, & Jefferson 1974). Oh-prefacing responses to questions is a practice which is part of a set dealing with the relative claims to knowledge that speakers unavoidably register in their interactions (Heritage & Raymond 2005), and is part of the management of the epistemic relations between speakers (Heritage 2008). Polarity in question design is a part of the preference organization of interaction, through which actors privilege or favor certain actions over other alternatives, often in ways that maximize solidarity and minimize conflict (Heritage 1984b, 2008, Pomerantz 1984, Sacks 1987, Schegloff 2006, 2007).

In sum, the basic tradition of conversation analysis involves identifying particular conversational practices and pinning down their contexts of occurrence, their meanings and consequences, and their place within larger orders of conversational organization. The outcome of this research is an understanding of how basic social actions are produced and recognized, and how their production and recognition are located and shaped within the institution of interaction.

Institutional CA

In the second type of CA – institutional CA – research builds on these basic findings about the institution *of* talk as a means to analyze the operations of other social institutions *in* talk. There is an important shift in perspective here. One can study interaction between 911 emergency and callers as *conversation* by focusing on generic interactional matters, how they take turns, or how one action invites another to form interactional sequences. Or one can study this talk as *emergency call interaction* in particular, that is, as something shaped by the concerns and exigencies of the emergency service (Heritage 2005). Institutional CA takes this second approach.

Institutional CA first emerged with Atkinson and Drew's *Order in Court* (1979), a classic study of courtroom interaction. Atkinson and Drew were interested in how the specialized turn-taking system for courtroom interaction solved problems connected with the large number of people in the courthouse during a hearing. They examined how questions were produced by lawyers and heard by witnesses to be building up towards an accusation, and how defenses could anticipate and forestall this kind of build-up. In short, they were concerned with how the tasks and substance of court business are transacted through interaction. This involves a distinctive approach to interaction relative to basic CA. Interaction remains the focus of investigation but it is examined for how specific practices of talk embody or connect with specific identities and institutional tasks. Over time, this perspective spread into studies of 911 emergency calls (Zimmerman 1984, 1992), classroom lessons (McHoul 1978), doctor–patient interaction (Heath 1986, ten Have 1991), news interviews (Heritage 1985, Greatbatch 1988, Clayman 1988) and an ever-widening range of social institutions and contexts (Boden & Zimmerman 1991, Drew & Heritage 1992).

In all this work, the same basic question – *why that now?* – was applied to the data. However, the analysis centered on how specific types of turns and actions were being implemented to achieve institutional objectives. For example, returning to our doctor–patient example, it is evident that at line 11 the doctor redirects the patient's attempts to respond to his question because he wants to arrive at a medically useful estimate of the frequency with which the patient consumes alcohol. The patient is finally brought to recognize this and supplies such a response at line 16. However the patient, for her part, is concerned to convey how she drinks and not merely how often: that she is a social drinker, and not one who drinks alone. And she deploys a specific practice – describing time in terms of biographical activities to achieve this end (Button 1990, Drew & Heritage 1992).

Ordinary Conversation and Institutional Talk

The boundaries between ordinary conversation and institutional talk can be surprisingly difficult to define (Schegloff 1999, Heritage 2005). However, the participants to interaction nonetheless make clear demarcations (Drew & Sorjonen 1997), as when doctors and patients orient to a dividing line between the pleasantries that may occur at the beginning of a medical visit and the "turn to business" which the doctor may initiate with "What's the problem?" (Robinson 1998, 2006). And, although the boundaries between institutional talk and ordinary conversation are not clearly fixed and demarcated, there are clear distinctions between classroom interaction, news interviews, mediation sessions, and medical visits on the one hand, and ordinary conversations between family, friends, and strangers on the other.

The relationship between ordinary conversation and institutional talk can be understood as that between an encompassing "master institution" and its more restricted local variants. Relative to the institution of conversation, the law courts, schools, news interviews, doctor–patient interactions, etc. are comparatively recent inventions that have undergone a great deal of change, some of it planned on an organized basis. Anyone who looks at news interviews from the 1970s or doctor–patient interactions of the same period will easily see major changes. Ordinary conversation, by contrast, exists, and is experienced as, prior to institutional interaction both in the life of the individual and the life of the society. Relative to institutional interaction, it is relatively stable: the interactional maneuvers in the plays of Shakespeare, sophisticated though some of them are, are perfectly intelligible to us four centuries later. The ordinary conversation of the 1970s does not look so very different from the interactions of today.

In addition to its stability, ordinary conversation encompasses a vast array of rules and practices, which are deployed in pursuit of every imaginable kind of social goal, and which embody an indefinitely large array of inferential frameworks. Institutional interaction, by contrast, generally involves a reduction in the range of interactional practices deployed by the participants, restrictions in the contexts they can be deployed in, and it frequently involves some specialization and respecification of the interactional relevance of the practices that remain (Drew & Heritage 1992).

Institutional Talk: Research Objectives

In its early development institutional CA focused on comparison. Treating the practices of ordinary conversation as primary, researchers asked how things were managed differently in particular institutional contexts (Schegloff 1991, 1992b). For example, it was clear that, in comparison with ordinary conversation, turn taking was managed completely differently in news interviews (and classrooms and courts). Some practices that are extremely common in ordinary conversation – for example, acknowledging an answer to a question with "oh" – are virtually nonexistent in many institutional contexts. From examples like this, it seemed that each institution might have a unique "fingerprint" of practices that contributed to the fulfillment of its unique tasks and which made it uniquely what it is. Although it has its limitations, this fingerprint idea is highly useful and we will explore it further in chapter 3.

But other interests have also been pursued within institutional CA. There is a concern with how particular institutional tasks are managed and discharged through talk, without regard for the similarities and differences to ordinary conversation. Indeed specific action choices can index particular institutional stances, ideologies and identities that are being enacted in the talk, as well as particular professional beliefs and institutional rules and guidelines (Heritage 2005). For example, health visitors open their first visits to young mothers in strikingly different ways depending on whether fathers are present. When the father is present, they open with questions about the name of the baby, or compliments about the baby's appearance. When the mother is on her own, they open in a different way – with a question about the mother's experience of labor, or her general health. Table 2.1 shows seven opening questions. In this situation, the health visitors are faced with distinctive and sometimes conflicting objectives (Heritage and Sefi 1992, Heritage & Lindström 1998, Heritage 2002a). On the one hand they want to establish a "befriending" relationship with the new mother, and to establish the basis on which the mother can feel able to turn to the health visitor for support in times of need. Beginning the relationship by sharing the mother's recent experience of the birth of her child is a virtually ideal vehicle for this, while also being a part of the medical fact gathering that the health visitor must engage in anyway. With the father present however, the health visitors can be concerned that such an intimate opening would shut out the father, and alienate his interest and support for the health visiting service.

Finally, institutional interactions have causes and consequences. Thus we can ask how the use of particular interactional practices matters for issues that lie "beyond the talk". These

Table 2.1 Health visitor openings

Father or "significant other" present	What you going to call he::r?	(HV 1)
	Lovely.=A little bo:y.=What are you ca:lling him.	(HV 4)
	.hhh She's beau:tiful isn't she.	(HV 4)
Father or "significant other" absent	Didju have an easy ti::me,	(HV 1)
	Anyway, what sort of time did you have?	(HV 3)
	How do you fee:l.	(HV 3)
	.hhh What sort of time did you ha:ve.	(HV 5)

Source: Heritage 2005

issues can concern causes: do external factors influence the deployment of interactional practices, or even give rise to the invention of new ones? As chapter 16 will show, the types of questions that are asked in presidential press conferences vary with a slew of economic and political factors. Similarly interactional practices have consequences: does the deployment of specific interactional practices influence the outcomes of interaction, for example decision making or attitudes? As chapter 11 shows, medical decision making is strongly influenced by specific features of interaction in the medical visit. And this research has direct practical applications: do particular interactional practices expedite or improve the effectiveness of particular activities and, if so, are there downside costs? In chapter 10, a study is described which shows that the wording of medical questions can drastically reduce the likelihood that patients will leave doctors' offices with problems that were not addressed, and that this can be achieved in visits taking the same length of time.

At this point, however, we have got ahead of ourselves. In the next chapter, we consider how interactional practices are deployed in connection with particular institutions.

For Further Reading

Erving Goffman's research is diverse and wide-ranging. His work on the interaction order is best represented by several papers: "On face work" (1955), "The neglected situation" (1964), "The interaction order" (1983), and "Felicity's condition" (1983). Two books – *Relations in Public* (1971) and *Forms of Talk* (1981) – add important additional content, and Goffman describes his perspective in a fascinating interview with Jef Verhoeven conducted in 1980 (Goffman 1993). Drew and Wootton (1987) have a strong collection of papers on Goffman's work: the contributions by Adam Kendon, Randall Collins, and Emanuel Schegloff are particularly useful.

There is quite a large literature on Harold Garfinkel. The tic–tac–toe experiment is reported in his "Trust" paper (Garfinkel 1963), and others of his experiments and demonstrations are reported in his *Studies in Ethnomethodology* (1967), and *Ethnomethodology's Program* (2002). Eric Livingston (1987, 2008) provides two wonderful views of ethnomethodology in practice, and Heritage (1984b, 1987) gives an account of ethnomethodology in relation to sociological theory. Garfinkel's idea that rules are involved in recognizing and understanding action as well as shaping it is echoed in John Searle's distinction between constitutive and regulative rules (Searle 1969).

The formation of CA can be traced in the collected *Lectures on Conversation* by Harvey Sacks (1992). One of the most influential early published papers in CA was Schegloff and Sacks' "Opening up closings" (1973). Schegloff recalls this period in his Introduction to Sacks' collected lectures (Schegloff 1992a), and in a more recently published extended interview in a collection devoted to his research (Schegloff 2003).

3

Talking Social Institutions into Being

In this chapter, we will start to connect sequences of interaction with the social institutions in which they occur. The basis on which we will do so was established in the previous chapter. There we saw that, first, social actions are produced in a methodical fashion and that this methodicalness is very stable. Second, these methods are resources for both *producing* and *understanding* actions. This is essential. Persons use the methodic character of their actions to *produce* them so as to be *recognizable* in a particular way. Third, quite a lot of this methodicalness is based in social rules. These rules are mainly tacit and taken for granted, but they are shared between persons, and this too is essential. A person who does not know the rules of football cannot produce or recognize football actions. Such a person cannot play the game, or even watch a televised game and understand what's going on. The game of football depends on each and every player sharing a knowledge of its rules. Similarly in interaction, if we didn't have shared access to the rules, it would be impossible to produce and recognize conversational actions, or make inferences from them. Intelligible interactional conduct would be impossible.

Accordingly, as we go about analyzing interaction from the point of view of how it is methodically produced, we essentially spend our time asking "Why that now?" (why that action, why that word selection, why that hesitation, why that look, why that gesture, and so on, *now*). And we ask that question as a way into studying interaction, because that is the question the participants are always asking themselves as they navigate through their interactions with one another and build a social world together, and we want to find out how they are doing that. When you ask the question "Why that now?", you overcome the tendency to view interaction as familiar and "natural". At the same time, you very quickly come to see how *methodical* social interaction really is – how deeply it is based on methods of reasoning and action that the participants share. As we analyze their interaction, we are trying to figure out their reasoning as they ask, and answer, this question about one another. And we're going to find that they answer this question by looking at the logic that's built into the conduct of interaction.

This logic is shaped by work settings. The production and understanding of actions is shaped and adjusted by the circumstances and tasks of institutions, and by the fact that the interaction is produced by people who have specific identities, like doctor and patient, attorney and witness, journalist and interviewee, to live up to. Of necessity then, we need to take a view on the relationship between interactions and the contexts in which they are produced.

Two Views of Talk and Social Context:
The Bucket versus the Yellow Brick Road

The traditional view of the relationship between interaction and its context is what we term the "bucket theory" of context. The dominant image of this relationship is of a container that "contains" interaction as a bucket contains water. In general the bucket theory assumes that interaction accommodates to fit the context rather as water does the bucket. At any rate the bucket is not significantly altered by the interactions it contains. It is easy to see how this image arises and seems so compelling. If we consider an institutional setting like a university lecture theater, the participants – professors, students, teaching assistants, etc. – enter the institutional space and behave in accordance with the norms appropriate to a lecture. The lecture hall, like the bucket, contains the actions and it does not seem to be affected by them.

This image of a situation containing its appropriate actions is a dominant one in many forms of structural theorizing in the social sciences, but it starts to appear profoundly mis-leading as soon as we encounter actions that depart in any way from the norm. For exam-ple, in the 1960s Harold Garfinkel had his undergraduate students bargain for the prices of goods at supermarket checkouts. This was temporarily confusing for all concerned, but the majority of the students were able to negotiate reductions in the price of goods whose starting prices varied from below \$2 to more than \$50 (Garfinkel 1967: 69). By their actions, these students *transformed* the situations they were in: what the situation came to be at the checkout was the *project* of their actions and the *product* of their actions. It did not exist inde-pendently of those actions. Similarly, we can argue that the normal supermarket checkout scenario is also the project and product of our actions: we ongoingly reproduce it and take its re-production for granted.

It is just as hard to sustain the credibility of the bucket theory in ordinary sociable inter-action. While there may be ongoing relationships and identities that persons attend to in these situations, these features do not mandate particular actions and so it is not at all clear what the "bucket" consists of. And when persons are encountering one another for a first time, whatever the interaction will come to is obviously a product of the parties' actions. A first date is the paradigm example of this: single actions can transform the content and meaning of the date, together with what it eventually comes to.

Our alternative to the bucket theory is summed up by an unforgettable image associated with the Beatles' *Yellow Submarine* movie. In this image the Beatles are walking along, and as they step forward a yellow brick road (like the one in *The Wizard of Oz*) materializes and forms under their feet. Their walking feet form the road. Their actions build the route they are traveling on. Applying this image to interaction, the view we will take is that social con-text is *never* independent of actions (Duranti & Goodwin 1992). To the contrary, persons are continuously creating, maintaining, or altering the social circumstances in which they are placed – regardless of how massively, even oppressively, "predefined" those situations appear to be – and they do so in and through the actions they perform. This is unavoidable because of the reflexive relationship between action and context that Garfinkel (1967) argued to be endemic to human action. And this is so even for the most "routine" actions because, given that the circumstances of today are going to be different from those of tomorrow, even repeated actions are done anew. Within this view of things, actions are reflexive, dynamic, and context-renewing. Situational stability is just as dynamic as situational change because both occur through the same reflexive processes. Situations do not "contain" actions; rather, situations are created, maintained, or altered through their constituent actions. "Context" is the project and product of the participants' own actions. The participants are continually enacting context, making its relevance available in and through their contributions to the interaction.

As we turn to interactions in institutions we want to maintain this focus. For example, if we analyze 911 emergency calls or news interviews, we want to be able to show that, and how, the participants are enacting the "emergency" dimension of their conversation and not some other dimension, or that they are oriented to the news interview context of their talk and not some other context. This means showing that the participants build the context of their talk in and through their talk. For example, we are not going to rely on the fact that the talk is located in a call to 911, or in a news studio. These aspects of the talk may help to make the interaction more quickly recognizable, but they are never criterial. There are personal calls to 911, and hoax calls, and calls from people who think 911 should find their car keys, or ward off attacks from outer space! The "emergency" status of a call and its "impersonal" character require a good deal more than calling 911. We want to find out how that is achieved. We want to see how the participants, one of whom may never have called 911 before, co-construct their circumstances as an emergency service transaction, incrementally advance it turn by turn as such, and bring it off in these terms. This involves asking and answering our crucial "Why that now?" question, because, in the ways that they ask and answer that question, the parties navigate through an interaction that will have become co-constructed as a call for emergency service by a credible citizen with a need for help.

Methods of Talking: A Simplest Case

In this section, we will take one of the most fundamental rules of interaction, and show how it operates as a method of producing actions, and of achieving intersubjectivity. The rule organizes the ordering of actions into pairs, and is called the adjacency pair rule. A large number of actions in conversation are organized as pairs: for example, greetings, goodbyes, how are you's, questions and answers, requests and acceptances or declinations, invitations and acceptances or declinations. For this reason adjacency pairs are a basic form of sequence structure in interaction (Schegloff 2007). Because questions and answers play an enormous role in institutional interaction we will focus on them.

We can introduce the idea of an adjacency pair with a little puzzle. Take an interchange like (1):

(1) [Levinson 1983: 102]
```
  1  A:      Where's Bill?
  2  B:      There's a yellow VW outside Sue's apartment.
```

The puzzle is that even though B's response is not formed up overtly as a response to A's question, A will not hear the response as irrelevant to his prior question. Rather, A will attempt to hear B's utterance as relevant and responsive. That is, he will try to interpret the meaning of B's utterance bearing in mind its context: that it occurs next to and presumably in response to his question. And it is only after having tried to hear it in that way and having failed, that A may finally shake his head and say "What's that got to do with anything?" Now plainly there's something that is getting A (and of course us) to understand B's response to A as an answer to A's question. Sacks and Schegloff termed this something an adjacency pair, and we will spend a little time exploring this form of social organization.

According to Sacks and Schegloff, the adjacency pair has five basic characteristics:

1 It is a sequence of two actions, which are
2 adjacent, and
3 produced by different speakers, and are
4 ordered as first pair parts and second pair parts (even when the parts are identical as in greetings like hello–hello), and
5 pair–type related so that a particular type of first pair part requires a particular type of second pair part.

The two actions are linked by a simple rule which states that, given the recognizable production of a first pair part, its producer should stop and a second actor should start to produce a second pair part of the type which the first pair part is drawn from.

Applied to questions and answers, this can just seem like a long-winded way of saying that questions are invariably or at least frequently answered. But, as a statement of invariance, the claim would be palpably false. Questions are manifestly not answered from time to time. Moreover, although it is true as a quantitative generalization across many languages (Stivers, Enfield, Brown, et al. 2009), the rule's true significance is not quantitative. Instead, its significance is normative. Questions invoke a *right* to an answer and place the recipient under an *obligation* to respond. Persons *should* answer the questions that are put to them. They are *normatively accountable* for doing so.

This normative accountability is apparent in two main ways. First, when an answer is not forthcoming, questioners assert their rights to an answer by repeating the question. For example in (2), which occurs at the beginning of a meal, the Mom's initial response (lines 2–3) does not answer her daughter's question:

```
(2)  [Stew Dinner]
  1  CIN:        Mommy if-I-if-I don't like the food do I have
  2               to ea:t i:t,
  3  MOM:        First you need to move this out of the way so we can get
  4               to the table,
  5  CIN:   →    Well do I: (.) I'd-[if-I
  6  MOM:                           [You need to at least try it,
```

Notice that Cindy's "repeat" of her question (arrowed at line 5) is really a partial repeat and does not reissue the substantive content of the question in lines 1–2. If her mother had not heard the original question, what Cindy says at line 5 would hardly have helped her respond. Knowing this, Cindy would have repeated the whole question. However, the renewed (partially repeated) question at line 5 is successful in getting an answer. Thus we can say that the form of Cindy's question at line 5 incorporates an analysis that her Mom deliberately had not (yet) responded to it – something conveyed by the Mom's "First you need . . ." – rather than that her question had not been heard.

A more extended version of this issue is presented in (3) where a child offers successively reduced versions of the same question, again conveying that her mother had heard the original question:

```
(3)
  1  Ch:    Have to cut the:se Mummy.
  2         (1.3)
  3  Ch:    Won't we Mummy
  4         (1.5)
  5  Ch:    Won't we
  6  Mom:   Yes
```

Again the Mom is brought to a response by her child's repetition. The child has asserted her right to an answer and that her mother has an obligation to provide it.

The second kind of evidence for the question–answer pairing as a norm arises from the fact that failures to answer are often explained: persons present reasons for not fulfilling their obligation to respond. In question–answer sequences (and many others [Heritage 1984b]) the most frequent, and primary, accounts used tend to involve inability, as in (4).

```
(4)
  1  A:    What happened at (.) wo:rk. At Bullock's this evening.=
  2  B:    .hhhh Well I don'kno::w::.
```

It is important to recognize in (4) that, though B responds to the question, she does not answer it. Instead her response is an account for *not* answering the question.

By their very production questions position the respondent as knowledgeable, or at least more knowledgeable, about something than the questioner. Accounts may then address the matter of why, unexpectedly, the answerer lacks such knowledge. In (5), Beth's daughter is about to get married and will be traveling to Paris by train from London. Ann's question concerns the mechanics of this process, and positions the bride-to-be's mother as likely to be knowledgeable about it:

```
(5)
  1  Ann:    But the trai:n goes. Does the train go o:n the boa:t?
  2  Bet:    .h .h Ooh I've no idea:. She ha:sn't sai:d.
```

Beth's response not only accounts for her failure to answer by reason of inability ("Ooh I've no idea:."), but also accounts for that inability itself with "She ha:sn't sai:d."

The idea that the failure to answer questions is accountable is familiar to every child, and it is known by them to be inferentially rich. Failures to respond without good reason are understood to be indicative of some ulterior motive for not responding, such as embarrassment or guilt. And this in turn is embedded in the legal systems of many Western societies which provide citizens with the legal right to refuse police questioning, without that refusal being legally admissible in court where it could easily attract inferences of guilt.

A Logic of Questions and Answers

We can now take a further step towards institutional talk by nailing down the basic logic of question–answer sequences. When persons ask questions in ordinary conversation, they normally commit to a number of basic propositions about themselves, their recipients, and

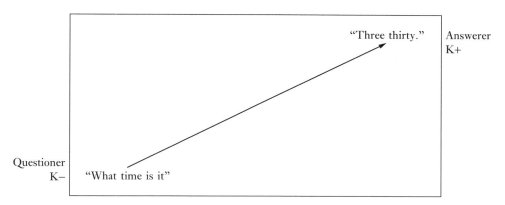

Figure 3.1 Epistemic gradient for a simple question

the topic of the question. In addition to the social right to ask the question, they claim to be unknowing about the state of affairs they are asking about *relative to the recipient*. We will represent this as the "K–" claim of a questioner. Simultaneously, they establish the recipient as relatively knowledgeable about the matter, which we will represent as "K+". Thus they establish an "epistemic gradient" between questioner and respondent, which is represented in figure 3.1. By projecting the respondent as knowledgeable, questioners generally commit to the idea that the response will be informative and that, once the response is provided, they will be informed (and the epistemic gradient will have been made level). A standard way that questioners indicate that this has occurred is through the use of the acknowledgment token "oh" (Heritage 1984a), as in (6):

```
(6)  [Frankel:TC]
  1  Shi:          .hh When do you get out.  Christmas week or the
  2                week before Christmas.
  3                (0.3)
  4  Ger:          Uh::m two or three days before Ch[ristmas,]
  5  Shi:      →                                    [ O h :  ,]
```

In this case, Shirley acknowledges the answer to her question with "oh," indicating that whereas she previously did not know when Geri's school broke up for the holiday, now she does.

The use of "oh" to register this "change of state" of information is not to be confused with surprise (Wilkinson & Kitzinger 2007). In (6) above, the questioner set a likely time scale for the end of term and the response fell within that time scale. In (7), the questioner, as she indicates in her question, has a good idea that her respondent will be working on the next day. She indicates this with a declarative question seeking confirmation of a third-party report about the respondent's intentions, and is not surprised by the answer. Here the initial epistemic gradient between questioner and answerer is much flatter than in (5) or (6):

```
(7)  [Rah:12:4:ST]
  1  Jen:          Okay then I was asking her and she says you're
  2                working tomorrow as well.
  3  Ivy:          Yes I'm supposed to be tomorrow yes,
  4  Jen:      →   Oh:::,
```

Nonetheless she indicates a shift in her state of knowledge with "oh," though here the shift is in the degree of certainty with which she holds the information – from third-party hearsay to first party information straight from the horse's mouth.

This use of "oh" to acknowledge new information is extremely prevalent. It is recurrent in the next example where Nancy is asking her friend Hyla about a new boyfriend who is a student in San Francisco:

```
(8)  (HG:II:25)
  1  Nan:   a→  .hhh Dz he 'av 'iz own apa:rt[mint?]
  2  Hyl:   b→                              [.hhhh] Yea:h,=
  3  Nan:   c→  =Oh:,
  4               (1.0)
  5  Nan:   a→  How didju git 'iz number,
  6               (.)
  7  Hyl:   b→  I(h) (.) c(h)alled infermation'n San
  8          b→  Fr'ncissc(h)[uh!
  9  Nan:   c→              [Oh::::.
 10               (.)
 11  Nan:      Very cleve:r, hh=
 12  Hyl:      =Thank you[: I- .hh-.hhhhhhhh hh=
 13  Nan:   a→            [W'ts 'iz last name,
 14  Hyl:   b→  =Uh:: Freedla:nd. .hh[hh
 15  Nan:   c→                       [Oh[:,
 16  Hyl:                                [('r) Freedlind.=
 17  Nan:   d→  =Nice Jewish bo:y?
 18               (.)
 19  Hyl:   e→  O:f cou:rse,=
 20  Nan:   f→  ='v [cou:rse,]
 21  Hyl:          [hh-hh-hh]hnn .hhhhh=
 22  Nan:      =Nice Jewish boy who doesn'like tih write letters?
```

In this case the first three question–answer–oh sequences (labeled a, b, c) clearly involve new information that was unknown by Nancy. However, her fourth question (d→) is a little different: it is hearable as a *likely inference* about the boyfriend's ethnicity, possibly derived from his last name ("Friedland") and/or from beliefs about Hyla's taste in boys. Hyla's response ("O:f cou:rse,=") treats this conclusion as self-evident, and Nancy's acknowledgment – an echoing "='v cou:rse," – does *not* treat this as new information in the way that "oh" would have done. Instead she also treats it as self-evident that the boyfriend would be a "nice Jewish boy".

With this sequential outcome, there has been an important shift in how line 17 is to be understood. Line 17 could have been understood as a real question indexing a real information gap. If Nancy had wanted her question to be understood in that way, then she could have acknowledged Hyla's answer with "oh". However, since Nancy did not do so, Hyla can see that Nancy had not intended her line 17 to be a question at all, but rather a comment on the self-evident likelihood that Hyla's new boyfriend is Jewish.

The upshot of this analysis is that, while a second speaker may infer that a preceding turn was a question in search of information, the second speaker can't be sure that they were right until their response is acknowledged to be "informative" with "oh" or a response like "oh". In short, it takes a three-turn sequence for an initial "questioning" turn to be fully and intersubjectively ratified as having been a real question (Heritage 1984a, Schegloff 1992c). This process of retroactively reconfirming the meaning of actions is absolutely central to the management of interaction in general and of intersubjective understandings in interaction in particular. It is critical to the participants' ability to make joint sense of their actions and of the contexts in which they occur. It is also a significant element in how the parties in institutional interactions talk their institutions into being.

In the next section, we will look at the ways in which the tasks and constraints associated with particular social institutions are apparent in quite elementary features of their question–answer sequences.

The Sequential Organization of Questions and Answers: Four Institutions

Classroom interaction

A good deal of what McHoul (1978) terms formal classroom talk (see also Mehan 1979) has involved question–answer–evaluation sequences (Sinclair and Coulthard 1974; see also Lee 2007, 2008). The example below is fairly representative. The sixth grade class has read a poem by Ralph Hodgson (1917) called "Time, you Old Gypsyman" and the teacher begins the class discussion of the poem by asking "Now then (.) has anyone anything to say (.) what d'you think this poem's all about?" As it transpires, he is attempting to get the class to recognize that the true topic of the poem is time:[1]

```
(9)  [Gypsyman:3]
 1  Tea:        Okay (.) now then (.) has anyone anything to say (.)
 2              what d'you think this poem's all about?
 3              (2.9)
 4  Tea:        Miss O'Neil?
 5  Stu:        The uh:m gypsyman they want him to stay one more day
 6              longer.
 7  Tea:        The gypsyman they want him to stay one day longer,
 8              (.) Don't be afraid of making a mistake, if you've
 9              got any thoughts you put your hand up.=No-one's
10              gonna laugh at ya.=I shall be very grateful for
11              anything you have to say. Miss O'Neil said it's a
12              poem about a gypsyman (.) an' somebody wants him to
13       →      stay. (0.3) Any other ideas.=She's not right.
14              (3.1)
15  Tea: →      That's the answer I expected but she's not right.
16              (0.9)
17  Tea:        Kate my love what are your thoughts?
18              (4.3)
19  Tea:        Mister Williams?
20              (2.5)
```

```
21  Tea:        Don't be frightened don't be frightened. This is a-
22              not an easy poem. (1.3) Miss Cotrell my dear,
23  Stu:        They want him to com:e (1.0) just come anyway they
24              want him to come and stay [with them.
25  Tea:                                  [Uhr who- they want who to
26              come?
27  Stu:        The gypsy.
28  Tea:        The gypsy. You say (.) we are talking about a gypsyman.
29              (1.1)
30  Tea:        You are arn'tcha?
31  Stu:        ((nods))
32  Tea:    →   Well we're not. (1.1) We are not talking about a
33              gypsy living in a caravan, (.) Not really. They-
34              the- the word gypsyman is there and the caravan
35              etcetera etcetera etcetera. (.) But (.) ehr this
36              is not really what the poem is all about.
                ...
                ...(Six lines Omitted)
                ...
43  Tea:        Mister Roberts.
44  Stu:        Could it be some kind of- pickpocket or something-
45              always on the move so he doesn't get caugh[t
46  Tea:    →                                            [No:: it
47              is not a pickpocket pocket- on the move. (.) Mister Amos?
48  Stu:        Is it about a bird that flies around.
49  Tea:        About a:?
50  Stu:        A bird that flies [around
51  Tea:    →                     [A bird flying around.=No,
```

The teacher's evaluations of the students' responses are arrowed at lines 13, 15, 32, 46, and 51. These evaluations instantiate the social relations of the classroom. For, as they make very clear, the teacher's questions do not embody a K− position; rather they embody the kind of K+ position that entitles the teacher to evaluate the correctness or otherwise of the students' responses. These then are the familiar "known answer" or "exam" questions whose object is to discover what the recipient knows (correctly), rather than to learn anything new about the topic (Searle 1969, Levinson 1992).[2] The teacher's assertion of epistemic supremacy is so clear that, by line 31, a student is reluctant to verbally confirm her earlier claim and, by lines 44 and 48, students are overtly guessing by framing their responses as questions using interrogative syntax.

As this example shows, the contrast between a third-turn "oh" (Q–A–Oh) and a third-turn evaluation (Q–A–E) could not be starker. In the Q–A–Oh sequence, the "oh" retroactively confirms that the previous question was a "real" question offered by a relatively uninformed questioner. In the Q–A–E sequence, the evaluation confirms the epistemic supremacy of the questioner, and that the question was designed to test the answer. Thus we can see that the Q–A–E sequence *constitutes* a pedagogic context. If we remove the desks and chairs of the classroom, and substitute a family breakfast table, the sequence will still constitute a teaching relationship between a more knowing questioner and a (possibly) less knowing respondent. Here then there is a tight fit between basic sequence organization in the classroom and the institutional functions of classroom interaction.

News interviews

In news interviews, sequence organization is again very different. Here questioners – the news interviewers (IR in the transcript) – rarely acknowledge interviewee (IE) responses at all, as in the following segment in which a US Treasury official (Robert Rubin) was being questioned about the price of gasoline:

(10)   [US ABC This Week with David Brinkley May 1996] (Interview with Treasury Secretary
Robert Rubin – the initial question concerns the price of gasoline)
```
 1  IR:      =Well tell me where you would like (for) it to go.
 2           (.)
 3  IE:      We:ll David let me take it- a s:lightly different approach if I
 4           ma:y,=And that is tha:t (.) thuh president took sensible
 5           action this past week, and I think action that was very
 6           sensitive¿ (.) to thuh concer:ns of very large numbers of
 7           Americans with respect to gas prices,
 8      →    (0.3)
 9           He ordered an accelerated sale of: twelve million barrels of oil
10           that co:ngress had mandated that we sell.=As part of thuh
11           budget,
12      →    (0.3)
13           As a consequence I think we'll get good prices f'r thuh
14           ta:xpayers,
15      →    (.)
16           He asked thuh secr'tary of energy to take a look at thuh whole
17           situation, report back in forty five days, .hh and independently
18           (0.2) I (re)stress: independently, (.) thuh Justice Department
19           to try to take a look at thuh=situation: and (0.2) draw their
20           own conclu:sions.
```

In this case, we have used arrows to highlight the absence of response by the interviewer (David Brinkley) at pauses in Rubin's talk (lines 8, 12, and 15). Here "oh" is clearly missing but so are other kinds of conversational responses such as "uh huh", "mm hm", and "Yes" which are also used to acknowledge preceding turns at talk.

These missing responses instantiate a distinctive institutional reality. First, the role of interviewers, at least in "hard news" interviews, is to elicit information not for themselves, but for the "overhearing" news audience for whose benefit the interview is being conducted (Heritage 1985, Clayman & Heritage 2002a). In such a context, acknowledgments of any kind will suggest that the interviewer and not the news audience is the primary target of the interviewee's statements, getting between the interviewee and the audience, and destroying the audience's sense that they are the people for whom the interview is being presented. Exactly the reverse relationship is aimed at in chat shows where interviewers do acknowledge interviewee statements, and the sensation of eavesdropping on a semi-private conversation is contrived for the audience.

Significant though these considerations are they do not entirely account for the absence of "oh" in news data. For this we need to recall that news personnel are generally expected to be objective, neutral or "neutralistic" towards the interviewee's response (Clayman & Heritage 2002a; see chapters 15 and 16). Now the "change of state" (K– → K+) proposal embodied in Q–A–Oh sequences also implies acceptance of, or belief in, what the answerer said. Patently this would undermine the impartial stance which journalists and their employers strive to maintain. Thus the interviewer–interviewee–audience relationship is constructed in part by interviewers who withhold acknowledgments to interviewee statements. Simultaneously these withholdings avoid actions which could be construed as supportive of the interviewee's stated positions and as compromising the neutrality of the broadcasting organization.

Courtrooms

A similar pattern, in which questioners do not acknowledge witness responses, holds in courtroom trials. For example, in the cross-examination of a witness by the defense attorney for an alleged rapist, the attorney simply moves from one question to the next (arrows at lines 5, 10, 19, 22, 33):

```
(11)   [Oulette 45/2B:2]
  1  Def:        A' February fourteenth of uh: (0.4) nineteen seventy
  2              fi:ve you were (0.3) what eighteen years old. (0.3)
  3  Def:        At that time?
  4  Wit:        Ye:s.
  5         →    (1.7)
  6  Def:        Now: (0.7) February fourteenth of nineteen seventy
  7              five you were (0.3) you were down a- (.) in Bo:ston.
  8              (.) Is tha- Is that ri:ght?
  9  Wit:        Ye:s
 10  Def:   →    An' you went to a: uh (0.9) uh you went to a ba:r?
 11              (in) Boston (0.6) Is that correct?
 12              (1.0)
 13  Wit:        It's a clu:b.
 14              (0.3)
 15  Def:        A clu:b?
 16              (1.0)
 17  Def:        There was liquor served there wasn't there?
 18  Wit:        Ye:s
 19         →    (0.5)
 20  Def:        You had so(me) liquor didn't you?
 21  Wit:        Ye:s.
 22         →    (3.1)
 23  Def:        It's a: uh singles club. Isn't that what it is?=
 24              =((sound of striking mallet))
 25  Pro:        (                    )
 26              (0.9)
 27  Jud:        No you may have it,
 28              (1.1)
 29  Def:        It's where uh (.) uh (0.3) gi:rls and fellas meet.
 30              Isn't it?
 31              (0.9)
 32  Wit:        People go: there.
 33         →    (4.9)
```

Here the issues overlap with the news interview situation. The role of trial attorneys is to elicit and test the witness's account of events in a fashion favorable to their client for the benefit of an "overhearing" and largely non-participant audience: the judge and jury. These participants are not eavesdroppers to a trial; rather, they are the persons for whose judgment the trial is being conducted. Attorneys thus should not "stand between" the witness and the jury, as would be the case if they acknowledged witness statements. Nor should they endorse them as true with "oh" acknowledgments, since judgment of the case is the job of judge and jury. Again then we can say that there is a clear fit between the specific patterning of question–answer sequences in courtroom interaction and the basic functions and ideology of the court system.

Doctor–patient interaction

The pattern is a little different in doctor–patient interaction where, after all, there is no overhearing audience. Here, as (12) shows, doctors willingly acknowledge patient responses to questions but they do not do so with "oh":

```
(12)  [History Taking]
  1  Doc:          Has he been coughing uh lot?
  2                (0.2)
  3  Mom:          .hh Not uh lot.=h[h
  4  Doc:     →                     [Mkay:?,
  5  Mom:          But it- it <sound:s:> deep.
  6                (1.0)
  7  Mom:          An' with everything we heard on tee v(h)ee=hhhh
  8                £we got sca:re.£
  9  Doc:     →    Kay. (An fer i-) It sounds deep?
 10                (.)
 11  Mom:          Mm hm.
 12  Doc:          Like uh barky cough?
 13  Mom:          .hh (1.1) Uhhhm=hhh It sounds very:=uhm (.)
 14                (I don't know:=wwlike:) (0.2) It sounds- (2.5) Tlk
 15                .hh Tlk Not like that like:
 16  Doc:          [Not (barky.)
 17  Mom:          [Like when someone has bronchitis that it sounds
 18                (     )
 19  Doc:     →    Okay.
 20  Doc:          Does he sound like uh dog er uh seal barking?
 21  Mom:          No.
 22  Doc:     →    Okay.
```

In this pediatric visit, the doctor mainly responds to the Mom's statements with "okay." This is one of a set of acknowledgments, including "I see" and "Mm hm", which doctors use frequently. We will discuss this further in chapter 8, but for now it is sufficient to note that "okay" is agnostic as to whether the child's symptoms are "new" or "unexpected" or whether, alternatively, they are the predictable symptoms that any doctor would expect of a coughing patient. "Oh" responses to patient statements are extremely rare in doctor–patient interaction, but the reasons for their rarity are distinct in this environment. It is not a matter of believing the mother or not, but whether to register patient symptoms as new, unexpected or unusual. "Oh" responses might convey this with dire consequences for patient peace of mind: for either the doctor is highly knowledgeable and the patient has an unusual complaint, or the doctor is so inexperienced as to find a reported symptom unusual. Neither inference would inspire confidence in the average patient! In this context, the agnostic "okay" or the apparently omniscient "I see" may tend to inspire greater confidence.

Conclusion

We titled this chapter "talking institutions into being". We do not mean by this to suggest that every time persons talk they invent institutions from scratch. Far from it: the institutions of education, news, courts, and medicine plainly antedate the lives and actions of the persons who participate in them. But these institutions do draw life from, and are reproduced in, those actions. The word we have used for this in this chapter is "instantiate". By this we mean that the sequences of talk we have examined are aligned with, and embody, some of the basic imperatives of the institutions within which they are found. Talking in these ways is, in part, how these institutions are realized: that is, are rendered observable and consequential in everyday life as the real entities that persons take them to be. Talking in these ways is part of being a teacher or a student, an interviewer, a lawyer or a doctor. These roles are enacted by talking in these ways. Failing to talk in these ways, by contrast, can lead to difficulties in realizing, or being recognized in, these institutional roles and activities. Speakers in these institutions are accountable for bringing off their question–answer sequences in these ways, and institutions are accountably reproduced in these sequences.

This chapter has deployed arguments that are fairly typical of the rest of this book. These arguments are several. (1) Small behavior sequences are deeply aligned to the workings and ideology of large institutions, and changes in these sequences can have great significance for the nature of the institution and how its workings are managed. (2) Understanding the logic of these sequences is central to grasping how embedded many of them are in institutional contexts and processes, and how "locked in" some of this embeddedness is. (3) None of this can make sense without accepting the context-shaped, context-renewing power of sequential organization. In the ways that actors build sequences they are also building institutional context, roles, and identities as well. These building processes are unavoidable and ceaselessly at work. To abandon the bucket theory of context and accept a context-renewing one in which actions reflexively build context is to accept the point of view that stability and change in institutional life are *both* the products of human interaction.

For Further Reading

The idea that games are only a very approximate model for real-life situations is discussed in Garfinkel (1963), while the radical insufficiency of rules as specifications of real-world activities is really one of the central topics of his *Studies in Ethnomethodology* (1967). What we have described here as the bucket theory of context is closely related to Garfinkel's critique of sociological analysis as implying a view of human beings as "judgmental dopes" (Garfinkel 1967), and is also part of a more general revision of the idea of "context" in the social sciences (Duranti & Goodwin 1992). The question–answer analysis was developed by Heritage (1984a, 1984b).

Notes

1 The opening stanza of the poem reads as follows: "TIME, you old gypsy man, / Will you not stay, / Put up your caravan / Just for one day?"

2 That learning this agenda for classroom questions is a central aspect of early classroom socialization is illustrated by an anecdote told by Peter French about a first grade classroom in which a child is looking down a microscope. Asked by the teacher what he could see, the child replied "Have a look!" French commented that almost all students abandoned this response within a week or two of starting formal schooling.

4

Dimensions of Institutional Talk

In this chapter, our objective is to describe some fundamental features of institutional talk and, building on chapter 2, to lay out a basic framework of analysis for subsequent chapters.

What is "Institutional Talk"?

Consider the ceremony in which the President-Elect of the United States is sworn in as President. Such a ceremony, appropriately enacted, involves the participants – President-Elect, Chief Justice, and other witnesses – speaking in a particular order (or withholding speech), and producing actions that are precisely specified. The swearing-in ceremony embodies three basic elements of institutional talk:

1 the interaction normally involves the participants in specific goal orientations *which are tied to their institution-relevant identities*: President-elect and Chief Justice, doctor and patient, teacher and student, etc.;
2 the interaction involves special constraints on what will be treated as allowable contributions to the business at hand; and
3 the interaction is associated with inferential frameworks and procedures that are particular to specific institutional contexts.

These features are summarized in table 4.1.

Although the formal swearing-in ceremony is a good example of institutional talk, it is far too scripted to be of much interest to conversation analysts. Instead the general focus of research has coalesced around interactions between lay people and the representatives of occupations, professions, or public bureaucracies: thus the courts, education, police, social services, medicine, business meetings, and mass media have all been major areas of "institutional talk" research during the past twenty years. These kinds of interactions allow the participants much more freedom to maneuver than highly scripted events like rituals and ceremonies. But this freedom tends to be quite strongly reined in by the limits of goal orientation, special constraints on contributions, and special inferences listed above. This is what inhibits, for example, news interviewees from asking questions of their interviewers, doctors

Table 4.1   Characteristics of institutional talk

Characteristic	*Example: US presidential swearing-in ceremony*
Participants	Chief Justice of the Supreme Court
	President-Elect
Identity-based goals	Officially inaugurating the presidency of the President-Elect
Special constraints on contributions to the business at hand	Participants must enact the ceremony as written in the US constitution. No departures are allowable
Special inferences that are particular to specific contexts	Sticking to the ceremony constitutes the President-Elect as the President of the United States. Departing from it may void this outcome.[1]

from complaining to patients about their own illnesses, and callers to 911 emergency from asking for marriage guidance.

The conceptualization of "institutional talk" (Drew & Heritage 1992) with which we began this chapter was developed to encompass these basic situations. It was not developed to provide a definition of institutional talk. A full definition and conceptualization of institutional talk is probably impossible. This is partly because the range of institutions is very varied. Within conventional social science, the family, science, and magic are also "institutions", and so a discussion of astronomy or astrology around the family dinner table should present itself as a target for analysis as institutional talk too. The difficulty of definition is further compounded by the fact that institutional talk is not confined to particular physical or symbolic settings such as hospitals, offices or classrooms (Drew & Heritage 1992): institutional talk can occur anywhere, and by the same token "ordinary conversation" can emerge in almost any seemingly institutional context. Finally, the vast majority of interactional practices that are deployed in institutional talk are also deployed in ordinary conversation.

But even fuzzy boundaries can be extremely useful. Though the boundaries between "conversation" and other types of talk are difficult to define exactly (Schegloff 1999), the distinction is still worth making. The most important reason for this is that the participants clearly orient to the distinction. For example, the beginning of doctor–patient encounters often involves some social conversation before there is a recognizable turn to business. In (1), for example, the doctor asks about a hike the patient went on (line 1) and, in the course of arriving at a response ("Saturday"), the patient talks about a hailstorm that took place the same evening (lines 9–10), which the doctor then recollects (lines 15 and 17). At line 24, the doctor turns to the patient's medical records and begins the medical business of the visit:

```
(1)  [MidWest 3.2:1]
 1  Doc:     When didju do that hike.
 2           (0.2)
 3  Pat:     Oh:: ((door slams)) (1.1) (around) two:: three
 4           weeks ago,
 5  (Doc):   hhhh
 6  Pat:     .hh An' I mean it was h:otter than uh (        )
 7  Doc:     (Cu-) Did that on uh Sunday?
 8  Pat:     .hh Saturday.
```

```
 9 Pat:   ((sniff)) That- that- that night (0.2) (it)
10          started tuh rai:n, an' then it hailed. [Oh my go:hd.
11 Doc:                                             [Mm hm,
12 Doc:   Mm [hm,
13 Pat:      [.hh
14          (0.5)
15 Doc:   Oh I- Yeah: I remember what night that was(,)
16          (.)
17 Doc:   It was uh real bad storm.
18 Pat:   Yeah.
19 Doc:   Yeah,
20          (.)
21 Doc:   Kay. (.h[h
22 Pat:           [hhhh .hh
23          (2.8)
24 Doc:   hhhh (.) Well let's see what we need tuh do:.
25        #Hm hm#.
26          (13.0)
27 Doc:   Tlk=.hh Your medicines're- are thuh sa:me,
```

This kind of initial "non-business" conversation is common in medicine and in other institutional contexts as well (Drew & Sorjonen 1997). In doctor–patient interaction, non-medical business is often marked by the use of practices, such as oh-acknowledgments, which are completely absent in actual medical business (ten Have 1991, Drew & Sorjonen 1997). Thus both in their boundary work, and in the different practices deployed in the business and non-business aspects of their interaction, the parties orient to the relevance of the distinction. They are attentive to the distinction between the two types of talk, and they work to construct their purely sociable remarks as distinct from the business at hand.

Dimensions of Distinctiveness in Institutional Talk

Despite the fact that, as already noted, institutional talk embodies many practices of mundane or ordinary conversation, it is also distinct and distinguishable from ordinary conversation. A number of dimensions of difference were systematized by Drew and Heritage (1992):

1 turn-taking organization
2 overall structural organization of the interaction
3 sequence organization
4 turn design
5 lexical or word choice
6 epistemological and other forms of asymmetry

In the next several sections we will outline and exemplify these major levels of organization. Notice that the overall structure of the interaction is made up of sequences, which are made up of turns, which are made up of words, so these dimensions nest inside one another like the

Russian "matryoshka" dolls. As we shall see however, turn-taking organization is distinct from this nesting pattern. This chapter will address epistemological asymmetries only in passing, though the issue will be prominent in subsequent chapters.

Turn taking

All interactions involve the use of some kind of turn-taking organization (Sacks, Schegloff, & Jefferson 1974), and many kinds of institutional interaction use the same turn-taking organization as ordinary conversation. Some, however, involve very specific and systematic transformations in conversational turn-taking procedures. These special turn-taking systems can be very important in studying institutional interaction because they have the potential to alter the parties' opportunities for action, and to recalibrate the interpretation of almost every aspect of the activities that result. For example, the opportunities to initiate actions, what the actions can be intended to mean, and how they will be interpreted can all be significantly shaped by distinctive turn-taking systems.

In conversation, very little of what we say, the actions we perform, or the order in which we do things is determined in advance (Sacks, Schegloff, & Jefferson 1974). In this sense, conversations are unpredictable. In some forms of institutional interaction – debates, ceremonies, and many kinds of meetings – the topics, actions, and order of speakership are organized from the outset in an explicit and predictable way. This kind of organization involves special turn-taking procedures that are systematically different from conversation.

The most intensively studied institutional turn-taking organizations have been those that obtain in the courts (Atkinson & Drew 1979), news interviews (Greatbatch 1988, Clayman & Heritage 2002a), and classrooms (McHoul 1978, Mehan 1985). As these examples suggest, special turn-taking organizations tend to be present in large-scale formal environments involving many potential speakers and hearers. However, special turn-taking systems can be found in more private, and less formal, contexts. For example, Peräkylä (1995: ch. 2) has described turn-taking practices within counseling contexts that are designed to implement special therapeutic processes, including the elicitation of thoughts about death. Similarly Garcia (1991) has shown that mediation can involve special turn-taking practices as a means of limiting conflict between the participants. Finally, there are other turn-taking organizations in non-Western societies that order speakership by age, rank or other criteria of seniority (Albert 1964, Duranti 1994), though, perhaps because CA has focused mainly on conduct in industrialized societies which may be less hierarchical than others in the world, these systems have so far been less studied.

Special turn-taking procedures fall into three broad groups: (1) action (or "turn-type") pre-allocation which is characteristic of courtrooms, and news interviews (Atkinson & Drew 1979, Greatbatch 1988, Clayman & Heritage 2002a), (2) mediated turn-allocation procedures characteristic of business and other forms of chaired meetings (Cuff & Sharrock 1985), and (3) systems that involve a combination of both processes, which are common in mediation (Garcia 1991) and some forms of counseling (Peräkylä 1995). These are summarized in table 4.2. The most pervasive form of action pre-allocation involves the restriction of one party to asking questions and the other to responding to them. This form of pre-allocation is characteristic of interactions in courtrooms, news interviews, and classrooms. Its effect is to severely restrict when and which persons may speak (the addressee of the question) and the type of

Table 4.2   Types of institutional turn-taking systems

Turn-taking system	Location	Broad function
Turn-type pre-allocation	News interviews, courts, formal classroom	Management of talk for overhearers, normally in large-scale settings
Mediated: a "chair" mediates turns as the addressee and initiator of talk by other participants	Meetings	Management of turn-taking traffic in a large group
Mixed pre-allocated/mediated	Specialized counseling techniques, dispute mediation	Management of conflictual or sensitive interactions

contribution they may make (responding to the question). In all three institutions, formal and informal sanctions – ranging from contempt of court to informal chastising – exist for persons who talk out of turn or who fail to be responsive to questions.

This type of restriction is often deployed in contexts where large numbers of people are co-present, and it is necessary to restrict their initiative to speak – a necessity that is reinforced when the others co-present are the non-addressed targets of the dialogue between primary protagonists (Levinson 1988). In circumstances such as mediation or news interviews, where two or more persons may be in opposition, this restriction also works to prevent direct opposition or argument between the opponents by forcing them to present their positions to a third party (Garcia 1991, Greatbatch 1992). The restriction of "rights to initiate" also permits the institutional representative to maintain control over the substance of the interaction, as well as its overall structure, particularly its beginning, end, and internal phase transitions.

In addition, restrictions may be placed on the types of turns that the institutional representative may perform. The most common of these is to restrict the institutional representative to turns that question; this is the case in both courtrooms and news interviews. It deprives them of rights to make statements, to overtly evaluate responses to previous questions, and even to engage in the kind of routine acknowledgments ("mm hm", "uh huh", etc.) which are commonplace in ordinary conversation. The effect of these constraints is that the institutional representative is understood to be the elicitor of responses, but not the addressee of those responses, which are, instead, understood to be targeted at the non-addressed news or courtroom audience. It also enforces a kind of neutralism on the institutional representative, who is deprived of the opportunity to "editorialize" on the answers that are produced (Clayman & Heritage 2002a).

In mediated turn-allocation systems, there are often fewer restrictions on the content and type of contributions that can be made, but at the end of each contribution the mediator (often the "chair") of the proceedings allocates the next turn. The functions of this system are similar to those of turn-type pre-allocation systems: within the context of a large group, control over topic and speakership is restricted to a single "guiding" individual, whose authority is thereby reinforced. In the context of contentious meetings, ranging from mediations involving three or four individuals to parliamentary proceedings involving several hundred, conflict can be controlled by avoiding direct address between opposed persons. These constraints are augmented in "mixed" systems (Garcia 1991), where a controlling mediator may also police initially established restrictions on the contributions made by other participants (Dingwall 1980, Greatbatch & Dingwall 1989).

How do we identify interactions in which a distinctive and institutionalized turn-taking system is in place? Most special turn-taking systems in contemporary industrial societies exploit question–answer exchanges to form particular turn-taking systems, so we will concentrate on these. To identify special turn-taking systems, we must distinguish interactions in which the pursuit of immediate interactional goals involves the participants in lengthy question–answer [Q–A] chains, such as medical history taking (Mishler 1984, Boyd & Heritage 2006) or the interrogative series in 911 emergency calls (Zimmerman 1992), from interactions in which Q–A chains are mandatory. Although it might seem otherwise, statistical studies indicate that it can be difficult to distinguish these two kinds of interactions on a quantitative basis (Linell, Gustavsson, & Juvonen 1988).

Rather than a quantitative criterion, the decisive identifying feature of a special turn-taking organization is that departures from it – for example departures from the order of speakership, or the types of contributions individuals are expected to make – are treated as normative and vulnerable to sanctions. This happens when a person asks to speak out of turn, or indicates that their talk will defer an answer to a question (Clayman & Heritage 2002a). Similarly this happens in meetings when speakers are ruled "out of order", and in the courts when persons are sanctioned for answering when they should not, or failing to answer appropriately, and when children in classrooms are punished for "shouting out" answers, or talking when the teacher is talking. These explicit sanctions are very important analytically. They tell us that the rules which we initially hypothesize from empirical regularities in the participants' actions are in fact rules that the participants recognize that they *should* follow as a moral obligation. In short, explicit sanctions show that a turn-taking system is being treated as a normative organization *in its own right*.

Earlier, it was suggested that turn-taking systems offer particular interactional affordances to the participants. As an illustration, consider the design of questions in news interviews and press conferences (Clayman & Heritage 2002a, 2002b). The constraint that interviewees may only respond to questions is exploited by interviewers to preface their questions with "background" statements. These may be relatively innocuous and transparently motivated by an interest in informing the news audience, as in (2):

```
(2)   UK BBC Radio World at One: 25 Jan 1979: Letters
IR: Anna Sebastian, IE: Harry King, Librarian
 1   IR:    1→   .hhh The (.) price being asked for these letters
 2                is (.) three thousand pou::nds.
 3   IR:    2→   Are you going to be able to raise it,
```

But this practice can be exploited, as in (3), to include background information which is quite damaging to the interviewee, then-presidential candidate Phil Gramm:

```
(3)   [Face The Nation 16 Apr. 1995 Senator Phil Gramm (Texas, R)]
 1   IR:       I just wanta get to thuh politics of this McNamara book. .hh
 2             a→  Ah President Clinton avoided thuh draft,
 3             b→  and he seemed to suggest that this book in some way:: ah
 4                 vindicates that draft avoidance and almost removes Vietnam
 5                 as a political issue now and forever more.
 6             c→  .hh You avoided thuh draft, .h
```

```
 7     d→   do you feel .h that this ih- this book is gonna help inoculate
 8          you from say Bob Dole, who has this war record, in your own
 9          competition?
10 IE:      I don't think so. I don't- I don't think I need vindication,
11          (0.3) and I don't think books vindicate you.
```

In both these cases, the interviewer has the room to make background statements, knowing that the interviewee should not respond until a question is put (Clayman and Heritage 2002a).

Distinct turn-taking systems are by no means definitive of institutional interaction. Indeed, as indicated earlier, most forms of institutional talk do not manifest specialized turn-taking systems at all. However, specialized turn-taking systems profoundly structure the frameworks of activity, opportunity, and interpretation that emerge within them. It is for this reason that the determination of their existence (or not), and investigation into their features constitute an important first step in the analysis of institutional talk.

Overall structural organization

With "overall structural organization", we address the fact that most interactions have phases of activity that ordinarily occur regardless of the interaction's particular content. In ordinary conversation, the openings and closings of the conversation are just this: pre-specified phases of action that are ordinarily features of almost every conversation and have dedicated sets of practices assigned to them (Schegloff 1968, 1986, Schegloff & Sacks 1973). Otherwise, however, conversation embodies an exceptionally open, fluid, and diverse set of activities and practices which combine and recombine in many unpredictable forms in line with the objectives and inclinations of the participants. For this reason, once we move outside openings and closings in conversation, we do not find other pre-specified phases of overall structure to identify.

Matters are rather different in institutional interactions where, as often as not, the overall task of the interaction involves recurrent phases of activity. For example, as chapter 5 will show, the overall structure of calls to 911 emergency consists of five parts of which the core is a request–response sequence with an intervening "interrogative series" (Zimmerman 1984, 1992). Similarly, as chapter 8 will outline, the acute primary care visit can be construed in terms of a six-part structure that is straightforwardly task-focused (Byrne & Long 1976, Robinson 2003).

To illustrate overall structural analysis we will look at a call in which a school truancy officer (Off) calls the mother of a child who has been absent from school:

(4)   Arroyo 1 (from Heritage 1997)
```
 1 Mom:      Hello.
 2           (0.5)
 3 Off:      Hello Mister Wilson?
 4           (0.8)
 5 Mom:      Uh: this is Missus Wilson.
 6 Off:      Uh Missus Wilson I'm sorry. This is Miss Matalin
 7           from Arroyo High School calling?
 8 Mom:      Mm [hm
```
-------End of section 1

```
 9  Off:         [.hhhhh Was Martin home from school ill today?=
10  Mom:         =U:::h yes he was in fact I'm sorry I- I didn' ca:ll
11               because uh::h I slept in late I (.) haven' been feeling
12               well either. .hhhh And uh .hhh (0.5) u::h he had uh yih
13               know, uh fever:
14               (0.2)
15  Mom:         this morning.
16  Off:         U::h hu:h,
17  ( ):         .hhh=
18  Mom:         =And uh I don' know y'know if he'll be (.) in
19               tomorrow fer sure er no:t, He's kinna j'st bin laying
20               arou:nd j(hh)uhkno:w,=
-----------End of section 2

21  Off:         =Okay well I'll [go ahead en:' u:hm
22  Mom:                         [( )
23  Off:         I won' call you tomorrow night if we don' see 'im
24               tomorrow we'll just assume he was home ill.
25               (.)
26  Mom:         nnRig[ht ( )
27  Off:              [A:n-
28  Off:         Send a note with him when he does return.
29  Mom:         I will.
-----------End of section 3

30  Off:         O:kay.
31  Mom:         Okay=
32  Off:         =Thank you
33  Mom:         Uh huh Bye [bye
34  Off:                    [B'bye
-----------End call
```

Here Ms. Matalin, the school truancy officer, places the call and Martin's mother answers the phone. Although there is only one task to perform, the call falls into four basic sections:

1 Opening: The first section (lines 1–8) is an "opening" section in which the parties enter into a state of interaction and establish their identities for one another (Schegloff 1986).
2 Problem initiation: In the second section (lines 9–20), Ms. Matalin gets to the "business" of the call by raising the question of Martin's absence and the mother explains it. I have termed this the "problem initiation" section, because although Martin's mother resolves the problem in this call, simple resolutions of this kind don't always happen.
3 Disposal: In the "disposal" section (lines 21–9), Ms. Matalin details the bureaucratic action she will take towards Martin's absence in the light of the mother's account, and describes the action that the mother should take. In other calls, she describes what the child should do as well.
4 Closing: The final section of the call (lines 30–4) is devoted to managing a coordinated exit from the conversation (Schegloff and Sacks 1973).

Each of these four sections involves the pursuit of a particular sub-goal within the interaction and is jointly oriented to, indeed co-constructed by, the speakers with that task in view.

In this call, all tasks are fulfilled to the apparent satisfaction of both parties, but this does not always happen and it is not essential to identifying sections of institutional talk. What we are identifying here are goal- or task-oriented sections, which the parties co-construct and identify as somehow relevant to the completion of their business together.

Identifying these main sections of the call allows us to notice other features as well:

1   Doing the sectional analysis forces us to see that the call is focused on a single topic – dealing with Martin's absence from school. Other interactions may have more than one item of business to transact: a patient, for example, may have several ailments to be dealt with, or a family may have several difficulties that require social worker support. This distinction can be important in analyzing institutional interaction.

2   The sectional analysis allows us to see significant stages in the *parties'* co-construction of the tasks and goals of the conversations, and that for the parties these are incremental moves towards the completion of the business of the call. This is significant. For example, in medicine the ways in which patients present their medical problems may already anticipate a possible diagnosis both implicitly (Stivers 2002a) and explicitly (Heritage and Robinson 2006a), and in these ways indicate an orientation favoring a particular treatment recommendation (Stivers, Mangione-Smith, Elliott et al. 2003). Particular behaviors during problem presentation pointing towards a physical examination, diagnosis or treatment (Robinson & Stivers 2001, Ruusuvuori 2001) may be used to indicate that, from the patient's point of view, the problem presentation is complete. Physician conduct during the physical examination may "forecast" (Maynard 1996) a final diagnosis (Stivers 1998, Heritage & Stivers 1999, Mangione-Smith, Stivers, Elliott et al. 2003). In all of these ways, the overall structure of an encounter may be evoked as a resource for moving the encounter forward.

3   Within each section, we can examine how the parties progressively develop (or not) a joint sense of the task that is to be accomplished and look at the roles each party plays in this process.

4   We can look at whether the parties agree about "where the boundaries are" as they shift from one section to another (Robinson & Stivers 2001). In this call, the parties make very clean transitions from one section (and one component of their "business") to the next. But confusion and foot-dragging are also possible: one party may want to move on the next issue while the other party is reluctant to quit the current one. Or one party may not recognize that a "next issue" is now relevant, while another is trying to press on with it. Different interests (and clear conflicts of interest) may be involved in these clashes.

Using this four-phase framework, it is relatively easy to identify the same sections, occurring in the same order, in most of the phone calls Ms. Matalin makes. However, the purpose of identifying these sections is not to exhaustively classify every piece of every one of Ms. Matalin's interactions in these terms. Still less is it to assert that these sections will always occur in her conversations in this order, or even that they will always occur. In other cases of these school calls, we can find the participants *reopening* sections and *reinstating* task orientations that they had previously treated as complete. The same applies to 911 calls and doctor–patient interactions. So we are not trying to find invariance or even statistical regularity in the presence or ordering of these sections. The purpose of describing these sections is to identify task orientations which the *participants* routinely co-construct in routine ways, and to see how they depart from these orientations as well. Overall structural organization, in short, is not a framework – fixed once and for all – to fit data into. Rather it is something that we're looking for and looking at only to the extent that the parties orient to it in organizing their talk.

The kind of complex internal structural organization of talk described in this section is not to be found in all forms of institutional talk. In news interviews, as in ordinary conversation, only the opening and closing activities of the interview are clearly structured in this way, though with very substantial differences from ordinary conversation itself (Clayman 1989, 1991, Clayman and Heritage 2002a). The kind of standardized, repetitive phases of activity that parties can use and rely on in their dealings with one another tends to be found in highly focused monotopical task-oriented encounters, including many kinds of bureaucratic and service encounters and interactions which involve requests for help of various kinds.

Sequence organization

Sequence organization is the engine room of interaction. It is through sequence organization that the activities and tasks central to interaction are managed. Sequence organization is the primary means through which both local interactional identities and roles (story teller, news deliverer, sympathizer) and more enduring social and institutional roles (woman, grandparent, Latino, etc.) are established, maintained, and manipulated. This role for sequence organization is true for both ordinary conversation and institutional interaction. In chapter 3, we saw this role for sequence organization: the presence and type of third turns to Q–A sequences was a significant (and recurrent) index of the social context of the interaction and the social identities of its participants.

To further illustrate the role of sequence organization, we return to a passage in our truancy call.

(5)   Arroyo 1 (detail)
```
  6  Off:   Uh Missus Wilson I'm sorry. This is Miss Matalin
  7          from Arroyo High School calling?
  8  Mom:   Mm [hm
  9  Off:      [.hhhhh Was Martin home from school ill today?=
 10  Mom:   =U:::h yes he was * in fact * I'm sorry I- I didn' ca:ll *
 11          because uh::h I slept in late * I (.) haven' been feeling
 12          well either. .hhhh And uh .hhh (0.5) u::h he had uh yih
 13          know, uh fever:
 14          (0.2)
 15  Mom:   this morning.
 16  Off:   U::h hu:h,
 17  ( ):   .hhh=
 18  Mom:   =And uh I don' know y'know if he'll be (.) in
 19          tomorrow fer sure er no:t, He's kinna j'st bin laying
 20          arou:nd j(hh)uhkno:w,=
```

Here, having finally secured Mrs. Wilson's identity after using a form of address ("Hello Mister Wilson?" that indicates a likely "business" call, Ms. Matalin introduces herself using a parallel form of address which she elaborates with an institutional identification "from Arroyo High School". This identification presupposes that she is unknown to her recipient in a way that "This is M̲iss Matalin. I'm Martin's violin teacher" would not. Finally she adds the "redundant" word "calling?", which carries a rising (continuing) intonation. The entire turn conveys that Miss Matalin is a school official, personally unknown to the Mom, and calling on official business that she is ready to go ahead with. The Mom responds with a "go ahead" continuer response at line 8. However, once Ms. Matalin has asked her the question about her son, the mother begins an elaborate response at line 10. In particular the Mom goes far beyond the basic task of filling the "information gap" raised by the question, and launches into a quite elaborate apology and account for her own actions (cf. Stivers & Heritage 2001).

Having given an initial response that confirms her child is at home ill, Mrs. Wilson continues with an apology for not calling (line 10), to which she adds an account (line 11) – she slept in late, to which she adds a further account – she hasn't been feeling well herself. These components are added in such a way as to interdict any intervention by Ms. Matalin. We have marked each potential terminal unit in her turn with an asterisk (*). None of them is brought to a clear intonational boundary (for example, falling "period" intonation), and the Mom even avoids taking an in-breath of air at these places. Moreover she only pauses at a grammatical place where Ms. Matalin would be unlikely to start a turn at talk (line 11).

All of this is significant because, given the turn-taking system for conversation (which is in play in this interaction), a sentence boundary is a place where Ms. Matalin could intervene with a question or a new observation, and thus disrupt the explanation that the mother is piecing together. It seems clear that the mother talks in the way she does so as to avoid creating these opportunities, and that she does this so that she can conclude her explanation for why she hasn't called the school without being interrupted. Thus it is only *after* she has completed her explanation that she hasn't been feeling well "either", that she takes a deep breath (as indicated by the four h's) at a sentence boundary.

If the mother's talk to this point is managed so as to retain the turn in progress, her subsequent elaboration seems to emerge because she is unable to relinquish it. Extending her turn at lines 12–13 with a description of the child's illness, she pauses at line 14, only to find no uptake from Ms. Matalin. In response to this, she re-completes her turn with an incremental (and redundant) time specification ("this morning"), and then encounters a response from Ms. Matalin ("uh huh") that is prototypically used to indicate an understanding that the previous speaker (in this case, the mother) is not yet finished. In the face of this response, the mother continues with a prognosis of her son's condition (lines 18–20), finally coming to a halt at line 20.

Thus in this exchange of question and answer-plus-elaboration, we can see that the mother treats Ms. Matalin's question as implicitly pointing to a fault in her conduct, a fault for which she is accountable, and for which she is at pains to supply an explanation. Rather than treating the question as a casual inquiry, this response embodies a particular – and specifically "institutional" – understanding of the question's relevance. Her subsequent extension of this account is the product of an implicit sequential negotiation over who will take the conversational initiative. The detailed internal structure of the mother's rather lengthy turn is thus the product of a complex sequential negotiation. There are many other aspects of the sequences making up this exchange that merit analysis of the institutional relevancies that inform their production. We will catch some of these aspects as we move on to the fourth area where initial analysis might proceed: turn design.

Turn design

Sequences are made up of turns and cannot, therefore, be completely analyzed without a major consideration of turn design. This section deals with some ways that institutional contexts are implicated in the design of turns and of the actions they implement. This is a massive topic and only glimpses of its ramifications can be presented in a short review. It is worth beginning, however, by remembering that in much institutional interaction a highly practiced institutional representative is talking with a very much less practiced layperson. Thus sheer repetition generates a kind of "knowhow" about dealing with the general public, and in particular how conflict or confrontation can be avoided. This is clearly illustrated in our truancy call. We particularly focus on the question at line 9: "Was Martin home from school ill today?"

```
(6)   Arroyo 1 (Detail)
 1  Mom:    Hello.
 2          (0.5)
 3  Off:    Hello Mister Wilson?
 4          (0.8)
 5  Mom:    Uh: this is Missus Wilson.
 6  Off:    Uh Missus Wilson I'm sorry. This is Miss Matalin
 7          from Arroyo High School calling?
 8  Mom:    Mm [hm
 9  Off:       [.hhhhh Was Martin home from school ill today?=
10  Mom:    =U:::h yes he was in fact I'm sorry I- I didn' ca:ll
11          because uh::h I slept in late I (.) haven' been feeling
12          well either. .hhhh And uh .hhh (0.5) u::h he had uh yih
13          know, uh fever:
```

Here the social context is delicate. Either the child is home sick and the mother has failed in her obligation to notify the school of this fact, or the child is a truant from school, and the mother is unaware of this fact. Neither contingency reflects well on the family. At line 9, Ms. Matalin uses a highly designed turn to initiate the "move to business" which manages the delicacy of the situation in various ways.

1   Her question clearly implicates that the child was not at school, but it is not explicitly occupied with "informing" the parent of that fact (cf. Pomerantz 1988, 2004). Instead, by implying that the child is absent as part of a question, this turn avoids an asserting the absence in a way that might be heard as accusatory (e.g., "I'm calling because Martin wasn't at school today.").
2   The question offers the most *frequent* and *legitimate* account for a child to be away from school – sickness – using a question form that is designed for the mother to respond to affirmatively.
3   Even if it turns out that the child is in fact truant, the inquiry avoids any direct reference to, or implication, of that possibility. That possibility is, however, put in play by the inquiry.
4   Finally the question does not directly thematize the parent's responsibility to inform the school, but rather leaves it to the parent to assume the responsibility, where relevant, which this parent does in fact do (lines 10–11).

This school official begins many of her routine calls with this question, and it is not difficult to see why. Almost any other opening might attract greater resistance, or cause disagreements or arguments to emerge. If she was not directly taught this opening, the official will likely have developed it through experience, because it is a question design which evokes least resistance. As in the design of a car, the aerodynamics of this question has gone through a wind tunnel of testing by repeated use. This judicious, cautious, even bureaucratic question design is the kind of design that develops in contexts where officials have to do interactionally delicate things on a repetitive basis.

As Drew and Heritage (1992) note, turn design involves two distinct elements of selection: (1) the action that the talk is designed to perform and (2) the means that are selected to perform the action.

The first sense in which a turn is "designed" concerns the selection of the action which someone wants to accomplish in a turn at talk. In work on health visitors' home visits to mothers of newborns, we came across the following sequence in the health visitor's opening visit. The father and mother respond to what looks like a casual observation by the health visitor by performing quite different actions:

```
(7)  [HV:4A1:1] [Heritage and Sefi 1992: 367]
  1  HV:        He's enjoying that [isn't he.
  2  F:    →                      [°Yes, he certainly is=°
  3  M:    →    =He's not hungry 'cuz (h)he's ju(h)st (h)had
  4             'iz bo:ttle .hhh
  5             (0.5)
  6  HV:        You're feeding him on (.) Cow and Gate Premium.=
```

The health visitor's remark "He's enjoying that" notices the baby sucking or chewing on something.[2] In response the father immediately and simply agrees. The mother responds quite differently. By replying with "He's not hungry", the mother treats the health visitor's remark as implying that this is why the baby is "enjoying" whatever he's sucking or chewing – an implication which she further opposes by observing that the baby has just been fed. The mother's response, then, is defensive in rejecting an unstated implication which she treats the health visitor's remark as having. The father, by contrast, simply agrees with the health visitor.

Thus in "constructing" their responses (quite apart from the particular designs of their turns), the mother and father have elected to perform alternative activities. Both activities, of course, have a logic as relevant next actions. The father treats the health visitor's remark as innocent while the mother finds in it an implied criticism regarding the proper care of her baby. They thus construct their responses differently by selecting different next actions. These two actions may well reflect a division of labor in the family, in which the mother is treated as having the primary responsibility for her baby (reflected in her defensiveness), while the father, with less responsibility, can take a more relaxed and innocent view of things.

The second aspect of turn design arises from the fact that the same action can be performed in a variety of different ways. Thus speakers must also select among alternative ways of performing an action. The following extract, from the same health visitor interaction as the previous one, illustrates this clearly. In this extract, the mother and father each perform a broadly similar activity – agreeing with the health visitor's suggestion that they'll be "amazed" at the child's progress (in physical development) – and they do so nearly simultaneously (lines 5 and 6). But they design their agreements rather differently. While the mother's agreement refers to the development of children in general ("They learn so quick don't they"), the father refers to their experience of their own child's progress ("We have noticed hav'n't w-"). While the father's utterance exhibits a commitment to noticing their own child's behavior and development, the mother's response does not.

```
(8)  [HV:4A1:2] [Drew and Heritage 1992: 34]
 1   HV:        It's amazing, there's no stopping him now, you'll be
 2              amazed at all the di[fferent things he'll start doing.
 3   F:                            [(hnh hn)
 4              (1.0)
 5   M:    →    Yeh. They [learn so quick don't they.
 6   F:    →              [We have noticed hav'n't w-
 7   HV:        That's right.
 8   F:    →    We have noticed (0.8) making a grab for your bottles.
 9              (1.0)
10   F:        Hm[::.
11   HV:          [Does he: (.) How often does he go between his feeds?
```

Significantly, the mother's response avoids the "expert–novice" stance that the health visitor's remark might be seen as expressing, while the father's agreement(s) (at lines 6 and 8) seem designed to prove to the health visitor that they are observant and alert about their new baby. The different ways in which they design their actions may also point to the same underlying division of labor in the family that we suggested earlier. The father, who is putatively the junior partner in the family's child care arrangements, appears eager to prove their competence in noticing the details of their child's behavior. The mother's agreement, by contrast, seems to avoid taking the "inferior" and "inexpert" position of proving anything to the health visitor, but rather asserts an agreement in bland and general terms.

Lexical choice

Turn designs are implemented with words that have to be selected. Our "Why that now?" question can certainly embrace this process of selection. We have already noted the significance of word selection when we commented that Ms. Matalin's choice of her "last name + organizational ID" projected a business call. And we can add that when she asked "Hello Mr. Wilson?", her addressee chose a parallel form of identification when she responded "Uh: this is M̲issus Wilson." Lexical choice implies that alternative lexical formulations are available to reference the same state of affairs. For example, speakers can reference themselves using "I" or "We", the latter choice often being used to index that they are speaking on behalf of an institution (Sacks 1992). Again, law enforcement can be referred to as "police" or "cops", but the selection between these two terms may be sensitive to whether the speaker is appearing in court (Jefferson 1974), or talking with adolescent peers (Sacks 1979).

To illustrate lexical choice, we will focus on uses of the word "notice" in two institutional contexts. The first is from a call to 911 emergency:

(9)   [Zimmerman, 1992: 440]
```
  1   C:          .hh Yeah hi, uh this is Mary Cooper .hh um: my sister and I
  2               left our house earlier tonight (.) and we were certain we
  3               locked thuh doors and .hh when we came back .hh oh: about a
  4        →      half hour ago oh twenty minutes ago .hh we noticed thuh
  5               front door was open hhh an so we jus' didn' feel like uh
  6               checkin' aroun: so I thought we'd call you
```

Here a caller is reporting something suspicious about her house: she left the doors locked, and when she returned the front door was open. This discovery is reported as something that she and her sister "noticed" (line 4). When persons describe something as a "noticing", what they are conveying is that coming upon it was unmotivated: it was not something they were "looking for" (Halkowski 2006). In this case, what seems to be suggested with this verb is that the discovery was inadvertent, unexpected, and not the product of a witness who is on the lookout for problems.

A similar usage is also apparent in the following case, from a pediatric primary care visit. A mother is presenting her eleven-year-old daughter's upper respiratory symptoms. The time is Monday afternoon, and the daughter has not attended school. The mother begins with a diagnostic claim (lines 1–2, 5) which strongly conveys her commitment to the veracity of her daughter's claims about her symptoms, and may imply the relevance of antibiotic treatment (Stivers 2002a, Stivers, Mangione-Smith, Elliott et al. 2003):

(10)   [Pediatric Visit]
```
  1   MOM:        .hhh Uhm (.) Uh- We're- thinking she might have an
  2               ear infection? [in thuh left ear?
  3   DOC:                       [Okay,
  4   DOC:        Oka:y,
  5   MOM:        Uh:m because=uh: she's had some pain_
  6               (.)
  7   DOC:        [Alrighty?
  8   MOM:        [over thuh weekend:. .h[h
  9   DOC:                               [No fever er anything?,
 10   MOM:        Uhm[:
 11   DOC:           [Mkay:[:?
 12   MOM:                 [An' uh sore throat_
 13               (0.2)
 14   MOM:        An:' like uh (.) cold.
 15               (.)
 16   DOC:        Wow.
 17   MOM:        (An' thuh)/(Kinda thuh) cold symptoms, huhhh.
 18   DOC:        Was it like that over thuh weekend too?
 19               (0.2)
 20   MOM:   →    Uh:m: When did you notice it.
 21               (.)
 22   MOM:   →    <Yesterday you mentioned it.
 23   PAT:        Yesterday.
 24   DOC:        M[kay.
 25   MOM:         [It started yesterday. (     )/(0.5)
 26               (0.2)
 27   DOC:        °#Lemme write that i:n,#°
```

After some elaboration of the child's cold symptoms (lines 12–17), the doctor asks about their duration (line 18), and the mother refers the question to her daughter at line 20 ("Uh:m: When did you notice it."). As in the previous case, her use of the word "notice" conveys a quite distinct notion of attention and cognition. It conveys that the child's perception of her symptoms emerged in an unlooked-for and, hence, unmotivated way. Its use is one of several ways in which the mother conveys her commitment to the factual status of her daughter's symptoms. It helps to convey that the symptoms were genuine, and to offset any suspicion that they were fabricated as a means of not attending school – an issue that can hang heavily over Monday visits to the pediatrician! Subsequently the mother distinguishes between the child's noticing her symptoms and "mentioning" them – thus opening up the possibility that the child has endured them for longer than 24 hours, which would further underwrite the unmotivated nature of their discovery and report. Here then what is at issue is how the "discovery" and "recognition" of the child's medical symptoms are to be portrayed (Halkowski 2006).

Lexical choice and person reference (Drew & Sorjonen 1997, Enfield & Stivers 2007) are profoundly complex aspects of institutional talk. They embody highly general principles which are nonetheless exquisitely linked to the interactional projects in which the participants are engaged. As Schegloff (1972) showed years ago, lexical formulation is strongly impacted by considerations of "recipient design", having to do with the particular circumstances and individuals involved in the interaction. This is just as true of institutional contexts as it is of ordinary conversational interaction. Examining participants lexical choices, therefore, can give a very exact window into how they are oriented to the states of affairs they wish to describe, the circumstances they are in, and the ways in which those circumstances are to be navigated.

Conclusion

An abiding feature of many forms of institutional interaction is the discrepancy in experience between professionals – whether they be school officials, health visitors, 911 call-takers, doctors, or teachers – and lay persons. For example, an emergency call center in a mid-sized US city may take upwards of one million calls per year, but the individual caller may be making his or her once-in-a-lifetime call to the call center. An average patient makes an average of three office medical visits per year, while a physician may easily deal with thirty times as many visits in a week. These are very substantial discrepancies in experience, and they are associated with very extensive differences in technical knowledge, institutional knowhow, and rights to express knowledge by the participants. Added to this are the potentially very great differences in the emotional involvement of the participants in the topics of institutional interaction (Whalen & Zimmerman 1998). A call to 911 emergency may be a matter of routine for the call-taker, but of life and death to the caller (Whalen, Zimmerman, & Whalen 1988). A condition which is "unusual" or "interesting" to a physician may threaten a patient's entire well-being, and her sense of a future (Maynard 2003). A professor whose interest is primarily in subject matter may be faced by students whose primary interest is in their grades. These topics are generally handled under the rubric of "asymmetry" in institutional talk. Asymmetry and its dysfunctions have animated many studies of the doctor–patient relationship (see Mishler 1984, West 1984, Waitzkin 1991, and Fisher & Todd 1993, amid many others). It is implicit in many studies of pedagogy and its dysfunctions (Rosenthal &

Jacobson 1968, Rist 1970), and in numerous studies of organizational decision making. In all of these areas it is generally recognized that interactional practices both reflect and embody differential access to resources and to power. A summary of the many strands of research in this domain is beyond the scope of this chapter (see Drew & Heritage 1992, Drew & Sorjonen 1997). But it is highly significant in our treatment of the institutional domains, which forms the subject matter of the rest of this book.

In conclusion, we revisit the idea that there are layers of organization within institutional talk that we can examine. These layers nest within one another. The selection of words (lexical choice) contributes to turn design and the building of actions within turns. Turn design contributes to sequence organization which, in turn, contributes to the phases of inter-action which make up its overall structural organization. All of these activities are pervaded by the turn-taking system that is in play within a given type of interaction. These layers, or orders, of organization can also be viewed as "keys" that can be used to unlock institutional data. Our "Why that now?" question can be used to ask questions about why particular words were chosen, why turns were designed that way, how and why particular sequences were built, and how and why the phases of the interaction took the exact form that they did. In the process, we start to understand the constraints under which institutional participants operate, how the participants situate themselves within the institution, and how they build and rebuild their institutional contexts within a framework of agency and constraint.

For Further Reading

Although this chapter has cited a very large array of studies, the actual number of studies of interaction in institutions is vast and completely exceeds the scope of this chapter. Accordingly we focus here on two areas of research that are not touched on in this chapter, but which are nonetheless important. The first of these is the workplace studies initiated by conversation analysts in business schools and corporate think tanks like Xerox Parc. These often focus on high-tech situations and computer-mediated interaction, for example Lucy Suchman's pioneering *Plans and Situated Actions* (1987), and Christian Heath and Paul Luff's *Technology in Action* (2000). A second important line of research has focused on the embodiment of work activities. Heath and his group have been important in this domain as well, but the pioneering studies have been performed by Charles Goodwin. Amid a large variety of papers, Goodwin's "Seeing in depth" (1995) – a study of work on an oceanographic vessel – and his "Transparent vision" (1996) – a study of an airline's operations control room – are part of a series of papers on concerted practices of action and cognition inside workplace environments. (We discuss another paper in this series, "Professional vision" (1994), in chapter 12.) Finally, an institutional context of questions and answers that is of particular interest to social scientists is the survey interview. For CA studies of social surveys, see Houtkoop-Steenstra (2000), and Maynard, Houtkoop-Steenstra, Schaeffer et al. (2002).

Notes

1   When Chief Justice Roberts departed from the oath of office as prescribed in the United States Constitution at the swearing in of President Barack Obama in January 2009, the ceremony was repeated the following day at the White House to pre-empt any claim that Obama was not the legal president of the United States (Washington Post, January 22nd, 2009).

2   Unfortunately, we don't have a videotape, but certainly this is how the mother understands the word "enjoy" when she responds "He's not hungry . . ." (lines 3–4).

II

Calls for Emergency Service

5

Emergency Calls as Institutional Talk

After leaving work one evening, a man discovers that his car's passenger window has been broken. He calls 911 to report the apparent vandalism, and a police car is dispatched to the scene.

A woman glances out her living room window one evening and notices an unfamiliar vehicle idling suspiciously in the street near her house. She calls 911, but since there could be a benign explanation, the call-taker urges her to call back if something else transpires.

A man returns home to find his wife bleeding from a self-inflicted gunshot wound. He calls 911 and paramedics are sent to administer medical assistance and transport her to a hospital.

Every day, in countries all around the world, many thousands of telephone calls like these are made in pursuit of some type of police, fire, or medical assistance. Sometimes these calls are placed to specific public safety organizations like the local police or fire department, but many are placed to general emergency dispatch centers like 911 in the US, 999 in the UK, and 112 in most of Europe. Some involve urgent and life-threatening emergencies, while others are occasioned by less serious troubles. Some concern problems that are absolutely clear-cut, while others involve situations that are ambiguous or only potentially problematic. In some instances the request is for information only and assistance may be rendered over the phone, but often the request is more substantial, requiring the dispatch of a patrol car, fire truck, or paramedic unit. Such calls are typically quite brief, with most lasting less than fifteen seconds from start to finish, although they can also be considerably longer.

On the surface, emergency calls are remarkably varied, with differences in the type, severity, and urgency of the problem at hand as well as the remedial service being sought. But if one looks beyond the surface *content* of the talk to the underlying *activities* of which it is composed, the activity framework exhibits a striking degree of uniformity. Emergency calls as a group are distinguished from ordinary conversational telephone calls by the narrowness and specificity of this framework. Their hallmark is that there is a single order of business or task that occupies the participants from the beginning of the call until the end. The participants come together only in order to discharge this task, so their relationship to one another – such as it is – is essentially anonymous, purely instrumental, and does not extend beyond the call itself. Correspondingly, they act exclusively under the auspices of their institutional roles as citizen caller and emergency call-taker. This in turn establishes a framework of relevance that powerfully shapes both the allowable contributions that each party may make, and the inferences that may be drawn on the basis of those contributions.

Calls for emergency service thus exhibit all of the identifying features of institutional talk outlined in the previous chapter, and they do so in a particularly stark and transparent way. In the continuum from open-ended and sociable conversation to task-oriented forms of institutional talk, the emergency call falls at the extreme latter end. It is also, we might add, an enormously consequential form of talk, one that plays a pivotal role in delivering vital services to members of the public. For all of these reasons, the domain of the emergency call stands as an ideal point of departure.

For this tour of emergency calls, we draw on a range of conversation analytic research studies, and we are particularly indebted to pioneering research conducted by Don Zimmerman (University of California, Santa Barbara), Marilyn Whalen (Palo Alto Research Center), Jack Whalen (Palo Alto Research Center), and Jörg Bergmann (University of Bielefeld).

Background: Public Safety Communication Centers

Specific public safety organizations like police and fire departments have existed for centuries, but the general-purpose public safety communication center is a relatively recent development, one that emerged following the invention of the telephone. The British system dates back to the 1930s, while the American system developed over the course of the 1960s and 1970s. Most industrialized countries now have a system of this kind, with a single telephone number – typically a three-digit number – that enables those with public safety problems of various kinds to solicit help efficiently.

There is a tremendous demand for the services dispatched through public safety communication centers, and the centers themselves process an enormous number of incoming calls. Large cities like New York, Los Angeles, and London can get more than a million calls per year. In recent years the volume of calls has risen with the spread of cell phones, which has made the telephone readily and continuously accessible to most people. To alleviate the pressure on emergency call centers, some locales have implemented a second telephone number (e.g., 311 in the US) dedicated to less urgent calls for governmental and other social services.

The work involved in processing emergency calls may be subdivided into two basic tasks: (1) *call taking*, or dealing with the citizen caller and soliciting information relevant to the provision of assistance, and (2) *dispatching help* by relaying the relevant information to the appropriate police, fire, or paramedic facility. Call centers differ in terms of how they co-ordinate these tasks. In some centers, the tasks of taking calls and dispatching help are entirely separate, performed by different people in different locations. Alternatively, the tasks may be done in the same room, with call-takers and dispatchers in close proximity (see figure 5.1). The latter arrangement enables workers to monitor one another's activities, and facilitates the simultaneous interweaving of the two tasks. As the call-taker is dealing with a citizen caller, nearby dispatchers can "eavesdrop" and may begin to dispatch help even as the call is unfolding (Whalen & Zimmerman 2005).

Thus, even though only a single person is actually on the phone talking with the caller, the work of processing the call can be a team effort involving a multiplicity of public safety communications personnel. This collaborative work environment can in turn reach into the calls themselves and affect their course and trajectory, as when call-takers loudly repeat and highlight certain key terms used by callers – terms like "fire", "gun", and "heart attack". For instance, here "gun" is repeated with marked emphasis.

Figure 5.1 Atlanta emergency call center. Source: Georgia Tech Research News, Aug. 14, 2002. http://gtresearchnews.gatech.edu/newsrelease/DRIVEATL.htm

(1) [from Whalen 1995: 204]
```
 1  Clr:      . . .he's got a gun and he's comin' back
 2  911:    → He's got a gu::n?
```

In one sense, such repeats are addressed to the caller and their manifest function is to seek verification for important details in the caller's report. But they also have a latent function, namely to inform overhearing dispatchers and enable them to take action promptly. Indeed, there is good evidence that dispatchers actively monitor for key work-related terms of this sort, and call-takers may produce them with an eye toward their overhearability (Whalen & Zimmerman 2005).

Finally, emergency calls have been impacted by the advent of the computer. Most call centers in the US now use *computer aided dispatch* (CAD),[1] which supplies call-takers with an onscreen form in which to enter the information they receive from callers. The data entry form has fixed fields for the type of incident or problem, its location, and various supporting details (see figure 5.2 for a typical example). The fields are arranged in a specific configuration on the form, and some fields are obligatory in that they must be filled before the information can be electronically relayed. Experienced call-takers are artful and skilled at navigating this onscreen form. Nevertheless, the data entry form, coupled with the changing position of the computer cursor as a given call unfolds, is an important contingency affecting

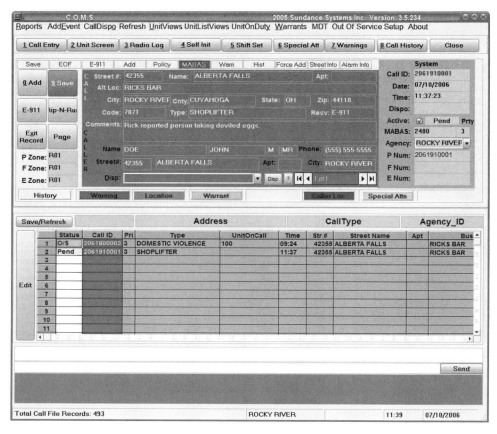

Figure 5.2 Computer aided dispatch, data entry form. Source: http://www.sundance-sys.com/
images/CADScreenCallEntryLarge.jpg

both the order of call-takers' questions and their sensitivity – or lack thereof – to callers'
previous talk (Whalen 1995).

Most callers are, of course, wholly unaware of the social ecology and technological infrastructure of emergency call centers, and most are also novices with this type of interaction.
Although service calls of other kinds are more commonplace, for the vast majority of callers
placing an emergency call is an exceedingly rare if not entirely unique event. By contrast,
call-takers receive calls of this sort routinely, and they have a thorough understanding of
the social and technological circumstances. They know precisely what must transpire in
order for a given call to progress to a satisfactory conclusion. As was noted in chapter 4,
asymmetries of knowledge and experience characterize most service provider/client
encounters, but here the asymmetry is enormous. As we examine emergency calls in the pages
and chapters to follow, it is important to bear in mind the sheer magnitude of the gulf
separating participants. For the caller this is apt to be a new venture into unfamiliar interactional territory; for the call-taker it is utterly routine, the umpteenth call he or she has
received that day.

The Overall Structure of Emergency Calls

Turning now to the calls themselves, we begin at the most macroscopic level by considering the overall structure of emergency calls. Calls of this sort follow a specific arc or trajectory consisting of five basic components (Zimmerman 1984, 1992). These are best under-stood as phases of activity that recurrently unfold in the same predictable order, with each phase distinguished from the next by the specific task occupying the participants. They are:

1 opening
2 request
3 interrogative series
4 response
5 closing

The phases are mapped onto a typical emergency call in the following example.

```
(2)  [Zimmerman 1984: 214]
  1  911:   Midcity Emergency::,
  2          (.)                                    Opening
  3  Clr:   U::m yeah (.)
     ------------------------------------------
  4          somebody just vandalized my car,       Request
     ------------------------------------------
  5          (0.3)
  6  911:   What's your address.
  7  Clr:   three oh one six maple
  8  911:   Is this a house or an apartment.
  9  Clr:   I::t's a house                          Interrogative series
 10  911:   (Uh-) your last name.
 11  Clr:   Minsky
 12  911:   How do you spell it?
 13  Clr:   M I N S K Y
     ------------------------------------------
 14  911:   We'll send someone out to see you.      Response
 15  Clr:   Thank you.=
     ------------------------------------------
 16  911:   =Umhm bye.=                             Closing
 17  Clr:   =Bye.
```

It bears emphasis that the boundaries between phases in this illustration are approximate. A single turn (and sometimes a sequence of turns) may "pivot" between phases, functioning as the last turn in one phase and the first turn in the next. For instance, the "thank you" in line 15 is just such a pivotal turn – in accepting the promise of assistance it is part of the response phase, but in completing the sole task of the call it also moves toward closing. Nevertheless, the diagram provides a rough guide to how these phases are manifest in an actual emergency call.

The opening and closing phases will be discussed later on, so for now let us zero in on the meat of the call sandwiched in between. Much of the call is organized around a single adjacency pair sequence consisting of a request for help (phase 2) and a response to that request (phase 4), which typically involves a granting of the request in the form of a promise of assistance. All normal emergency calls have this simple request–response sequence at their core, even though some are very short (less than 15 seconds) and others are much longer (several minutes). Most of the variation in length stems from the phase intervening between the request and its granting or refusal, namely a succession of questions and answers or inter-rogative series (phase 3). Although this phase may contain just a few simple questions (as in excerpt 2 above), as we shall see in the next chapter it can expand like an accordion into a lengthy interrogation. Extended interrogative series arise recurrently when the problem at hand is atypical, complex, or ambiguous. Conversely the series may be shortened when callers build additional information into the initial request turn (e.g., details about the problem, its location, caller's own name), thereby anticipating and forestalling subsequent questions on these matters.

Regarding the interrogative series, notice that it is the call-taker who launches this phase and instigates most of the questioning. Call-takers are in the interactional driver's seat during most of this phase, and this is not coincidental; there are both interactional and insti-tutional reasons for this arrangement. As recipients of a request for help, call-takers are charged with responsibility for dispensing a desired service. Moreover, as agents of a bureaucratic entity that interfaces with a variety of public safety organizations, they are attentive to established operating procedures specifying when and how scarce police, fire, and paramedic resources should be mobilized (Zimmerman 1984). Thus, most of the questions that call-takers ask are necessary to deal with the request – to determine whether assistance is warranted, and if so to extract the information necessary to render that assistance in an appropriate and effective way. They seek information about the problem itself (the type of problem, degree of urgency, etc.), its location (the street address, type of dwelling, how to gain access, etc.), and sometimes other details such as the caller's identity, involvement, and basis for believing that the problem is genuine. In excerpt (2) above, the type of prob-lem (vandalized car) is already conveyed in the initial request (line 4), so the call-taker's subsequent questions (lines 6–13) concern locational information and the caller's name. This is, in turn, a prelude to the subsequent promise of assistance (line 14).

If call-takers take the lead in driving the interrogative series, callers are typically quite willing to be driven. In excerpt (2), notice that the caller not only answers the questions, but does so straightforwardly and without protest or complaint. That callers are generally co-operative during this phase is remarkable given that an unrealized request for help remains on the table. As we saw in chapter 2, sequence-initiating actions obligate their recipients to provide an appropriate response, so that if it is not immediately forthcoming the first speaker can insist on the called-for response. Emergency callers, however, typically do not insist that their requests be granted (or refused) straightaway. Underlying such patience is the inference that the call-taker's questions, while not immediately fulfilling the request, are nonetheless dealing with issues raised by it and are thus broadly relevant and responsive to the agenda that the request set in motion. Callers can, in other words, see that the questions are moving in the right direction. In general, then, when call-takers start asking questions, callers fall cooperatively into line.

There are, of course, occasional exceptions to this generalization. When callers are highly distressed in the face of disturbing or life-threatening circumstances, they may fail to grasp the relevance and import of the call taker's questions. In an infamous call to the Dallas Fire Department (discussed further in chapter 7), the caller's response (arrowed) to the very first question challenges the relevance of that question and suggests by implication that it is an unnecessary diversion from the task at hand (Whalen, Zimmerman, & Whalen 1988).

```
(3)   [Dallas Call]
  1  FD:        Fire department
  2             (0.8)
  3  Clr:       Yes, I'd like tuh have an ambulance at forty one
  4             thirty nine Haverford please?
  5             (0.2)
  6  FD:        What's thuh problem sir.
  7  Clr:    →  I: don't know, n'if I knew I wouldn't be ca:lling
  8             you all.
```

A failure to grasp the relevance of the questions can be manifest in more subtle ways. Later in the same call, when the caller is asked by the fire department nurse if he is in a house or an apartment, his response – "It is a home" – declines to choose from among the alternatives and fails to provide the information that paramedics will need to locate and gain entry to the residence.

```
(4)   [Dallas Call]
  1  N:         Okay iz this uh house or n' apartmen'?
  2  Clr:       It- it is a ho:me
```

This response is indicative of a caller who is so distressed (indeed, his mother is deathly ill) that he simply cannot maintain a grasp on the larger agenda that motivates the call-taker's questions. Exceptional cases of this sort demonstrate the fragility of the interrogative series in distressing circumstances, while at the same time highlighting the interpretive work that underlies the successful navigation of this phase in routine calls.

Now this basic five-phase structure is not unique to emergency calls. The same basic structure may be found in calls for other kinds of service, as in this call to an airline reservation service (Zimmerman 1984). Here the request is for information regarding the cost of a round trip flight from Portland to DC.

```
(5)   [Zimmerman 1984: 216]
  1  CT:        Federated Airlines Reservations Joanne        Opening
  2  Clr:       Hi
     ------------------------------------------------------------
  3  Clr:       Could you tell me what your cheapest fare would be    Request
  4             from Portland to Washington, DC?
     ------------------------------------------------------------
  5  CT:        Mhm? You're travelling one way or round trip?
  6  Clr:       Round trip
  7  CT:        And when are you planning on travelling
  8  Clr:       Uh probably in the summer sometime              Interrogative
  9  CT:        Okay So it would be after the fifteenth of June   series
 10             you'd be leaving?
 11  Clr:       Yes
 12  CT:        All right About how long'r you planning on staying
 13  Clr:       Um two or three weeks?
     ------------------------------------------------------------
 14  CT:        Okay Okay I can tell you right away the lowest rate
 15             that we can offer um would be our Super Saver fare   Response
```

```
16                 (.) You would have to make your reservation at least
17                 a week before you travel
18   Clr:         Mhm
19   CT:          Okay for the lowest fare (.) you'd have to stay at
20                 least seven days (.) and not more than fourteen days
21   Clr:         Okay
22   CT:          'Kay An' that's going to be a round trip of three
23                 ninety nine
```

Much of the same activity structure can also be found in ordinary conversational telephone calls between acquaintances, when a request of some kind is involved (Schegloff 1990). Here a young girl calls a friend and asks to borrow his BB gun for use in a school play. This request (at line 1) gives way to a lengthy round of questioning (lines 3–23) in which the gun owner asks which gun is being requested, why it's needed, and so on, before finally granting the request (line 24).

```
(6)   [Schegloff 1990: 56–7]
  1   B:          .hhh 'n I was wondering if you'd let me borrow your gun.
  2               (1.2)
  3   J:          My gun?
  4   B:          Yeah.
  5               (1.0)
  6   J:          What gun?
  7               ((Repair sequence omitted))
  8   J:          What- I meant was which gun.
  9               (0.5)
 10   B:          tch .hhh Oh (0.4) uh::m (0.4) t .hhh (0.5)
 11               D'j'have a really lo:ng one,
 12               (0.8)
 13   J:          A really l:ong one .hh[h
 14   B:                                [Yeah.
 15               (0.2)
 16   B:          't doesn't matter what ki:nd.
 17               (1.0)
 18   J:          Why:: would you like a >really long one.
 19               ((repair sequence omitted))
 20   B:          I am doing a pl- a thing. (0.3) .hhh in drama....
 21             .
 22             . ((More talk about the play, B's part within it, etc))
 23             .
 24   B:          Yeah: you can use 't,
```

So at least at the level of the core request sequence, the emergency call resembles other service calls, including those that are not specifically "institutional" in character.

There is, however, a critical element that distinguishes *institutional* service calls from *conversational* calls that happen to *contain* a service request. In the BB gun call above, the request sequence is just one part of a much longer call encompassing many topics and tasks. The two friends converse about all sorts of things, and for good reason. When friends and relations call each other to request a favor of some sort – a ride to school, a borrowed jacket, a sum of money, etc. – talk about other matters serves to acknowledge an interpersonal relationship beyond the purely instrumental one of delivering and providing a service. Callers, in other words, seek to avoid treating their friends and relations as if they were nothing more than chauffeurs, loan officers, or other service providers. Indeed, not only do conversational callers make a point of introducing other topics, but they may prioritize those topics by raising them first in the course of the call. They thereby treat the other (non-request) subject as the official reason for the call, while deferring the request and allowing it to "come up naturally" later on (Schegloff & Sacks 1973). Conversational calls, furthermore, have built-in opportunities for prioritizing unplanned, non-instrumental, and purely sociable talk, most notably the *how are you* sequences that are typically exchanged before callers introduce the official reason for calling (discussed further below; see also Schegloff 1986). All of this results in a class of telephone calls that are relatively unpredictable and, in the aggregate, lack a standardized overall shape.

We return, then, to our initial observation about the five-phase structure of emergency calls. It may have seemed at first like an obvious point, but it goes to the heart of what makes such calls prototypically institutional. Unlike ordinary conversation, where the range of actions and opportunities for action reflect broader forms of sociability and more fully developed social relationships, in an emergency call the exclusive focus on a singular task is both relevant and appropriate. The recurrent five-phase structure organized around a single request–response sequence is thus a concrete embodiment of the "strictly business" orientation that runs like a spine through emergency calls from start to finish.

Openings: Constraints on Contributions

Just as a focused orientation to task shapes the overall structure of the emergency call, it also reaches into the design of specific phases of activity. Here we take a closer look at the opening phase, and we begin with a brief sketch of openings in ordinary conversational telephone calls, drawing on research by Emmanuel Schegloff (1968, 1979, 1986). This will reveal with greater specificity how the practices of ordinary conversation get reduced and specialized in the emergency call environment.

Conversational call openings normally contain four basic components before the introduction of the first official topic. These components, each of which is addressed to a specific interactional problem, ordinarily unfold in the order exemplified in the following excerpt.

```
(7)  (Schegloff 1986: 115).
 1              ((ring))
 2   Res:       Hallo,
 3   Clr:       Hello Jim?
 4   Res:       Yeah,
 5   Clr:       's Bonnie.
 6   Res:       Hi,
 7   Clr:       Hi, how are yuh
 8   Res:       Fine, how're you,
 9   Clr:       Oh, okay I guess
10   Res:       Oh okay.
11   Clr:       Uhm (0.2) what are you doing New Year's Eve.
```

First comes the *summons–answer* sequence, here consisting of the telephone's ring and the recipient's first "hallo" (lines 1–2). This sequence opens the channel of communication, establishes each party's availability and readiness for talk, and brings them into a state of mutual engagement.

Next comes the *identification/recognition* component (lines 2–6), wherein the parties arrive at an understanding of who they are talking to. While this can be facilitated by the technology of caller ID, it is otherwise accomplished through the interaction itself by either of two basic methods: (1) recognition by voice sample, and (2) self-identification. Both methods are used in the preceding example. The caller recognizes the call recipient merely by hearing the initial "hello" (line 2), and she subsequently displays her recognition by guessing the recipient's name ("Jim" in line 3). The call recipient, by contrast, merely confirms the name guess (line 4) and hence does not display any recognition of the caller from the voice sample provided through that guess. This, in turn, leads the caller to resort to the other method to convey her identity to the recipient, that of self-identification (line 5). While the parties utilize alternate methods to achieve identification/recognition, the method of recognition by voice sample is treated as preferred over self-identification (Schegloff 1979), and personal names are utilized whenever possible (Schegloff 1996).

The third and fourth components, the exchange of *greetings* (the reciprocal "hi" in lines 6–7) and *how are you* queries (lines 7–10), are both straightforwardly observable in this example. Greetings are often intertwined with the identification/recognition process, because issuing a greeting can be a way of claiming to have recognized the other person. And *how are yous* provide each party with an opportunity to introduce some pressing matter in advance of the official reason for the call.

After these four components are completed, the caller introduces the reason for calling, which here (line 11) involves a prelude to an invitation.

Turning now to openings in emergency calls, such as the next example, it is immediately apparent that there are enormous differences (Whalen & Zimmerman 1987).

(8) [Midcity 21: Midnight–1:00am: 5a]
```
1              ((ring))
2  911:   Midcity emergency?
3  Clr:   Yes uh::=I need a paramedic please,
4  911:   Where to.
```

Perhaps the most obvious difference is the greater brevity and compactness of the opening. Two of the four components are entirely absent here, namely the exchange of greetings and *how are yous*. It may be tempting to explain this by reference to the urgency of the problem and the impetus to get to the point quickly – here, in the second turn at talk – and that may indeed be a factor in cases like this one where paramedic assistance is requested. But similar absences are found also in calls for non-urgent matters such as minor acts of vandalism (see example (2) above) and loud parties:

(9) [Midcity 21: Call 24 (15.43)]
```
1  911:   Midcity emergenc(h)y,
2  Clr:   Yes I'd like tuh report a loud party.
3  911:   ((keyboard)) Where is it ma'am.
```

It is as if someone had used the *find/replace* function on the entire set of emergency calls, systematically deleting the greetings and *how are yous* from all (or almost all) of the openings.

This, too, may be understood in terms of the task-oriented and impersonal character of the talk (Whalen & Zimmerman 1987). Greetings and *how are yous* are primarily geared toward sociability rather than instrumental tasks. They are normally relevant for acquaintances who have a personal relationship grounded in shared biography, although greetings may also be used by those seeking to establish relationships with others. Correspondingly, greetings and *how are yous* are generally absent not only from emergency calls but from impersonal occupational encounters of many kinds. When they do appear in such encounters, their presence can impart an element of sociability and warmth to what would otherwise be a purely instrumental transaction. Indeed, they may be exploited by telemarketers and other sales personnel (e.g., "Good morning Mister Smith, how are you today?") in an effort to establish a sense of personal relationship and thereby make it more difficult for a prospective customer to reject whatever is being sold. Plainly, none of this is relevant in emergency calls, which involve the impersonal pursuit of a singular task.

The exceptions are, as always, revealing. When the caller to an emergency dispatch center happens to be acquainted with the call-taker, these missing components tend to reappear (Whalen & Zimmerman 1987).

```
(10)  [Whalen and Zimmerman, 1987: 177]
  1  911:       County Dis:patch
  2             (0.4)
  3  Clr:       Hi.
  4             (1.0)
  5  911:       Hi! (0.2) How are you?
  6  Clr:       .hh Fine howya doin'
  7  911:       Fine...
```

Here the call-taker answers the phone with the usual institutional self-identification (line 1), indicating that she is in work mode at this point and is expecting the caller to be an anonymous person seeking help. But the caller, instead of proceeding with a request for help, issues a greeting (line 3) and a particularly informal greeting at that ("Hi."). In so doing, this caller strongly claims to have recognized the call-taker from her voice sample, and by implication he presents himself as a personal acquaintance. But the caller is also being rather coy here: he greets but does not self-identify, thus putting the ball back in the call-taker's court and inviting reciprocal recognition. After a substantial silence (line 4), the call-taker finally claims recognition by coming forth with a greeting of his own and a *how are you* question (line 5). As it turns out, the parties are organizational colleagues, and their shared biography is reflected in an interlude of sociable small talk that defers the business of the call. Greetings and *how are yous* can thus reappear when the parties are acquainted, thereby transforming what began as a purely task-focused call into a more sociable encounter.

Beyond these systematic absences, the opening components that remain present in emergency calls are adapted to the thoroughly impersonal character of the transaction. Consider the identification/recognition process, focusing first on the identification of call-takers. Call-takers answer the phone by self-identifying with the name of the public safety organization (e.g., "midcity emergency", "911 emergency", "bigcity police and fire", etc.).

```
(11)  [Midcity 21: Midnight–1:00am: 5a]
  1             ((ring))
  2  911:       Midcity emergency?
```

```
3 Clr:       Yes uh::=I need a paramedic please,
4 911:       Where to.
```

(12) [Midcity 21: Call 24 (15.43)]
```
 1                ((ring))
 2 911:          Midcity emergenc(h)y,
 3 Clr:          Yes I'd like tuh report a loud party.
 4 911:          ((keyboard)) Where is it ma'am.
```

Recognition by voice sample is thus avoided in favor of self-identification as the primary method in this environment, with institutional names rather than personal names as the primary vehicle for call-takers' self-identification (Zimmerman 1984, Whalen & Zimmerman 1987, Zimmerman 1992).

If call-takers convey their identities to callers by institutional self-identification, how do callers discharge this same task? While they occasionally self-identify by name at this juncture, more often they engage in a much more minimal practice. As can be seen in examples (8) and (9) above, following the call-taker's self-identification, callers typically issue a brief acknowledgment – "yes" or "yeah" – before proceeding to the reason for the call (Zimmerman 1984). This might not seem to convey identifying information, but in fact it does in an implicit way. Consider that by acknowledging call-takers' self-identification, callers treat it as unproblematic and, by implication, they present themselves as someone who intended to call the emergency service and is thus seeking relevant assistance. This analysis is further supported by cases where callers are not sure that they have reached the appropriate service port. Callers then withhold acknowledgment as they seek to rectify the problem.

(13) [Midcity 21: Midnight–1:00am: 37]
```
 1 911:          Midcity emergency hh
 2 Clr:    →     (Uh) it's not an emergency I was just trying tuh reach
                 the police.
```

(14) [Midcity 21: Midnight–1:00am: 26]
```
 1 911:          Midcity emergency
 2 Clr:    →     Can I 've the police=please=
```

Merely by acknowledging and accepting the call-taker's self-identification, then, callers manage to project an identity of their own for the call. Moreover, it is an anonymous categorical identity – service-seeker – that corresponds to the call-taker's identity. This projected identity is subsequently crystallized and reinforced when the caller launches into the actual request for help. In a variety of ways, the identification procedures used by both callers and call-takers are fitted to their anonymous categorical identities as seekers and providers of emergency service.

Requests for Help: Special Patterns of Inference

We've seen that a focused task orientation is manifest in the overall phase structure of emergency calls, and in the markedly reduced and specialized opening phase. Now we consider how this same task orientation is manifest in special patterns of inference associated with the next phase of the call, wherein callers present the reason for calling (Whalen & Zimmerman 1987).

Earlier it was noted that callers ordinarily request some form of assistance at this juncture, but that generalization glosses over the wide range of formulations that callers can employ as their reason for calling. Callers may offer explicit requests for help ("Please send a patrol car ...", "I need an ambulance at ..." as in example (15) below), problem reports ("I'd like to report a ..." as in example (16)), or unadorned descriptions of trouble (as in example (17)).

```
(15)  [Midcity 21: Midnight–1:00am: 5a]
 1                ((ring))
 2  911:         Midcity emergency?
 3  Clr:    →    Yes uh::=I need a paramedic please,
 4  911:         Where to.
```

```
(16)  [Midcity 21: Call 24 (15.43)]
 1  911:         Midcity emergenc(h)y,
 2  Clr:    →    Yes I'd like tuh report a loud party.
 3  911:         ((keyboard)) Where is it ma'am.
```

```
(17)  [Zimmerman 1984: 214]
 1  911:         Midcity Emergency::,
 2               (.)
 3  Clr:    →    U::m yeah (.) somebody just vandalized my car,
 4               (0.3)
 5  911:         What's your address.
```

Despite such variation, all of these formulations attract the same kind of response from the call-taker – a question about the location of the problem ("Where", "where to", "What's your address"). This response, which seeks information necessary to send help, reveals that the call-taker understands all three of these formulations as requests for help.

That understanding is not remarkable for the case of explicit requests, and perhaps not for problem reports either, but what about unadorned descriptions? There is nothing natural or inevitable about hearing a problem description as a request for help. Consider that the very same formulation used by the caller in example (17) – "Somebody just vandalized my car" – may be heard very differently depending on the social context in which it is produced (Wilson 1991). If said to a doctor's receptionist on the morning of an appointment, it might be heard as an account for canceling out, which might in turn prompt the receptionist to offer a new appointment timeslot. If said to a close friend in response to a "how are you" question, it might be heard as a purely expressive act, the unloading of a personal trouble, and may attract a sympathetic response ("Gee that's awful!") and perhaps a request for elaboration ("So how bad is it?"). Depending on the social relationship between caller and recipient, their geographic proximity, joint plans, and other contextual particulars, such an utterance might be heard to be hinting at the need for assistance and may indeed prompt an offer of help (Schegloff 2007). In the emergency call environment, however, such descriptions are transparent requests for help and are routinely treated as such.

This pattern of inference is perhaps more striking when the caller says nothing at all to the call-taker, so that only distant shouting, dogs barking, or other background noises may be heard. In the next example, after ambient noise of this kind is followed by the phone being disconnected (lines 2–3), the call-taker articulates an understanding of the situation ("Oops! Sounds like a domestic" in line 4), and she then calls back and asks if there is a problem (lines 5–6).

```
(18)  [M. Whalen and Zimmerman, 1987: 179]
  1  911:         Nine one one emergency
  2               ((Loud voices in the background—screaming and arguing))
  3               ((Click))
  4  911:     →   Oo:::ps! Sounds like a domestic
  5               ((Dispatcher calls number from which call originated))
  6  911:     →   This is thuh Sheriff's Department. Is there a problem?
```

Even silence on the line may be understood and treated in this way (arrowed below).

```
(19)  [M. Whalen and Zimmerman, 1987: 179]
  1   911:        Nine one one emergency
  2                ((pause))
  3   911:        HELLO:::, Nine one one (.) HELLO.
  4          →    What's thuh problem
  5                ((click))
```

Also revealing are calls that are "coming from left field", so out of sync with expectations that the call-taker has difficulty making sense of what the call-taker is seeking. For instance, a request for a decidedly non-emergency type of service (a tow truck to remove a car from caller's parking space) embodies such a breach of expectations that the call-taker is momentarily confused (arrowed).

```
(20)   [Zimmerman 1992a: 40]
  1  911:         Nine one one emer:gency.
  2               (0.6)
  3  Clr:         Yes, I need a towing tru:ck for one car away (    )
  4               they di:d park in my parking spa:ce the who:le day and
  5               overni:ght (0.6) 'n they won't mo:ve.
  6               (0.5)
  7  911:     →   I'm I'm sorry?
  8               (1.2)
  9  Clr:         Okay, I need a towing truck (0.6) for towing.
 10  911:     →   You need a TOW TRUCK?
 11  Clr:         Yes.
 12  911:         Then call a tow company.
```

Sense-making difficulties of this sort also arise in the following prank call to 911. Not only is the initial slurred speech and ambient noise treated by the call-taker as a possible request ("Wadidja want?" in line 8), but even when the caller launches into sexual talk (line 10) and an explicit preface to a riddle (lines 14, 17), the call-taker struggles to hear what is being said as somehow implicating or deferring a possible request for help (lines 16, 19) (Zimmerman 1998).

```
(21)  [MCE 20-10: 196]
 1  911:        Midcity police an' fire
 2               ((background noise and music on the line))
 3  Clr:        (YA::H ) Thiz iz thuh (    ) ((voice is very slurred))
 4               (1.5) ((loud background noise))
 5  911:        Hello:?
 6               (0.4)
 7  Clr:        YEA::H?
 8  911:     →  Wadidja want?
 9               (0.5)
10  Clr:        Yea::h we- we wan' forn'ca:y (h) heh
11               (0.6) ((background voices, noise))
12  911:     →  'Bout wha::t?
13               (5.3) ((noise, voice: "hey gimme dat..."))
14  Clr:        Hey=I've=uh ri:ddle for ya:
15               (0.3)
16  911:        HU:::H?
17  Clr:        I have uh ri:ddle for ya
18               (0.3)
19  911:     →  I don't have ti:me f'r riddles=do=ya wanna squa:d 'rno:t=
```

Taken together, these responses to inexplicit, ambiguous, and incongruous events power-fully demonstrate that call-takers act under the default assumption that whoever dials the emergency service number must be seeking to obtain appropriate assistance (M. Whalen & Zimmerman 1987). This assumption stands as a basic frame of reference in terms of which caller's first turn – or whatever might be happening at the juncture where the caller's first turn *should* be – is heard and understood. Call-takers will try to make sense of what is happening as relevant to a request for public safety assistance. To be sure, that frame of reference can be overturned (as we saw in examples (10) and (20) above), but considerable effort may be required for that to be achieved. The default impetus to hear the caller as seeking assistance represents a distinctive framework of inference tied to the focal task of the emergency service environment.

Conclusion

We began by proposing that the emergency telephone call is a prototypical instance of institutional talk. We have demonstrated that point by contrasting emergency calls with ordinary conversational telephone calls. The comparison highlights many ways that the participants' orientation to a singular task, and to anonymous identities associated with that task, shapes their conduct. The parties draw upon their general interactional skills and practices, but they do so in a selective and context-sensitive manner. Thus, a vast array of commonplace conversational practices are systematically absent here, while the remaining practices are adapted to the particulars of the emergency service environment. The result-ing configuration of practices constitutes what we earlier termed an interactional "fingerprint" that distinguishes the emergency call from other forms of institutional talk, and from the general-purpose mode of interaction embodied in ordinary conversation.

In this brief summary, the emphasis has been on the weight of the institutional context and its power to constrain normative patterns of action and inference. But it is equally important to emphasize the other side of the coin, namely the constitutive and transformative power of action. It is through the fingerprint of practices analyzed in this chapter that the institution of emergency service dispatch is activated and talked into being. This happens incrementally, moment by moment and turn by turn. Moreover, when such practices are *not* performed – as we saw when the caller turned out to be an acquaintance of the call-taker – the institution is deactivated as the parties pursue some other interactional project.

The case of the emergency telephone call underlines the inadequacy of the bucket theory of context while reinforcing the yellow brick road perspective. Clearly social contexts are not independent entities that contain human actions; contexts are incrementally realized through actions and are transformable at any moment. Thus, even when there is a dedicated emergency telephone line, and a professional call-taker poised to deal with incoming problems, together with all of the social and technological infrastructure of emergency service, that entire institutional matrix can be rendered irrelevant, or at least held at bay, through humble turns at talk.

For Further Reading

The overall structure of 911 emergency calls, and the reduction and specialization of specific phases, has been the subject of several key papers (M. Whalen & Zimmerman 1987; Zimmerman 1984, 1992). A useful account of the technological and social ecology of emergency call centers can be found in J. Whalen (1995). For the broader field of research dealing with institutional help lines more generally, see the edited collection by Baker, Emmison, and Firth (2005), the special issue of *Research on Language and Social Interaction* edited by Derek Edwards (2007), and Torode (1995).

Note

1   This generalization is derived from the "Facts and Figures" webpage of Dispatch Monthly, the trade magazine for US public safety communications workers: www.911dispatch.com/info/fact_figures.html.

6

Gatekeeping and Entitlement to Emergency Service

Calling 911 is Not Like Ordering a Pizza

Emergency call centers and public safety organizations can be a source of information and advice (Raymond & Zimmerman 2007), but often they dispense more tangible forms of assistance such as police, fire, and paramedic units. Incoming calls requesting material services are sometimes refused. One study of police department calls documented a refusal rate of 10% for those calls requesting officer assistance (Percy & Scott 1985). Since refusals are recurrent if not commonplace, emergency calls embody a gatekeeping process wherein call-takers screen incoming calls to determine whether material assistance is warranted or justified, and callers are accountable for providing an adequate justification (Sharrock & Turner 1978, J. Whalen, Zimmerman, & M. Whalen 1988, Whalen & Zimmerman 1990, Bergmann 1993a).

This gatekeeping process, and callers' accountability within it, is apparent in how the initial request is designed and dealt with. Non-justified requests by callers – those lacking any reference to a specific problem – prompt the call-taker to respond with a question on the order of *What's the problem?* For instance, when this caller requests a squad car without specifying why it's needed (lines 2–3), he receives just such a question from the call-taker (line 4).

```
(1)  [MCE 21:12–1:22]
 1  911:   Midcity emergency.
 2  Clr:   Ye::s uh if you gotta squa:d care could you send one
 3         over to Wake Street and Lowen Avenue?  ((keyboard))
 4  911:   Whatsa problem there.
```

This pattern characterizes not only commonplace emergency calls from ordinary people, but also momentous calls involving eminent personages. Consider the call that was placed during the US presidential campaign of 1968 when Robert Kennedy was shot. Here the caller goes so far as to indicate that "an emergency" is involved (line 8), but she does not specify its nature, prompting the call-taker to probe for a specification (line 10).

```
(2)  [Zimmerman, 1992: 436–7]
 1  PD:    Police Department.
 2         ( )
```

```
 3 Clr:    Yes This is the Ambassador Hotel Em- Ambassador Hotel?
 4         ((echo: Hotel))
 5 Clr:    Do you hear me?
 6         (.)
 7 PD:     Yeah _I hear you.
 8 Clr:    Uh they have an emergency=They want thuh police to thuh
 9         kitchen right away.
10 PD:     What kind of an emergency?
11 Clr:    I don't know honey They hung up I don't know [what's happening
12 PD:                                                  [Well find out,
13         (.)
14 PD:     We don't send out without=
15 Clr:    =I beg your pardon?
16         (0.5)
17 PD:     We have to know what we're sending on.
```

A little later in this call, the pivotal importance of this question, and the gatekeeping process that it adumbrates, become quite explicit. When the caller indicates that she doesn't know what the problem is (line 11), the call-taker moves to reject the request by invoking a general rule (lines 14, 17): "We have to know what we're sending on."

In both of these examples, the caller provides all of the basic information that would in principle enable assistance to be dispatched to the scene of the problem. That is, the caller indicates both *what* is being requested ("squad car" in example (1), "the police" in example (2)) and also *where* it should be sent (an address is given in example (1), and a well-known establishment in example (2)). And yet the call-taker responds not with a promise of assistance, but with a query aimed at determining *why* the requested assistance is needed. This question may, of course, be multifunctional, yielding supplementary information that will enable public safety personnel to gear their assistance more effectively to the specifics of the problem at hand. But it's more fundamental function is to enable the call-taker to determine whether the problem is actionable, and hence whether the request should be granted in the first place.

Many callers tacitly grasp the need for an actionable problem, for they often include a report or description of the problem from the outset. This was noted in the previous chapter, in our discussion of the various forms that requests for help may take; now we highlight the justifying import of problem-focused reports and descriptions. Here the caller first issues an explicit request for help (line 1), but he then proceeds without pause to indicate why it's needed (line 2).

(3) [Zimmerman, 1992: 436]
```
 1 Clr:    Can you get somebody over here right away.
 2         We've got a gal that's just ready to pass out
```

And in the next example, the caller goes one step further, providing only a description of the problem that itself stands as a request for help, prompting the call-taker to respond cooperatively (line 3).

(4) [Zimmerman, 1992: 438]
```
 1 Clr:    Somebody jus' vandalized my=ca:r,
 2         (0.3)
 3 911:    What's your address.
```

So a problem-based justification is required. Many callers supply it on their own initiative, but if they don't the call-taker will request it, and failure to furnish one is – as we saw in example (2) – grounds for rejecting the request for help.

That an adequate justification is required may seem unremarkable, but there is nothing natural or inevitable about this. Other kinds of service requests need not be justified (J. Whalen, Zimmmerman, & M. Whalen 1988). When one calls an airline to obtain a fare quote or purchase a ticket, one would not be asked to explain the purpose of the trip; and when one orders a pizza for delivery, one would not be asked to certify as to a sufficient state of hunger. Services of this sort are, in effect, available on demand. Against this backdrop, the accountability of callers for emergency service is distinctive.

This framework of accountability is rooted in the distinctive economy of public safety organizations. Unlike commercial services, police and fire departments are publicly financed, so that callers do not directly pay for the services they receive. At the same time these services are a critical and intrinsically scarce resource. The number of squad cars, fire trucks, and paramedic units is limited, so dispatching to one locale necessarily makes these resources unavailable elsewhere. Thus, while many commercial services are available on demand to anyone able to pay for them, the services of public safety organizations have a more restricted availability, and any given caller's entitlement to such services is contingent and defeasible.

The contingent nature of service entitlement in this context is at least tacitly recognized by many callers, and is often built into the design of the initial request. Explicit requests that treat the service as a matter of casual preference (e.g., "*I'd like to have* a squad car at . . ."), although extremely common in commercial service environments, are almost never used here. (Some extraordinary cases are discussed in the next chapter.) By contrast, parallel formulations indexing a compelling need (e.g., "*I need* . . .") are used recurrently (arrowed in examples (5) and (6)).

(5) Midcity 21: CALL 33 (22.05)
```
1  911:         Midcity emergency.
2  Clr:    →    Yes I need a ambulance. hh
3  911:         Tuh where.
```

(6) Midcity 21: CALL 5A (1.53)
```
1  911:         Midcity emergency?
2  Clr:    →    Yes u::h=I need a paramedic please,
3  911:         Where to.
```

Beyond the specific language of *need*, the same idea may also be indexed (as we saw earlier in examples (3) and (4)) by the problem-focused reports and descriptions frequently included within the request. In this example, both elements converge in a single request formulation.

(7) Midcity 17: Call 13 (17.3)
```
1  911:         Midcity p'lice and fire,
2              (0.4)
3  Clr:    →    Yeah (.) say we've got an emer- u::h(hh) an acciden'
4          →    over here (a) car an' a:(h) (0.5) (h:it) a motorcycle
5          →    we need=an ambulance(h), .h[hhhh
6  911:                                     [Whe:re?
```

In the remainder of this chapter, we explore two basic gatekeeping considerations that inform conduct in emergency service calls. The first, which we term *the genuineness issue*, concerns whether or not the problem that motivated the call is in fact real. The second, which we term *the relevance issue*, concerns whether or not the nature of the problem places it within the domain of responsibility of the service provider – that is, the emergency service call center or specific public safety organization – targeted by the call.

The Genuineness Issue: Is There Really a Problem?

Not every *report* of a public safety problem reflects an *actual*, bona fide problem. A degree of skepticism toward incoming reports is part of the occupational culture of public safety communications. When *Dispatch Monthly*, a leading trade journal in the field, assembled a training manual from instructional materials used at various community call centers, they advised new call-takers and dispatchers to be vigilant and ready to probe reports that are excessively vague.

> Citizens report all types of events to the police when they think that something illegal is going on. Usually the event is innocent, but only personal evaluation by a police officer can determine this is so. Callers who say "I see a suspicious person/car/etc." should be questioned as to WHY they feel it is suspicious. (*Dispatcher Training Manual*, no date)

Incoming reports can turn out to be faulty for a variety of reasons. There are, first of all, *normal mistakes* made by callers who are reasonably competent and essentially sincere. The sound of a prowler in the bushes outside a bedroom window may turn out to be nothing more than a coyote, a raccoon, or the neighbor's cat. An open back door may be an indication, not that the house has been burglarized, but that the door was inadvertently left ajar by the owners themselves. And smoke billowing from a kitchen window may not be an indication of a house fire in progress so much as an overcooked dinner.

Then there are *malicious reports*. Callers may intentionally phone in a false report to cause trouble for some belligerent neighbors, or for public safety personnel themselves. Studies of police work (Rubinstein 1973) document the strategic use of false reports by those who are "cop-wise" or knowledgeable about police procedures. If certain problems – such as a robbery in progress or an officer in need of assistance – are known to generate a massive police response, someone who is planning a robbery or burglary can call in a false report of this sort in another neighborhood as a diversionary tactic. Correspondingly, those seeking revenge against the police may make false reports to waste departmental resources and, perhaps, place officers at risk of getting into accidents.

Finally, there are instances of *irrational paranoia*, in disturbed or mentally ill individuals who see sinister goings-on wherever they look. Police departments and emergency call centers are aware of those individuals who call frequently, and call-takers may develop routinized techniques for managing and disarming what are termed "chronic callers". Don Zimmerman (personal communication) recounts one disturbed individual who routinely called 911 to report that she was being bombarded by rays from some malevolent source. Call-takers at this dispatch center devised a solution for the caller – they would instruct her to wrap aluminum foil around her forearms as a shield against the bombardment. Occasionally, specific paranoid fears can spread through a community, generating episodes of "mass hysteria" and flurries of misguided police and emergency calls (Cantril 1940, Johnson 1945).

Call-takers are thus alert to the possibility that, for a variety of reasons, any given caller's account may be erroneous. Rather than accept all incoming problem accounts at face value, call-takers monitor for some indication of how the caller knows there is a problem, and more generally for signs that the caller is reliable and his or her account genuine. The next example, involving the report of a rape in progress (from M. Whalen & Zimmerman 1990), clearly illustrates this monitoring process.

```
(8)  [M. Whalen and Zimmerman 1990: 473, edited]
 1   911:   Midcity emergency
 2   Clr:   Would you send thuh police to eleven six oh Arvin Avenue north?
 3   911:   Eleven six oh Irving Avenue north?
 4   Clr:   Yes there's been raping goin' on
 5   911:   WHERE
 6   Clr:   Eleven si[x oh
 7   911:           [Inside ur outside?
 8   Clr:   Inside thee house.
 9   911:   There's somebody being RAPED?
10   Clr:   Yup=
11   911:   =How do you know this?
12   Clr:   I live next door. Two ladies bein raped, eleven six oh=
13   911:   =Di- How do you know they're BEing raped inside that house.
14   Clr:   Because they was shoutin'. They was shoutin' "rape." They was
15          shoutin' "help."
16   911:   What is yur address
17          .
18          . ((locational sequence omitted))
19          .
20   911:   Okay wull get som[e
21   Clr:                    [They were shoutin "rape" (.) and "fire, help."
22   911:   Da you know- are you sure they're not just playing around?
23   Clr:   No I- I- I- know, they're cryin
24   911:   O:kay, wull get somebody there. Thank you for calling.
```

Here, after the caller requests police assistance and gives an address (line 2), he describes the problem this way: "there's been raping goin' on" (line 4). The description, while clear enough about the problem itself, is uninformative as to how the caller knows this is taking place at what turns out to be a private residence. He's said nothing about who he is, where he is, or how he is connected to the parties involved. His basis for knowing what he reports is, at this point, opaque.

It is in this context that the call-taker asks "where" in line 5. As is apparent from the caller's response (line 6), he interprets this location question as geared to the address provided earlier, but the call-taker appears to have had something else in mind by the query. She cuts him off to reformulate her question in different terms ("inside or outside" at line 7) designed to get a better fix on the situation and the caller's access to it.

The caller, however, doesn't seem to grasp the investigatory import of this question either, leading to still more investigatory questions from the call-taker. He provides only a minimal answer to the inside-or-outside question ("inside" at line 8), one that does little to clarify his basis for knowing. Consequently, after the call-taker confirms that it is indeed a rape being reported (lines 9–10), she asks specifically how he knows this (line 11). At this point the issue of genuineness, which had been implicit in the previous line of questioning, rises to the surface as an explicit theme.

The caller makes one brief stab at providing a basis for his belief ("I live next door" in line 12), and then assuming this to be adequate, he proceeds to re-present the basic problem and the address ("two ladies being raped, 11 6 0 . . ."). But from the call-taker's point of view, his account remains inadequate. She cuts him off to ask a more specific version of the "how do you know" question: "How do you know they're being raped *inside that house?*" (line 13, emphasis added). His subsequent reference to shouting "rape" and "help" finally seems to do the trick, as the call-taker then proceeds to verify the address (line 16) apparently as a prelude to the dispatch of service.

But then the caller does something that derails this forward progress. Just as the call-taker begins to issue a promise of assistance (line 20), the caller interjects to elaborate on the shouting (line 21) in a way that again raises doubt. He adds "fire" to the list of what was shouted. This prompts the call-taker to backtrack and ask yet another investigatory question (line 22). Only after receiving an acceptable response (line 23) does she complete her promise of assistance and move toward closure (line 24).

The overall trajectory of this call suggests that the type of question being asked during the interrogative phase can be indicative of the call-taker's evolving assessment of the problem's genuineness. Correspondingly, different question types have different implications for the forward movement of the call and its resolution. While questions targeting the address or other details (e.g., lines 3, 16) may be neutral or may even presume the reality of the problem, investigatory questions (e.g., lines 11, 13, 22) can suggest an attitude of doubt or skepticism on the part of the call-taker. Once the reality of the problem is called into question, other questions get deferred until that issue is resolved. Conversely, when the call-taker shifts from investigatory questions to more routine questions – as in line 16 – that may be taken as a sign that the problem has been accepted as genuine and that the call is moving forward toward a favorable resolution.

Accomplishing Genuineness: Epistemic Access, Inferential Cautiousness, and Motivational Propriety

As an illustration of the genuineness issue and its management, the preceding example is rather exceptional. Because the caller does such a poor job of furnishing a basis for his belief in the reported problem, the issue of its genuineness surfaces in an unusually explicit way. In most instances, overtly investigative questions are unnecessary because callers usually take steps to indicate their relationship to the problem from the outset and, more generally, to present themselves as reliable and their accounts as genuine (M. Whalen & Zimmerman 1990).

The following excerpt illustrates some of the key dimensions involved in this process. The call begins with a routine request for the police at a specific place of residence (lines 2–3), followed by a "What's the problem" query from the call-taker (line 4).

(9) [MCE: 12–1: 34]

```
 1  911:        Midcity emergency.
 2  Clr:        .hhh Yes. (.) would you (send) th'police: (.) please to:
 3              thirty four twenty two Jones north .hhh downstairs.
 4  911:        Whatsa problem ma'am.=
 5  Clr:   →    Uh::: (.) I just went by there
 6         →    and my son lives there an' his wife an:: thuh family,=
 7  911:        =Uh huh,=
 8  Clr:        =An' uh (.) there's some kids throwin' knives at their house.
```

Notice that in response to this query, the caller doesn't actually characterize the rather unusual problem (kids throwing knives at a house) until line 8. Most of the intervening talk bears on the display of genuineness, and it does so in two distinct stages. First the caller indicates her *physical access* to the problem ("I just went by there" at line 5) and, by implication, how she was able to observe it.

Even as this account solves one problem for the caller involving her epistemic access, it seems to create another centering around her motivations. *Why* did she "just go by" a house that does not seem to be her own? And why is she now calling 911? These are salient issues for the call-taker because of the previously noted problem of mistaken, malicious, and paranoid callers. Is the caller a wholly uninvolved bystander who is doing a good deed by phoning the authorities? Or might she have an ulterior motive of some sort? Could she be a nosey neighbor with a general tendency to spy on nearby residents? Or might she have an unhealthy preoccupation with the residents of this particular house? Or to consider a more Machiavellian interpretation, could she herself be somehow implicated in the offending group?

The caller's very next utterance (line 6) resolves all of these motivational puzzles in a single stroke. By situating herself *socially* vis-à-vis the problem – her son's family lives there – she indicates that she is neither paranoid nor malicious, and that her motives for being on the scene and for calling 911 are innocuous and legitimate.

In general, callers may display their physical proximity to the problem and by implication how they were able to observe or experience it, as well as their social relationship to the problem as victim, acquaintance or relative, neighbor or passerby, and so on (M. Whalen & Zimmerman 1990). Relational information may in turn have both epistemic and motivational implications. That is, it can indicate both how the caller could have known about the problem being reported, and their reasons for being on the scene and getting involved. And as the preceding example illustrates, most callers work to portray themselves as both knowledgeable and properly motivated.

The motivational dimension tends to be particularly problematic for detached witnesses and passers-by, perhaps because the lack of an obvious personal stake in the matter (as victim, friend/relation of victim, etc.) can raise questions regarding the caller's intentions. Thus, detached witnesses recurrently go to extra lengths to account for such matters as their presence on the scene, their witnessing of the incident, and their decision to place the call. In the next example, the caller's motivational accountability is addressed head-on when he characterizes himself as a "good neighbor calling" (arrowed) about an escalating playground fight. It doesn't take much imagination to see that an adult's presence at a children's playground may indeed require an account.

(10)   [Meehan 1989: 127 (modified)]
```
 1  PD:         Bigcity police three five seven
 2  Clr:    →   Yea::h this is just a good neighbor callin' up and I'd
 3              I'll advise you to send a pa- crowd car over here to
 4              the Green Street playground (.) in Subcity (0.5) hh to stop
 5              these kids because I think they're gonna have a big fight
 6              over here
```

The next caller addresses the motivational issue as well, but in a more subtle way. Instead of *claiming* to be properly motivated, this caller *shows* it by recounting how she came to have witnessed an accident (arrowed).

(11)   [MCE 17: 11–12: 20]
```
 1  911:        Midcity p'li̱ce an' fi̱re,
 2              (0.5)
 3  Clr:        Ye̱:s, I̱'d like to repo̱rt an a̱:cciden'
 4              (0.8)
 5       →      igh- augh- I̱ was just wa̱lking up University Avenue
 6       →      an' jus' seen two cars colli̱:de...
```

She portrays her presence on the scene and her witnessing of the accident as utterly routine and normal. As she puts it, she was "*just* walking" up the road and "*just* seen two cars collide" (lines 4–5, emphasis added). By implication, she was not out "looking for trouble"; she was otherwise occupied when her attention was drawn to the accident (cf. Bergmann 1993b; Halkowski 2006). Notice that these formulations emerge as the caller begins a chronological narrative of what transpired, which she launches after her initial problem report (line 3) fails to elicit a response from the call-taker (line 4).

In general, chronological narratives of this sort are rich environments for the accomplishment of genuineness because they enable callers to speak at length without interruption (Zimmerman 1992, Bergmann 1993a). The opportunity space provided by narratives is something that callers exploit by painting an elaborate picture of exactly where they were, what they were doing, and how they came to observe the incident being reported, as well as the course of reasoning they went through before concluding that something problematic is, or may be, taking place, and before deciding to place the call. All of this has obvious epistemic and motivational implications, and makes the narrative format particularly useful for ambiguous troubles whose actionability may be subject to doubt. Consider the next example, wherein the caller's narrative begins at line 8.

(12)   [MCE Call 30 20:18]
```
 1  911:        .hh Midcity emergency.
 2  Clr:        .hhh Yeah uh(m) I'd like tuh:- report (0.2) something
 3              we̱ir:d that happen:ed abou:t (0.5) uh(m) five minutes
 4              ago, 'n front of our apartment building?
 5  911:        Yeah?
 6  Clr:        On eight fourteen eleventh avenue southeast,
 7  911:        Mm hm,=
 8  Clr:        =.hh We were just (.) uhm si̱ttin' in the room 'n'
 9              we heard this cla̱:nking y'know like (.) someone was
10              pulling something behind their ca̱:r.='N' we
```

```
11              looked out the window'n .hhh an' there was (this) (.)
12              light blue: smashed up uhm (1.0) .hh station wagon
13              an',=.hh A:nd thuh guy made a U-turn,=we live on
14              a dead end, .hh an:d (0.2) thuh whole front end of
15              the- (.) the car (is/w'z) smashed up. .hhh And (.) >he
17              jumped outta the car and I (r)emember< 'e- (.) he tried
18              to push the hood down (with/er) something and then he
19              jus' (.) started running an' he took o::ff.
20    911:      Mm hm,
21    Clr:      .hh A:nd we think that maybe 'e could've (.) you know
22              stolen the car and aba:ndoned it. er something,
```

Notice first that, from the beginning of the narrative and recurrently thereafter, the caller indicates that she *witnessed the incident together with at least one other person* ("we heard this clanking . . .", "we looked out the window", "we think maybe . . ."). Although she never explicitly names or refers to this person (or persons), her repeated use of the collective "we" casts her observations and inferences as intersubjectively validated.

Moreover, *she portrays her initial discovery of the incident as a specifically unmotivated act.* Her narrative begins not with the incident itself, but with what she was doing moments before that. She indicates that she was "just sitting in the room" (line 8) when she heard the noise that led her to "look out the window" (line 11). Thus, much like the caller in the previous example, she presents herself as otherwise occupied and in effect minding her own business when her attention was drawn to events outside.

She also indicates that she *first made sense of the sound in a comparatively ordinary or at least non-criminal way* ("like someone was pulling something behind their car" in lines 9–10). Correspondingly, it wasn't until some time later that she entertained a more extraordinary interpretation involving a possible crime (stolen and abandoned car in lines 21–2). As Sacks (1984b) and Jefferson (2004) have demonstrated, it is common for narratives of unusual experiences to unfold in this way, starting with a relatively normal first interpretation ("At first I thought . . .") that later gives way to an extraordinary realization. This pattern has ramifications for speakers' self-presentation as trustworthy and believable. By indicating that they first tried to interpret the incident in a more mundane or ordinary way, speakers present themselves as not jumping to wild conclusions, and hence as circumspect and trustworthy perceivers of reality.

This caller's inferential cautiousness is matched by *the care with which she formulates and delivers her conclusion* regarding a stolen/abandoned car (lines 21–2). Not only is her conclusion deferred until the very end of a lengthy narrative in which she sticks mainly to "just the facts" of what she observed, but her conclusion is offered only after her narrative receives minimal uptake from the call-taker (line 20). Furthermore, the conclusion itself is massively hedged and marked as uncertain: "*We think that maybe he could've* you know stolen the car and abandoned it *er something*" (emphasis added). She thereby presents herself as just as cautious and trustworthy in stating her conclusions as in the course of reasoning that led to them.

Finally, *her decision to place the call is also portrayed as carefully considered.* She notes that the original incident occurred "about five minutes ago" (lines 3–4). By indicating the elapsed period of time, she implies that this was something she had to think about, and perhaps discussed with her associate(s), before finally deciding to call in a report.

Given the massive and multidimensional utility of chronological narratives for displays of genuineness, it is perhaps not surprising that this caller works to secure the interactional space in which to offer such a narrative. Returning to the beginning of the call, notice that she initially frames her request as a succinct problem report ("I'd like tuh:- report" at line 2). But just as she arrives at the point where a definitive police-relevant categorization would be relevant (i.e., a stolen vehicle), she hesitates and then produces the much more vague characterization "something weird". This is hearably incomplete as a request, and indeed it elicits only the most minimal forms of acknowledgment from the call-taker (lines 5, 7). This in turn enables the caller to continue and clarify by launching into her much more cautious and designedly "genuine" narrative account.

The Relevance Issue: Is It a Matter of Public Safety?

We turn now to consider the other main gatekeeping consideration that informs emergency calls, which has to do with the relevance of the problem being reported. Even if the problem is regarded as genuine, it may not be the responsibility of the police or fire department, or the emergency dispatch line that interfaces with them. Of course, most people who place an emergency call, or who call the police or fire department directly, have problems that fall squarely within the organization's domain of responsibility, but a substantial number of problems are more marginal and hence of questionable relevance. As we shall see, these marginal problems pose special problems for the participants, and how they are dealt with can be consequential for how organizational identities are reproduced and, at times, transformed.

These processes were explored by Jörg Bergmann (1993a) in a study of calls to a community fire department that involved non-fire problems of various kinds. For instance, here the problem is a plumbing leak coming from an upstairs business establishment (lines 4–5), a problem – though about water – that is about as far from fire as one can get. The request (line 3) is for firefighters to open the locked door so the plumber can gain entry.

```
(13)  [Bergmann 1993a]
  1  FD:     Fire department,
  2  Clr:    .hh Yes this is Bessler market place and seed merchant.
  3          Good morning, (0.6) Excuse me could you open a door for us
  4          because of the following_ We had water dripping down that is
  5          it comes from the sun bathing studio .hh and I don't have a key
  6          for that and even privately I can't reach them.
  7  FD:     (mh[m)
  8  Clr:       [Now I called the plumber and he will come in a minute
  9          but he said h .hh he'd prefer if y- uh you would open the door.
```

Not only is the content of the request unusual, but so is the manner in which it is expressed. In a variety of ways, the caller is attentive to the extraordinary nature of what he is seeking. First he issues a *token of apology* ("excuse me" in line 3) just before launching into the request. Following the request he provides an *elaborate account* (lines 4–9) that explains not only what the problem is but also why he's chosen to deal with it by calling the fire department. The account is launched immediately and without a hitch upon completion of the request ("could you open a door for us because of the following . . ."), thereby blocking the call-taker from responding to the request until at least some of the explanation is provided.

The account includes two elements that are recurrent in calls involving marginal problems. First there is reference to *previous efforts to solve the problem*. The caller indicates that three possible solutions were tried or at least considered – he does not have a key (line 5), he can't reach the owners (line 6), and he called a plumber first (line 8) – all of which casts the call to the fire department as a dispreferred last resort (cf. Edwards & Stokoe 2007). Moreover, *the decision to call the fire department is attributed to a third party*, the plumber in this case (line 9), which further justifies the call while also diffusing responsibility for it. All of these elements are linked to the delicacy involved in making a request that plainly does not fall within the fire department's usual domain of responsibility.

Many of the same elements appear in the next example, involving a report of "two swans tormenting a third one" (line 5).

```
(14)  [Bergmann 1993a]
  1  FD:     Fire department
  2  Clr:    Yes good morning my name is Kelcher, (0.5) the following matter,
  3          This morning I drove past Mainsteig, I live near there.
  4  FD:     M[hm
  5  Clr:     [.hh and I saw .h that two swans were tormenting a third one
  6  FD:     (w)e[ll
  7  Clr:        [And at first I thought (.) maybe they were mating,
  8          In spring evidently you think of something like that .hh
  9          But that was not the case- obviously violated their territory
 10          .hh and h thus I had the impression they were really going to
 11          kill it. h.hh And it always had- one of these swans kept trying
 12          to push (.) the weaker one underneath the water and the weaker
 13          one just couldn't get away.
 14  FD:     mhm
 15  Clr:    could only escape to the shore.
 16          .hh Now I called the vet and he suggested (.) that I call the
 17          fire department they could help in cases like that
```

Here again the caller provides an elaborate account that references previous attempts to solve the problem – the caller first contacted a veterinarian – while also citing the veterinarian as responsible for the decision to call the fire department (lines 16–17).

Notice further that all of this is packaged in the form of a chronological narrative, which is launched when the caller refers to an event in the past ("This morning I drove past Mainsteig . . ." in line 3). Just as narratives are useful for managing problems of questionable genuineness (as we saw in example (13) above), they are also useful for managing problems of questionable relevance. In both contexts the key issue is the capacity to speak at length without interruption about a problem that is not easily categorized in specific actionable terms, and to engage in elaborate forms of accounting. When relevance is at issue, the narrative account is geared toward portraying prior efforts to deal with the problem, as well as the exogenous input that led to the decision to place the call.

In calls to 911 and other emergency service centers, the relevance issue can take on an additional dimension. Not only are incoming requests assessable in terms of their organization-specific fit (e.g., is it an actionable police, fire, or paramedic request?), but requests are also assessable by reference to a criterion of urgency. Callers here are accountable for having problems that are sufficiently pressing and hence require a timely response. This standard poses

a challenge for callers when the urgency of the problem is less than transparent, a challenge
that becomes particularly salient when the rubric of "emergency" figures in the call-taker's
opening self-identification.

```
(15)  [MidCity 21: midnight: 37]
  1  911:        Midcity emergency hh
  2  Clr:    →   (Uh) it's not an emergency I was just trying tuh reach
  3                the police. hh=
  4  911:        This is police.
  5  Clr:        Okay. There seems to be some sort of argument or potential
  6                fight uh:: about to happen in the alley:...
```

Here the caller is reluctant to proceed in response to the call-taker's "Midcity Emergency"
self-identification (line 1), invoking a distinction between having an emergency as opposed
to "just trying to reach the police" (lines 2–3). But as soon as the call-taker modifies her
self-identification to one that is police- rather than emergency-focused (line 4), the caller proceeds without a hitch (line 5). What changes at this juncture isn't the institution, but rather
the manner in which it has been formulated or labeled.

Sensitivity surrounding the language of "emergency" may actually thwart efforts to stream-
line emergency calls. Some call-takers answer the phone with an utterance like "911, what
is your emergency?", apparently in an effort to solicit a problem straightaway and thereby
get down to business as quickly as possible (Zimmerman 1992). But this practice can have
the opposite effect, the "emergency" term prompting hesitation and reluctance to proceed
(e.g., "Well, it's not an emergency . . .").

More generally, when callers have problems of marginal urgency, they often engage in
mitigating and accounting work not unlike that seen in non-fire calls to the fire department.
In the next example, a bar manager reports a conflict with some belligerent customers. What
makes this problem marginal is that the conflict is thus far mild and nonviolent.

```
(16)  [Midcity 21: midnight: 16]
  1  911:        Midcity emergency.
  2  Clr:        Uh:: yeah hi. This is uh:: hh thuh Valley:: (.) Pub.=
  3  911:        =Mm[hm,
  4  Clr:           [An::d .hh I'm thuh manager here tonight [an::
  5  911:                                                    [mmhm,
  6  Clr:        .hh there's not re:ally:: any trouble going on
  7                except that I've asked a few people tuh lea:ve (.)
  8                they aren't (.) drunk they're just belligerent...
  9                .
 10                .
 11                .
 12  Clr:    →   ...I don't really wanna have any trouble with'em (but)
 13          →   I'm afraid if they don't go I will have trouble with them?
```

Notice that the caller, after self-identifying (line 4), launches into a problem description
(line 6) by providing a disclaimer that "there's not really any trouble going on . . .". So from
the very start, he acknowledges explicitly that what he is about to report falls short of what
is expected in this environment. Later on, as the fact-based description is winding down,

the caller moves to justify the request by *expressing concern* about the developing incident and the possibility that it may escalate ("I'm afraid . . ." in line 13).

Expressions of concern or fear are, it turns out, commonplace in calls of this sort, that is calls involving virtual, impending, or not-yet-actualized problems (Meehan 1989: 130). The next example involves another potential fight, although the caller initially describes only a large gathering of kids at a public intersection (lines 2–4).

```
(17)  [Meehan 1989: 128 (modified)]
 1  PD:         Bigcity Police three oh eight
 2  Clr:        Yeah at the corner of uh:: Walton Way and Beaumont
 3              Street there's a kid there Harry O'Donnell (.) (in fact)
 4              there's a whole group of kids but this one kid in
 5              particular has got a gun
 6  PD:         He's gotta gu:n?
 7  Clr:    →   Yeah and they're startin' a fight up there and
 8          →   I'm afraid that someone's really gonna get hurt.
 9  PD:         This is on Beaumont Street and wha[::t?
10  CLR:                                          [Beaumont and Walton Way
11              (2.5)
12  PD:         Walton Way?
13  Clr:        Yeah (.) ((Subcity)) I can hear them from my window
14              I live here [( )
15  PD:         And they're fighting right now?
16  Clr:        Yeah they're startin' right now and the kid's got a gun
17  PD:         Didya see the gun?
18  Clr:        Yeah I SAWR it
19              (1.0)
20  Clr:        As a mat- fact he's bra::ggin' about it
```

The caller takes steps to justify the call by reference to what may yet transpire. He does so first by noting the presence of a gun (line 5), and then by expressing fear of a fight with serious injury to come (arrowed, lines 7–8).

In this case, the expression of fear doesn't settle the issue, as the call-taker subsequently pursues a line of investigatory questioning. It begins with "And they're fighting right now?" (line 15), which problematizes the not-yet-actualized nature of the fight. The caller initially answers in the affirmative ("yeah" at line 16), seeming to confirm that the fight is now in progress, but his elaboration implicitly backs away from this position ("Yeah they're *starting* right now", emphasis added) while also re-invoking the presence of a gun. Still unconvinced, the call-taker asks whether the caller actually saw the gun (line 17), which the caller confirms as something that he not only saw (line 18) but also heard the kid "bragging about" (line 20). This appears to satisfy the call-taker, who switches from investigatory to more routine questions thereafter.

In both of the preceding examples, expressions of concern or fear are introduced to justify requests for help with a problem that is emerging and hence not yet fully realized. In the absence of a fully developed "objective" problem, expressions of this sort provide alternative subjective grounds for the request. In both cases, moreover, the subjective grounds are introduced by the caller only after the objective facts of the situation, suggesting an order of preference in the presentation of such materials.

In addition to the marked justificatory work evident in the preceding examples, marginal problems are also associated with request formulations that are mitigated and hence markedly less forceful. Thus, when this caller asks the police to help a neighbor who accidentally locked herself out of her house, his request is framed with "I was jus' wondering" (line 4).

```
(18)  [Sharrock and Turner 1978: 176]
  1  PD:          Newton Police.
  2  Clr:         Eh my neighbor ah up the street ah thirty o::ne (1.0)
  3               ( ) forty five has locked herself out.
  4        →      (I was jus') wonderin' if you could send a man up to
  5               help her to get in, she's an old lady over eighty.
```

Similar language ("I'm wondering if you could") prefaces this request for help with a similar problem involving keys locked in the caller's car.

```
(19)  [Midcity 17: 11–midnight: Call 2]
  1  911:         Midcity p'lice an' fire,
  2               (0.2)
  3  Clr:    →    .hhh Hello: (.) I'm wondering if you could send somebody
  4               to open up my c:ar door, cz my keys are locked insi:de,
```

In general, this way of formulating a request treats the granting of the request as contingent, thereby casting the caller as having a somewhat diminished entitlement to what is being requested (Curl & Drew 2008). Accordingly, through the use of such formulations here, callers show themselves to have a realistic assessment of the marginality of the problem that they are now bringing to official attention.

Opening the Gates: Promising Assistance and Saying "Thank You"

When issues of genuineness and relevance are resolved to the call-taker's satisfaction, material assistance is in order. This favorable outcome may be foreshadowed, as we have seen, when call-takers shift from investigatory to routine questions, but it becomes explicit when call-takers come forth with an actual promise of assistance. At this juncture, the matter of the caller's involvement and motivations, which informed the initial request and problem description, emerges once again through the practice of expressing appreciation by saying "thank you".

When *callers* take the lead in expressing appreciation, they portray themselves as the beneficiaries of a service provided by the call-taker on behalf of the organization he or she represents (Bergmann 1993a). For instance (arrowed):

```
(20)  [MCE 17: Call 1 (modified)]
  1  911:         Midcity p'lice an' fire
  2               (.)
  3  Clr:         In the YWC:A parking lot there bunch a
  4               teenagers right now v:andalizing my car:
  5               .
  6               . ((interrogative series))
```

```
 7                      .
 8  911:      Alri' we'll be right the[re.
 9  Clr:   →                         [Thank you.
```

Here the caller's self-presentation as a service beneficiary (line 9) is indeed appropriate given that the problem concerns vandalism to the caller's own car (lines 3–4).

While this might seem to be the natural state of affairs in emergency calls, the process can unfold differently, particularly when the caller is a detached witness or is otherwise less involved. *Call-takers* may then take the lead in expressing appreciation, as in the next example (line 35) concerning a fire across the street from the caller's home. Here it is the call-taker who says "thank you" immediately after promising assistance (line 35), while the caller aligns with a corresponding "you're welcome" (line 36).

```
(21)  [Bergmann 1993a: 13]
33  FD:       So you live right across [from Spenc[er.
34  Clr:                               [Yes      [Yes
35  FD:    →  Right, [we'll drop by:, Th[ank you so much [Good bye
36  Clr:           [Yes                [(    ),          [You're welcome
```

Both parties thus collaborate in portraying the call-taker as the beneficiary of a service altruistically provided by the caller – namely the service of having brought a problem of public safety to official attention.

It is important to recognize that expressions of gratitude do not simply reflect the participants' "objective" benefactor/beneficiary status. As Bergmann (1993a) has suggested, saying "thank you" is by no means mandatory even for callers standing to benefit from the service, and callers may avoid this practice in an effort to portray themselves as altruistically motivated. Indeed, callers may take additional steps to maintain an altruistic self-presentation (recall the "good neighbor" self-characterization in example (10)). In the next example, an uninvolved caller, having not received a "thank you" from the call-taker, nonetheless responds to the promise of assistance with "you are welcome" (arrowed).

```
(22)  [Bergmann 1993a]
 1  FD:       Okay we'll drive there, [right?
 2  Clr:   →                          [Okay. You are welcome, bye bye,
```

By responding *as if* he had been thanked, this caller goes out of his way to highlight and dramatize his status as an uninvolved and selflessly motivated benefactor of the public safety organization.

Further complicating matters is the fact that "thank you" is not only a display of appreciation; it is also a powerful resource for bringing the call to a close (Zimmerman & Wakin 1995). This partially explains its frequent use by callers following the promise of assistance, as well as its use in environments involving overly talkative recipients. In the next example, it is exploited by the call-taker as a way of exerting pressure on the caller to end the call. The caller had previously responded to the promise of assistance not with a closing-implicative action (such as "okay" or "thank you"), but by attempting to specify and in effect reopen the request (line 2). The call-taker, however, merely thanks the caller (line 3), thereby avoiding either accepting or rejecting the specification and once again placing the call on a "downhill" or closing trajectory.

```
(23)   [Zimmerman and Wakin 1995]
  1   911:          We'll get somebody there right away.=
  2   Clr:          =Maybe emergency rescue?
  3   911:     →    Thank yo[u.
  4   Clr:                   [Thank you.=
  5   911:          =Mm bye.
```

In cases like this one, the pro-social expression of gratitude becomes a strategic resource for exiting the call, and may thus have no systematic relationship to the caller's "objective" level of involvement.

Finally, in some marginal calls, when it's not clear that there is a genuine actionable problem at hand and when no promise of assistance is actually forthcoming, "thank you" may be avoided by both parties. In the last example, the caller reports only that a suspicious car has been "sitting across the street from the house" with its headlights on. The call-taker is skeptical, suggesting that it "doesn't sound too suspicious" and offering various innocuous explanations for an idling car (lines 7–10). Despite this, the caller continues to press for help, at one point invoking her fear of the situation ("It's making me nervous" in line 15). After delayed and minimal uptake from the call-taker (lines 18–19), the caller issues an explicit albeit markedly low-pressure request ("Just send somebody around to check maybe" in line 20).

```
(24)   [MCE: Car with Headlights]
  1   911:    It's jus' s:itting there with the headlights on huh(h),
  2   Clr:    Yeah jus' s:ittin' there with the headlights on, all the tail
  3           lights or: whatever you wanna call'em on the back of-
  4           (thuh-/wuh-) I: dunno whatchu call'em [(there's-) (.) the=
  5   911:                                          [Well if
  6   Clr:    =lights are o:n on the rear end too .h[hh
  7   911:                                          [.hhhh W'l if it izn't
  8           (.) ugh=i:f it's only been there a short time, it doesn't really
  9           sound too suspicious they could be waitin' to pick somebody up,
 10           or drop som:ebody o:ff, er_
 11           (1.8)
 12   Clr:    Yeh I don't know exactly know how long its been there m:inutes
 13           wi:se, but I know its been sittin' here fur a l- little bi:t.
 14           (0.7)
 15   Clr:    It's jus' makin' me nervous ez it's sittin' there not knowin'
 16           u- if: (.) .hhhh what it- what's in- if:- anything's wro:ng or
 17           what, you know.
 18           (0.5)
 19   911:    mt .hh O:[kay(h)
 20   Clr:             [(Just) send s:omebody around to ch:eck maybe,
 21           (.)
 22   911:    Alright.
 23           (1.0)
 24   Clr:    Alright.
 25   911:    Umhum bye
```

This low-pressure request receives only a minimal and in context noncommittal "alright" from the call-taker (line 22), which is subsequently matched by the caller (line 24).

Throughout the closing phase, with no explicit promise of assistance offered and no clearly actionable problem at hand, neither party deigns to say "thank you".

Conclusion

The gatekeeping considerations that inform public safety and emergency calls are generally taken for granted by the participants, and are most often addressed in ways that are succinct and embedded within the routine activities that comprise such calls. These tacit considerations become more prominent in ambiguous, marginal, or otherwise problematic cases where the genuineness or relevance of the trouble is subject to doubt. Such cases find caller-takers asking questions that are investigatory rather than routine, and callers engaging in a variety of remedial practices, some of them quite elaborate, geared toward establishing that the problem is actionable despite appearances to the contrary. The various practices used by callers, and the considerations to which they are addressed, are summarized in table 6.1.

Table 6.1   Callers' practices in ambiguous and marginal cases

Gatekeeping considerations	Dimensions	Practices in ambiguous/marginal cases
Genuineness	Caller's reliability Caller's access to the problem Caller's social involvement Caller's motivations	Narrative accounts and extended tellings geared to establishing reliability Antecedent activities portraying unmotivated discovery of the problem Inferential cautiousness, including "at first I thought . . ." Conclusion avoided, deferred, hedged Decision to call portrayed as delayed Reference to other observers
Relevance	Appropriate problem type Sufficient urgency	Narrative accounts and extended tellings geared to justifying the call Previous efforts to solve the problem Expressions of concern or fear Diffusion of responsibility for the call Mitigated request formulations marking reduced entitlement to service Apology tokens

Upon reflection, it is apparent that characterizations and descriptions ostensibly focusing on the *problem* have significant implications for the *caller*. The thorough intertwining of callers' problem presentation with their own self-presentation is particularly evident in chronological narratives. Here the problem is embedded within an elaborate account detailing how the caller came to discover it, how they made sense of it, and how they came to conclude that something officially actionable might be taking place and that a call to the authorities might be warranted. Such accounts overwhelmingly portray the caller as circumspect, benignly motivated, and reliable, and hence entitled to public safety assistance.

These issues of gatekeeping and entitlement are by no means unique to the emergency call environment. Although the particulars may vary, similar considerations and methods for addressing them arise in a wide range of other service encounters, including primary care encounters between doctors and patients (as we shall see in chapter 9).

For Further Reading

The issue of genuineness in emergency calls and the potential for call-taker doubt is broached by Sharrock and Turner (1978). M. Whalen and Zimmerman (1990) offer an extensive analysis of how callers deal with this issue and thereby present themselves as sincere and their problems as genuine. The relevance issue and its management is examined in the context of calls to a small-town fire department (Bergmann 1993a), and is further developed in Meehan's (1989) insightful analysis of the problematics of urgency in emergency calls. Relatedly, Raymond and Zimmerman (2007) offer an intriguing study of how the default framework of an emergency service call can be transformed into one facilitating the distribution of information and advice. Both Bergmann (1993a) and Zimmerman and Wakin (1995) examine the complex issues surrounding the benefactor/beneficiary distinction and the role of "thank you" in the closing process.

7

Emergency Calls under Stress

An emergency call can be an intensely charged encounter. When callers find themselves in dangerous or life-threatening circumstances, they may be highly distraught, sometimes to the point that it impedes or derails the forward progress of the call. Calls of this sort are relatively uncommon. Public safety communications personnel generally refer to them as "hot calls" and treat them as a departure from routine, and the subset of hot calls that become interactionally problematic is even smaller.

What can be gained from studying calls that are plainly extraordinary and non-representative of the general run of emergency calls? Problematic calls are of interest for a variety of reasons stemming precisely from their extraordinary character. Perhaps most obviously, they provide a window into the role of human emotions within structured work environments. The emergency call is an arena where strong emotions are recurrent if not commonplace, and yet it is also a bureaucratically organized arena that requires the regulation and suppression of emotion in the service of a practical task. Emotionally charged calls can reveal how the participants manage this tension between the demands of the caller's internal state and the demands of the interaction, which here involve the transfer of essential information from caller to call-taker so as to enable the dispatch of assistance.

There is also a practical dimension to studying problematic calls, where communication practices can have serious real-life consequences. If the caller is unable or unwilling to participate effectively in the call, then necessary information may not be conveyed and help may not be sent. Dealing with distraught callers is thus a crucial skill for professional call-takers, albeit a skill whose particulars tend to be taken for granted. Looking closely at such calls – examining the consequences that follow from different courses of action – can shed light on the communication practices that are most effective in calming distraught callers and moving the call toward a favorable resolution.

Finally, such calls can also feed back into our understanding of more routine emergency calls. In general, the study of extraordinary or "deviant" cases can shed light on what is ordinary or routine. So although it may seem paradoxical, problematic emergency calls can be revealing as to the practices and forms of reasoning that underlie the most commonplace and ordinary of calls.

Emotion Displays and Information Transfer

Some callers are highly distressed early on with anxiety, fear, or grief triggered by the problem about which they are calling. The display of such emotions can affect the transfer of
necessary call-processing information (J. Whalen & Zimmerman 1998). To illustrate, here
a man is calling because his wife has just shot herself with a shotgun.

```
(1)   [Whalen and Zimmerman 1998: 146 (modified)]
  1   911:      Nine one one what is your emerg-   ((cut off by static))
  2              (0.2)
  3   Clr:      GO::D!, MY WIFE (JUST SHOT HERSELF)! ((howling/shrieking voice))
  4              (0.3)    THIRTY EIGHT FIFTY NINE (     ) AVENUE HURRY U::::::P!
  5              (0.2)
  6   911:      What happened?
  7              (0.2)
  8   Clr:      ((howling/shrieking voice)) (AR:::)-SHE JUS' SHOT HERSE::LF!=
  9   911:      =SHE FELL?
 10              (0.2)
 11   Clr:      SHE SHOT HER SELF WITH'A SHOTGUN!
```

The caller is so agitated that the call-taker has difficulty making out the nature of the problem. His first attempt at characterizing the problem (lines 3–4) is completely missed by the
call-taker (line 6), and his second attempt (line 8) is heard incorrectly (line 9).

    The displays of extreme emotion that appear in cases of this sort fall into two broad cat-
egories. *Verbalizations* include exclamations (e.g., *oh my god* or simply *god* as in line 3 above)
and pleading or beseeching remarks (e.g., "hurry up" in line 4). *Paralinguistic behaviors* include
screaming, gasping, and sobbing. While verbal emotion displays may delay the transmission
of information, paralinguistic behaviors can occur simultaneously with informational statements and can render them unintelligible, as the preceding example demonstrates.

    Callers may be perceived as in control of their emotions, or as overwhelmed or consumed
by them. Recognizable differences in emotional involvement depend not on the sheer
magnitude or quantity of the emotion displays themselves, but on whether they impede
the transfer of necessary information to call-takers (Whalen & Zimmerman 1998). The
following example illustrates these varying possibilities.

```
(2)   [Whalen and Zimmerman 1998: 149]
  1   911:      Nine one=on:e what is your emergen[cy
  2   Clr:   →                                   [>Oh my God ( ) gunshot=hh<
  3              (0.3)
  4   911:      Whe:re
  5              (0.3)
  6   Clr:      Uh:m (0.1) eighteen ten Halston Street .hh apartment (0.2)
  7              three fourteen=hhh[.hhh    ]
  8   911:                        [Anybody] shot?=
  9   Clr:   →  =Ye:s we've gotta hh .hh <my roomate's (hurt)
 10          →  Oh: my: Go:d ple:a[se co-
 11   911:                        [Okay just stay on the li:ne,
 12              is the gun- <is the gun put away?
```

The more controlled display of emotion appears in lines 9–10. Here the caller first answers the "Anybody shot?" question, and then produces an emotion display in the form of an exclamatory "Oh my God" followed by a pleading "please come". By answering the question first, the caller shows himself to be attending to the interaction and subordinating his display of emotion to the normative obligation to answer the question.

By contrast, in line 2 the succession of events is reversed: in response to the "what is your emergency?" question, the caller first produces an exclamation ("Oh my God") and only then answers the question, or tries to, by referencing a gunshot. In comparison to the previous exchange, here the caller shows himself to be at risk of losing control of his emotions, prioritizing them over the interactional obligation to answer. Indeed, the turn-initial display of emotion here bleeds into the answer itself, garbling it to the point that the call-taker is unable to fully grasp what he is trying to say (cf. line 8).

What is the temporal relationship between a caller's outward display of emotion, and the inner feeling-state that the display indexes? Common-sensically, it might be assumed that the two occur simultaneously, but close analysis suggests a more complicated picture. Emotion displays are often *precisely placed* in relation to other interactional activities. This is obviously so for the relatively controlled displays exemplified in lines 9–10 above, which are deferred until the caller has produced an interactionally appropriate response to the prior action. But even turn-initial or free-standing displays of emotion, which ostensibly overwhelm or consume the caller, may be precisely placed relative to the call-taker's prior turn at talk. Consider the very first exchanges in examples (1) and (2) above. In both cases, the call-taker's initial exclamation is deferred until the call-taker has self-identified ("Nine one one") and completed a problem question ("What is your emergency?"). In the second example, the exclamation is launched just as the question is winding down, overlapping only the very last syllable (lines 1–2). The ensuing exclamations may be a way of indicating "shock" on the part of the caller (Whalen & Zimmerman 1998), but their precise timing and placement suggest that they are sensitive to the demands of the interaction and not only the caller's internal state of arousal (cf. Heath 1989).

Responding to Emotion Displays

In the face of callers' displays of emotion, call-takers remain oriented to the task of securing the information needed to dispatch help. Responses that would be normal and expected in ordinary conversation – sympathetic or empathetic remarks such as "oh my" or "I'm so sorry" – are systematically absent in emergency calls. In their place are remarks geared toward realigning the caller to the task at hand (Whalen & Zimmerman 1998).

This is particularly evident in the next example (a continuation of excerpt (1) above) wherein a new call-taker (CT) is being monitored and assisted by a veteran (CT2). Notice that the veteran counsels the new call-taker to urge calm ("tell him to quit shouting" in line 17), and the latter complies although in slightly more polite terms (line 19). When the caller persists in shouting (line 20), the call-taker takes a different approach, twice interjecting to summon his attention ("Sir" in line 21), and then reassuring him that help is on the way (line 22) before asking the next question.

```
(3)   [Whalen and Zimmerman 1998: 146]
15  Clr:          HURRY: U:::P!
16                (0.4)
17  911b:    →    Tell'im to quit shouting. ((Spoken to CT))
18                (0.3)
19  911a:    →    Please stop shouting sir we're here ta-=
20  Clr:          =(WE:LL WHO'[S: ] BO:THERING), GO:D[DA:MN] FUCKIN' S[H-
21  911a:                    [Sir]               [Sir ]            [We're-
22           →    we're (gettin') an ambulance there, where did she shoot herself?
23                (0.4)
24  Clr:          SHE SHOT HERSELF IN=THE CHEST HURRY U::P!
```

All of these measures – summoning the caller's attention, urging calm, and issuing reassurance
– are general practices of interaction, and are here mobilized in the service of realigning the
caller toward a specific institutional task. Call-takers thus deal with the situation not as a
trouble to be worked through, but as a problem to be solved (cf. Jefferson & Lee 1981) via
emergency service dispatch.

When call-takers act to reassure callers, they appear to be attentive to the possibility that
callers might then hang up prematurely, before critical information is acquired. This is apparent in what call-takers do next. After reassuring the caller, they recurrently proceed either
to resume questioning (as in line 22 above, "where did she shoot herself?"), or to instruct
the caller to "stay on the line" (line 3 below).

```
(4)   [Whalen and Zimmerman 1998: 149]
1   Clr:          =Ye:s we've gotta hh .hh <my roomate's (hurt)
2                 Oh: my: Go:d ple:a[se co-
3   911:     →                      [Okay just stay on the li:ne,
4            →    is the gun- <is the gun put away?
```

The reassurance here is minimal, limited to an "okay" response to the caller's "please come".
Nevertheless, the call-taker subsequently urges the caller to "stay on the line", and asks another
question. Both practices constitute efforts to re-engage the caller, and they are offered
immediately and without pause following the reassurance. Their effect is to forestall a
premature hang-up.

The possibility of the caller hanging up at this juncture is linked to the fact (demonstrated
in chapter 5) that emergency calls are organized around a single order of business. It is a
general feature of monotopical or monofocal telephone calls that the completion of the primary business of the call establishes the relevance of closing as the next course of action
(Schegloff & Sacks 1973). Correspondingly, in emergency calls it is the promise of assistance that typically completes the focal agenda launched by the caller's request and paves
the way for closing (Zimmerman 1984). And indeed, the parties, led by the caller, quickly
move to end the call soon thereafter.

```
(5)   [Midcity 21: Call 5a]
1   911:          We'll get somebody there right away.=
2   Clr:          =o:kay thank yo[u.
3   911:                         [<mm bye>
4                 ((end call))
```

```
(6)  [Midcity 21: Call 24]
  1  911:    .hhh We'll send someone out.
  2  Clr:    Tha:nk you.
  3          ((end call))
```

Against this backdrop, concern about the caller hanging up following reassuring remarks seems well founded, since reassurances from the call-taker (e.g., "we're getting an ambulance there") bear a striking resemblance to promises of assistance. While the seriousness of call termination depends on whether crucial information remains outstanding, call-takers work to avoid that eventuality.

Labeling Callers' Emotions

Thus far the analysis has focused on how the caller's emotions are displayed and responded to, and this in turn suggests that such emotions are socially organized and regulated. But there is another social dimension to emotions within emergency calls, and this has to do with how they come to be named or labeled.

Whalen and Zimmerman (1998) examined the emotion labels that call-takers occasionally enter into the call record form (see, for example, figure 5.2). This record of the call, which may be electronic or paper, contains information that is relayed to the dispatcher and used to coordinate an organizational response. Emotion labels, when included, typically appear in an open field used to record any supporting details that may be seen as relevant to the dispatch of assistance – including details that explain or elaborate on entries in other fields.

Whalen and Zimmerman observed that some callers are characterized as "hysterical". This label is most closely associated, not with the sheer quantity of emotion displays within the call, but rather with blank or incomplete fields elsewhere on the call record form. The *hysterical* label appears to provide a way of accounting for the missing information, one that deflects responsibility away from the call-taker and onto the distressed caller. In one instance analyzed by Whalen and Zimmerman (1998: 156–7), the caller's responsibility for missing information about a reported fire is made quite explicit by the call-taker, who types: "UNK [unknown] WHAT'S ON FIRE – SHE'S TOO HYSTERICAL." The *hysterical* label is thus the call-taker's way of saying to the dispatcher – who is in turn put in the difficult position of having to coordinate a response with incomplete information – "It's not my fault."

In a broader discussion of the occupational culture of public safety communications, Whalen and Zimmerman (1998) also point out that the problem of *hysterical callers* figures prominently. Training manuals devote extensive attention to such callers and the challenges they pose, while also emphasizing the importance of the call-taker *taking control of the call* to ensure that necessary information is obtained.

This analysis elaborates and deepens our sense of the social organization of emotions within emergency calls. What might elsewhere be termed fear, grief, or distress, is in the emergency service environment labeled as *hysterical*. This label highlights not merely the emotion-state itself, but the caller's consequent inability to participate effectively in the focal task. It is, moreover, deployed within an occupational framework of accountability, where it serves as a resource by which call-takers maintain a stance of professional competence before their colleagues.

Angry Callers

There is a specific type of problematic call that is quite unlike the calls examined thus far. This type is marked by a different trajectory of events and different emotional content. A call of this sort begins more or less straightforwardly and only becomes problematic as the call develops, and the principal emotion that emerges is not fear or grief but anger. Although real-world events may be a contributing factor, the caller's emotions appear to be triggered by and targeted at events within the interaction itself, most notably the "bureaucratic" requirements imposed by call-takers during the interrogative phase of the call. Such callers may be seen by call-takers as *unwilling*, rather than *unable*, to answer their questions.

To illustrate, following this caller's request for an ambulance, the call-taker asks two questions (line 1, line 7) probing the nature and cause of the caller's injury. After the second question is repaired and answered, the caller registers a complaint (line 15, arrowed) regarding "too much information and shit, man?" This is spoken with a marked intonation contour characteristic of challenging and other oppositional moves (M. Goodwin 1983, Günthner 1996) and suggesting aggravation or incipient anger.

```
(7)  [Fire Dept.: Fell Off Stairs]
  1  FD:        Yeah what ha- what happened to you.
  2  Clr:       Uh I fell dow:n.=I want them to fuckn' check my he:ad
  3             er my- .h my finger cuz I'm- I'm kina cut an' shit.
  4             (0.9)
  5  FD:        kay.
  6             (.)
  7  FD:        Y[ou fell off what.
  8  Clr:        [( )
  9  Clr:       What?
 10  FD:        Wha'dju fall off of.
 11             (0.4)
 12  Clr:       Fuck'n stairs:'n shit like [that. (   )
 13  FD:                                   [(   )
 14             (0.5)
 15  Clr:   →   Eh: too much inforMAtion 'n shit.=man?
 16  FD:        Well we need to get the information so we know what
 17             uh: what ambulance to send.
```

The caller's complaint can be understood as an argumentative move (Maynard 1985) which, if responded to in kind, could lead to further argumentation disruptive of the interrogation. The call-taker, however, moves to defuse the incipient conflict (lines 16–17) by explaining that the questions are necessary to dispatch help. Moreover, he declines to match the caller's agitated intonation, and instead delivers his explanation in a low, steady, and hence manifestly calm tone of voice. Subsequent questions are answered without complaint.

In chapter 5 it was noted that most callers answer the questions straightforwardly, apparently grasping the relevance of the questions as a necessary prelude to the provision of assistance. However, when callers are distressed and anxious, they may be less inclined to view such questions as relevant and cooperative with the agenda set by the request. The interrogative phase can thus be a source of tension in emergency calls, requiring work by call-takers to defuse incipient conflict and return to the task at hand.

Extended Conflict: The Case of a Failed Emergency Call

Next we consider a highly conflictual emergency call that was *not* successfully defused. This fateful call, which was perceptively analyzed by J. Whalen, Zimmerman, and M. Whalen (1988), reveals how extended conflict can upset the otherwise stable architecture of the emergency call. It is, in other words, a case study in the vulnerability of emergency calls when emotions run high. The following account draws heavily from the Whalen, Zimmerman, and Whalen analysis.

Early in 1984, a Dallas resident sought emergency assistance for his elderly stepmother who was having difficulty breathing. The call began normally enough, but it soon deteriorated into an argument between caller and call-taker, an argument that continued as the caller was transferred first to the fire department nurse and later to her supervisor. Here is the first half of the call.

```
(8)  [Dallas Call]
  1  FD:      Fire department
  2           (0.8)
  3  Clr:     Yes, I'd like tuh have an ambulance at forty one
  4           thirty nine Haverford please?
  5           (0.2)
  6  FD:      What's thuh problem sir.
  7  Clr:     I: don't know, n'if I knew I wouldn't be ca:lling
  8           you all.
  9           (0.5)
 10  FD:      Are you thuh one th't needs th'ambulance?
 11  Clr:     No I am not.=It's my mother.
 12           (0.7)
 13  FD:      Lemme letya speak with thuh nurse?
 14  Clr:     Oh bu:ll shit!
 15           (1.7)
 16           ((in background)) Nurse, line one (1.0) Nurse, line one
 17           (1.2)
 18  Nrs:     This is thuh fi:re department nurse, what iz thee
 19           address?
 20           (0.3)
 21  Clr:     Forty one thirty nine Have:ford
 22           (1.4)
 23  Nrs:     For[t y -](.) one thirtynine what's thuh street?
 24  Clr:        [Drive]
 25           (0.3)
 26  Clr:     Haverfo:rd Drive ((spoken with irritated tone))
 27           (0.3)
 28  Nrs:     H. a. v. e. (c.) o. r. [d.
 29  Clr:                           [No, H. a. v. e:.
 30           r. f. o. r. d. Drive ((exasperated tone))
 31           (1.6)
 32  Nrs:     Okay iz this uh house or n' apartmen'?
 33  Clr:     It- it is a ho:me
 34           (0.6)
```

```
35  Nrs:       What street crosses Haverford there on thuh corner?
36             (0.4)
37  Clr:       Uh: it's Lincoln, you (c'n cut) off at Lincoln
38             (1.9)
39  Nrs:       And thuh pho:ne number?
40             (0.6)
41  Clr:       Thuh phone number, three two nine, three two
42             two fi:ve.
43             (0.8)
44  Nrs:       And whatiz thuh problem there.
45  Clr:       I don't kno:w, if I knew I wouldn't be needin'
46             [y-
47  Nrs:       [Si:r:, I a- would you answer my questions please?
```

This call was enormously consequential. The ambulance was delayed, and when it finally arrived the caller's mother was already dead. The caller subsequently sued the city of Dallas for $300,000 in damages, and many of the parties involved were either fired or demoted.

Can a conversation analytic approach shed any light on this tragic event? It can, provided we bear in mind that our primary goal is not to pass judgment or take sides, but to understand what transpired and why by reference to the communication practices – the methods of action and inference – employed by the participants themselves as the interaction developed toward its unfortunate outcome.

Opening troubles

The call begins in an unremarkable and seemingly routine way.

```
(9)
 1  FD:        Fire department
 2             (0.8)
 3  Clr:       Yes, I'd like tuh have an ambulance at forty one
 4             thirty nine Haverford please?
```

The call-taker answers the phone with a standard categorical self-identification ("Fire Department" in line 1), and the caller acknowledges this ("yes" in line 3) and then issues his request for an ambulance. The request is spoken somewhat tersely, but otherwise lacks any overt display of anger, or fear or grief for that matter. The caller thus appears outwardly calm at this point.

The trouble begins with the next exchange, when the call-taker asks the very first question about the nature of the problem (line 6). Recall that this question is the standard follow-up to an unelaborated request (see chapter 5), and it launches the interrogative series as a prelude to what would typically be a granting of the request. While the question is routine, the caller's response (lines 7–8) is not.

```
(10)
 6  FD:        What's thuh problem sir.
 7  Clr:    →  I: don't know, n'if I knew I wouldn't be ca:lling
 8          →  you all.
 9             (0.5)
```

```
10  FD:      Are you thuh one th't needs th'ambulance?
11  Clr:     No I am not.=It's my mother.
12           (0.7)
13  FD:      Lemme letya speak with thuh nurse?
14  Clr:     Oh bu:ll shit!
```

The caller claims not to know what the problem is, and he then proceeds to challenge the relevance of the question: "If I knew, I wouldn't be calling you all." In effect, he implies that as a 911 caller he shouldn't be asked a question of this sort. Then, when he's transferred to the fire department nurse (line 13) he curses sharply (line 14).

Misunderstanding the "What's the problem?" question

Part of the difficulty appears to be a misunderstanding of the call-taker's initial "What's the problem?" question. The caller treats this question as if it were seeking something on the order of a formal medical diagnosis, rather than an informal layperson's account of the problem at hand. Indeed, this apparent misunderstanding persists – when the nurse asks essentially the same question much later in the call (line 44), the caller responds in much the same way (lines 45–6)

```
(11)
44  Nrs:     And whatiz thuh problem there.
45  Clr:  →  I don't kno:w, if I knew I wouldn't be needin'...
```

Divergent orientations

This semantic misunderstanding is, however, merely the surface layer of a deeper misapprehension regarding the fundamental nature of the transaction in which they are engaged. Recall that the police and fire departments are public services for which requests must be justified (chapter 5). This caller, however, is treating the fire department as if it were a consumer service available on demand. The resulting clash of perspectives – that Tracy (1997) has identified as a recurrent difficulty in emergency calls – is manifest in the caller's challenging response to the "What's the problem?" question, which seems premised on the assumption that he shouldn't have to justify his request.

   Although the caller's "consumerist" orientation becomes obvious in his challenging response (lines 7–8), it is foreshadowed earlier in the call. Consider the design of his initial request (lines 3–4).

```
(12)
 1  FD:      Fire department
 2           (0.8)
 3  Clr:  →  Yes, I'd like tuh have an ambulance at forty one
 4           thirty nine Haverford please?
 5           (0.2)
 6  FD:      What's thuh problem sir.
```

The form of this request ("I'd like to have . . .") is rather unusual. As noted in the previous chapter, while this request form is commonplace in restaurants and other commercial service environments, it is extremely rare in emergency calls. Unlike explicit request forms that acknowledge the contingencies of response (e.g., "*Could you* send an ambulance . . ."), and others that assert the necessity of response (e.g., "*I need* an ambulance . . ."), this form is distinctly casual in seeming to frame the request as a matter of mere preference. This may in fact be an attempt by the caller to maintain a calm demeanor in the face of a frightening situation, but it can be taken as indicative of a problematic orientation to the emergency service. Thus, what would later emerge explicitly was implicit in the caller's very first turn at talk.

The emergence of call-taker doubt

It is clear that the fire department nurse doubts the caller's claim regarding his mother's pulmonary illness. This is apparent in her investigatory lines of questioning, which include a request to speak with the mother (line 59), and a demand for further explanation when the caller refuses on the grounds of his mother's "incoherence" (lines 60–3).

```
(13)
55  Nrs:   Where is she now.
56         (0.3)
57  Clr:   She is in thuh bedroom right now
58         (0.4)
59  Nrs:   May I speak with her, please.=
60  Clr:   =No you ca:n't, she ca- (can't) (.) seems
61         like she's incoherent.
62         (0.5)
63  Nrs:   Why is she incoherent,=
64  Clr:   =^How thuh hell do I:: kno::w.=
```

The skepticism implicit in such questions soon becomes quite explicit when the nurse asserts (in response to caller's "why don't you just send an ambulance out here" in line 70): "we only come out on life-threatening emergencies" (lines 72–3).

```
(14)
65  Nrs:   =Sir, don't curse me
66  Clr:   Well I don't care, you y- y' stupid ass
67         (king-) questions you're asking,
68         (3.0)
69  Clr:   Gimme someone that knows what they're doin',=
70         why don't you just send an ambulance out here.
71         (0.6)
72  Nrs:   Si:r, we only come out on life threatening
73         eme:r[gencies,      okay?]
74  Clr:        [Well this is li]fe threatening emergency.=
```

What is the basis of her skepticism? This might seem puzzling since the caller has taken many of the steps (noted in the previous chapter) geared to securing a problem's genuineness, having indicated both his social relationship (the victim is his mother) and epistemic access (she is in the next room) to the problem. However, other practices may have undermined his credibility. Consider the exchange immediately preceding the investigatory questioning in segment (13) above. Responding to the problem query (line 44 below), the caller first asserts unequivocally that he doesn't know what the problem is (line 45); but when the nurse then insists on an answer (lines 47–8) he immediately reverses himself and supplies one ("difficulty in breathing" in lines 49–50).

```
(15)
44  Nrs:     And whatiz thuh problem there.
45  Clr:     I don't kno:w, if I knew I wouldn't be needin'
46           [y-
47  Nrs:     [Si:r:, I a- would you answer my questions
48           please? whatiz thu[h problem?
49  Clr:                       [She is having difficult in
50           breathing
```

This complete reversal is unmarked by "oops", "oh", "oh, I see", or any other indication of the caller having undergone a shift in understanding (cf. Heritage 1984a). In light of the caller's unmarked about-face, his initial response is vulnerable to being heard in retrospect not as a sincere misunderstanding of the problem query, but as a capricious and willfully uncooperative act. Consistent with such a hearing, the nurse makes no attempt to clarify or explain her problem query (cf. example (7) above); she merely insists on an answer (lines 47–8) and then launches the implicitly skeptical investigatory line of questioning that will culminate in her request to speak directly to the mother.

"The runaround"

The nurse's skeptical questioning is experienced as frustrating to the caller, but not merely because it delays the dispatch of assistance. Recall the distinction (introduced in the previous chapter) between routine and investigatory questions, and the observation that a shift from investigatory to routine questions may be taken by the caller as a sign that the problem has been accepted as genuine and that the call is moving forward. Recurrently in the Dallas call, hopes are raised in this way but then subsequently dashed.

For instance, after the caller is initially asked to justify his request by reference to a specific problem (excerpt (8), line 6), he is transferred to the nurse who then asks a lengthy series of locational questions (lines 18–42). The shift to non-investigatory questions can be taken to indicate progress toward a favorable resolution, and indeed the caller answers these questions impatiently but without overt protest. Then, however, he is asked essentially the same *what's the problem* question that launched the interrogation (line 44; cf. line 6). From the caller's point of view, this question takes him back to square one, and he answers it with the same angry challenge.

The caller is again pulled in different directions with the next course of questioning (example (13)). Questions regarding the mother's age (not shown) and exact location (line 55) can be seen as relatively neutral or in the latter case presumptive of a genuine problem, and indeed the caller answers these questions straightforwardly. But the subsequent request to speak directly with her (line 59) and the refusal to accept the caller's rejection (line 63) are pointedly skeptical, especially given the caller's earlier claim that his mother is having breathing difficulties. And the caller's responses to these skeptical questions (challenging in the first case, profane in the second) are correspondingly uncooperative.

Being repeatedly whipsawed between the opposing stances embodied in routine versus investigatory questions, and shuttled from call-taker to nurse to supervisor, appears to have contributed to the caller's frustration.

Activity contamination

Turn by turn, the Dallas call was transformed from a routine emergency call into an argument. And an argument is a recognizably distinct order of activity in its own right, one organized around a succession of oppositional acts that dispute, reject, or otherwise counter what came before (Goodwin 1983, Maynard 1985, Kotthoff 1993, Dersely & Wootton 2000).

Once the Dallas call took on the contours of an argument, this was consequential for how the caller's remarks were understood. As Whalen, Zimmerman, and Whalen (1988) have observed, the caller did say many things that contain information of the sort that call-takers need. Here is a partial list of the caller's information-bearing utterances that focus on the problem itself.

```
(16)  [Whalen, Zimmerman, and Whalen 1988: ]
She is having difficult in breathing
She...seems like she's incoherent
Well this is a life threatening emergency.
[She's dying]
[She] can't breathe.
Sh'having difficult in breathing. She cannot talk,
She is incohe:rent.
She can not talk at all
```

However, it is misleading to consider these remarks in isolation from the specific sequential environments in which they were produced. Here are three key utterances, now re-embedded in their sequential contexts.

```
(17)
 59  Nrs:   May I speak with her, please.=
 60  Clr:   =No you can't, she ca- (can't) (.) seems
 61         like she's incoherent.

122  Nrs:   Okay sir, I need to talk to her still
123  Clr:   You ca:n't, she is incohe:rent

 89  Sup:   Well I'll tell you what.=If you cuss one more time
 90         I'm gonna hang up the pho:ne.=
 91  Clr:   =We- I'll tell you what.  What if it was your mother
 92         in there and can't breathe.What would you do.
```

In context, it is clear that the informational content of these utterances is subordinate to the action of countering and opposing whatever the call-taker (or nurse or supervisor) had just done. In the first two exchanges the caller characterizes the mother as "incoherent", but he does so in response to, and as a way of refusing, a request to speak to her. The third exchange finds the caller saying that his mother "can't breathe", but this is offered as a way of defending himself against the charge of having cursed. In short, notwithstanding their informational content, all three utterances are oppositional moves and are understood and treated as such.

Therein lies the corrosive effect of an argument. It is an activity framework that shapes the production and understanding of subsequent contributions, and thus embodies its own form of inertia. Threats to face may also be implicated, further contributing to an argument's persistence (Tracy & Tracy 1998, Tracy 2002). Accordingly, once the activity framework of an emergency call becomes contaminated by argument, additional work is required to repair the damage and set things right. And for whatever reason, such restorative work was not successfully undertaken in the Dallas call.

Coda: The Emergency Call as an Achievement

The stressful circumstances that motivate some emergency calls can spark powerful emotions in callers, emotions that range from anxiety about the problem itself to anger targeted at the bureaucratic hurdles that stand in the way of obtaining help. The expression of emotions is often restrained by the demands of the interaction, but emotion displays can also impede the transfer of information necessary for the dispatch of service, and can in some instances derail the call altogether. Fortunately, call-takers have various methods for defusing callers' emotions and reorienting them to the task at hand.

As we wind down this tour of emergency calls, let's return once again to the basic activity framework of such calls, the five-phase structure outlined at the beginning as a hallmark of such calls.

1 Opening
2 Request
3 Interrogative series
4 Response
5 Closing

This is, in one sense, a commonplace interactional routine, familiar to anyone who has participated in an emergency call, or a service call of almost any kind. Even many face-to-face service encounters have much the same general shape.

It should now be clear that a tremendous amount of concerted effort is required to make this routine happen, to bring it off across a succession of actual occasions. The work includes not only the positive engagement in activities comprising the five phases, but also the avoidance of alternative and incongruous actions. A wide range of behaviors that would be absolutely normal in ordinary conversation are systematically withheld or minimized here. Everything from greetings and *how are you*s (as we saw in chapter 5) to displays of emotion, sympathy, and argumentation (as we've seen in the current chapter) can, if produced, begin to divert the interaction along a different track. And indeed, the emergency call's activity framework – its architecture – is recurrently subject to stresses and strains. While it may occasionally give way under stress, countervailing procedures are available to maintain it across a variety of exigencies. Consequently, the institution embodied in this activity framework is made to persist and do its work, discharging vital services to those who need them.

For Further Reading

A wide-ranging overview of issues surrounding the display and control of emotions in emergency calls can be found in Whalen and Zimmerman (1998). These issues have been further illuminated by in-depth case studies of high-profile failed calls, most notably Whalen, Zimmerman, and Whalen's (1988) analysis of the Dallas call, and Garcia and Parmer's (1999) complementary analysis of a derailed emergency call involving "misplaced mistrust" of the caller. Recurrent sources of conflict in emergency calls have also been investigated. These include the problem of frame mismatch between callers expecting service on demand and call-takers requiring justification (Tracy 1997), and the ever-present and potentially toxic role of face and face threat (Tracy & Tracy 1998, Tracy 2002).

III

Doctor–Patient Interaction

8

Patients' Presentations of Medical Issues: The Doctor's Problem

In the 1970s two major studies established doctor–patient interaction as a systematic research domain. The first, conducted by Barbara Korsch and her colleagues at the Children's Hospital of Los Angeles, examined 800 pediatric visits. They found that nearly a fifth of the parents left the clinic without a clear understanding of what was wrong with their child, and nearly half were left wondering what had caused their child's illness (Korsch & Negrete 1972). A quarter of the parents reported that they had not mentioned their greatest concern because of lack of opportunity or encouragement. The study uncovered a strong relationship between these and other communication failures and non-adherence to medical recommendations, showing that 56 percent of parents who felt that the physicians had not met their expectations were "grossly noncompliant".

On the other side of the Atlantic, *Doctors Talking to Patients* (Byrne & Long 1976), based on some 2500 audio recordings of primary care encounters, anatomized the medical visit into a series of stages, and developed an elaborate characterization of doctor behaviors in each stage. Drawing on Balint's (1957) proposal that the primary care visit has therapeutic value in its own right, Byrne and Long argued that doctor-centered behaviors – behaviors that focused more on the expertise of the doctor than the needs of the patient – were prevalent and undermined the visit's therapeutic value to the patient.

These two highly influential studies inaugurated a whole field of research. And as we move from our focus on emergency calls to the field of medicine, we encounter a vast expansion in the amount of research to draw from. If as many as fifty articles on emergency calls have been published in the last twenty years, at least a hundred times as many have been published on doctor–patient interaction! The field is large because medicine is a large and important part of society and its economy, in the US for example absorbing approximately 14 percent of gross national product. It is also large because of the wide range of sites in which medicine is practiced: general practice, specialist clinics, emergency rooms, operating rooms, patients' homes, hospices, and so on. The range of specialties is equally large: cancer, heart disease, genetic counseling, psychiatry, childbirth, eating disorders, etc., and the numbers of research objectives are correspondingly vast.

Faced with this enormous range of choice, we will focus on primary care. Primary care is the largest single branch of medicine and something we have all experienced first hand. Within this general area, we will focus on three main topics: (1) how patients present problems to their doctors; (2) how doctors question patients about those problems, and (3) how doctors present patients with diagnoses and treatment recommendations. Underlying these topics are two major sociological themes which were established in foundational writings in medical sociology (Parsons 1951, Freidson 1970). These concern (1) how patients manage the visits so as to present themselves as legitimately in search of medical help, and (2) how doctors wield medical authority in their dealings with patients.

In order to provide a general context for the materials in this part of the book, we begin by distinguishing between several broad categories of primary care visits. First there are *acute care* visits. These are visits in which patients present newly arising problems to their doctors for the first time. Second there are *follow-up* visits in which, as the name suggests, patients return for an additional visit to review the progress of an illness or its treatment. Third, there are *routine visits* which patients make on a periodic basis, often for chronic problems, such as diabetes or heart disease, for review and adjustments in treatment. Finally, there are *well visits*, often made on an annual basis. The premise of these visits is that the patient is well, and is present at the doctor's office for a check-up that will confirm that there are no problems. The different assumptions that inform these visits are highly significant for their structure and trajectory, and are often clearly indexed from their opening moments (Robinson 2006). In the following chapters, we will focus on acute care visits.

Acute Care Visits

Acute care visits have a basic phase structure that is taught to doctors in medical school and learned by patients through experience in primary care. The six-phase structure below, described by Byrne and Long (1976), like the phase structure for emergency calls described earlier, has a simple functional logic (see figure 8.1). Visits must be opened, together with certain ancillary activities (Robinson 1998). A presenting problem is normally a prerequisite for the launching of medical business. And this problem must be investigated through history taking and physical examination. This investigation will ideally culminate in a diagnosis and treatment recommendation, after which the visit can be terminated. This structure is one that doctors and patients clearly orient to in the course of acute visits (Robinson 2003). For example, as we shall see, patients are fully oriented to their ownership of the conversational floor during problem presentation and its imminent loss as the visit transitions into physician-directed history taking (Robinson & Heritage 2005). And they recurrently treat diagnosis as a prelude to the recommendation of treatment or some other procedure or service. However, departures from this structure are quite common because patients may have more than one problem to be dealt with, or because additional concerns surface during the visit.

We will begin our survey of acute care interaction near the beginning of the visit, at the point when the patient presents a medical problem, the "presenting concern" or reason for the visit, to the doctor.

The Importance of Problem Presentation

The problem presentation phase of the medical visit is the primary opportunity for patients to describe their problems in their own terms and in pursuit of their own agendas. At the

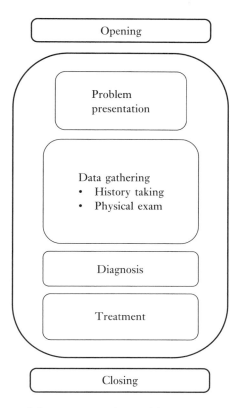

Figure 8.1   Phase structure of the acute care primary visit

end of the problem presentation, when the doctor shifts into history-taking questions, the patient loses control of the content and direction of the talk and becomes more or less constrained by questioning that is physician-directed (Beckman & Frankel 1984, Mishler 1984, Boyd & Heritage 2006). In a word, the patient loses the interactional initiative.

Problem presentation has been much studied because it is important for a number of reasons. Some of these are biomedical: patients who are able to give relatively complete accounts of their problems will likely contribute to improvements in the doctor's ability to diagnose and treat their diseases correctly (Arborelius, Bremberg, & Timpka 1991). Moreover, as part of that account, they may convey information about their own theories of their illness and its causation, and about underlying anxieties and fears which may not otherwise surface (McKinley & Middleton 1999). Additionally, although medical visits can have therapeutic value in their own right, this will not be realized if patients do not feel that their concerns were adequately heard and addressed (Byrne & Long 1976, Orth, Stiles, Scherwitz, et al. 1987, McWhinney 1989). Problem presentation is a crucial facet of this process. Finally, patients' effective communication of their problems is associated with favorable health outcomes (e.g., recovery from headaches, upper respiratory infections, and high blood pressure), and together with greater patient comfort and satisfaction with the visit itself (Silverman, Kurtz & Draper 2005, Roter & Hall 2006).

The Brevity of Problem Presentation

These benefits notwithstanding, most problem presentations are comparatively brief. In a classic study, Beckman and Frankel (1984) found that the average problem presentation in their data set lasted only about 18 seconds, and this finding was reproduced by Heritage and Robinson (2006b) who found an average of 21 seconds in a larger sample. A further study by Marvel, Epstein, Flowers, and Beckman (1999) found a mean of 23 seconds, but their data included a subset of physicians who were trained in communication and counseling skills and whose patients generally spoke somewhat longer.

What accounts for this brevity? The first place to look is the design of the question used by the physician to elicit the presenting concern. A study by Heritage and Robinson (2006b) distinguished between question designs according to (1) whether they convey that the doctor does or does not know the patient's problem, and (2) whether they invite the patient to describe the concern, or merely confirm what the doctor already knows. These question designs are presented in table 8.1. The "general inquiry" questions convey that the doctor does not know the patient's problem and invites its description. The other two question types convey that the doctor already has some idea of the patient's problem (perhaps from the practice receptionist or a nurse or another member of the practice team). They invite confirmation of this while creating a more (type 2) or less (type 3) hospitable context for patient elaboration. Heritage and Robinson (2006b) found that responses to the first type of general-inquiry question averaged 27 seconds, while responses to the second type (16 seconds) and the third type (8 seconds) were very much shorter, and described fewer symptoms.

While question design obviously contributes to the extent of problem presentation, it is clear that it does not tell us the whole story. After all, problem presentations to the most inviting of general-inquiry questions only last for an average of 27 seconds. In their discussion of this issue, Beckman and Frankel (1984) defined completed problem presentations as those in which the patient said everything they had to say, as indexed by patients' use of units of talk specifically designed to complete the problem presentation, like "So that's why I'm here today" or "Do you think it could be serious?" Beckman and Frankel argued that physicians curtailed patients' problem presentations before these completion points by interrupting or redirecting them before they were complete, mainly by asking

Table 8.1   Types of opening questions and extent of patient responses

Question type	Example	Average length of response (n = 302)
"General inquiry" questions	How can I help? What can I do for you today? What's the problem.	27 seconds
"Gloss for confirmation" questions	Sounds like you're uncomfortable. So you're sick today, huh?	16 seconds
"Symptoms for confirmation" questions	So having headache, and sore throat and cough with phlegm for five days?	8 seconds

Source: Heritage and Robinson 2006

history-taking questions, such as "How long has this been going on?" However, the cogency of this suggestion is weakened by Marvel, Epstein, Flowers, and Beckman's (1999) finding that fully complete problem presentations (defined in the same way as Beckman and Frankel) lasted an average of only 6 seconds longer than redirected ones. This suggests that doctors are timing their follow-up questions relatively close to where the patient would otherwise have completed their problem presentation anyway. Evidently we need to develop a more comprehensive approach to problem presentation as a whole.

Problem Presentation: The Doctor's Dilemma

We begin with the observation that the question with which the doctor begins the medical business of the visit (e.g. "What can I do for you today?") opens up a space for the patient's problem presentation that will be effectively closed when the doctor asks a first history-taking question (e.g., "So what kind of pain is it?"). Although the doctor opens and closes this space, it is important to recognize from the outset that problem presentation is best considered as a *co-construction* between doctor and patient. Within this framework, the doctors have a very specific issue to deal with as they listen to their patients' presentations: *Is the patient's presentation intended to be complete yet?* In principle, this issue arises at the end of each and every unit of the patient's problem presentation, *including the very first unit.* This is because a considerable number of problem presentations consist of only a single sentence:

```
(1)  [Dog Bite]
  1  Doc:        What happened here. huh?
  2               (1.5)
  3  Pat:    →   Got bitten by thuh dog.
  4               (0.2)
  5  Doc:        Your dog? Somebody el[se's.
  6  Pat:                            [My dog.
  7               (.)
  8  Doc:        What happened.
```

```
(2)  [Eczema]
  1  Doc:        .hhh So what's goin' o:n today. What brings
  2               you i:[n.
  3  Pat:    →         [Well- I have this lip thing again:,=
  4  Doc:        =Aga:in. [Huh?
  5  Pat:                 [ Yes:[:.
  6  Doc:                       [>When was< thuh las' time we
  7               saw you (.) for that.
```

This means that physicians must be continually prepared to recognize that and when problem presentations are complete. This process of recognition is not always straightforward:

```
(3)  [Bad Foot]
  1  Doc:        Whatcha up to:.=h
  2               (0.2)
```

```
 3  Pat:    →  I've gotta bad foot that I can't: get well.
 4             (0.2)
 5  Doc:       Which part.
 6  Pat:       >Okay.< About ↑five weeks ago I went to Disneyland
 7             and I wore uh pair of sandals that weren't very
 8             supportive.... ((continues))
```

In this case, the doctor thinks the patient has completed the presentation at the end of line 3 and begins data gathering at line 5. However the patient resists this and, at line 6, begins an extended narrative.

At the opposite extreme are problem presentations that are built from the outset to be extended. In (4) the patient, who is presenting this problem in August, begins the presentation by starting with events in June, clearly projecting some kind of narrative.

```
(4)  [Ringworm]
 1  Doc:      What happened.
 2            (.)
 3  Pat:      Well I got (.) what I thought (.) in Ju:ne (.)
 4            uh was an insect bite.=in thuh back of my neck here_
 5  Doc:      Okay,
 6  Pat:      An' I (0.2) you know became aware of it 'cause
 7            it was itching an'=I (.) scratched at't,
 8            (0.2)
 9  Pat:      An' it persisted fer a bit so I tried calamine
10            lotion,=
11  Doc:      =Okay,
12            (0.2)
13  Pat:      An' that didn't seem to make it go away
14            completely, an' it=s:tayed with me,=w'll its
15            still with me. Thuh long and thuh short of it.
16  Doc:      [Okay.
17  Pat:      [Cut to thuh chase is its- its still with
18            me, .hhh but (its) got a welt associated °with it.°
19  Doc:      Okay,
20            (0.5)
21  Pat:      It's got a welt that's (.) no:w increased in
22            size to about that big=it was very (.) small
23            [like a di:me initially you know, an' now
24  Doc:      [Okay,
25  Pat:      its (0.3) like a (.) bigger than a half do:llar
26            (I bet [it's like-) [(       )-
27  Doc:             [ And    you [said  it's no: longer
28            itchy. Is that correct,
```

Moreover, the patient's use of an "at first I thought" version of events at the beginning of the narrative (line 3), clearly conveys that this initial idea about his problem was not correct, and that a more complicated problem is at hand (Jefferson 2004).

We have already seen enough to know that the completion of patient problem presentations is a site of negotiation and manipulation. The primary locations at which these occur are at the beginnings and endings of problem presentations, to which we now turn.

Beginnings: patients' resources for indicating an extended presentation

How do physicians anticipate the likely extent and shape of patients' problem presentations? If they must form these judgments by the end of the patient's first unit of talk, then resources for such judgments must emerge within that unit. It turns out that patients ordinarily format these initial units in ways that reliably project whether they will extend over one, or more than one, turn-constructional unit of talk.

One resource in this process is the use of "well" as a preface. "Well" prefaces, when used in response to questions, commonly indicate that the response will not be straightforward (Schegloff & Lerner 2009) and, in the medical context, they indicate that the first turn-constructional unit of the response will almost certainly not be the last (Robinson and Heritage 2005).

A second resource that patients can use to indicate an extended problem presentation is an initial response that is rather general and lacking in relevant detail – that is, coarse in terms of what (Schegloff 2000) calls "granularity". In the following case, both practices are deployed by a patient (line 3) to produce the interactional equivalent of a newspaper headline for her problem. She goes on to illustrate the severity of her symptoms by describing problems in everyday living (at arrows a and b):

```
(5)  [Breathless]
 1  Doc:       ='hhhhh So::. What's the problem.
 2             hhh[hhhhhhhhhhhhhhhhhhh
 3  Pat:   →     [Well me breathin's shockin'.
 4  Doc:       Ri:ght.
 5  Pat:   a→  As I'm wa::lkin' [ah- (0.3) I 'av ta sto:p.
 6  Doc:                        [Yeah, (.) Yeah,
 8  Doc:       Yeahs.
 9             (.)
10  Pat:   b→  An' even when- >do you know when ya go< ta
11             shake the pillas up,
12  Doc:       Yeah
13             (0.3)
14  Pat:   b→  I ga- I go out a bre:ath.
15  Doc:       Mm
```

The patient headlines her problem with "Well me breathin's shockin'." In contrast to single sentences like "Got bitten by thuh dog." which adequately describe the patient's problem, this description is hearably (and designedly) insufficient as an account of her problem. This insufficiency, together with the "well" preface, is the means by which the patient indicates to the doctor that her problem presentation will be extended.

In the case of narratives, "well" prefaces combine with opening statements located in the historical past (arrow a) to project an extended report, as in the "Ringworm" narrative. With overwhelming frequency patient narratives culminate in either an account of the decision to come to the doctor's office or an account of the patient's symptoms in the here and now.

```
(4)  [Ringworm]
 1  Doc:       What happened.
 2             (.)
```

```
 3 Pat:   a→  Well I got (.) what I thought (.) in Ju:ne (.)
 4            uh was an insect bite.=in thuh back of my neck here_
 5 Doc:       Okay,
             .......((nine lines omitted))
14 Pat:   b→  ...........an' it=s:tayed with me,=w'll its
15            still with me. Thuh long and thuh short of it.
16 Doc:       [Okay.
17 Pat:   b→  [Cut to thuh chase is its- its still with
18            me, .hhh but (its) got a welt associated °with it.°
```

It is the latter that emerges at lines 14–18 of the patient's narrative, though he will go on to detail the special nature of the welt, which is now large and prominent.

Endings: finding a place to shift into history taking

If there are relatively straightforward ways to indicate that a problem presentation will be extensive or not, indicating a point where the doctor should take the initiative and begin to question the patient is a more complex business. Transitioning from the problem presentation is far from an exact science. Robinson and Heritage (2005) analogized this transition to the passing of a baton in a relay race. And, just like a relay race, the baton may be offered but not accepted, it may be reached for prematurely, or it may be fumbled in other ways during the transfer. In a relay race, there is a baton-passing area – a part of the track where it is legitimate and appropriate for the baton to be passed. In the medical visit, as we shall see, this area is defined by the patient's description of currently existing concrete symptoms in the present tense. At this point patient and physician enter a mutually understood baton-passing zone of transition (see figure 8.2). The shift to history taking can occur after the patient articulates a first concrete symptom. Physician and patient proceed deeper into this zone with a second and a third symptom presentation, at which point the problem presentation will likely be terminated either by a physician's history-taking question, or a patient's use of an "exit device" (e.g. "So that's why I came in today.").

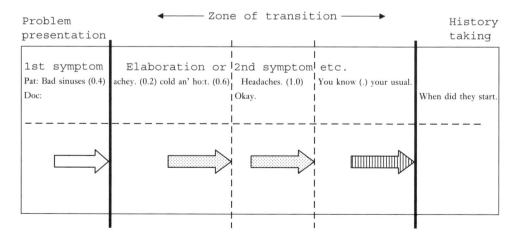

Figure 8.2 Passing the baton: transition from problem presentation to history taking

If this view is correct, then patients who present past tense symptoms or non-concrete glosses of symptoms will be treated as incomplete. This is overwhelmingly the case (Robinson & Heritage 2005). In (6), the patient's initial presentation at line 3 is both non-concrete and in the present perfect tense (a tense which is often used when a time period has not finished). Using this tense, the patient presents a symptom as situated in the past, yet ongoing. The presentation is treated as incomplete by the doctor's "uh huh?" and the patient continues at line 6:

```
(6)  [Ear Problem]
  1  Doc:        What's goin' on.
  2              (0.3)
  3  Pat:        'ell my ear's been acting up. hh[hh
  4  Doc:    →                                    [Uh huh?
  5              (0.4)
  6  Pat:        Thuh: >Friday< evening it started to: (.) to
  7              ring real loud,
```

By contrast, in (7) the patient's presentation of a single concrete and current symptom is treated as an occasion to begin history taking (line 3):

```
(7)  [Sore Throat]
  1  Doc:        How >can I< help you today.
  2  Pat:        Got=a #sore thro:at,# ((#=hoarse))
  3  Doc:        .hhh How long ['as it  been the[re.
  4  Pat:                       [It's kuh-     [.hh #Since Monday.#
```

Given the importance of whether the patient begins in the present or the past tense for how the problem presentation will unfold, we would expect patients to shift from one to the other as part of a project to redesign the presentation, as in (8):

```
(8)  [Flu Symptoms]
  1  Doc:        What=in thuh world's goin' o:n.
  2              (0.2)
  3  Pat:    →   W'll (.) ↑I ha:ve↓ (.) da- ta back up ta thuh very
  4              beginning. I think I had like an upper respiratory
  5              flu:.
  6  Doc:        Ri:[ght, ((while nodding))
  7  Pat:           [L:ike- (.) a week ago. I was running a fever...
```

In this case the patient starts in the present tense with what may have been going to be a description of symptoms or a self-diagnosis (W'll (.)↑I ha:ve↓), but subsequently abandons this beginning, in favor of a historicized narrative ("ta back up ta thuh very beginning . . ."), thus holding off the moment at which history taking will begin.

Similarly, when physicians attempt to move into history taking before patients have arrived at concrete current symptoms, patients may resist this as premature. In (9), the patient evidently intends his initial "My back doc" as a gloss of his problem and he proceeds to elaborate ("I uh"):

```
(9)  [Back Pain]
  1  Doc:        So:, tell me. what brings you in here today (      ).
  2  Pat:        My back doc. I: uh (0.3)
```

```
3  Doc:      Back pa:in?
4  Pat:      Yeah lemme tell you what ha:ppend.
5  Doc:      Sure.
6  Pat:      I: uh (1.7) (have) one=a those little electric scooters?...
```

Here the doctor's question at line 3 is resisted by the patient in the interest of giving an account of how his problem came about.

In short, current, concrete symptoms are presented, and responded to, as appropriate objects of medical inquiry, and they are the overwhelming site at which history-taking questions begin, as table 8.2 shows.

Table 8.2   Ending the problem presentation

Point at which doctors initiate history taking	*Percentage (n = 302)*
After one current symptom	25
After two or more current symptoms	53
After patient has confirmed a current symptom-for-confirmation opening question, e.g. "Sore throat for three days huh?"	16
None of the above	6

Source: Robinson and Heritage (2005)

With these observations in mind, some of the difficulties and fumbled transfers from problem presentation to history taking can become more understandable. For example, if we return to (3), we can see significant ambiguity in the patient's problem presentation:

```
(3)  [Bad Foot]
 1  Doc:          Whatcha up to:.=h
 2                (0.2)
 3  Pat:    →     I've gotta bad foot that I can't: get well.
 4                (0.2)
 5  Doc:          Which part.
 6  Pat:          >Okay.< About ↑five weeks ago I went to Disneyland
 7                and I wore uh pair of sandals that weren't very
 8                supportive.... ((continues))
```

Here the patient is sitting on the examination table with her shoe off and her foot up on the table. Though lacking the full concrete granularity of a classic "current symptom", her announcement "I've got a bad foot", when combined with the foot that is apparently prepared for examination, seems to be one of those designedly brief one-line problem presentations. On the other hand, her continuation "that I can't get well" hints at a history of trouble with the foot and efforts at remedy that she may want to describe. After a short silence (line 4), the doctor takes it that he should start the history. But the patient then begins a narrative which will describe the history of her foot problem. Here an ambiguous problem presentation results in the doctor anticipating a transfer to history taking long before, as it turns out, the patient is ready to do so. The transfer is fumbled.

During problem presentation: negotiating incompleteness

The physician's responses to problem presentations during the course of their actual production is an important source of information – to patients and to conversation analysts – of how they view its progress towards completion. Although these responses tend to be brief acknowledgments of what has been said, these acknowledgments embody subtle, but clear, distinctions.

For example, acknowledgments like "mm hm" and "uh huh" are continuers (Schegloff 1982). They register that the previous speaker has arrived at a unit boundary in their talk, forgo an opportunity to take a turn, and thereby permit the previous speaker to continue. In this way, they simultaneously embody an analysis of what the previous speaker has said as incomplete, and invite its continuation. These features are particularly marked when acknowledgments are intoned with a rising, or "comma", intonation. In the context of medicine this combination strongly suggests that the doctor understands that the patient has not yet completed what he or she has to say.

Acknowledgments like "okay" and "right", by contrast, are "shift-implicative" (Beach 1993). While they also register that the previous speaker has arrived at a unit boundary in their talk, they are associated with, and communicate, a preparedness to shift to a new topic or to a new primary speaker. In contrast to the continuative acknowledgments such as "mm hm", the shift-implicativeness of "okay" and "right" embody an analysis that the previous speaker could be complete and ready for such a shift. This shift-implicativeness can be tempered with the use of rising "comma" intonation ("Okay," rather than "Okay."). Here the "comma" intonation indexes a continuative orientation that counteracts the shift-implicativeness of the acknowledgment token itself. "Okay," (with comma intonation) permits doctors to hedge their bets as to whether a patient is complete. They can index a willingness to shift but without insisting on it.

Thus when doctors choose either "okay." or "mm hm" to acknowledge what a patient is saying, they are indicating an analysis that a patient is, or is not, complete (or has said, or not said, enough). These acknowledgments, then, are not neutral. They may quite strongly curtail, or alternatively prompt, the continuation of the problem presentation.

Doctors frequently (and unavoidably) use these acknowledgments during problem presentation. For this reason, and because these acknowledgments tend to prompt, or alternatively curtail, continuation, problem presentations must necessarily be considered as co-constructions between doctor and patient, rather than as under the control of the patient alone. Problem presentations that begin with background information, or in the historical past, tend to be acknowledged continuatively. However, once they approach the description of current symptoms, entering the zone of transition where the initiation of history taking becomes imminent, shift-implicative acknowledgments become more common. Whenever the patient's willingness to relinquish the problem presentation role is unclear, doctors also have available the comma-intoned "okay," which hedges on where the patient is in the presentation, and whether transition into history taking is to be attempted.

These features are clearly shown in the following example. The patient begins in the historical past with an account of a visit three weeks previously and its outcome, which the doctor acknowledges continuatively (1→).

```
(10)  [Sore Throat]
  1  Doc:      An' what can we do ↑for ya↓ today.
  2  Pat:        'hh Well I was here on September=h <twenty third>
```

```
 3                    because I had <bronchial> (.) >an' I< was put on
 4                    zi:throma[x.
 5  Doc:   1→              [Mm hm,
 6  Pat:             'hh thuh following: Tuesday Wednesday I had such a
 7                    sore throat I could hardly swallo[w.
 8  Doc:   1→                                         [Mm [hm,
 9  Pat:                                                  [ 'hh I came
10                    i:n fo:r a culture an' it was negativ[e.
11  Doc:   2→                                              [(n)Okay,
12  Pat:             'hhhhhh it wa- started on this si:de it went ta both
13                    si:des (an') >I can hardly swallow< thuh culture was
14                    negative.
15  Doc:   1→         [Mm hm,
16  Pat:             ['hh  So I been takin' i:buprofin (.) using
17                    sa:lt=h 'h zinc lozengers 'hh an' it won't go away
18                    from this side.
19  Doc:   2→         (n)[Oka:y,
20  Pat:                 [It gets really sore in this side an'
21                    then its feels like its up in to my ear.
22  Doc:   2→         Okay,
23                    (.)
24  Doc:   2→         [Okay,
25  Pat:             ['h An' that's why I'm here today. 'Cause its been
26                    (.) long.
27  Doc:   2→         O:kay,
28  Doc:             >'hh< Well that sounds like a pretty good history
29                    there, that's [pretty-] pretty concise,
30  Pat:                           [Yes.   ]
31  Doc:             'hh Uh: any problems with hay fever er allergies in
32                    thuh pa:st.
```

At lines 9–10, the patient describes a second visit two weeks previously and a negative test for strep throat, which the doctor acknowledges with a "hedging" comma-intoned "okay," (2→). However, as the patient enlarges on the description of the second visit and reiterates the negative strep finding, the doctor "reverses" into a more continuative stance (line 15). Subsequently, as the patient first details her self-medication (lines 16–18), and then her current symptoms (lines 20–1), the doctor moves back into a hedged shift-implicative stance. A repeat of this hedged "okay," at line 24, which leaves a further opening for continuation, prompts the patient to boundary off her account with a summary (lines 25–6) designed to manage exit from the problem presentation (".h An' that's why I'm here today. 'Cause its been (.) long."). At this point the doctor shifts into history taking (lines 28–32).

A second case shows a similar pattern. Here the patient starts by summarizing how he came to the clinic: he was referred by another facility for a shoulder problem. Following the doctor's hedged "Okay," (line 7), he elaborates with a brief history of his problem, and the doctor acknowledges its component units with rising comma-intoned "mm hm"s (lines 12, 14, 18).

(11) [Shoulder Pain]

```
1  Doc:   Well what brings you to thuh clinic t'day.
2  Pat:   O:kay:. Here uh: Tuesday I was up at U C I:.
```

```
 3  Doc:    Uh huh,
 4  Pat:    An' they'd- uh: (0.5) told me tuh come over here.
 5          (0.2)
 6  Pat:    About my:=#b:# left shoulder here.
 7  Doc:    O[kay,
 8  Pat:     [.hh
 9          (0.5)
10  Pat:    Okay it started out: here s:at- last Saturday just
11          bein' so:re.
12  Doc:    M[m hm,
13  Pat:     [Up in through here.
14  Doc:    Mm [hm,
15  Pat:        ['hh
16  Pat:    (Then) it just worked its way up intuh my n:e:ck up
17          [in here, .hh an' down my left arm. [(a little.)
18  Doc:    [Mm hm,                             [O:kay.
19          (1.0)
20  Doc:    °Okay.° How old are you?
21  Pat:    Yeah I'm forty seven.
```

As the patient's account of his symptoms approaches the "here and now" of the visit, the doctor shifts to the form of downward-intoned "Okay." which is clearly shift-implicative (lines 18 and 20), and then transitions into history taking.

Although not all doctors deploy this differentiated use of acknowledgments, and may not always do so consistently, this shift from continuative to shift-implicative acknowledgments in extensive problem presentations as patients move into the zone of transition to history taking is both common and significant.

The Transition from Problem Presentation to History Taking

The actual transition into history taking is overwhelmingly accomplished through doctors' questions. As we think about this transition, it is worth looking at whether the initial problem presentation was brief or extended. This is because the extent of a problem presentation indexes a commitment to the interactional "floor" of the medical visit and to the interactional initiative and control which go with it. Extended narratives show a strong commitment to this kind of interactional initiative, in which the patient controls the content and direction of the talk, while brief "symptoms only" (Stivers 2002a) problem presentations exhibit a much lesser degree of this commitment. When the doctor commences history taking, the visit enters into a phase in which medical questioning controls the content and direction of the talk. Thus the baton which is passed in the zone of transition is, in an important sense, control over the content and direction of the interaction – the interactional initiative.

Research by Gail Jefferson (1984a) documents an interesting sequence of events in contexts where persons want to change the direction of conversations in which troubles have been reported by the other person. They begin with "other-attentive" questions that focus on a facet of what has previously been said. However, these other-attentive questions are frequently vehicles by which the questioner will, after the answer, shift the conversation onto a different track. A similar pattern can be discerned in initial history-taking questions, though there is an important contrast between brief and extended problem presentations. Brief problem presentations that simply describe current symptoms tend to attract questions that elaborate on the medical problem by inviting more details, such as duration, location or intensity of symptoms (e.g., examples (3) and (7)), or which ask about other, potentially related, symptoms.

Extended problem presentations, by contrast, tend to attract more other-attentive initial and transitional history-taking questions. Other-attentive history-taking questions include those that summarize or recapitulate something the patient has already said, build the question as a continuation of the patient's own account, or support the patient's reasoning or decision making in some way. For example, in the following case, the patient's extended account of her flu symptoms culminates in an account of her decision not to go to work:

```
(12)
 1  Pat:           A:n' uh: (0.4) >so I called< thuh secretary today
 2  said           I'm not coming in today, or tomorrow.
 3  Doc:    1→     Good.
 4  Pat:           '(C)ause I figured thuh less I (.) use my voice (.)
 5                 thuh be:tter.
 6  Doc:    1→     °You're right.° An' you('ve) got some fever no::w,
 7  ( ):           ·hhh
 8  Doc:           (        )-
 9  Pat:           W'll I ran a fever over thuh weekend. too:.
10  Doc:    2→     When you cou:gh does anything come up?
11                 (0.2)
12  Pat:           Ye:s.
```

The physician responds with two statements (1→) that support the patient's decisions. The first (line 3) positively assesses the patient's decision, and the second offers confirmation of the patient's reasoning and adds an additional symptom: the patient is currently running a fever. Subsequently, the doctor shifts into history taking (2→).

And in the next case involving an out-of-hours call to her primary care provider (Drew 2006), a wife narrates an account of her husband's illness which began the previous evening and is presently ongoing. As the doctor transitions into history taking, he begins with a question that renews the time frame and duration of the symptoms mentioned by the caller (at lines 2 and 9):

```
(13)   [Stomach Pain]
 1  Doc:      How can I help.
 2  Clr:      .hhh Well- (0.3) all of a sudden yesterday evening
 3            having been perfectly fit for (.) you know
 4            ages, [.hh
 5  Doc:            [Ye:[s,
 6  Clr:                [My husband was taken ill: (wi') th'most awful
 7            stomach pains, and sickness, h[h
 8  Doc:                                     [Ye:s,
 9  Clr:      .hh An' it's gone on a:ll night.<He has vomited once.
10            hh! .hh[h
11  Doc:             [Right,

......((seven lines of problem presentation omitted))
```

```
18  Clr:        Uhm: (.) an:d (.) you know he just feels he ought to s
19              a doctor. hhh [˙hh
20  Doc:                      [(b)R:ight, ih- h[e's actch-
21  Clr:                                       [He's ly:ing in be:d
22              really absolutely wre:tched. hhh
23  Doc:    →   And he's had thuh pain in 'is tummy all night
24          →   (h)as ['e?
25  Clr:              [Y:es,
```

Here the doctor's question at line 23 ("And he's had thuh pain in 'is tummy all night (h)as 'e?"), in addition to recycling already presented information, is built with the "and" preface as a continuation of the caller's own account. This is also a feature of the doctor's "An' you('ve) got some fever no::w," in (12) above.

The recycling of elements of patients' accounts, which are especially common when the duration of symptoms has been mentioned, may seem redundant. However, patients do not ordinarily treat them as such. The use of this kind of question to transition into history taking is recommended in some text books of medical interviewing, but its fundamental role as other-attentive means to transition into a more doctor-directed topical agenda derives from more fundamental processes, first described by Jefferson (1984a), that are a part of how interaction works in the lifeworld of the ordinary society.

Conclusion

Problem presentations, as we have seen, represent the primary institutionally ratified opportunity for patients to describe their problems and to tell the story of their illness in their own words. This is an important opportunity for patients to be heard and for their doctors to listen and come to grips with their concerns. However, whether this opportunity is taken, and the corresponding problem presentations are long or short, are highly variable. In this chapter, we have explored the basic ground rules that patients and their doctors orient to in the construction of problem presentation. This is, as we have seen, a co-construction. Problem presentation is shaped by the doctor's opening question and, immediately afterwards, its extent and structure are projected by the patient from the very first unit of talk. Thereafter its extension is an object of negotiation organized by the practices through which patients design, and doctors acknowledge, each new element of the presentation. At length, the participants enter a zone of transition into history taking. This zone of transition is effectively entered once the patient has described at least one current symptom in concrete detail. These "current symptom" parameters are clearly oriented to by both physicians and patients as indexing the zone of transition, regardless of whether current symptoms are entered into at the very beginning of the problem presentation or only after an extended narrative.

As the visit enters into the history-taking phase, there is a transfer of the interactional initiative. While the patient holds the initiative during problem presentation, history taking is another matter. For here the physicians' questions set the agenda for patient responses, and constrain how they may present additional information and concerns. We will discuss these issues in chapter 10. But because we have so far considered only the structure of problem presentation, we turn next to consider its content.

For Further Reading

Byrne and Long (1976), whose work we discuss at the beginning of this chapter, were pioneers in the movement for patient-centered care that began in the 1970s. Other pioneers were George Engel (1977), Elliot Mishler (1984), and Howard Waitzkin (1991). Patient-centered care has now become a focus of national medical policy in the United States and elsewhere, although there remain difficulties in defining it (Mead & Bower 2000, Epstein, Franks, Fiscella, et al. 2005), and in determining how it should be implemented (Emanuel & Emanuel 1992, Frosch & Kaplan 1999).

In her pioneering study, Barbara Korsch (Korsch and Negrete 1972) used a method of coding interactional data which was derived from the sociologist Robert F. Bales. This coding system was developed by Debra Roter in directions that improved its fit to medical interaction and it is now widely used (Roter & Larson 2002). Roter and Hall (2006) give a detailed overview of the results of many of their studies using this coding system.

Critics identify the central weaknesses of the Roter system in its lack of sensitivity to the details of interaction and its failure to incorporate the perspectives of the participants. This criticism is voiced by Mishler (1984), Tuckett, Boulton, Olson, and Williams (1985), Stiles (1989), and Charon, Greene, and Adelamn (1994). Conversation analysts who stress the specificity of interaction and the need to get at the participants' perspectives share the critics' point of view. Heritage and Maynard (2006b) provides an overview, while Heritage and Maynard (2006a) provides a set of studies modeled on Byrne and Long's original attempt to describe the primary care visit in its entirety.

9

Patients' Presentations of Medical Issues: The Patient's Problem

In this chapter we examine how patients present the specifics of their medical problems. These presentations are very diverse: patients vary in their portrayals of how symptoms came to be discovered (or not), how they were identified (or not), and how they are named. Patients differ in whether they describe theories of what the illness might be, and how they acquired it. They also diverge in whether they describe the anxieties and underlying concerns which their symptoms may be causing them. They differ too in whether they present just a simple enumeration of symptoms, or a narrative of symptom development. And they will vary in the extent to which they convey that they are entitled to medical help.

Faced with this diversity, the organizing principles of problem presentation can be difficult to disentangle. However, it is useful to begin from Talcott Parsons' classic discussion of the doctor–patient relationship in *The Social System* (1951). Parsons argues that becoming sick involves entering a special social role – the "sick role" – which has particular rights and obligations that can be summarized thus.

Rights

1   Depending on how ill the person is, there is an entitlement to some exemption from normal activities.
2   Freedom from personal responsibility for the illness and for recovery. The sickness is not treated as the patient's own fault and s/he is not expected to recover through an act of will. The patient can't help it and needs to be taken care of.

Obligations

1   Being sick must be viewed as undesirable. The patient should strive to get better. There must be no resignation to the illness state and the patient must not seek to take advantage of the "secondary gains" of being the center of attention and concern.
2   The patient must seek technically competent help and co-operate in the treatment process.

According to Parsons, the sick role is special for two main reasons: (1) it entitles persons to social support from others and is a means by which they are protected from the consequences of sickness, and (2) it provides a basis on which persons are entitled to withdraw from their normal social obligations. However, for these very reasons, the sick role is one that can be exploited by persons to get social, economic, and psychological support from others, and it can also be exploited as a means to withdraw from social obligations. Our language is replete with terms to describe people who exploit the sick role or look for medical help inappropriately – hypochondriac, malingerer, crock, and so on – and the pathological disposition to do so (as manifested in Munchausen's Syndrome) is itself treated as a medical condition. There are significant consequences for the evaluation of patients' moral and social character if they are found to be looking for medical help too frequently, or without adequate justification.

Parsons also stressed that patients enter into a relationship of dependency with their physicians. This dependency arises out of either the experience of pain or fear of life-threatening or life-curtailing conditions, and may be intermingled with feelings of embarrassment and humiliation associated with bodily malfunctions. Much of the normative patterning of the role relationship he described is plausibly associated with the need to manage this dependency so that it is not exploited by either party. These two Parsonian themes, of fear and dependency on the one hand, and the need for legitimacy on the other, infuse the organization of problem presentation and contribute to its special dynamics. They play out, first of all, through the kinds of medical problems that patients are dealing with.

Patients who have made an appointment for a medical visit and come to the doctor's office have, by those very actions, committed themselves to the position that they have a legitimate medical problem. Heritage and Robinson termed this a "doctorable" problem and defined it as one that is "worthy of medical attention, worthy of evaluation as a potentially significant medical condition, worthy of counseling and, where necessary, medical treatment" (Heritage & Robinson 2006a: 58). Drawing on a distinction of Eliot Freidson's (1970: 298), we can distinguish between unconditionally and conditionally legitimate illnesses.

Unconditionally legitimate illnesses involve conditions that are treated as self-evidently problematic without any need for medical validation of the patient's illness status. In (1) the patient's problem is obvious and is immediately raised by the doctor as he comes in the room:

```
(1)  [Shooting Accident]
  1  Doc:       So what happened tuh your ha↑:nd.
  2             (1.0)
  3  Pat:       We wen:t shooti:ng to uhm=
             ...
             ...((22 lines omitted))
             ...
 26  Doc:       So this was uh bullet that (blew) right
 27             [through (there.)
 28  Pat:       [Yeah it went through.
 29             (.)
 30  Pat:       I got shot.
```

Patients may similarly formulate illness as unconditionally legitimate:

```
(2)  [Dog Bite]
  1  Doc:       What happened here. huh?
  2             (1.5)
  3  Pat:    →  Got bitten by thuh dog.
```

```
4              (0.2)
5   Doc:       Your dog? Somebody el[se's.
6   Pat:                          [My dog.
7              (.)
8   Doc:       What happened.
```

In both these cases, both doctor and patient are oriented to the transparent nature of the patient's problem. But less clearly legitimate problems may also be presented in ways that index the patient's commitment to their unconditional legitimacy:

```
(3)  [Bronchitis]
1   Doc:       What can we do for you toda:y. What brings ya i:n.
2   Pat:       Uh:=I wanna get rid=a this: stuff in my
3              °lu:ng[s.°
4   Doc:            [O:kay, >'hh< how long have you been sick for.
5              (0.5)
6   Pat:       Four (weeks.)
```

Here the patient's response is brief, and frames the problem in terms of a desired solution that presupposes the reality of his problem. This framing, together with the absence of history or explanation, and the sense of entitlement conveyed in the use of the word "wanna" (Curl & Drew 2008), communicates that from the patient's point of view his visit is unconditionally legitimate.

Freidson (1970) observed that conditionally legitimate illnesses frequently require legitimation by an authoritative practitioner. Sometimes this legitimation is quite explicit as in (4):

```
(4)  [Ear Pain] (050)
1   Doc:       Mkay¿ (.) mtch! .hh So::, you c'n tell me about yer::
2              head. nhh
3   Pat:       tch! U:m, (0.4) I: woke up last night, an:' ihm- ihm-
4              it hurts tih touch this side uh my fa:ce, and my ear:
5              (.) is really botherin' me,
6   Doc:       M[m h:m.
7   Pat:        [Sometimes it- (.) I can feel thuh pai:n, other times
8              it's just touching it.an' it hurts. .hh An' u:h (0.6)
9              I didn't sleep much last night, so I figured maybe some-
10             yi- maybe had the ear infection.er something.=
11  Doc:    →  =So this woke you from your sleep.
12  Pat:       Yeah.
13  Doc:    →  That's important enough.  Okay.
```

Alternatively, a more tacit legitimation process may arise as the doctor treats the problem presentation as a basis for further investigation. This second kind of legitimation is often treated by patients as provisional and may be re-problematized later in the visit (Heritage 2009).

As we consider more conditionally legitimate patient concerns, we can make a fundamental distinction between what are presented as "known" and "unknown" medical problems. "Known" medical problems fall into two main groups: (1) routine illnesses which patients and the population more generally are familiar with and can give vernacular names to like colds, flu, strep throat, and (2) recurrences where patients believe that the problem they are presenting is a return of a previously diagnosed illness. "Unknown" problems, by contrast, are framed as beyond the patient's previous experience and as manifesting in symptoms that the patient does not have the vocabulary to describe: in Zimmerman's (1992) terminology they have low "codeability". This distinction between "known" and "unknown" problems is a fundamental feature of patients' problem presentations because it is central to whether patients name their illnesses or not.

"Known" Problems: Routine Illnesses

Routine illnesses are medical problems that most, if not all, of the population has experienced and can give vernacular names to. Upper respiratory illnesses (colds, strep throat, bronchitis, and ear infections) are perhaps the classic examples of routine illnesses, and account for about 30 percent of medical visits for new problems in the United States (Cherry, Woodwell, and Rechtsteiner 2007). These conditions will normally resolve on their own, and patients' presentations often show an orientation to their conditional legitimacy. Following Stivers (2002a), we can distinguish between "symptoms only" presentations of these problems, and presentations that embody "candidate diagnoses". In symptoms-only cases, patients simply describe the various symptoms they are experiencing and leave it to the clinician to form a judgment about them:

```
(5)  [URI]
  1  Doc:         What's been goin' o:n.
  2  Pat:    →    Ba:d sinuses (0.4) achey. (0.2) cold an' ho:t.
  3               (0.6) ((physician gazes at patient and nods once))
  4  Doc:         °Okay.°
  5  Pat:    →    Headaches.
  6               (1.0) ((physician gazes at patient and nods twice))
  7  Pat:    →    °You know.° (.) your usual.=
  8  Doc:         =When did they start. do you think.
```

By contrast, in problem presentations involving candidate diagnoses, patients go beyond the symptoms to propose that they are suffering from treatable illnesses, as in (6) and (7):

```
(6)  [Sinus Infection]
  1  Doc:         e=Uh#::# Sounds like you haven't been feelin'=so spiffy?
  2  Pat:         No::.
  3               (1.9)
  4  Pat:         Thought=it was goin' awa:y, an' it come back over
  5               thuh wee:kend.
  6  Doc:         Uh huh_
  7               (.)
  8  Pat:    →    Jill's like you got=a sinus infection a year
  9          →    ago. (.) it's got=a be:_=
 10  Doc:         =(Uhh/Oh). How's Jill doin' these days,
```

(7) [Sore Throat]
```
1  Doc:        So you're having a bad sore throat huh.
2  Pat:        Yes:: um (.) a- a girl friend of mine kinda made me
3         →    paranoid about it. =She said u:m (.) uh it could be
4         →    strep throat but I've never had it before
5              [so I have no idea what that is but um (.) I was just=
6  Doc:        [Uh huh
7  Pat:        =explaining to her that my throat's been hurtin' up.
```

These candidate diagnoses "raise the bar" in terms of the claim to legitimacy. Rather than presenting symptoms for evaluation, the diagnoses they present embody a tacit claim for prescription medication (in these cases, antibiotics) as the basis for legitimizing the visit. For this reason, this kind of presentation can imply that the patient would not have made the appointment if he or she had not thought that medication was necessary. This is often heard by physicians as exerting pressure for a prescription (Stivers, Mangione-Smith, Elliott, et al. 2003), and may even imply that a failure to prescribe will delegitimize the visit.

Other practices may also be used to shore up questionably legitimate visits. In the next two cases, patients describe how they have waited before coming to the doctor, and also point to a questionable new symptom – "green phlegm":

(8) [Cold]
```
1  Doc:        What can I do for you,
2  Pat:        It's just- I wouldn' normally come with a cold,=but I
3              'ad this: co::ld. (0.4) fer about.hh >m's been< on
4              (Fri:day).=I keep coughin' up green all the time?
```

(9) [Chest Cold]
```
1  Doc:        What's been goin' o:n?
2  Pat:        I just got (0.4) chest cold a:nd it's been uh
3              goin' on for a week- I don't seem to be able to
4                  [shake it-
5  Doc:        [O:kay
6  Pat:   →    And uh what caused me to call is uh 'bout fourth
7         →    or fifth day in a row in thuh morning- [I was
8  Doc:                                              [Mm hm
9  Pat:   →    tryin' to get the engine started-
10 Doc:        Mm hm
11 Pat:   →    Coughin' up a buncha green stuff.
12 Doc:        Oka:y.
```

In (8) the patient indicates that she would not ordinarily treat a cold as a legitimate reason for a medical visit. With this claim, she is on her way to implying the special status of the symptoms she has. She documents these in terms of duration (since last Friday), indicating that she showed fortitude and "troubles resistance" (Jefferson 1988) in the face of her symptoms, before deciding to visit her doctor with the appearance of green phlegm, which most patients associate with bacterial illness and antibiotic treatment (Mainous, Zoorob, Oler, & Haynes 1997). In (9) the patient is still more explicit about his attempt to wait out his symptoms, and about the appearance of "green stuff" as the grounds for his visit.

Visits for routine illness can also be accounted for by reference to patients' expectations about how the illness will progress. In (10), the patient offers such a prognosis:

```
(10)  [Strep Throat]
 1  Doc:        .hh U:m: (2.0) what's been goin' o:n.
 2  Pat:        Ah just achiness sore throat, an' .h I jus' thought
 3         →    rather than wait, um (0.2) I just have seen up a
 4         →    predisposition t' pick up strep throat durin' the school
 5              year.=I teach kindergarten.=
 6  Doc:        =Oh you do.=
 7  Pat:        =So but thuh ↑school year hasn't [↑started yet,
 8  Doc:                                         [eh heh heh heh heh heh
 9              heh ((laughs)) [.hhh
10  Pat:    →                 [I jus' thought rather than wait, °I want
11          →   to stop in and check.°
```

In this case the patient justifies her current visit, not by her current symptoms, but by reference to her past history of upper respiratory illnesses which she offers as grounds for what her symptoms might come to. As she portrays her reasoning process (lines 10 and 11), she indicates that she wants to "check" if she has a problem, justifying the visit in a preventative, proactive modality.

We can end this discussion of routine illness problem presentations by noting that patients may further bolster the legitimacy of the visit by claiming that the decision was not simply theirs, but was rather made in concert with others. As Freidson (1970), Zola (1973) and others have noted, medical decision making is often a social process. In these cases, shared decision making is invoked as a support to medical legitimacy. Indeed, in (6) and (7) another person is invoked as a prime mover in the decision and responsibility for the judgment is diffused away from the patient (Heritage & Robinson 2006a).

"Known" Problems: Recurrent Illnesses

Patients who visit their doctors with what they believe are recurrences of previously diagnosed illnesses have a completely different set of opportunities for problem presentation and for the legitimation of the visit. The presentation of the previous diagnosis is prima facie grounds for the legitimacy of the visit, the more so as the diagnosis has already been authoritatively validated by a doctor. Moreover, even if the patient is wrong about the current condition, they may be seen to be justified in making the visit unless their belief is seen to be without any foundation. However, with the presentation of a fully medicalized diagnosis, the patient steps onto terrain that is the authoritative province of medical professionals and may encounter sanctions. In (11), for example, the patient downgrades her diagnostic claim with a slightly delayed "I think," and the sanction (lines 6–8) is mild and joking:

```
(11)  [UTI]
 1  Doc:     >How do you do.<
 2           (0.9)
 3  Pat:     I got a 'U' 'T' 'I',
```

```
 4                 (0.2)
 5  Pat:           I think,
 6  Doc:           Uhh huh ((laugh)) £Okay look. that makes
 7                 my job easy,£ y(h)ou've a(h)lr(h)ead(h)y
 8                 d(h)i(h)ag[n(h)osed (h)it.
 9  Pat:                     [I know.
10  Doc:           ˙hhh £Okay.£ ˙hh £have a seat over here.£
```

But in (12), the patient is challenged to account for the diagnosis and, as the form of the challenge makes clear, is treated as lacking the requisite authority to make it:

```
(12)  [Torn Rotator Cuff]
 1  Doc:           .hh So: can you tell me:=uh what brings you
 2                 in today?
 3  Pat:           Uh=I got=uh- torn (roto cuff:.)
 4                 (.)
 5  Pat:           in my left shoulder.
 6                 (1.0)
 7  Doc:      →    (Ok[ay) who told you tha:t.
 8  Pat:             [An:'
 9  Pat:           Uh: family doctor,
10                 (.)
11  Pat:           I: did it about: nine months ago:=I really don't
12                 even know how I did it.
```

Patients who do not wish to encounter this kind of challenge may phrase their self-diagnoses with more subtlety. For example, in the following case, the self-diagnosis is conveyed inexplicitly with the single word "again" (line 5) which evokes a previous diagnosis without referencing it as such:

```
(13)  [Alopecia]
 1  Doc:           [.hh [W'[l what brings you in today. Thuh nurse [wrote
 2  Pat:                [Yea:h.                                   [We:ll
 3  Doc:           down that you're havin' some trouble with your [ha:ir.
 4  Pat:                                                          [Y:ea:h.
 5            →    [Aga:in. I'm [really   [upse:[t.
 6  Doc:           [(    )      [(Okay)   [.hh  [When was thuh la:st time.
 7                 It w's- its been a whi:[le.
```

After this one-word self-diagnosis, the physician immediately goes to the patient's medical records to investigate (lines 6 and 7).

In the case of more serious possibly recurrent illnesses, patients may fully justify the visit by reference to the gravity of the previous episode.

```
(14)  [Actinic Keratosis]
 1  Pat:           =Now look it here.
 2                 (0.2)
 3  Pat:           I got cancer here.
 4                 (.)
```

```
 5  Doc:       Uh hu[h,
 6  Pat:           [I know it's cancer because it=was told to me
 7             from a doctor one time before [he said you have a
 8  Doc:                                      [Uh huh,
 9  Pat:       touch, .h I had some here an' they >cut it
10             out< over at [HMO Name] ye[ars ago.
11  Doc:                                 [Oka:y,
12  Pat:       .hh But n:ow I think it's coming in here, here,
13             and over there.
```

Here the patient has every reason to visit his doctor, and every reason to explain the visit by reference to his previous diagnosis. Indeed whatever the outcome of the visit, including complete reassurance, the visit will have been justified.

Yet not all patients will take this stance. In the following case, also involving a possible return of skin cancer, the patient is transparently preoccupied with the possibility that her concern is a false alarm and that her visit is illegitimate. Her initial "headline" statement projects this possibility, and her subsequent narrative strongly implicates her husband in the decision to make the visit. She also disaffiliates from his concern at lines 15–17:

```
(15)
 1  Pat:  →   I'm here on fal[se pre- pretenses.<I think.
 2  Doc:                     ['hh
 3  Doc:       [<Yes.
 4  Pat:       [ehh! hih heh heh heh!
              . ((Five lines omitted))
 6  Pat:       I asked my husband yesterday 'cause I could feel: (0.8) (cause)
 7             I: could feel this li'l mo:le coming. An:d: uh (0.5) (he) (.) I:
 8             hh thought I better letchya know-<uh well I asked my husband 'f
 9             it was in the same place you took off thuh (0.5)   °thee (mm)
10             thee:°( [                        )
11  Doc:               [That's why you've come in be[cause of the mo:le.
12  Pat:                                            [that's why I ca:me, but=
13  Doc:       =H[ow long 'as it been-]
14  Pat:         [t h i s   m o r ning-] I: I didn' I hadn't looked yesterday
15             he said it was in the same place but 'hh but I: can feel it
16             nah- it's down here an' the other one was up here so I don't
17             think it's: th'same one at a:ll.
18  Doc:       Since when.
19             (0.8)
20  Pat:       Y(h)ea(h)h I(h) just felt it yesterday 'n
21  Doc:       Does it hurt?
22  Pat:       No?
23             (.)
24  Pat:       No it's just a li:ttle ti:ny thing bu:t=I (.) figured I
25             sh(h)ou(h)ld l(h)et y(h)ou kn(h)ow .hhh i(h)f i(h)t was (on)
26             the same pla:ce, b't
27  Doc:       So when you push [on it it doesn't hur[t.
28  Pat:  →                     [(Right.)            [No it's
29  Pat:  →   just a little- li:ttle tiny skin: [(tag) really.
30  Doc:                                        [I: (.) see=
31  Doc:       =Yeah it's different than whatchu had be[fore.
32  Pat:                                               [Uh huh.
```

```
33  Doc:         Your scar is up here,
34  Pat:    →    Yeah that'[s what I figured (an-)
35  Doc:                  [An'
36  Doc:         An' this is down below.
37  Pat:    →    .hh When he s- When he told me it was in the same place I
38               thought Uh: Oh: I better ca:ll a(h)nd te(h)ll yo(h)u .hhh
39  Doc:         Ri:ght.
40               (.)
41  Doc:         That's- I'm <ve:ry gla:d that you uh> did that.
```

By line 31, the physician has already examined the lesion and ruled out a recurrence of cancer. At this point, the patient is at pains to convey that her concern arose from her husband's judgment (the lesion was on the back of her neck), and the sequence closes with the
physician reassuring the patient that what she did was appropriate.

"Unknown" Problems

A patient with a new and unknown condition has an altogether more complex set of issues
to deal with in problem presentation. On the one hand, an unknown or inexplicable
symptom is a legitimate thing to present to a doctor even if it is benign. On the other hand,
several kinds of difficulty arise in the presentation of unknown symptoms. These include,
first, how to name and describe symptoms that may never have been experienced before
and, as part of this, whether the symptoms truly are symptoms of anything at all. In the
following case, the patient struggles to describe unfamiliar sensations. She begins with a
highly generalized gloss of her concern: "I fee:l like (.) there's something wro:ng do:wn under-
neath here in my rib area." and then tries to analogize her problem to a condition – "cracked
ribs" – that as she subsequently acknowledges (line 9) she has never experienced:

```
(16)  [Costochondritis]
 1  Doc:        What can I ↑do↓ for you today.
 2              (0.5)
 3  Pat:        We:ll- (0.4) I fee:l like (.) there's something
 4              wro:ng do:wn underneath here in my rib area.
 5  Doc:        Mka:[y,
 6  Pat:            [I don't tuh:m (0.4) I thought I might'a cracked 'em
 7              somehow but I have no clue ho:w,
 8              (0.4)
 9  Pat:        An' I don't even know what cracked ribs £f(h)eel like.£ I jus'
10              know that there's a pa:in there that shouldn't be. ˙hh an' as
11              I'm sittin' here its not (.) not as ba:d but when I'm up an'
12              active an' (.) movin' around an' breathin' an' (.) doin' all
13              that (.) you=know (.) extra (.) [heavy breathin' it (w's)
14  Doc:                                       [ Mm hm:,
15              really bo:therin' me.
16  Doc:        ˙tch=˙hh So- (.) when you take a deep
17              breat[h, does that make it wo:r[se.
18  Pat:             [Y:eah.                   [Yeah.
```

The patient finally asserts that her symptoms are real and problematic with her claim that "I jus' kn<u>o</u>w that there's a p<u>a</u>:in there that sh<u>o</u>uldn't be." (line 10) before describing circumstances in which the pain worsens (lines 11–15).

Second, patients have to deal with how they came to register certain symptoms and decide to present them to a physician. As Halkowski notes (2006: 89), it is often the case that a problem presents itself over time and, as it presents itself, the patient has to decide whether it is part of an illness process or not, and whether it might resolve if left alone. Relatedly, should patients present themselves as acutely aware of, and monitoring, bodily processes for signs of change, or as persons for whom changes force themselves into attention? And finally, how should patients present their reasoning about these unknown symptoms – in terms of best-case or worst-case hypotheses?

These problems are recurrently addressed in accounts of symptom discovery which often take the form of narratives. In the following case, the patient's presentation of a substantial abdominal swelling is careful both in balancing his inferences (line 5) about its causation between relatively benign (a hernia) and more serious ("something inside"):

```
(17)  [Halkowski: 108]
 1  Pat:        (.hh) I have ah- ah little swelling here.
 2               (0.3)
 3  Doc:        Oka:y,
 4  Pat:    →   annd ah (.hh) I don't know whether its ah (hh)
 5          →   ah hernia, (0.4) or (ah) (.) something inside
 6               there causing it ((cough)) but ah ((cough)) it-
 7               is- ah little lop sided (.) maybe I'm just
 8               growing that way.
 9  Doc:        Hm hmm,=
10  Pat:        But I think maybe its something ought ah be
11               looked at.=
12  Doc:    →   =You just noticed it two weeks ago,
13  Pat:        Yeah.
14  Doc:        Okay.=
15  Pat:        =(Hey) it coulda been there for ah year. (.hh)
16          →   I don't look at myself very much.
```

When confronted with the clinician's apparent surprise (line 12) that, as he described earlier in the visit, he has only noticed it recently, the patient defends himself by explicitly asserting that "I don't <u>look</u> at myself very much." Subsequently, he presents his discovery of the symptom as an unmotivated noticing:

```
(18)  [Halkowski: 108]
 1  Pat:        But I was shaving or something an I (0.4) I do
 2               some side to side exercises an I guess I was
 3               doing it an kindah maybe in front of ah (0.3)
 4          →   mirror or something [an I just noticed that
 5  Doc:                            [hm hmm,
 6  Pat:        this side is (1.0) extended
 7  Doc:        Okay.
 8  Pat:        rather than this side. ((Pat continues))
```

In other cases, the initial noticing is presented as the first in a sequence of more intrusive experiences:

(19) [Halkowski: 101]
```
 1  Doc:        When did it initially start.
 2  Pat:        ahhhh (.) it started two weeks before I saw
 3              Marion.
 4  Doc:        mm hmm,
 5  Pat:   →    I noticed I would have this pressured feeling in
 6              the bottom of my stomach.
 7  Doc:        mm hmm
 8  Pat:   →    and then one day I went to the bathroom and it
 9              just literally set me on fire to use the
10              bathroom like I had bathed myself in antiseptic
11              or something
12  Doc:        mm [hmm,
13  Pat:           [cause it was burning just that bad. (.hh) an
14              it did that one day and then it didn't do it
15         →    again (0.5) then thuh next thing I notice I go
16              to thuh bathroom to use thuh bathroom to urinate
17              and (0.2) I'm spotting blood.
18              (1.2)
19  Pat:   →    So then I f:igured it was time to call (0.2) the
20              doctor to get in to see an appoint- to have an
21              appointment that's when I went to see her. (0.8)
22              when I started spotting.
23  Doc:        Alright, (3.4) ((cough)) Now today (.) you are
24              having symptoms of what now.
```

Here the third (and most alarming) in a sequence of symptoms is presented as a turning point in the patient's decision to go to the doctor.

Third, many accounts of unknown symptoms embody narratives in which patients present themselves as having reasoned about their condition and self-medicated based on that reasoning, often for considerable periods, as in the following case:

(20) [Ringworm – Expanded]
```
 1  Doc:        What happened.
 2              (.)
 3  Pat:        Well I got (.) what I thought (.) in Ju:ne (.)
 4              uh was an insect bite.=in thuh back of my neck here_
 5  Doc:        Okay,
 6  Pat:        An' I (0.2) you know became aware of it 'cause
 7              it was itching an'=I (.) scratched at't,
 8              (0.2)
 9  Pat:        An' it persisted fer a bit so I tried calamine
10              lotion,=
11  Doc:        =Okay,
12              (0.2)
13  Pat:        An' that didn't seem to make it go away
14              completely, an' it=s:tayed with me,=w'll its
```

```
15              still with me. Thuh long and thuh short of it.
16   Doc:       [Okay.
17   Pat:       [Cut to thuh chase is its- its still with
18              me, .hhh but (its) got a welt associated °with it.°
19   Doc:       Okay,
20              (0.5)
21   Pat:       Its got a welt that's (.) no:w increased in
22              size to about that big=it was very (.) small
23              [like a di:me initially you know, an' now
24   Doc:       [Okay,
25   Pat:       its (0.3) like a (.) bigger than a half do:llar
26              (I bet [it's like-) [(        )-
27   Doc:              [ And    you [said it's no: longer
28              itchy. Is that correct,
```

Here the patient presents an initial conclusion (that he had been bitten by an insect) and
a course of treatment (calamine lotion) which failed (lines 13–14). These narratives are
"troubles resistant" in Jefferson's (1988) sense of the term: They present the patient as
able to cope without assistance and without involving others in their problems. In this case,
the patient contracted the problem in June but has waited until mid-August (the date of this
medical visit) before bringing it to the doctor. This delay raises a presentational difficulty:
given that the patient has been reluctant to bring this problem to the doctor's office, why
are they bringing it in now?

A common presentational solution to this problem is to focus on a turning point: an
event which crystallized the decision to seek medical care. In (19) the turning point was
when the patient started to find blood in her urine. In (20), the turning point is a "welt"
(lines 18–25) which is growing dramatically from the size of a dime to bigger than a half
dollar. In the following case, the turning point is the advice of an unnamed other person
(lines 23–4):

```
(21)  [Back Pain]
 1   Doc:       .h How I can help you [today.]
 2   Pat:                             [   .hh]h We:ll=hh- I:=h uh:m
 3              (0.5) .tlkhh (.) -developed an ek-stre↑:me [pai:n=
 4   Doc:                                                 [ (Mm_)
 5   Pat:       =on mu-=uh Monday.
 6              (.)
 7   Pat:       <uh-
 8   Doc:       O[kay.
 9   Pat:        [overni:ght.=or: I should say: .h Sunday night.
10              tuh Monday night.
11   Doc:       O[kay.
12   Pat:        [↑Terrible pain.
13   Pat:       .hh An' I could:: ide↑ntify where it was_ [It was=
14   Doc:                                                 [Mm hm,
15   Pat:       =certainly in this area(,)/(.)
16   Pat:       .hh An:d very difficult to- to move arou:nd,
17   Doc:       Mm [hm,
18   Pat:          [An' I- took some ibuprofen_
19   Pat:       .hh (I've) been:=really busy at school: an' I
```

```
20                 <could no:t> (0.4) tend to i:t,
21   Pat:          [.hh
22   Doc:          [Okay:.=
23   Pat:    →     =Uh: an- and=hh I p=h been encouraged then to te↑nd
24           →     to it so I- I call:ed then. .h yesterda:y.=a[n:d=uh
25   Doc:                                                      [Okay.
26   Pat:          .hh but- (.)
27   Doc:          Were you able tuh wa:lk?
```

Another turning point is presented in the following, very troubles-resistant presentation:

(22) [Bad Foot]
```
 1   Doc:          Whatcha up to:.=h
 2                 (0.2)
 3   Pat:          I've gotta bad foot that I can't: get well.
 4                 (0.2)
 5   Doc:          Which part.
 6   Pat:          >Okay.< About ↑five weeks ago I went to Disneyland
 7                 and I wore uh pair of sandals that weren't very
 8                 supportive.
 9                 (.)
10   Pat:          .hh And after that I started tuh have trouble.
11                 (.)
12   Pat:          It hurts in here,
13                 (.)
14   Doc:          (°Mm hm.°)
15                 (0.8)
16   Pat:          (Now s)=it's uh lot better than it was because I've
17                 been wearing an ace bandage.
18   Pat:          .hh But it still swells,
19                 (0.2)
20   Pat:          #An'# I don't know (.) what's wrong.
21   Pat:          .hhhh Every day I've been wearing an ace bandage.
22                 (0.2)
23   Pat:    →     But what r:eally made me come in here is that
24           →     this morning (0.5) when I woke u:p_ (0.5) it was
25           →     kind=of- reddish blue, right here?
26   Pat:          .hh An' it hurts terrible tuh walk on my toe: an'
27                 this part here.
28   Pat:          .hh Now if I press it it don't hurt very much but
29                 when I walk on it (h) (But) I don't walk on it. I
30                 walk on (th') side uh my foot which is no good
31                 for this:.
32                 (1.5)
33   Doc:          Yeah:.=h
34                 (0.2)
35   Doc:          #eh# I hope you didn't- may have uh s:mall fracture
36                 there er something.
37   Pat:          Well how could I get uh fracture from just walking.
```

The patient begins with an account of a trip wearing sandals "that w<u>e</u>ren't very supp<u>o</u>rtive." This implies a benign theory of her problem as something that can be treated with over-the-counter remedies – in this case, an "ace bandage" which was only partially successful. By line 20, she returns to her initial claim that the problem is not resolved and that she doesn't know what the problem is. At lines 23–7, she presents a clear turning point. On the morning of the medical visit, her foot changed color to a "reddish blue" and walking is very painful.

This last case will also help to introduce a final theme in this discussion of the presentation of unknown problems. We have seen that a number of these narratives offer benign interpretations of symptoms. But if the patient has started to entertain a less benign theory of the condition, should the patient now articulate it? The evidence strongly suggests that patients tend to avoid this course of action. Returning to (22), we can see at the end of the segment (line 37) that the patient resists the doctor's suggestion that she may have a "small fracture". As it turns out, she has an alternative hypothesis which she states later in the visit in the following fashion:

(23) [Bad Foot cont.]
```
 1  Pat:   Th<u>i</u>s uhm (0.4) .hhh ↑This feels like ya know I don't
 2          if I gi- I'm gi- I have (phleb<u>i</u>tis) in that- uh blood
 3          vessel there? or wh<u>a</u>t.
```

Here we see the upshot of the patient's reasoning about the sudden appearance of the "reddish blue" color on her foot: she thinks it may be a blood clot (phlebitis) which has formed in her foot. The patient is a diabetic and blood clots are a common, and dangerous, side effect of this condition. None of this, however, is directly stated in the patient's problem presentation. Here is a different dimension of "troubles resistance". This patient, and the others with unknown problems discussed in this chapter, do not describe their worst fears during problem presentation. Rather they leave these unstated, and content themselves with descriptions of how their more benign ideas about the condition have not worked out. Both aspects of problem presentation are, in Maynard's (2003) terms, stoic and, in Jefferson's (1988), "troubles resistant".

Conclusion

In the last chapter we saw that problem presentation is comparatively brief, and that it is organized by reference to the emergence in the patient's account of concrete current symptoms that can form the starting point for the clinician's investigations. In the present chapter we can begin to see why it may be that many problem presentations are so brief. Put simply, patients who believe that they have a clear-cut and legitimate medical condition that they have experienced before tend to present their problems with a brief overview of symptoms or a candidate diagnosis. It is only patients who cannot "place" their medical experiences, or who feel they may be of questionable legitimacy, who tend to present problems in extended narrative-style presentations. In this regard, medical patients are not unlike the callers to 911 emergency we described earlier who, encountering problems that are hard to define or which may only marginally seem to warrant an emergency call, also present their emergency through narration.

For problems that are hard to put into words, or which seem to be only marginally legitimate, the use of narratives has real advantages. Narratives allow the patient to tell the story of their problem in their own words, in an order of their own choosing, incorporating elements of sensation and context, the reactions of others, the reasoning process by which some interpretations were discounted and others entertained, and by which revisions in perspective emerged. Because medical narratives almost always end in the "here and now" of the doctor's office, they can, and frequently do, culminate in descriptions of the thinking that led the patient to make an appointment and come in for visit and, of course, they can portray this thinking as reasonable. In short, narratives permit the patient to give an account of illness that is completely under their own control.

Narratives portray a course of events over time. And as part of this they can be used to evidence the patient's troubles resistance in the face of adversity. "Troubles resistance" is a feature that Gail Jefferson (1980) argued was characteristic of the disclosure of troubles and difficulties to others in everyday life. In a troubles-resistant description, persons portray their problems as "self-manageable" and their difficulties as things that they will in fact be able to cope with.

There is of course a real sense in which a patient who has come to a doctor with a medical problem has already ceased to be troubles-resistant in this sense. And yet patients frequently make considerable efforts to portray their "pathway to the doctor" (Zola 1973) as an embodiment of successive struggles to sustain a troubles-resistant stance. They do so even though the "virtue" of troubles resistance may, as Halkowski (2006) points out, be understood as manifesting a deficiency in the common sense that would otherwise take a less resistant person to the doctor rather earlier. The same troubles resistance also emerges in the ways that patients very regularly avoid describing their fears about symptoms, or hunches about worst-case scenarios during the problem-presentation phase of the visit, even though it may later emerge that they are entertaining very alarming conceptions of the causes of their medical problems. Because the elaboration of these fears and concerns is not properly undertaken in the everyday world without significant support and encouragement (Jefferson 1980), these more emotion-laden aspects of patients' concerns are unlikely to be volunteered in the environment of problem presentation without careful and facilitative questioning (Silverman, Kurtz, & Draper 2005).

As we have commented before, the norms organizing social interaction are among the true bedrock structures of social life. They are not lightly departed from, and when departures consistently occur they are usually mandated by institutional imperatives. The interactional norms that shape the description of troubles and problems are among these bedrock structures. They are not relinquished at the entrance to the doctor's office: instead they continue to shape patient conduct in the context of the visit. They most likely do so because, as we noted in connection with calls to the emergency service, presenting a problem is unavoidably interconnected with what Goffman (1959) called the presentation of self. As patients present their problems they must have regard for how this presentation will be understood, whether as rational, misguided or deluded, as courageous or cowardly, knowledgeable or ignorant, as oriented to short-term or long-term outlooks and as reasonably or unreasonably so, as too much or too little concerned about health consequences, as indicative of a "good" or a "bad" attitude. In short, one of the things that may be put to the test during problem presentation is the patient's own moral character.

For Further Reading

The idea that patients may be concerned with legitimizing their visits to the doctor goes back to Parsons' classic discussion in *The Social System* (1951), and other medical sociologists have taken up the issue from time to time (Zola 1973, Bloor and Horobin 1975, Wolinsky and Wolinsky 1981). The notion that describing a medical concern is simultaneously a "presentation of self" of course derives from Goffman (1959), though he did not pursue it in the study of medical interaction. Papers dealing with the management of legitimacy in problem presentation and beyond include those by Drew (2006), Heath (1992), Heritage (2009), Heritage and Robinson (2006a), Peräkylä (1998), and Stivers (2007a: ch. 3).

10

History Taking in Medicine: Questions and Answers

Most medical visits involve a significant number of physician questions. Roter and Hall (2006: 119) estimate that physician information gathering occupies a little over 20 percent of the total visit, and studies by West (1984: 81) and by Stivers and Majid (2007) report mean numbers of history-taking questions ranging between 20 and 33 with maximum totals of 80 or more questions per visit.

Most physician questions emerge during the history-taking phase of the visit. These questions are often developed in a branching structure in which specific clusters of diagnoses are successively pursued, or ruled out, in the process of differential diagnosis: a hypothesis-testing procedure that begins early in history taking (Elstein, Shulman, & Sprafka 1978, Kassirer & Gorry 1978). Because illness can often be diagnosed simply through effective history taking (Hampton, Harrison, Mitchell, et al. 1975), it is a critically important dimension of medical care that is essential for accurate diagnosis and appropriate treatment (Stoeckle & Billings 1987, Bates, Bickley, & Hoekelman 1995, Cassell 1997).

Doctors' questions pursue information, but they do so in a particular way. Although this may seem an odd comparison, consider the kinds of questions that are used to obtain information in social surveys: for example, "What is your marital status? Are you single, married, divorced, separated or widowed?" This "objective" or "neutral" question form is used to reduce respondent bias which could invalidate survey results. But in the process it communicates an attitude of neutrality (bordering on indifference) towards the content of the response and, cumulatively, an "essentially anonymous" or bureaucratic social relationship between questioner and respondent (Heritage 2002a, Boyd & Heritage 2006). It is for just this reason that physicians and other medical professionals ordinarily do not ask questions this way.

Consider the following case. Here the patient is a middle-aged woman living in the mid-West of the United States and she has an adult daughter. In this context, the doctor's question about marital status looks like this:

```
(1)  [Midwest 3.4.6]
  1  Doc:    Are you married?
  2          (.)
  3  Pat:    No.
  4          (.)
```

```
 5  Doc:    You're divorced (°cur[rently,°??)
 6  Pat:                       [Mm hm,
 7          (2.2)
 8  Doc:    Tl You smoke?, h
 9  Pat:    Hm mm.
```

Here the doctor invites an affirmative response to what is, given the patient's age and the existence of an adult daughter, the patient's most likely marital status. This question involves "recipient design" – a term referring to the "multitude of respects in which the talk by a party in a conversation is constructed or designed in ways which display an orientation and sensitivity to the particular other(s) who are the co-participants" (Sacks, Schegloff, & Jefferson 1974: 727). It is the absence of this kind of recipient design that conveys the bureaucratic neutrality of the survey version of this question. Conversely, its presence indicates a questioner who is listening to and thinking about the circumstances of the answerer. One consequence of this, however, is that the physician's reasoning, beliefs and expectations about patients and their illnesses are communicated to patients through the design of their questions. Thus, as Cassell (1985: 4) notes,

> Even when we physicians ask questions, the structure of the questions and their wording provides information about ourselves, our intent, our beliefs about patients and diseases, as well as eliciting such information about patients; "taking a history" is unavoidably and actually an *exchange* of information. (italics in original)

In this chapter, we pursue this theme, focusing on elements of question design that communicate information to patients.

Dimensions of Question Design

We begin with an outline of four fundamental features of question design, which are summarized in table 10.1. In what follows, we briefly review these major dimensions of question-answer sequences.

Table 10.1   Dimensions of questioning and answering

Physician questions	*Patient responses*
set agendas:	conform/do not conform with
(i) topical agendas	(i) topical agendas
(ii) action agendas	(ii) action agendas
embody presuppositions	confirm/disconfirm presuppositions
convey epistemic stance	display congruent/incongruent epistemic stance
incorporate preferences	align/disalign with preferences

Agenda setting

Our first dimension concerns the "agenda-setting" function of questions. Self-evidently, questions set agendas (Mishler 1984, Clayman & Heritage 2002a, b, Heritage 2002a) that embrace both the kind of action that is required of a respondent and the topical content to which that action should be addressed. This kind of agenda setting is apparent in any straight-forward sequence of questions. Thus in (2), the clinician asks a series of questions about the patient's parents. The first three of these set a topical agenda that concerns her father's mortality, and the final one starts to develop the same set of issues in relation to her mother. Two of the questions (lines 1 and 11) are polar and set the action agenda for response within the narrow limits of "yes" and "no". The other wh-questions (lines 3 and 5) set action agendas a little wider.

```
(2)   [Midwest 3.4.4]
 1  Doc:      Tlk=.hh hIs your father alive?
 2  Pat:      (.hh) No.
 3  Doc:      How old was he when he died.
 4  Pat:      .hh hhohh sixty three I think.=hh
 5  Doc:      What did he die from.=hh
 6            (0.5)
 7  Pat:      He had:=uhm:: He had high blood pressure,
 8            (.)
 9  Pat:      An:d he 'ad- uh: heart attack.
10            (4.0)
11  Doc:      Is your mother alive,
```

Although the topic and action dimensions of agenda setting are not always easy to tease apart, perspicuous cases can be informative. For example in (3), the patient replies to a "where" question with a "where" response, but the two "wheres" have little in common save that they concern her mother:

```
(3)
 1  Doc:       Is your mother alive,
 2  Pat:       No:.
 3             (1.0)
 4  Pat:       No: she died- in her: like late (.) fifties: or:
 5             I'm not sure.
               ......
 7  Doc:  →    Whe[re was her cancer.
 8  Pat:         [( -)
 9  Pat:  →    .hhh Well:- she lived in Arizona an:'- she::
10             wouldn't go tuh doctor much. She only went
11             to uh chiropracter. (h[u-)
12  Doc:                             [Mm [hm,
13  Pat:  *→                             [An:d she had(:)/('t)
15        *→   like- in her stomach somewhere I guess but (.)
16             thuh- even- that guy had told her tuh go (into)
17             uh medical doctor.
```

```
18  Doc:        [Mm hm,
19  Pat:        [.hhh An:' she had- Years before her- (.) m- uh
20              hh mother in law: had died from: waitin' too-
21              or whatever ya know (on-) in surgery, .hh an'...
```

Using Raymond's (2003) terms, the patient here conforms with the question's action agenda – answering a "where" question with a location – but the location concerns where her mother lived, and not the question's actual topical agenda: where in her mother's body her cancer was located. In this case, the patient designs her response to launch a narrative and it is notice-able that, once the physician acknowledges that the narrative is under way with a continu-ative "mm hm" in line 12, the patient responds to the question (lines 13–14) before continuing with the narrative she had previously started. Here the agenda-setting function of the physician's question is set aside, then briefly addressed within the narrative, and then sidelined as the patient proceeds with her story.

Raymond (2003) has shown that yes/no questions set up agendas for yes/no answers in which the words "yes" or "no" should properly occur as the first item in a response. Given this, it is possible to identify cases of nonconformity or deferred conformity to yes/no questions, in which patients resist the terms the questions set to pursue, if only briefly, other agendas. For example, in (4) the patient's departure from the question's agenda communicates that not all her siblings are alive which the physician immediately picks up on:

(4)
```
1  Doc:        Do you have brothers 'n sisters?
2  Pat:    →   Ah there was eight in our family. hh
3  Doc:    →   How many are there now:.
4              (.)
5  Pat:        Ah: seven.
```

In (5) the patient defers her type-conforming "no" response to a yes/no question as a means of qualifying her answer:

(5)
```
1  Doc:        Do you have any drug aller:gies?
2              (0.7)
3  Pat:        .hh hu=Not that I know of no.
```

And in (6) the patient uses a brief departure to intimate a "lifeworld" circumstance (Mishler 1984). The question concerns a restaurant which she owns and manages and her prefatory "aside" ("How long has it had me.") intimates the burden it imposes on her:

(6)
```
1  Doc:        How long have you had that?,
2              (0.8)
3  Pat:        hhhuhhh How long has it had me.=[hh<No: it-
4  Doc:                                        [(Yeah.)
5  Pat:        We had it aba- - We built thuh building #abou:t#:
6              ten years ago. [(I think.)
7  Doc:                       [Mm.
```

Given that the agenda-setting aspects of questions establish relatively severe constraints on what patients may do in the next turn (Schegloff 1972, 2007, Sacks 1987), these responses communicate unasked-for elements of the patient's perspective to the physician and to the researcher.

Presupposition

The second dimension of question design concerns the presuppositional content of questions. All questions embody presuppositions about the states of affairs to which they are directed. For example, in (7) the question linguistically presupposes that the patient uses contraceptives. Associated with this presupposition are some implied cultural assumptions: that the patient is heterosexually active, is still capable of bearing children, and does not want any more of them:

(7) [Cassell 1985:101]
```
 1  Doc:    What kind of contraception do you use?
 2  Pat:    None, since my menopause.
```

The patient's response undercuts the question's presupposition and rejects the second of its associated assumptions (rendering the third of them moot): it does not address the first of them. In (8), by contrast, another physician is more cautious. His first question conveys his view that the patient might be using contraception but does not presuppose it:

(8)
```
 1  Doc:    Are you using any contraception? Is that
 2          necessary [for you?
 3  Pat:            [Huh uh (not now.)
 4  Doc:    °(Okay.)°
```

His second question ("Is that necessary for you?"), however, revises the position taken in the first question by addressing assumptions that underlie it (that the patient is heterosexually active, capable of bearing children, etc.). It thus goes some way towards retracting the relevance of the assumptions mobilized in the first question.

A similar variation in the presuppositional weighting of lifestyle questions is reported by Sorjonen, Raevaara, Haakana, et al. (2006) in the Finnish primary care context. The questions concern alcohol use – an issue which has in the past been a significant social problem in the Nordic countries. Whereas female patients are normally asked "Do you use alcohol?", Finnish males are asked "How much alcohol do you use?" Here the patient's gender is evidently the basis for questioning, which clearly varies in terms of its presuppositional loading, with the much more presumptive question about alcohol being reserved for men. And yet another variation in the communication of presuppositions was discussed in chapter 8. In American medical visits where patients are seen by nurses or medical assistants before their doctor visits, nurses frequently enter the patient's presenting concern into the patient's chart. Physicians thus commonly confront a choice between beginning the visit as if in ignorance of this information ("What can I do for you today?"), and conveying that they already have this information ("Sore throat and runny nose for a week, huh?").

As we saw in chapter 7, a number of medical visits are opened in this second way, and patients' responses to them are very much shorter and contain less information (Heritage & Robinson 2006b).

Epistemic stance

The design of questions communicates the extent to which the questioner may already have some access to the information solicited: the questioner's epistemic stance. Although questions ordinarily solicit information and convey a relatively unknowing (or what we have termed a K−) stance towards the respondent, we can distinguish questions in terms of the epistemic gradient they establish between questioner and respondent (Heritage 2010, Heritage and Raymond forthcoming). Consider the following three questions:

Q 1 Yes/no interrogative: Are you married?
Q 2 Statement + interrogative tag: You're married aren't you?
Q 3 Yes/no declarative question: You're married?

Each of these questions addresses information which is properly known to the recipient. That is, the recipient has primary epistemic rights to this information (Sharrock 1974, Heritage & Raymond 2005) or, in Labov and Fanshel's (1977) terms, the information being addressed here is "B-event" information. Nonetheless, the three questions index different stances towards it. The first of them conveys that the questioner has no knowledge of the respondent's marital status, and indexes a deeply sloping epistemic gradient between an unknowing (K−) questioner and a knowledgeable (K+) respondent (see figure 10.1). The second, by contrast, conveys a strong hunch as to the likelihood of a particular response, and a shallower "K− to K+" epistemic gradient. The third, declarative, question indexes a still stronger commitment to the likelihood that the respondent is married and a correspondingly shallow "K− to K+" epistemic gradient.

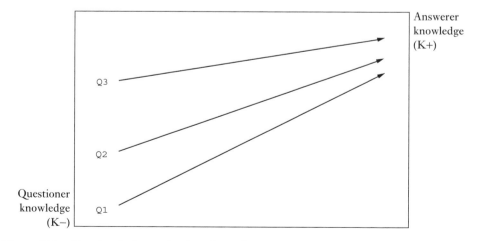

Figure 10.1   Question designs and epistemic gradients

The significance of these question designs is twofold. First, taking the "unknowing" stance of a yes/no interrogative (Q 1) can invite elaboration and sequence expansion, while the "knowing" yes/no declarative form (Q 3) merely invites confirmation of "known information" by the recipient, who is projected as an authoritative source (Turner 2008, Raymond 2010, Stivers forthcoming). These differences are clear in the following sequence involving a British community nurse (known as a health visitor [HV]) and a new mother. The nurse's first question (line 1) about the father's work as a painter, is in interrogative form and attracts an expanded response (lines 2 and 4) from the mother:

```
(9)   (5A1:9)
  1  HV:          Has he got plenty of wo:rk on,
  2  M:           He works for a university college.
  3  HV:          O:::h.
  4  M:           So: (.) he's in full-time work all the ti̠:me.
  5  HV:          °Yeh.°
  6               (0.4)
  7  HV:      →   And this is y'r first ba:by:.
  8  M:           Ye(p).
  9               (0.3)
 10  HV:      →   .tch An' you had a no:rmal pre:gnancy.=
 11  M:           =Ye:h.
 12               (1.1)
 13  HV:      →   And a normal delivery,
 14  M:           Ye:p.
 15               (1.4)
 16  HV:          °Ri:ght.°
```

The nurse's subsequent questions (lines 7, 10, and 12) are in declarative form, and attract unexpanded confirmations whose brevity is accentuated by the labial-stopped variant ("yep") of "yes", which underscores that the mother will not continue.

Second, as Raymond (2010) has shown, these question design choices index the state of social relations between physician and patient, and the relative information states of the parties at any particular moment. Turner (2008) discusses (10), from an after-hours call to a doctor's office (Drew 2006), in which a caller who claims to be pregnant is experiencing vaginal bleeding. After his inquiry about when the pregnancy test was done, the doctor is evidently concerned that the test could be a false positive, perhaps associated with faulty test administration (line 4).

```
(10)  DEC 2:1:8
  1  Doc:          ˙hhhhh! Aum:: (.) i::when didju actually have your: (.)
  2                t! eh:m: pregnancy test.
  3  Clr:          Eh:n: las' Thurs- Thursday, just gone.
  4  Doc:          The doctor did that, [or:
  5  Clr:                               [No, I ha- took a: a sample
  6  Clr:          intuh the chemist an' they done it.
  7  Doc:      →   ˙hhhhh Ri:ght. <Ehm: (.) an' they- i' was definitely
  8                positive then.
  9  Clr:          Yeah, yeah. [(Zuh) ('cause) the doctor didn' want me to
 10  Doc:                      [(°Well,)
```

```
11  Clr:      do another one (an') 'e said no, (as) 'e said they're
12            not wrong when they're positive, it's only when
13            they're negative that it- (   ) can be wrong.
```

Having discovered that the test was performed at a pharmacy, the doctor formulates the upshot of this line of questioning in declarative form: "i' was definitely positive then." In this context, interrogative syntax would put either the pharmacy's expertise or the caller's veracity into question. And even the declaratively formed upshot is sufficient to galvanize the caller into a defense of her conclusion (lines 9–13).

So powerful is declarative syntax that, as Turner (2008) has shown, it can also be used to convey that something has been specifically not mentioned, as in (11). Here another out-of-hours caller is concerned about a child's extensive vomiting:

(11)   Doctor's Emergency Calls, Tape 1, Side 1, Call 12 (37:20–40:35)
```
 1  Clr:        U::h we:ll basically since dinner i-tha' 'e's
 2              actually bringin'the milk up,
 3  Doc:        [Right,
 4  Clr:        [(    while), you know, it's sort'us: () comin'
 5              up all the while at the minute,
 6  Doc:   →    Is it? What-w: it's just milk coming up, no: 'hhh
 7         →    no blood or anyt'ing gree[n or anything¿
 8  Clr:                                 [No:,
```

The doctor's declarative question (lines 6–7) about what the child is bringing up invites confirmation that the caller's previous account has relevantly *not* mentioned "blood or anything green" (line 7) and that he was relevantly informed by these omissions. Because the question designs described here are associated with the strength of expectations for a particular response, epistemic stance is closely related to preference, to which we now turn.

Preference

Our final dimension of question design concerns the preference organization of questions. The conversation analytic term "preference" is used, in relation to questions, to address the bias or tilt of questions that are designed for, favor, suggest an expectation of, or "prefer" an answer of a particular type. A majority of physicians' questions are yes/no, "closed", or "polar" questions (Roter, Stewart, Putnam, et al. 1997, Roter & Hall 2006), and the grammatical design of these questions unavoidably favors one or another of the alternatives that the question problematizes (Heritage 2002a, Boyd & Heritage 2006). Thus the following grammatical designs favor "yes" responses:

1   Straight interrogatives, e.g., "Are you married?"
2   Declarative + negative tag, e.g., "You're married, aren't you?"
3   Declarative questions, e.g., "You're married currently."
4   Negative interrogatives, e.g., "Aren't you married?" (Bolinger 1957, Heritage 2002b, Heinemann 2006).

Similarly, there are a set of grammatical designs that favor "no" responses:

1   Negative declaratives, e.g., "There's no blood in the diarrhea."
2   Negative declaratives + positive tag, e.g., "There's no blood in the diarrhea is there?"
3   Straight interrogatives with negative polarity items (any, ever, at all, etc.), e.g., "Was there ever any blood in the diarrhea at all?"

In addition to conveying a questioner's orientation towards potential responses, these designs can exert a significant influence on how recipients may respond to them. A recent study of the questions "Are there [some/any] other concerns you would like to talk about today?" investigated responses to these questions among patients who had indicated in a pre-visit survey that there were additional concerns that they wanted to discuss. While 90 percent responded affirmatively to the "some" version of the question, only 53 percent responded affirmatively to the "any" version (Heritage, Robinson, Elliott, et al. 2007). Strikingly, this effect was entirely independent of other social variables like age, gender and ethnicity, and indeed these variables had no impact on the results in their own right.

Congruent and Cross-cutting Preferences in Medical Questioning

So far we've considered simply the grammatical design of questions as conveying expectations favoring a particular response. But, in addition to their grammatical design, the *content* of questions embodies social or medical preferences in favor of particular desired (or at least desirable) outcomes. For example, in a patient's medication request to a doctor that runs "Do you have some samples?", the fact that the question is asked at all suggests that the questioner is looking for a "yes" response and that the question is asked in the hope of getting free samples of medicine. In this instance, the grammatical polarity of the question, which favors a "yes" response, is *congruent* to the objective of the question which is in search of free medicine (Schegloff 2007: 76). However, a question with the same objective could have been designed with negative polarity: "You don't have any samples do you?" This format grammatically invites a "no" and thus respects the recipient's right to reject the request. It embodies negative politeness (Brown & Levinson 1987). It does so by deploying what Schegloff (2007: 76) calls "cross-cutting preferences": the action is designed for a "yes", but its grammatical format is designed for a "no". The choice between congruent and cross-cutting preferences is a key resource through which physicians communicate and patients apprehend the communication of information in questioning.

Optimization

Looking at history-taking questions in primary care, it is easy to find sequences like (12) below, that involve the following pattern: where a "yes" response is a favorable health outcome, the question is grammatically designed for a congruent "yes" (lines 1 and 9). Conversely, where a "yes" response would be an unfavorable health outcome for a patient, the question is grammatically designed for a congruent "no" (line 5).

(12)
```
 1  Doc:    →   Are your bowel movements normal?
 2              (4.0) ((patient nods))
 3  Pat:        °(Yeah.)°
 4              (7.0)
 5  Doc:    →   Tlk Any ulcers?
 6              (0.5) ((patient shakes head))
 7  Pat:        (Mh) no,
 8              (2.5)
 9  Doc:    →   Tl You have your gall bladder?
```

We will refer to this congruent pattern of alignments which favor responses embodying positive health outcomes as expressing the *principle of optimization*, which is a fundamental "default" principle of medical questioning: (Heritage 2002a, Boyd & Heritage 2006). This principle embodies the notion that, unless there is some specific reason not to do so, medical questioning should be designed so as to allow patients to confirm favorably framed beliefs and expectations about themselves, their health, and their circumstances. It is for this reason that patients are more rarely asked questions that grammatically prefer negative outcomes: "Is your father alive?" is the normal form for this question about mortality. "Is your father dead?" is comparatively rare and only asked when this circumstance is highly probable.

The following case – this time from a community nurse (HV) to a new mother – embodies this pattern of optimization:

(13) [4A1:17]
```
 1  HV:    →   Uh::m (.) .hh So your pregnancy was perfectly
 2         →   normal.
 3  M:         Yeh.
 4  HV:    →   And did you go into labor (.) all by yourself?
 5  M:         No: I was started o[ff because uh:m (0.8) the blood
 6  HV:                           [Induced.
 7  M:         pressure (0.7) went up in the last couple of weeks.
 8              ...
 9              ... [Segment dealing with why mother was induced]
10              ...
11  HV:    →   And was he alright when he was born.
12  F:         Mm[:.
13  M:           [Yeah.
14  HV:    →   He came down head fi:rst.
15  F:         Mm h[m,
16  HV:    →       [No:rm- no:rmal delivery?=
17  M:         =Ye:h.
18              (2.2)
19  HV:    →   And did he stay with you all the time.=
20         →   =He didn't go to special care baby unit.
21  M:         No:.
```

Here all six of the community nurse's questions are designed to favor responses that will articulate a normal pregnancy and an unproblematic delivery. The questions at lines 19 and 20 are particularly interesting: both the initial "yes"-preferring and the subsequent "no"-preferring versions of the question embody the principle of optimization – it would be better for the baby to have stayed with the mother and not gone to a special neonatal unit.

Optimization is a default feature of medical questioning: unless the physician has reason to believe something to the contrary, a question should be optimized.

Problem attentiveness

If the principle of optimization is the default principle of medical questioning, there are still many occasions on which it is clearly inappropriate. Most prominently, this is so when the questioning concerns the symptoms which are the patient's reason for seeking medical care. It would clearly be inappropriate to ask "You don't have a fever do you?" of a patient presenting with cold and sinus symptoms! Stivers (2007a), focusing on acute care visits, has formulated this as the principle of problem attentiveness. Drawing on Levinson's (2000) account of generalized conversational implicature, she observes that "doctors appear oriented to the assumption that if the parent did not mention particular symptoms, they are not likely to exist (Q principle). And, if particular symptoms were mentioned, then questions broadly in line with those symptoms should be designed to presuppose a problem (I principle)."[1]

The principle of problem attentiveness makes it inappropriate for physicians to question patients about their primary symptoms using optimized questions (Stivers 2007a). In (14) an 11-year-old patient presenting with pain in her left ear is asked a series of questions that invite affirmative responses to pain symptoms (lines 1, 9, 13):

```
(14)  [Heritage and Stivers 1999: 1511]
 1  Doc:   →  Which ear's hurting or are both of them hurting.
 2             (0.2)
 3  GIR:      Thuh left one,
 4  Doc:      °Okay.° This one looks perfect, .hh
 5  ( ):       (U[h:.)
 6  Doc:         [An:d thuh right one, also loo:ks, (0.2) even more
 7             perfect.
 8  GI?:       ( )
 9  Doc:   →  Does it hurt when I move your ears like that?
10             (0.5)
11  GIR:      No:.
12  Doc:      No?,
13  Doc:   →  .hh Do they hurt right now?
14             (2.0)
15  GIR:      Not right now but they were hurting this morning.
16  Doc:      They were hurting this morning?
17             (0.2)
18  Doc:      M[ka:y,
19  MOM:   ⇒  [(You've had uh- sore throat pain?)
```

The child's "no" responses at lines 11 and 15, are substantially delayed and hearably reluctant. Moreover, her response to the doctor's positively polarized follow-up question at line 13 (".hh Do they hurt right now?"), while reaffirming a "no pain" scenario, incorporates additional detailing that defends the decision to go to the clinic (Stivers & Heritage 2001, Drew 2006, Stivers 2007a, Heritage 2010). It can be noticed that the child's mother introduces a new symptom at the end of this sequence (line 19), most likely to defend the decision to make the medical visit.

A similar case described by Stivers (2007a) involves a child presenting with a cough. The parents have heard about a local meningitis outbreak on the television news, which they allude to at lines 7–8:

```
(15)
 1  Doc:        Has he been coughing uh lot?
 2              (0.2)
 3  Mom:        .hh Not uh lot.=h[h
 4  Doc:                          [Mkay:?,
 5  Mom:    →   But it- it <sound:s:> deep.
 6              (1.0)
 7  Mom:    →   An' with everything we (heard) on tee v(h)ee=hhhh
 8          →   £we got sca:re'.£
 9  Doc:        Kay. (An fer i-) It sounds deep?
10              (.)
11  Mom:        Mm hm.
```

Here again, the question at line 1 is polarized in a problem-attentive direction and the mother, finding herself responding in the negative at line 3, defends the significance of the symptom with an account of the sound of the cough and the collateral concern which the media had stimulated.

In ordinary acute care situations, there is often an alternation between problem attentiveness and optimization in the way symptoms are addressed. Such a case is (16), where an evening out-of-hours caller (Drew 2006) describes her child's extensive bouts of vomiting and diarrhea:

```
(16)
 1  Doc:        .hh Fine. 'h So: ho:w ho:w: this was: all just
 2              started tonight, is it?
 3  Clr:        Yes.<Well I didn't come in from wo:rk unti:l uh: ten past
 4              past seven and she'd already been sick three times,
 5  Doc:        'hhh Ri:gh[t,
 6  Clr:                  [(And) since then, (.) [been sick [another three
 7  Doc:                                         ['hhhh     [mYeah,
 8  Clr:        ti[mes,
 9  Doc:    →     [Another three time 'hh What's she bringing up?=
10          →   =any[thing exciti°n-
11  Clr:           [(like just)       [Just fluid rea[lly,
12  Doc:                              ['hhh           [hhh  Just fluid.
13  Clr:        [Nothing now. I don['- obviously I don't know what it was=
14  Doc:        [Nuh-               ['hhh
15  Clr:        =earlier on,  I wasn't here, you know,=
16  Doc:    →   =Right, but the: th I mean- n:othing nasty no blood er
17          →   anything 'hhh and the diarrhea: you say is quite (0.9)
18  Clr:        Very strong, yeah.
```

Having established that the onset of the child's illness is recent, the doctor proceeds to question the caller about the content of the vomiting and diarrhea. As he moves towards symptoms that might be indicative of a serious medical condition, his questions (e.g., "What's she bringing up?==anything exciti°n-" [lines 9–10]) become negatively polarized (via the use of "anything") and hence optimized. In response to this question, the parent responds "Just fluid." and the doctor pursues the issue using a declarative question design that, as we have seen, treats her as having specifically not mentioned anything "nasty" such as "blood". This negatively polarized declarative is, then, somewhat optimized.

Recipient design

In circumstances, such as "well visits" and information-gathering medical interviews, where there is no specific medical problem to drive the principle of problem attentiveness, the principle of optimization may nonetheless be tempered by more general considerations of recipient design. This, as noted earlier, involves managing talk so as to show sensitivity to the other(s) present, their interests and what has been said already. It is this principle which, directed to a patient who works 60-hour weeks in her owner-managed restaurant and has gained eleven pounds since her last medical visit, mandates a "no"-preferring, non-optimized question about exercise:

```
(17)
 1  Doc:    →  Tlk Do you exercise at all?
 2             (2.5)
 3  Pat:       N::o, uh huh huh huh (.hh-[.hh) huh [huh (.hh huh huh)
 4  Doc:                            [Hm          [£Not your thing
 5             [ah:,]
 6  Pat:       [.hh ] £Would you believe me if I sai(h)d y(h)e(h)s,=
```

That the physician's non-optimized design of this question was appropriate is very thoroughly validated by the patient's response (especially line 6).

Balancing the principles of optimization and recipient design creates a pointed dilemma for the community nurse in (18), whose questions are directed to the completion of check-list information about the mother's recent birthing experience. This sequence follows a lengthy period of conversation in which both parents described how the baby's shoulders had become stuck in the birth canal. The nurse has reached a point in her pre-printed checklist where the text reads "Type of delivery" and there is a blank space to be written in: the choices are, broadly speaking, "normal", "forceps", "caesarian", etc. The nurse's turn at line 1 was likely headed towards an optimized version of this question – "So you had a normal delivery?" – which is the normal form of the question asked at this point (see (13) above line 16, (22) below line 13, and, more generally, Linell & Bredmar 1996, Bredmar & Linell 1999, Heritage 2002a):

```
(18)  [1A1:14]
 1  HV:        =So you had a- uh:
 2             (1.0)
 3  HV:    →  You didn't- Did you- You didn't have forceps you had a:
 4  M:         =Oh [no:: nothing.
 5  F:            [(    )
 6  HV:        An- and did she cry straight awa:y.
```

```
 7  M:          Yes she did didn't sh[e.
 8  F:                               [Mm hm,
 9              (1.0) ((Wood cracking))
10  HV:         Uhm (.) you didn't go to scboo: you know the
11              spe[cial care unit.
12  M:             [Oh: no: no:.
```

Belatedly recognizing the possible inappropriateness of this question just at the point that the word "normal" would be due, the nurse stops for a whole second, and then (line 3) tries for a rephrasing of the question which would acknowledge the possibility of a forceps delivery but, through the use of a negative declarative, would treat it as specifically not mentioned previously – thus optimizing the question: "You didn't- [have forceps]". She then reverses away from the (optimized) negative polarity of that question with the beginnings of a positively polarized interrogative replacement: "Did you- [have forceps]". This format would imply that this was not ruled out by the parents' previous account, and would treat this outcome as a genuine, if unknown, possibility. Finally, she returns to the initial formulation, which is shaped to be doubly optimized: "You didn't have forceps you had a:". The possibility of forceps is acknowledged with a negative declarative, while its alternative – a normal delivery – starts to be developed declaratively with positive polarity. Once again, however, the nurse hesitates at the point where the word "normal" is due, and the Mom intervenes with a strong confirmation, using an oh-preface (Heritage 1998) and repetition of her response (Stivers 2004), that forceps were not used (line 4). Here, in a situation of true uncertainty about the "real facts", the nurse repeatedly hesitates between question forms that are organized both by the principles of optimization and recipient design, and by whether enough has been said or implied to rule in, or rule out, a forceps delivery.

Dimensions of Question Design in Special Situations

Routine checklists

Medical questioning in "well visits" and information-gathering interviews normally does not involve the forensic pursuit of a differential diagnosis, but is rather aimed at achieving a routine overview of the patient's health or social information. This questioning is often styled in ways that exhibit this routine "checklist" objective.

For example, over the course of a sequence of questions, each successive question may be shorter than its predecessor in a process of ellipsis, as in (19). In this case, the first question (line 1) is a fully formed sentence. The second (line 5), by contrast, is contracted to a noun phrase with the negative polarity item "any". And in the third (line 8), the polarity item is deleted, though its relevance, in part assisted by the etiologic and semantic connections between "chest pain" and "shortness of breath", is clearly still in play.

```
(19)
 1  Doc:    →  Tlk You don't have as:thma do you,
 2             (.)
 3  Pat:       Hm mm.
 4             (1.1)
```

```
 5  Doc:   →   (hhh) .hh Any chest type pain?,
 6  Pat:       Mm mm.
 7              (3.4)
 8  Doc:   →   Shortness of brea:th,
 9              (1.0)
10  Pat:       Some: but that's: cuz I should lose weight (I know that,)
11              (.) I thin'.=<Not much.
```

Here, through successive contractions, a line of checklist questions is brought off as just that: brief questions aimed at ruling out domains of medical problems. This understanding is clearly indexed by the patient's responses at lines 3 and 6. These are nearly immediate, completely "closed-mouthed", and are among the most minimal and "pro forma" responses that can be used to execute a "no" response in English. Through their use, the patient treats the questions, and the relevancies they invoke, as involving pro forma matters that can be dismissed out of hand.

At line 10, by contrast, the patient delays a full second before responding to a negatively polarized question that, by content and design, is fully optimized. Her initial response is not type-conforming and is designed to mitigate the significance of an affirmative response. The subsequent expansion of her response is designed to show insight into the causes of her condition and to link it to her weight gain, which has already been topicalized in the visit (Stivers & Heritage 2001).

Another feature of question design that emerges in these kinds of contexts is and-prefacing (Heritage & Sorjonen 1994). And-prefacing is typically used to link a series of question–answer sequences, as elements of a common task or activity. For example, in (20) the task is entering a newborn baby's name onto a chart:

```
(20)  (3B1:2)
 1  HV:        What are you going to (.) call her?
 2  M:     →   Georgi:na.
 3              (1.0)
 4  HV:    →   An:d you're spelling that,
```

In these kinds of routine "face sheet" question sequences, which embody a convergence between medical interaction and social surveys (Heritage 2002a), the and-preface clearly links the two questions as elements in a common task. In (21) the activity link involves gathering face-sheet information about a husband:

```
(21)  (1C1:25)
 1  HV:        Okay so that's that's your clinic fo:rm.
 2  M:         (          )
 3  HV:        An' all I put on here is you:r (0.7) there's a
 4              bit about you::, (0.7) it sa:ys here that you're
 5              twenty o:ne is that ri:ght?
 6  M:         That's ri:ght.=
 7  HV:    →   =How old's your husba:nd.
 8  M:         Twenty s- uh twenty six in April.
 9              (0.5)
10  HV:    →   And does he wo:rk?
11  M:         He wo:rks at the factory yes.
```

Some of these activity lines can be quite extended. In (22) a community nurse links a sequence of seven questions by using "and" to preface six of them. Though these questions are somewhat linked in a broad topical sense, they relate to a single data entry page in a chart that the nurse is completing (Heritage 2002a), rather than to any strict topical or referential continuity.

```
(22)  (5A1:9)
  1  HV:            Has he got plenty of wo:rk on,
  2  M:             He works for a university college.
  3  HV:            O:::h.
  4  M:             So: (.) he's in full-time work all the ti:me.
  5  HV:            °Yeh.°
  6                 (0.4)
  7  HV:     →      And this is y'r first ba:by:.
  8  M:             Ye(p).
  9                 (0.3)
 10  HV:     →      .tch An' you had a no:rmal pre:gnancy.=
 11  M:             =Ye:h.
 12                 (1.1)
 13  HV:     →      And a normal delivery,
 14  M:             Ye:p.
 15                 (1.4)
 16  HV:            °Ri:ght.°
 17                 (0.7)
 18  HV:     →      And sh'didn't go into special ca:re.
 19  M:             No:.
 20                 (1.8)
 21  HV:     →      °An:d she's bottle feeding?°
 22                 (1.2)
 23  HV:     →      °Um:° (0.4) and uh you're going to Doctor White
 24                 for your (0.6) p[ost-na:tal?
 25  M:                            [Yeah.
```

The completion of this page of the chart, which is in plain sight of the mother and visually apparent, is verbally formulated as a single task-coherent activity in this sequence of and-prefaced questions.

Just as the progressively truncated questions in (19) conveyed a routine activity to which the patient responded with abbreviated responses, so in (22), as we have seen, the mother's responses are also abbreviated. Each declarative question formulates a "candidate answer" (Pomerantz 1988) as an item for the patient's confirmation ancillary to the entry of the information into the chart. Each of the mother's responses is a single word, sometimes completed with a labial stop (lines 8 and 14), that indicates that the response will not be elaborated. In this way the information being given is treated as a task-focused "pro forma" activity, and as non-indicative of any real interest or concern – as close, in fact, as we get in medicine to a "social survey" style of questioning.

Lifestyle questions

Lifestyle questions are a major exception to the principle of optimization sketched earlier. In this part of the medical visit, medically adverse responses may carry the additional burden of social stigma. Little linguistic intuition is required to see that an optimized question like "You don't smoke do you?" is unlikely to attract a "yes" response from an embarrassed smoker! The alignment of socio-medical and grammatical preference in such a question is surely too tempting, especially for the smoker who anticipates an exhortation to quit, or being chided for not having done so. Accordingly, lifestyle questions are rarely optimized. At the same time, non-optimized questions may permit non-smokers and non-drinkers to present their virtuous behavior quite emphatically. Thus in (23) a non-optimized question about smoking receives the flattest of rejections:

```
(23)
 1  Doc:      Are you a smoker?
 2            (.)
 3  Doc:      Or a past smoker?=
 4  Pat:      =Never.
```

Here the grammatical ("yes"-inviting) form of the question cross-cuts its negative socio-medical preference. The patient's emphatically negative response both is enabled by, and rebuts, the question's grammatical preference. In this way, the patient is able to construct himself as an upstanding, health-conscious, right-living member of the community. A similar effect can be achieved through minimized response:

```
(24)
 1  Doc:      tch D'you smoke?, h
 2  Pat:      Hm mm.
 3            (5.0)
 4  Doc:      Alcohol use?
 5            (1.0)
 6  Pat:      Hm:: moderate I'd say
 7            (0.2)
 8  Doc:      Can you define that, hhhehh ((laughing outbreath))
 9  Pat:      Uh huh hah .hh I don't get off my- (0.2) outa
10            thuh restaurant very much but [((awh:)
11  Doc:                                    [Daily do you use
12            alcohol or:=h
13  Pat:      Pardon?
14  Doc:  →   Daily? or[:
15  Pat:               [Oh: huh uh. .hh No: uhm (3.0) probably::
16            I usually go out like once uh week.
17            (1.0)
18  Doc:      °Kay.°
```

Here the patient's response at line 2 is dismissively minimal, though her designedly considered response (line 6) to the companion question is quite the reverse (Stivers & Heritage 2001). It can also be noticed that the elliptically designed question at line 4 – "Alcohol use?" – seems to be equivocal between the alternatives deployed in the Finnish consultations mentioned earlier: "Do you use alcohol?" and "How much alcohol do you use?" The physician's subsequent pursuit of a quantity, via the left-dislocated "Daily do you use alcohol or:=h", is also non-optimized and is resisted with a repair initiation at line 15 (Drew 1997) and a subsequent oh-prefaced response (Heritage 1998) which treats it as inapposite (Stivers & Heritage 2001).

Conclusion

Insofar as we have evidence of the effects of question design on patient responses, a central finding is that these effects are large and generally exceed the significance of other, more contextual, factors such as patient and provider characteristics, the medical practice, social attitudes, and other less proximate characteristics of the medical visit. These findings reaffirm a core tenet of conversation analysis: when considering the impact of context on action, the most primary aspect of this context is the immediately prior action to which the action responds. Question design in all its specificities is such a context, and as such it mediates the many particularities of medical interaction and its broader contexts. The result is that many of these elements of context exert their influence *through* features of talk such as question design, rather than in independence of them (Heritage, Robinson, Elliott, et al. 2007).

As we have stressed, a central tenet of conversation analysis is that the analyst should, for every aspect of an utterance, ask "Why that now?" This approach is illuminating because it raises the very same concerns that participants must address when they construct responses. The central theme of this chapter is that for precisely this reason, whether questioners like it or not, their questions are unavoidably communicative. Questions communicate through their topical and action agenda-setting properties: why that question on that topic? They communicate through their presuppositions: why was that presupposed? They communicate through their epistemic gradients: why was that question declaratively framed? And they communicate through their preference design: why was that question made yes-preferring rather than no-preferring?

In the medical context, these elemental features of question design cluster in ways that are structured by the institution of medicine, the nature of medical knowledge, the purposes of a medical visit, and the stage it has reached. In a "well visit" should this question be yes-preferring or no-preferring, optimized or recipient-designed? In an acute visit, should this question be problem-attentive or should it be optimized? As the visit is winding down, should it be a matter of "Do you have any questions?", "What questions do you have?" or just "Questions?"

But though these choices in question design are clustered and filtered through the institution of medicine, this does not exhaust their significance. Through these choices knowledge is conveyed, relationships are forged, identities are asserted, validated and rebuffed, risks are taken. And because physicians, and interactants more generally, are without a hiding place in these matters, these risks are unavoidable.

For Further Reading

Question design has been a topic of interest and concern to researchers in medical communication for many years. A classic early study is Elliot Mishler's *The Discourse of Medicine* (1984: ch. 3), which examined the role of questioning in the physician's control of medical discourse; related themes were sounded by West (1984), Silverman (1987), Todd (1989), and Waitzkin (1991). In general, yes/no (or polar or closed) questions are more constraining of patient response, and their proportion out of total physician questions is often used as an index of physician-centered styles in medical visits, e.g. Roter, Stewart, Putnam, et al. (1997). More general CA views of question design include Raymond (2003) and Heritage and Raymond (forthcoming).

Note

1   In the theory of generalized conversational implicature (Levinson 2000), the Quantity (Q) principle states both that speakers should provide the strongest possible statement of knowledge that they can and that recipients will assume that what is stated by their interlocutor is the strongest possible statement/description. The Informativeness (I) principle states that speakers should say as little as necessary to achieve communicative ends. The corresponding recipient's corollary assumes this and therefore allows recipients to assume the richest description possible consistent with what is taken for granted.

11

Diagnosis and Treatment: Medical Authority and its Limits

As social scientists and physicians have long noted, the exercise of authority is a central feature of the physician–patient relationship. An orientation to authority begins when the patient, who has experienced some symptoms and perhaps formed some theory of their nature and etiology, makes an appointment and visits the doctor. It continues during problem presentation where patients face the problem of justifying the medical visit to a more knowledgeable clinician. During the history-taking phase of the visit, patients' reported symptoms are validated (or not) as medical "signs" relevant to a diagnosis. And at the point of diagnosis, the patient's "illness" – "the innately human experience of symptoms and suffering" (Kleinman 1988: 3) – becomes a medically validated "disease" – "an alteration in biological structure or functioning" (ibid.: 5). All these activities are suffused with the exercise of authority, but its exercise arguably becomes most explicit during the physician's rendering of a diagnosis and subsequent recommendations for treatment.

In *The Social Transformation of American Medicine* (1982), Paul Starr argues that medical authority involves patients in what he calls "the surrender of private judgment" (p. 10). By that he means that when patients get a recommendation from their doctor, they abandon whatever personal beliefs, uncertainties, fears, and misgivings they may have about their medical condition, and accept the physician's diagnosis and treatment recommendation "on authority". This medical authority, Starr observes, has two main sources. First, there is the dependency of patients who are sick, demoralized, and fearful, and who are not capable of understanding or solving their health problems without expert assistance. The second derives from the cultural authority of science. Cultural authority, says Starr, involves the rights of certain individuals, groups or professions to make definitive pronouncements about the nature of the world and its properties. The cultural authority of physicians is based in training in regimes of seeing and recognizing and diagnosing complexes of medical signs (cf. Kuhn 1962, 1977, Barnes 1982), and formal certification in this training. Starr argues that medical authority derives not only from the fact that certain medical techniques work, but more importantly from the more general scientific basis of medical knowledge which empowers doctors both to describe and define the nature of illness and its causes, and to operationalize these in the practical evaluation of patients.

Doctors have not always possessed the kind of authority they wield today. As Edward Shorter (1985) observes, before the rise of scientific medicine in America, starting around 1880, patients avoided doctors as far as possible and only went to see them in very severe circumstances. Subsequent improvements in medical technique and technology resulted in improvements in diagnosis and prognosis, but in the early twentieth century, before the development of significant drugs like antibiotics and the emergence of effective surgical techniques, the status of the profession rested primarily in its ability to diagnose rather than to treat disease (Shorter 1985). In the opinion of many commentators (Starr 1982, Shorter 1985, Freidson 1986), medical authority and status, powered by the emergence of new drugs, surgical techniques and other treatments, reached its zenith around 1960 – the "golden age of doctoring" (McKinlay & Marceau 2002) – and subsequently entered a long process of decline. While many factors have contributed to this process, two stand out. First is the rise in "consumerist" attitudes among patients who are prepared to shop around for doctors and, empowered by direct-to-consumer advertising in the US and the internet more generally, to evaluate and disagree with medical recommendations. The second is the rise of managed care, which allows corporations to subject medical judgments to bureaucratic and financial evaluation, and involves sanctioning doctors for the use of inappropriate treatments (Light 2000).

In this chapter we examine medical authority in relation to the process of diagnosis and treatment recommendation. There is broad agreement among medical sociologists and practitioners that diagnostic reasoning in medical settings is an activity based on special knowledge possessed and controlled by the profession of medicine. A number of authors also argue that the knowledge gap between the physician and the patient is so wide that diagnostic reasoning is inherently opaque to the layperson. As Parsons (1951) put it, "The physician is a technically competent person whose competence and specific measures cannot be competently judged by the layman. The latter must therefore take these judgments and measures 'on authority'." So, then, it is when the physician counsels the patient and proposes treatment that patients arguably reach the point in the visit where they truly "surrender their private judgment", as Starr puts it. By the same token, it is at this point that physicians most completely deploy their cultural authority to define the nature of the patient's problem. Most medical sociologists therefore suggest that the patient is at best a marginal participant in the diagnostic process, and that physicians are not obligated to present, explain or justify their medical reasoning to patients or to persuade them of the rightness of their decisions. It is sufficient for them simply to pronounce a diagnostic judgment. To anticipate the conclusions of this chapter, there is substantial truth in this position but medical practice is significantly more varied than it suggests, requiring significant revision to the standard sociological position. A significant innovation in medical practice has been the movement for "patient-centered" medicine which aims to give more room for the voicing of patient concerns and perspectives in the medical encounter (Engel 1977, Mishler 1984, Emanuel & Emanuel 1992, Mead & Bower 2000).

Our questions in this chapter are: What are the interactional dynamics through which medical authority is expressed in diagnosis? And do these dynamics carry forward into the treatment recommendation phase? As we address these questions, recall that we are focusing on primary care and dealing only with moderate illnesses that are not normally life-threatening. Though we do not know for sure, the story is likely to be significantly different with more serious illnesses.

In what follows, we will explore the process of diagnosis and treatment recommendation as an interactional negotiation. We begin with three significant studies of the "diagnostic moment" in the medical visit which give strong, though qualified, support to the idea that patients show clear recognition of medical authority during the process of diagnosis. We then show data that suggests a rather different stance during treatment recommendations.

Finally, we further qualify these observations by reference to studies of diagnosis and treatment recommendations in patients with upper respiratory tract infections (URTIs) such as colds, flu, sinusitis, bronchitis and ear infections, which are common medical conditions in which many patients may claim some expertise.

The Interactional Management of Diagnosis: Three Studies

Patrick Byrne and Barrie Long: Doctors Talking to Patients *(1976)*

We begin with a classic British study conducted more than thirty years ago by Patrick Byrne and Barrie Long (1976). Byrne and Long's study was large-scale (over 2000 medical visits were examined), and pioneering in that it was among the first empirical studies to focus on the need for patient-centered medicine (see Mead & Bower 2000 for a review of contemporary literature on this topic). The study focused on a range of physician behaviors across the medical visit, but in relation to the diagnostic phase Byrne and Long focused on two main questions:

1 Did the physician identify and explain the diagnosis and treatment?
2 Did the physician design these descriptions so as to invite the patient to ask questions or participate in a discussion or negotiation of the treatment?

Using these criteria, Byrne and Long formulated seven diagnostic styles, which they categorized in terms of whether they were physician-centered (focusing on the physicians' knowledge and expertise) or patient-centered (focused on the patients' interests and concerns). As table 11.1 indicates, most of the cases fall into styles 1 and 2, which are the most doctor-centered styles. Below are some examples of these:

Style 1: [Diagnosis is not named, treatment is not explained]
Doc: Well now, take this along to the chemist. Take them three times daily after meals. Bye bye.
Doc: I'll make an appointment for you to have an X-ray. Now don't worry. We'll be in touch.

Table 11.1   Diagnostic styles

Diagnostic style	*Frequency (%)*
1 The physician makes a decision about the patient and his treatment and then instructs the patient to see some service.	31
2 The physician makes a decision and announces it.	36
3 The physician sells his decision to the patient.	4
4 The physician presents a tentative decision subject to change.	14
5 The physician presents the problem, seeks suggestions and makes decisions.	8
6 The physician defines the limits and requests the patient to make a decision.	4
7 The physician permits the patient to make his own decision	1

Source: Byrne and Long 1976: 106

Style 2: [Diagnosis is named, but not explained. Treatment is not explained, discussed, or negotiated]

Doc: Well now you seem to have nothing more than a bout of flu. Take this to the chemist
        on your way home. Go to bed for a few days and I'll look in from time to time.

Doc: This is an infection of the lung. I want you to go upstairs and have an X-ray now. When
        you've had that, come back here and I will detail some more treatment.

*Style 4: [Diagnosis is presented and explained: treatment options are given in a more exploratory,
tentative fashion]*

Doc: Now then, you appear to be having some more trouble with that leg of yours. This is,
        I think, a consequence of the fact that you're still trying to work as you did ten years
        ago. Now you are fifty five and you ought really to start taking things a little easier.
        I think you ought to have a long rest. Now then, how do you think you can cope
        with that?

As will be clear from these examples, physician-centered styles of diagnosis are those that involve little or no explanation to patients, and that invite little or no participation from them. Patient-centered styles involve more of both. In Byrne and Long's data, however, the two most physician-centered styles were by far the most common, amounting to a total of two thirds of all the diagnoses in their 2000+ recordings. And, as table 11.1 shows, in nearly a third of these, no diagnosis was actually presented. This study strongly reinforces the general claim from medical sociologists that physicians tend to be highly authoritarian in their delivery of diagnoses and that they in effect compel patients to surrender their private judgment by leaving the patient little other choice.

Heath: "The delivery and reception of diagnosis and assessment in the general practice consultation" (1992)

This idea that diagnosis involves the exercise of authority is also addressed in the second study. But whereas Byrne and Long focused on the physician's diagnostic announcement, Heath's investigation focuses on how patients respond to medical diagnoses (Heath 1992). His central observation concerns the remarkable passivity of patients in the face of diagnoses by physicians. In particular, he notes that, in a significant proportion of the videotapes he looked at, patients remained completely silent in the face of a diagnosis, or at most offered brief acknowledgments:

```
(1)  [Heath 1992: 240]
  1  Doc:         .hhhh You've got erm: (0.8) bronchitis::.
  2  Pat:    →    °er:.°
  3          →    (4.5) ((Dr begins to write prescription))
  4  Doc:         .hhh (0.3) I'll give you antibiotics: to take for a
  5               week. hhh
```

This is the more striking when Heath considers the range of response types that are largely absent. Patients could, for example, respond with "oh", a form of acknowledgment that, as we saw in chapter 3, treats what they have just heard as new information. Another response could be a "newsmark", for example "it is?" or "oh really". These brief responses invite some expansion of the announcement by the physician (Jefferson 1981, Heritage 1984a, Maynard

2003). And, of course, there are the substantive questions patients might ask in response to a diagnosis: "What's that?", "What causes it?", "Is it contagious?", "Is it serious?", "Can it be cured?", "How long will it last?" All of these response types are largely absent. These patients have just been given a diagnosis, but they don't even acknowledge it as new information.

Why is this the case? Heath considers the bodily and other nonverbal behavior of the physician. For example, the physician could be writing notes or a prescription, and appear unavailable. This, however, was not the case. Physicians were normally gazing directly at the patient – something which ordinarily solicits response (Heath 1986, Rossano 2009). Instead, Heath argues that patient passivity is directly related to the design of the diagnostic utterance – the feature stressed in the Byrne and Long study. For example, in (1) above the diagnosis is simply delivered as an authoritative assertion of fact. As expert opinion, authoritatively delivered, it does not offer a context that is ripe for subsequent enquiries. If we had to classify it in Byrne and Long's terms, we would probably suggest that it is a style 2 diagnosis that does not invite response.

Heath supports this notion by looking at cases in which the diagnosis is offered in a less authoritative way, as in (2):

```
(2)  [Heath 1992: 247]
  1  Doc:    →   .hhh It's not a totally typical story of a
  2          →   wear and tear arthritis, but I think that's:
  3          →   what it's going to turn ou[t to be::::.
  4  Pat:                                  [(Well that (.) but
  5              that en right wouldn') wife and nurse says hhh[h
  6  Doc:                                                      [Oh
  7              well [I think we ought to get an X-ray as a check.
  8  Pat:            [.hh heh
  9  Pat:        Yers
 10  Doc:        You've not had this done on that ankle before?
 11  Pat:        No:.
```

Here the physician offers a tentative diagnosis that will require confirmation by X-ray, and the patient responds quite actively.

Heath also shows that similarly active responses emerge when the physician's diagnosis is different from the patient's lay understanding of the problem. In (3), the patient has an eye problem that he thought was due to a vein: the physician determines that it is a muscle problem, and this engenders some discussion between physician and patient.

```
(3)  [Heath 1992: 250]
  1  Doc:    →   It's not a vein: (.) it's a muscle in spas:[m.
  2  Pat:    →                                             [Is it?
  3  Doc:        Yeah.
  4  Pat:    →   Oh:
  5  Doc:        And I think what's cau[sing it to be in spasm
  6  Pat:    →                         [I've had it for about
  7          →   three or fou[r weeks, and n[ow (or something like that.)
  8  Doc:                    [Yeah          [Yeah
  9  Doc:        You've got a low grade inflammation of the eye:::::
 10              (0.3) the front of the eye and this is probably
 11              making the spasm come.
```

In this case, the patient responds with the very kinds of responses (a newsmark at line 2, "oh" at line 4, and further commentary at lines 6 and 7) that are otherwise overwhelmingly absent in these data.

A third environment in which patients offer elaborate responses to physician's evaluations emerges when these evaluations undermine the legitimacy of the patient's reasons for visiting the doctor. In (4) the patient, who is in effect told he is well, counters with a report that his symptoms arise at night.

```
(4)  [Heath 1992: 255]
  1  Doc:        Well yer ches:t is:: (.) absolutely cle:ar: today::,
  2               (1.0)
  3  Doc:        which is helpful: (0.4) and your pulse is: (0.7)
  4               only eighty .thhhh (.) which is er:: (1.2) not so bad.
  5               (1.2)
  6  Pat:    →   (Right it's::) there:: night time (uh) (.) it's:: 'ts
  7          →   not clear there, I've got er::: ( ) (1.4) ( )
  8          →   (0.3) I've more or less gone to bed when it starts: on us:?
  9               (2.5)
 10  Pat:    →   I wake all the way through the night without getting
 11          →   any sleep (un open))
 12               (0.5)
 13  Doc:        Mm
 14  Pat:    →   (I don't know what's fetchin' it up) during the nights (.) but
 15          →   it comes in at the nights.
```

Even here the patient does not overtly challenge the diagnosis, but instead vigorously asserts that his – currently undetectable – symptoms emerge at night. Similar responses emerge when physicians offer diagnoses that appear to "question the severity of their symptoms and suffering" (Heath 1992: 255), though these rarely eventuate in overt disagreement or challenge.

To summarize, both the Byrne and Long and the Heath studies suggest that diagnosis is a prime site for the expression of medical authority. Byrne and Long show that the majority of diagnoses are delivered in a highly authoritarian fashion, offering little explanation and seemingly designed to occlude patient participation. Heath shows that patients respond to these diagnoses relatively passively. They rarely ask questions about the diagnosis and almost never question it or challenge it. So they tend to remain outside of and uninvolved in diagnostic reasoning. Heath finds only two types of exceptions to this: (1) if physicians offer uncertain or provisional diagnoses; (2) if the diagnostic process threatens the legitimacy of the patient's complaint.

The upshot of these two studies is that the default patient response to diagnosis is in fact non-response. Non-response defers to medical authority, and in particular to the cultural authority that physicians mobilize to pronounce on what is, and what is not, the case. This is underscored in subsequent work by Stivers (2007a), who showed that any form of questioning following the diagnosis – newsmarks (e.g. "Is it?"), questions about symptoms (e.g., "What about the green gunky stuff?") or questions about the diagnosis itself (e.g., "So you don't think it's in the ear?") – is understood as a form of *resistance* to the diagnosis. Questioning the diagnosis, she argues, forces the physician to reconfirm or expand the diagnostic section of the encounter, delaying the movement into treatment and the end of the medical visit. Thus, in a fundamental way, the cultural authority attaching to the act of diagnosis can result in any form of questioning by the layperson being viewed as an intrusion. Stepping over the line into the sphere of medical competence is ordinarily constituted as intrinsically resistant, and is avoided by patients for this very reason.

Peräkylä: "Authority and accountability" (1998)

More recently, a more modulated perspective on medical authority and diagnosis has been offered by Anssi Peräkylä. He begins by distinguishing between three main kinds of diagnostic statements. First, there are "straight assertions". They are the most common kind of diagnosis in primary care and they are illustrated in (5) and (6):

```
(5)  [Peräkylä 1998] "Plain assertion"
 1 Doc:    Here's (.) luckily the bone quite intact,
```

```
(6)  [Peräkylä 2006] "Plain assertion"
 1 Doc:    That's already proper bronchitis.
```

However, Peräkylä also notes two other ways in which physicians can frame their diagnoses. One involves reference to the experience of the physician in coming to a decision. This type involves the use of what linguists term "evidentials" (Chafe & Nichols 1986), expressions incorporating references to what the physician is seeing, feeling, hearing, or sensing. Evidentials normally emerge in verb form: the physician may comment that something "looks infected" (where the evidential is the word "looks") or that something "feels swollen" (where the evidential is the word "feels"). This type of diagnosis is illustrated by (7).

```
(7)  [Peräkylä 1998] "Evidential formulation"
 1 Doc:    Now there appears to be an (1.0) infection at the
 2         contact point of the joint below it in the sac of
 3         mucus there in the hip
```

Peräkylä remarks that in this type of diagnosis the physician makes an indirect or inexplicit reference to the sensory evidence on which the diagnosis is based (1998: 305), while simultaneously marking the diagnostic statement as tentative.

A third type of diagnostic format involves explicitly laying out some of the reasoning behind the physician's judgment. Peräkylä calls this the "evidence formulating pattern", as illustrated by (8).

```
(8)  [Peräkylä 1998] "Evidence formulating pattern"
 1 Doc:    As tapping on the vertebrae didn't cause any .pain
 2         and there aren't any actual reflection symptoms
 3         in your legs it corresponds with a muscle h (.hhhh)
 4         complication so hhh it's only whether hhh (0.4) you
 5         have been exposed to a draught or has it otherwise=
 6 Pat:    =Oh yes,
 7 Doc:    .hh got irritated,
```

Although the straight factual assertion format is the most frequent, the other two formats are also quite common (table 11.2).

Table 11.2 Frequency of types of diagnostic turns [Peräkylä 1998]

Turn design	Frequency	Percentage
1 Plain assertion	31	44
2 Evidential	12	17
3 Evidence formulating	28	39
Total	71	100

How are we to understand this general pattern? Peräkylä argues that we have to start from a different place than the traditional discussions of medical authority reviewed so far. He argues that physicians' diagnostic authority is not unbounded, but is balanced by their account-ability to patients. By accountability, Peräkylä means that physicians have the obligation to provide patients with at least a sense of the basis for their conclusions. This accountability of medical judgments is limited, Peräkylä argues, because laypersons cannot fully recognize the signs the physician is seeing, or make fully valid inferences about their causes. Nonethe-less, physicians' diagnoses incorporate a balance between the authority of their conclusions and the social accountability of their judgments in the more limited sense of indicating the general basis of the judgments they are making to patients.

Peräkylä argues that even the diagnoses that are formatted as straight factual assertions, and look really quite authoritarian, can embody this balance between authority and account-ability. He shows that when there is a close and relatively transparent relationship between the examination and the diagnosis that results from it, the diagnosis will be presented as straight factual assertion. For example, in (5) the physician's assertion "Here's (.) luckily the bone quite intact," is made while he is holding up an X-ray picture between himself and the patient. The patient can clearly see the evidence on which the diagnosis is based although, in keeping with his limited capacity to "read" X-ray pictures, he only briefly glances at it.

In this case there is a close relationship between the evidence and the diagnostic con-clusion: no great leap of inference is required to connect the two. Peräkylä calls this relationship between evidence and conclusion the "inferential distance" between the two, and in the X-ray example case this inferential distance is extremely short. In this case the authority of the physician's diagnosis is expressed in the *verbal design* of his diagnostic turn. The accountability of the diagnosis is managed through the *context* of his utterance which conveys, without stating so in so many words, that the diagnosis is based on the evidence that both parties have in front of them, even though they may have different capacities to make use of it.

Let us repeat here that Peräkylä is not claiming that patients have an exact understand-ing of the diagnostic reasoning involved in these diagnoses. But they do know what the physi-cian looked at in arriving at the diagnosis. In other words, they know that the diagnosis is based on something specific, even though they may not know exactly what its relevance is. As Peräkylä puts it, the patient knows from what "direction" the evidence comes.

Peräkylä shows that in the majority of cases where the inferential distance between exam-ination and diagnosis is short – for example, the physician looks in the patient's ear and then announces she has an infection, physicians tend to use the simple factual assertion format. And his argument is, as already suggested, that this does not embody flat-out authoritari-anism, but rather a particular balance between authority and accountability.

What are the contexts then in which physicians move away from the simple factual assertion to the more elaborated formats, using evidentials or evidence formulating? Let's start with the evidentials. Peräkylä argues that physicians use evidentials when the inferential distance between the examination and the diagnosis is greater. This greater distance can be the result of two factors, either separately or together. The first involves what Peräkylä calls temporal separation between the exam and the diagnosis. For example in (9), the physician conducted a physical examination of the patient, then he spent a while on the computer preparing a referral for an X-ray. At line 14, quite some time after the examination, he describes his diagnosis using an "evidential formulation" – "there *appears to be* an infection . . .".

(9) [Peräkylä 1998: Expansion of (7)]
((Before this extract, the physician conducted the physical examination, after which
he worked on his computer, telling the patient that he was preparing a referral to
the X-ray lab))

```
 1  Doc:    Has your hip ever been X-rayed before.
 2          (0.5) (Dr picks up some papers))
 3  Pat:    hhhh erm::hhh (1,0) I don't really rememb-
 4          I don't think it has.
 5          (0.8)
 6  Pat:    I don't think it has.=.hh My knee has been X-rayed
 7          as it #erm# yea:rs (0,2) .hh years ago as riding a
 8          bicycle was so painful that it couldn't put up (.)
 9          with it, .h but then nothing was found there.=As
10          far as I remember there has never been an X-ray of my
11          hip hh.
12          (1.2)
13  ?Pat:   .mth
14  Doc:    Now there appears to be an (1.0) infection at the
15          contact point of the joint below it in the sac of mucus
16          there [in  the hip.
17  Pat:          [Oh right .hh that's what I thought myself
18          too that <it probably must be an infection>.
19          [.hhhhh
20  Doc:    [And, because you have had trouble this [long we will
21  Pat:                                            [hhhhh
22  Doc:    make sure and take an X-[ray.
23  Pat:                            [Yes:.
```

Peräkylä argues that through this evidentialized turn design the physician verbally retrieves the earlier examination of the patient as a context for his diagnosis. In other words, the construction "there appears to be" re-invokes the evidence from the physical examination as the context for the diagnostic conclusion. The same is true for evidence formulating, where the diagnostic evidence and reasoning are explicitly retrieved. So when the diagnosis is temporally distant from the exam, physicians use the more expanded "evidential" or "evidence formulating" diagnostic designs (Peräkylä 2006: 227).

The second aspect of greater inferential distance between exam and diagnosis involves what Peräkylä calls the "opacity" of diagnostic reasoning. By using the term "opacity", Peräkylä means to refer to cases where the patient knows what was examined, but does not know why it was examined or what it was being examined for. This is what happens in (10). Here the patient complained about a pain in her foot and the physician has been looking at it.

```
(10)  [Peräkylä 1998] ((The physician has just examined the patient's foot))
  1  Doc:    Okay:. .h fine do put on your,
  2          (.)
  3  Doc:    The pulse [can be felt there in your foot so,
  4  Pat:              [Thank you.
  5  Doc:    .h there's no, in any case (.) no real circulation
  6          proble[m
  7  Pat:          [Yes I don't understand then
  8          [really .hh I was wondering whether (.) I should
  9  Doc:    [is <involved>.
```

Peräkylä reports that the patient's foot looks quite normal and that from a layperson's point of view the purpose of the examination is not at all clear. At the end of it, the physician describes a result of the examination, indicating that he was looking for, and found, a pulse in her foot. He then draws a diagnostic conclusion, explaining that the patient doesn't have a circulation problem. In this way, he connects his diagnostic conclusion to the physical exam, whose point is now revealed. Once again, Peräkylä finds that this is a quite general pattern where the purpose of physical examinations is opaque to patients.

Another kind of relationship between evidence-formulating diagnoses and their circumstances will be more predictable in light of Heath's findings. It occurs when the diagnosis is uncertain or controversial. By controversial Peräkylä means the diagnosis runs against the patient's beliefs about what is wrong with them, most often when the patient believes that the diagnosis is more serious than the physician seems to think, or the diagnostic evaluation may seem to undermine the legitimacy of the patient's medical visit. In both cases, physicians tend to do a lot more explaining, exhibiting just the kind of accountability for diagnosis that is central to Peräkylä's analysis.

What are the implications of Peräkylä's study? First, it revises our mindset about the nature of authority. If we do not look at interactional data, it is all too easy to see authority as an all-or-nothing phenomenon. Peräkylä reminds us that medical authority is not a blank check: accountability goes with authority – in the medical office just as much as the Oval office. And he also shows us how subtle that accountability can be. It can simply be a matter of the context in which a diagnosis is offered. And that kind of subtle accountability may be just enough when the problem isn't that serious and does not (or should not) require a vast amount of discussion or joint decision making.

Peräkylä also shows how physicians expand the verbal accountability of their diagnoses when the context cannot or will not do the job. He points out that physicians treat themselves as more accountable when their diagnoses are problematic, uncertain or disputed. Some researchers have believed that physicians restrict the flow of information to patients as a means of bolstering their authority. But research by Howard Waitzkin (1985) has also shown that when their diagnoses are tentative or under attack, physicians actually give more information to their patients. This finding is underlined by Peräkylä's study. Peräkylä shows that in these situations, physicians don't simply "assert their authority"; rather, they engage in persuasion: they treat their judgments as founded in an authority that is, after all, accountable.

Treatment Recommendations

In a significant paper on the overall organization of medical visits, Robinson (2003) suggests a further factor that may play into the relative lack of patient response to diagnosis in primary care: The patient is there in the first instance not for a diagnosis but for a remedy, and is ready to pass up the opportunity to discuss the diagnosis in the interest of getting to the treatment recommendation. In fact, looking back at cases like (1) and a mass of cases described in Heath (1992) and Stivers (2007a), it is clear that clinicians do not normally wait for patient response before proceeding directly into treatment recommendations; nor do patients object to this immediate forward movement from diagnosis to treatment. In sum, in the context of diagnosis, patients passively acknowledge the expert authority of physicians and, by doing so, permit the medical visit to advance to the next stage: the treatment recommendation.

Matters are rather different in the context of treatment. Here the patient's adherence to, and cooperation with, the treatment plan is critical for success, and both patients and physicians orient to the treatment recommendation as a bilateral process in which the physician proposes, but the patient disposes. In a series of publications on pediatric visits, Stivers (2005a, 2005b, 2006, 2007a) has shown that parents orient to treatment recommendations as *proposals* – that is, something to be accepted or rejected. For example, in (11), a parent who remains silent across an extended diagnosis (→) explicitly accepts the treatment recommendation (⇒):

```
(11)  [Stivers 2007a:107]
  1  Doc:        .hhh Uh:m his- #-# lef:t:=h ea:r=h, is infected,
  2        →     (0.2)
  3  Doc:        .h is bulging, has uh little pus in thuh
  4        →     ba:ck,=h
  5  Doc:  →     Uh:m, an' it's re:d,
  6  Doc:        .hh So he needs some antibiotics to treat tha:t,
  7  Dad:  ⇒     Alright.
  8  Doc:        Mka:y, so we'll go ahead and treat- him: <he has
  9              no a- uh:m, allergies to any penicillin or anything.
```

Similarly, when the treatment recommended is inaction, a parent will nonetheless endorse the decision:

```
(12)  [17-08-13]
  1  Doc:        But it's #hmh# one uh these things that antibiotics
  2              would be uh absolute waste of ti:me.
  3  Mom:  ⇒     Yeah,
  4              (.)
  5  Mom:  ⇒     I- I know_ I agree.
```

Conversely, when an acceptance or endorsement of a treatment recommendation is not forthcoming, physicians will commonly continue to add statements supporting the recommendation until the parent responds with an acceptance or some other action. In (13) the recommendation is simply "watchful waiting" – an appropriate recommendation when the illness is viral in origin. Having offered his recommendation (lines 1–3), the physician waits

for uptake (line 4) and then keeps adding additional statements supporting his original recommendation (lines 5, 6, 9, and 12):

```
(13)  [Stivers 2007a:110]
  1  Doc:        Unfortunately like most viruses we have to watch i:t?
  2  Doc:        .hh becau:se- you know- she (can)/(could) have uh fever::
  3              for another few days, and nothin' el:se.
  4       →      (.)
  5  Doc:  →     and jus- an' be fi:ne,
  6  Doc:  →     .hh Or else if she got uh fever an' got wor:se,
  7              and: started limping actually at that time we'd
  8              probably need 'er tuh come ba:ck,
  9  Doc:  →     .hh But at this moment since there's no swelli:ng?,
 10              or there's no: .hh you know <nothing else,
 11              th-uh most important thing t'do is tuh watch her.
 12  Doc:  →     .hh So we've had a fe:w people right no:w that have had-
 13              uh few of our kids are having tlk .h fever:s, for a few
 14              days, and not much other symptom:s.
 15  Dad:  ⇒     So can she go to preschool now?
```

The father's response (line 15) is quite hostile, and Stivers (2002b, 2005a, 2007a) also shows
that these passive "non-responses" to treatment recommendations frequently embody a resistant stance which, as in (13), may later surface in more overt signs of resistance. Importantly,
she also shows that, faced with these resistant kinds of non-response, clinicians may cave in
and alter their treatment recommendations in line with what they perceive the parent to want
(Stivers 2007a).

While the endorsement of treatment recommendations might seem to be a characteristic
only of pediatric visits where parents have the obligation to consider the best interests of
their children, Koenig (2008) has shown that the same kind of endorsement by patients, and
pursuit of it by clinicians, is operative in adult visits as well. The following case is representative of this conduct. Note that the patient responds minimally to the diagnosis (line 5).
The doctor's treatment recommendation emerges at lines 7–8. After the patient fails to acknowledge or endorse it, the doctor pursues uptake by explaining the purpose of the medication
(line 10), and subsequently elaborates on its effects (lines 12–16); having still received no
verbal uptake, he further expands on this (lines 19–20):

```
(14)  [Koenig 2008]
  1  Doc:        .ngHH=Well, ((clears throat)) (1.2) I think
  2              you got an ear infection.
  3              (.)
  4  Doc:        You knew that before you got here(h),
  5  Pat:        °Mm heh°
  6              (0.4)
  7  Doc:        Ah: what I'd like to do is put you on some
  8              antibio:tics, (0.2) and=uh give you a deconge:stant.
  9              (.)
 10  Doc:  →     See if we can dry out the pre:ssure.
 11  Pat:        ((slight head nod))
 12  Doc:  →     .hh U:hm, it is going to interfere with who
```

```
13                 you are for a while.=that will probably last
14                 for about two to three weeks.=°.hh=so:, what
15                 I would tell you is, <do:n't go::> (0.2) up to
16                 Big Bear=er don't do any uh=airplane trips.
17                 (0.4)
18    Pat:         ((slight head nod))
19    Doc:    →    'Cuz it'll be uh kind of uncomfortable for
20                 you if you do th[at.
21    Pat:                         [That's fine.
```

Thus it is only at line 21 that the patient verbally accepts the treatment recommendation that the doctor has been developing over eleven lines of transcript.

The upshot of this analysis is that patients and their doctors treat diagnosis and treatment as very different social events. Diagnoses are generally presented authoritatively and as not in need of affirmation from patients. Correspondingly, except under the special circumstances described by Heath, Peräkylä, and Stivers, patients tend to offer minimal responses to diagnoses and these rarely take the form of corroboration or endorsement. Treatment recommendations, by contrast, are overwhelmingly oriented to as requiring support and endorsement from patients.

A consequence of this difference is that patient resistance to diagnosis and treatment recommendations tend to take very different forms. Given that silence is treated as acquiescence in the context of diagnosis, a patient who wishes to question a diagnosis must do so actively. However, given that overt acceptance of treatment recommendations is required, patients can engage in passive resistance through silence and minimal acknowledgment.

How Authoritative are Physicians? A Case Study

The studies described so far have suggested that the traditional sociological understanding of medical authority may require subtle qualification. More recent studies of medical visits involving relatively mild conditions, e.g. upper respiratory tract infections (URTIs), suggest yet further adjustments to this picture.

A large body of research suggests that patients find ways to convey a demand for certain medications, particularly antibiotics, and that as a result the medical visit can take on the character of a tacit negotiation. The starting point for this research is that antibiotics are more commonly prescribed when physicians perceive that patients want them (Britten & Ukoumunne 1997). As Stivers and colleagues have shown, this desire is not normally conveyed explicitly (Stivers 2002a, 2002b, Stivers, Mangione-Smith, Elliott, et al. 2003). And yet, as table 11.3 shows, when physicians perceive such a desire they commonly adjust their diagnoses in the direction of bacterial illness, and they tend to prescribe antibiotics for viral cases (that do not justify an antibiotic prescription). Indeed, Mangione-Smith, McGlynn, Elliott, et al. (1999) found that the physician's perception that parents wanted antibiotics for their children was the *only* predictor of antibiotics prescribing for viral illnesses.

As we have seen, Stivers' research (2005a, 2005b, 2006, 2007a) shows that parents quite frequently contest treatment recommendations, and that this is one of the factors involved in inappropriate antibiotics prescribing (Mangione-Smith, Elliott, Stivers, et al. 2006). In one

Table 11.3   Impact of perceived parental expectations on diagnosis and treatment of pediatric upper respiratory infections

	Frequency of diagnoses and antibiotics prescribing (multivariate adjusted proportions)	
	Physician believes parent expects antibiotics (%)	*Physician believes parent does not expect antibiotics (%)*
Bacterial diagnosis	70	31 (p<.001)
Antibiotics prescribed (viral cases)	62	7 (p<.001)

Source: Mangione-Smith, McGlynn, Elliott, et al. 1999

of Stivers' examples, (15) below, it is clear from the way in which the physician formulates his diagnosis (lines 1–8) that he perceives that the parent would like an antibiotic for her child.

(15)   [Stivers 2000]
```
 1  DOC:   →   Well you know it's sort of one of those good news
 2         →   bad news scenarios. On one han:d thuh good news is
 3         →   that she [doesn't have any serious infection.   I=
 4  GIR:           [(                           ).
 5  DOC:   =mean her ears are fi:ne, so she can fly: an' .hh=
 6  MOM:   =(an-)=
 7  DOC:   →   =everything else looks okay_  Thuh bad news is that
 8         →   it's probably viral so we can't make it go away any faster,
 9             (.)
10  MOM:   Mkay.
11             (0.4)
12  MOM:   .hh -.h Now-
13  GIR:   (   [    )
14  MOM:   ⇒       [should I- (0.4) just as uh preventative thi:ng,
15         ⇒   should I give them some- antibiotics?, or:_ [(does that-)
16  DOC:                                                [It wouldn't
17             do anything for thi[s.
18  MOM:                      [No?=
19  DOC:   =An' if [anything it'd make: her diarrhea [worse=
20  MOM:        [Okay.                            [#huh huh#
```

Shortly after he has stated that the condition is viral "so we can't make it go away any faster," the mother makes a guarded request for antibiotics at lines 14–15. While the physician succeeds in resisting the mother's pressure for antibiotics in this case, in others physicians reverse their diagnoses and/or prescribe inappropriately (Stivers 2005a, 2007a). In such cases, patients have exerted pressure for prescriptions and coerced physicians into prescribing against their better judgment. This is the reverse of the "surrender of private judgment" with which we began, and represents, in effect, an abrogation of medical authority.

In related work, Heritage and Stivers (1999) suggested that "online commentary" might be a means of resisting patient pressure to prescribe. Online commentary consists of remarks about the physical examination as it is happening online. For example, a doctor may say "Her ears look good" during an ear examination, thus reassuring the parent that the child does not have an ear infection. Because a good deal of patient pressure is exerted through the problem presentation stage of the visit (Stivers, Mangione-Smith, Elliott, et al. 2003), physicians often perceive patient pressure early on. In these cases, online commentary can be a means of reshaping patient expectations along a non-antibiotic track. In the following case, for example, the physician describes what he is seeing, in the process indicating that the patient's signs are mild. While this may reassure the mother that her child is not very sick, it also builds a case against antibiotics prescribing and "forecasts" (Maynard 1996) an eventual "no antibiotics" treatment recommendation:

```
(16)   [Heritage and Stivers 1999]
   1  Doc:          Can you op'n your mouth for me agai:n,
   2                (0.3)
   3  Doc:          °'ats i:t°
   4                (0.7)
   5  Doc:      →   °Little bit re:d (.) hm°
   6                (1.6) ((moving sounds))
   7  Doc:          °°Alri::ght(h)°°
   8                (2.8) ((more moving sounds))
                    ...
                    ...((32 lines omitted))
                    ...
  41  Doc:          Ari:ght Michael. Can I loo:k >in your< ears
  42                (0.3)
  43  Mom:          °This o:n[e:°
  44  Doc:                   ['ank you
  45                (0.9)
  46  Doc:      →   'ats fi:ne the other one?
  47                (4.5)
  48  Doc:          ktch °okha::yh°
  49                (0.5)
  50  Doc:      ⇒   They're alri::ght(h). I mean there's a ju̱st a li:(tt)le
  51            ⇒   redness in his thro̲a:t an:d and just a little pinkness ther:e
  52            ⇒   which (.) means he's got one of tho:se co̲:lds that make them
  53            ⇒   cou:gh a lot .hh Because his chest is pe:rfectly all ri:ght
  54            ⇒   he ce̲:rtainly doesn't need (.) penici̲llin
  55  Mom:          N:o[:
  56  Doc:      ⇒      [°'r anything like tha:t°  .hhhh hh I think the c̲oughing...
                    ((talk continues))
```

Here the online comments (lines 5 and 46) forecast the diagnostic outcome. At the actual diagnosis, beginning at line 50, the physician explicitly retrieves his earlier comments as part of the case against prescribing (lines 50–4). Here, we might say, Peräkylä's evidence formulating starts earlier in the medical visit and is used as an ancillary to a "no treatment" recommendation. Preliminary findings suggest that this kind of online evidence formulating can reduce inappropriate prescribing (Mangione-Smith, Stivers, Elliott, et al. 2003, Heritage, Elliott, Stivers, et al. 2009).

Conclusion

What conclusions are to be drawn from this array of conversation analytic studies of diagnosis and treatment? First, it is clear that the act of diagnosis remains a fulcrum in the exercise of medical authority. None of the studies reviewed here shows that patients disagree with diagnoses to any significant degree. This is so even though the medical conditions being addressed are the relatively minor staples of primary care medicine and involve conditions in which patients may have some experience and expertise. It is all but certain that in more serious, unusual or life-threatening conditions the conclusion holds with still greater force.

The older Byrne and Long study shows physicians exercising medical authority in a fashion which is quite authoritarian, though this observation and those of Heath's later study need to be seasoned with Peräkylä's observations, which suggest more of a balance with social accountability than is traditionally observed in the sociological literature.

The studies of antibiotics prescribing further qualify these observations. They suggest that in cases of mild illness which patients have frequently experienced in the past, medical authority is compromised by a tacit bargaining process, in which the perception that patients may become dissatisfied with their medical care may outweigh the exercise of clinical judgment. Paradoxically, if the results of the "online commentary" studies are borne out by further research, physicians can redress the balance by a more fundamental exercise of the cultural authority of medicine: the capacity to "name the world", which in this case takes the form of unchallengeable observations about patient signs and symptoms. Yet this too involves a revision of physician authority. Online commentary is evidence-formulating because it reveals a process of diagnostic reasoning to the patient, thus further redrawing the balance between authority and accountability a little further in the direction of accountability.

At the beginning of this chapter we reviewed studies suggesting that medical authority may have been eroded since its zenith in the 1960s. The various interactional studies presented here seem to reinforce such a conclusion. The older data exhibits more authoritative, even authoritarian, physician behavior than the later. However, caution is in order here. The Byrne and Long and the Heath studies derive from Britain, Peräkylä's from Finland, and Stivers' work is based on American pediatric data. Without more evidence it will not be easy to separate the potential effects of time trends from the confounding effects deriving from national cultures, different insurance systems and other aspects of medical practice in these diverse countries. International comparisons of doctor–patient interaction are long overdue.

For Further Reading

The notion that diagnosis is a central site of medical authority is a fundamental tenet in medical sociology from Parsons (1951) and Freidson (1970) through Starr (1982) and Shorter (1985). The erosion of that authority is most comprehensively theorized by Light (2000). The empirical documentation of physician–patient "bargaining" over medications and the outcomes of that bargaining are to be found in Stivers (2007a) and Kravitz, Epstein, Feldman, et al. (2005).

IV

Trials, Juries, and Dispute Resolution

12

Trial Examinations

Spoken interaction is central to the legal system in most societies, although it has a special significance in societies where democratic ideals have been to some extent institutionalized. Everything from formal trials to informal legal proceedings (plea bargaining, mediation, etc.) is conducted through the medium of interaction. In the next two chapters we consider formal trial proceedings, focusing on two key phases of the trial process: the witness examination phase (this chapter) and the jury deliberation phase (next chapter).

Interaction in these environments is geared to an outcome with important social and moral ramifications: the determination of guilt or innocence. How consequential is the interaction itself for the particular outcome of any given trial? This is a matter of some controversy among legal scholars and social scientists. One point of view holds that interaction is of no particular consequence because it is the facts of the case and the relevant law that are determinative. From this vantage point, interaction is merely a neutral medium through which attorneys, witnesses, judges, and jurors determine what the facts are and how the law applies. The idea that interaction is in fact epiphenomenal has a normative counterpart in the philosophical viewpoint known as legal formalism, which holds that legal reasoning should be strictly constrained by the legal codes that bear on the facts of a given case.

An alternative point of view holds that interaction exerts an independent influence on judicial outcomes. From this vantage point, the facts and the law are not wholly determinative because neither "speaks for itself"; their import depends on how they are invoked and animated by the participants as the trial unfolds. Interactional practices are thus an important contingency bearing on the determination of guilt or innocence. This viewpoint is anti-formalist in character and is broadly consistent with the philosophical position known as legal realism. Legal realism is sometimes iconoclastically termed (following legal scholar Jerome Frank) "the breakfast theory of justice", for it is based on the insight that judicial outcomes may depend in part on a range of extra-legal contingencies, including what the judge had for breakfast that morning.

Our examination of courtroom trials in the next two chapters comes closer to the latter perspective, although our interaction-based approach departs from philosophical legal realism in several important respects. First, unlike the psychologism implicit in the "breakfast theory of justice", which views contingency as rooted in internal processes of judgment and interpretation, our emphasis is on what is actually said and done inside the courtroom, and in particular how language practices shape the way in which factual realities and legal codes are invoked, formulated, and rendered consequential. Secondly, unlike the wholesale arbitrariness and lack of constraint implicit in the "breakfast theory", our approach emphasizes the normative framework of accountability within which attorneys, witnesses, and jurors must operate as they build their actions and pursue their respective agendas. And finally, our approach is empirical rather than philosophical in character, grounded in the observation and analysis of actual legal proceedings and the language practices of which they are comprised.

But do these practices really matter? Can "mere words" materially affect trial outcomes? A long line of experimental research (e.g., Carmichael, Hogan, & Walter 1932, Loftus 1979) demonstrates that language practices are broadly consequential for perceptions, not only for those (like jurors) who learn about events second-hand, but also for those who were themselves first-hand eyewitnesses. In a series of studies by Loftus and her associates (summarized in Loftus 1979) with direct relevance to the courtroom, subjects were shown videorecordings of various auto accidents. When subsequently asked about specific details of what they had seen, minor changes in the wording of the question had a significant impact on subjects' recollections. The formulation of the accident itself mattered:

About how fast were the cars going when they *smashed into* each other?
About how fast were the cars going when they *hit* each other?

The first version ("smashed into") yielded substantially higher estimates of speed than the second version ("hit"). Even the contrast between definite and indefinite articles turned out to matter:

Did you see *the* broken taillight?
Did you see *a* broken taillight?

When the object in question did not in fact appear on the video, subjects in the definite article condition ("the") were significantly more likely to misreport it as having been present than subjects in the indefinite article condition ("a"). Correspondingly, the latter subjects were more likely to confess that they didn't know the answer to this question. Language practices, it would seem, embody ways of seeing the world, and even singular lexical choices can affect perceptions and memories, as well as the verbal accounts through which they find expression.

In this chapter we examine how such practices are mobilized within trial examinations. We begin with the general attributes of trial examinations as a form of talk. We then focus on the dynamics of cross-examination, exploring how attorneys build accusatory lines of questioning and how witnesses resist them. We conclude by considering how witnesses can also resist material evidence offered in court.

The Trial Examination as a Form of Talk

Trial examinations have several features that set them apart from ordinary conversation and from other forms of talk examined in previous chapters.

Talk for "overhearers"

First and perhaps most obviously, trial examinations are conducted for the benefit of an "overhearing" audience, typically the judge (who oversees the proceedings and adjudicates procedural matters) and the jury (whose members determines the trial's outcome). Even though most of the interaction takes place between attorneys and witnesses, and even though they address their remarks to each other, the whole exchange is being conducted for the benefit of these ratified overhearers.

This arrangement is consequential for the manner in which the interrogation unfolds. Attorneys usually have a pretty good idea of how the witness will answer any given question, so – using terminology introduced in chapter 3 – the attorney is in a K+ situation even before the question is launched. The whole point of the exchange is to solicit a response that will inform the jury, who are watching and listening and will eventually pass judgment on the case. This state of affairs is confirmed and reinforced by the attorney's practice of not responding to the answers with "oh", or indeed with any kind of receipt object (*yeah*, *uh huh*, etc.). To illustrate, notice how, in example (1), after each answer the attorney simply moves on to the next question without acknowledging the answer in any exposed way.

```
(1)  [Atkinson and Drew 1979: 108–9]
  1  A:     Then a message from you, Deputy Commissioner,
  2          "Ask people in Percy Street to go home as they can't
  3          stand there".
  4  W:     Yes.
  5  A:     Did you send that message?
  6  W:     Yes.
  7  A:     Were those people you were referring to there
  8          Protestant people?
  9  W:     Presumably they were.
 10  A:     Were they in fact a Protestant mob that was attempting
 11          to burst into Divis Street?
 12  W:     Prior to sending this message I must have known that
 13          there was a crowd of people there.
                   .
                   .
                   .
 14  A:     I want to ask you about the phraseology there, "Ask
 15          people in Percy Street to go home as they can't stand
 16          there." Was that your message?
 17  W:     Yes, that is my message.
 18  A:     That was a rather polite way of addressing a mob who
 19          had burned and pillaged a Catholic area, was it not?
 20  W:     I did not know that....
```

The complete absence of receipt tokens sustains a definition of the situation wherein attorneys are soliciting answers not for their own benefit, but for the benefit of the audience (Drew & Heritage 1992).

A specialized turn-taking system

In the institutional settings examined previously in this book – emergency calls and doctor–patient encounters – the procedures for taking turns at talk are not substantially different from ordinary conversation. Much as in conversation, there are no specific constraints on how long a speaker may occupy the floor at any given point, or who may speak next (Sacks, Schegloff, & Jefferson 1974). In more technical terms, turn order, turn length, and turn content are not fixed in advance, so these parameters of speech exchange remain to be determined by the participants within the interaction as it unfolds.

In trial examinations, however, these parameters of speech exchange are restricted by a special turn-taking system (Atkinson & Drew 1979). The system is organized around questions and answers, with attorneys restricted to asking questions, witnesses restricted to answering them, and other parties prohibited from speaking at all except under special circumstances. Compliance with this turn-taking system is monitored and enforced by the participants themselves, with the judge charged with the task of adjudicating procedural disputes. Although the procedures may differ in their particulars during direct and cross-examination, and in different legal environments, a question–answer system of turn taking is exceedingly widespread in formal legal proceedings.

Why such a specialized arrangement? The question–answer turn-taking system is, in effect, a solution to specific problems that emerge in this type of environment (Atkinson & Drew 1979). By pre-specifying who may speak at any given juncture, the system helps to manage the traffic of interaction in a situation where the large number of participants might otherwise lead to a cacophony of simultaneous speech. By prohibiting the "schisming" of proceedings into various separate interactions (cf. Egbert 1997), it sustains a collective focus on a single course of activity. Finally, by restricting attorneys to the act of questioning and thereby treating witnesses as the sole source of "factual" assertions, it is attentive to due process, rules of evidence, and other justice ideals. In general, as noted in chapter 4, specialized turn-taking systems are recurrent in settings involving multiple participants and strong professional norms, and the trial examination is no exception (see also news interviews in chapter 15).

Whatever its reasons for being, the turn-taking system operating here is experienced as restrictive and confining by the participants, and it endows the interaction with a distinctively "formal" character (Atkinson 1982). It is, moreover, thoroughly consequential for how trial attorneys build their cases.

The Dynamics of Examination and Cross-Examination

The basic dynamics of the examination process were first analyzed by Atkinson and Drew (1979). Although the overall objective is to establish the guilt or innocence of the accused, attorneys are not permitted to lay out the evidence in an uninterrupted monologue or speech. In accordance with the turn-taking system, each attorney must build his or her case step by step, in interaction with witnesses, through a series of questions and answers about specific facts of the case. Attorneys are in effect midwives to the facts, mobilizing questions to elicit relevant testimony from witnesses. One implication of this is that each question–answer sequence has a dual character. On the one hand, each is dealing with some specific fact of the case, but at the same time each is produced and understood by reference to how it bears on the overarching project of establishing guilt or innocence.

Example (1) illustrates these points. This is an excerpt from a British tribunal of inquiry in the 1970s – similar to a grand jury investigation in the US – occasioned by an outbreak of violence between Protestants and Catholics in Northern Ireland. The government counsel is cross-examining a deputy police commissioner who was responsible for keeping the peace in that neighborhood. Thus, the counsel may be understood as analogous to the "prosecutor" and the witness a key "defendant" in this investigative hearing.

```
(1a)   (Atkinson and Drew 1979: 108–9)
  1  A:      Then a message from you, Deputy Commissioner,
  2          "Ask people in Percy Street to go home as they can't
  3          stand there".
  4  W:      Yes.
  5  A:      Did you send that message?
  6  W:      Yes.
  7  A:      Were those people you were referring to there
  8          Protestant people?
  9  W:      Presumably they were.
 10  A:      Were they in fact a Protestant mob that was attempting
 11          to burst into Divis Street?
 12  W:      Prior to sending this message I must have known that
 13          there was a crowd of people there.
```

Notice how each question offers some particular fact for the witness to confirm or reject, but at the same time there is a broader prosecutorial agenda driving the line of questioning. That is, the attorney is building a case against the commissioner, suggesting through his questions that the commissioner was involved on a supervisory basis, and that he knew about the hostile crowd, but failed to take action to prevent the attack.

This is apparent not only in the particular facts offered for confirmation in each question, but also in the linguistic form of the questions and their arrangement into a line of questioning (Atkinson & Drew 1979: ch. 4). The first three questions lay the groundwork by offering comparatively "objective" facts for confirmation, namely the wording of the commissioner's message (lines 1–3), the fact that it was the commissioner who sent it (line 5), and the religion of those to whom the message was addressed (lines 7–8). After an initial verbatim quote, the second and third questions are designed as straightforward yes/no questions inviting confirmation. But the fourth question (at lines 10–11: "Were they in fact a Protestant mob that was attempting to burst into Divis Street") is somewhat different. At the level of content, this question is more interpretive in targeting the intentions or motivations of the group ("was attempting to . . ."). It is also accusatory in its import, for if they were indeed a "mob" with hostile motives, the officer should have taken preventative action. Correspondingly, this more interpretive and accusatory question also takes a distinctive form when the attorney inserts "in fact" before the characterization. This phrase seems to anticipate resistance on the part of the commissioner, for it frames the contentious interpretation as a "fact" and thereby increases the pressure for a confirmatory "yes" answer.

Across this line of questioning, the deputy commissioner plainly recognizes where the proffered "facts" are leading, for he struggles to resist their accusatory implications (Atkinson & Drew 1979: ch. 4). While he confirms the first two questions straightforwardly, with simple conforming "yes" answers, his resistance begins in response to the third question (lines 7–9). Although he confirms the "Protestant" characterization of the group, he avoids a conforming "yes" answer and interjects a bit of uncertainty into his confirmation: "Presumably they were." Correspondingly, in the next exchange (lines 10–13) the commissioner again confirms the attorney's characterization of events while also avoiding a conforming "yes" answer, and in this case he shifts the terms of the characterization from "Protestant mob" to the more innocuous "crowd of people". Both of these answers are thus defensive and exculpatory, suggesting that he knew less about the composition and intentions of the group than the counsel had implied.

A similar pattern of incrementally developed accusation and denial is woven into the next line of questioning. The first question (lines 14–16 below) is comparatively "factual", seeking confirmation only for the precise wording of the commissioner's message. A confirmation is subsequently provided (line 17), with a conforming "yes" answer followed by a faithful repeat of the terms of the question.

(1b)   (Atkinson and Drew 1979: 108–9)
```
14  A:    I want to ask you about the phraseology there, "Ask
15        people in Percy Street to go home as they can't stand
16        there." Was that your message?
17  W:    Yes, that is my message.
18  A:    That was a rather polite way of addressing a mob who
19        had burned and pillaged a Catholic area, was it not?
20  W:    I did not know that....
```

But the second question is more interpretive and accusatory, soliciting an evaluation of the message ("That was a rather polite way of addressing a mob . . ."), restoring the "mob" characterization and invoking the group's previous sectarian aggression. Moreover, all of this is packaged in the form of a positive assertion plus tag question, which (as noted in chapter 10) exerts greater pressure for a "yes" answer. So here again, just as the characterizations become more accusatory, the attorney anticipates resistance and chooses a form of question design that cranks up the pressure for confirmation. Resistance follows nonetheless (line 20): the commissioner not only avoids confirming, but he rejects the terms of the question altogether by challenging the presupposition that he knew about the crowd's hostile sectarian intentions.

This extended example illustrates the complex interplay between questions and answers on the one hand, and larger agendas involving the establishment of guilt or innocence. Attorneys and witnesses build their respective cases incrementally, brick by brick and in reaction to one another, through the exchange of questions and answers. For the case of cross-examination, a common pattern is for the attorney to proceed from relatively factual to more interpretive questions that bear more directly on guilt/innocence, and to employ question design forms that exert increasing pressure for a confirmatory response.

Resisting Attorneys' Questions

We focus next on cross-examination and in particular on the role of witnesses. It's tempting to assume that the attorney is all-powerful in this process. After all, attorneys are much more practiced in the "game" of cross-examination, and within this game they are perpetually able to "go first", setting the agenda through their questions to which the witness is obliged to respond (cf. Matoesian 1993). However, as we've already seen, witnesses are by no means without power and resources of their own, enabling them to resist even the most carefully constructed line of questioning.

Paul Drew's (1992) study of cross-examination in a US. criminal trial for rape demonstrates these themes. Drew focuses on the defense attorney's cross-examination of the plaintiff, the alleged rape victim, and more specifically on a line of questioning about events prior to the incident when the parties met during a night on the town. At issue is the status of the relationship between the plaintiff and the defendant – "who they were" to each other on that evening, and the level of intimacy involved.

```
(2)   [Drew 1992]
  1  A:        Now: (0.7) February fourteenth of nineteen seventy five
  2             you were (0.3) you were down a- (.) in ((City.)) (.) Is
  3             tha- Is that ri:ght?
  4  W:        Ye:s
  5  A:        An' you went to a: uh (0.9) uh you went to a ba:r? (in)
  6             ((City)) (0.6) Is that correct?
  7             (1.0)
  8  W:        It's a clu:b.
  9             (0.3)
 10  A:        A clu:b?
 11             (1.0)
 12  A:        There was liquor served there wasn't there? ((said fast))
 13  W:        Ye:s
 14             (0.5)
 15  A:        You had so(me) liquor didn't you?
 16  W:        Ye:s.
 17             (3.1)
 18  A:        It's a: uh singles club. Isn't that what it is?=
 19             =((sound of striking mallet))
 20  A2:       (                         )
 21             (0.9)
 22  J:        No you may have it,
 23             (1.1)
 24  A:        It's where uh (.) uh (0.3) gi:rls and fellas meet.
 25             Isn't it?
 26             (0.9)
 27  W:        People go: there.
 28             .
 29             .
 30             .
 31  A:        An' during that eve:ning (0.6) uh: didn't Mister ((Name))
 32             come over (to) sit with you.
 33             (0.8)
 34  W:        Sat at our table.
 35             (1.1)
 36  A:        Didn't he sit next to you?
 37             (0.6)
 38  W:        No (.) he sat across from me.
 39             (0.3)
 40  A:        Acro:ss from you?
```

```
41                (0.7)
42  A:            D'e (never) sa:t next to you:
43                (0.3)
44  W:            No?
45                (2.1)
46  A:            Didn' you da:nce with Mister ((Name))?=
47  W:            =N:o.
48                (1.0)
49  A:            D'y'ever dance with 'im (on that evening),
50  W:            No,
51                (0.9)
52  A:            D'y'ave any conversation with'im.
53                (0.5)
54  W:            Yeah.=I was talkin' to 'im, ((nonchalant tone of voice))
```

Here is a sustained tug of war over the relationship in question. Each yes/no question offers a specific detail for confirmation, a detail that suggests a degree of intimacy between plaintiff and defendant. The answers often contest these implications by downgrading the level of intimacy.

How exactly does the plaintiff enact her resistance? One method is to reject the attorney's version of events in an explicit manner by producing a "no" response, which may also be followed by a contradictory version of events. For instance (arrowed):

```
(3)  [Oulette 45/2b:2]
  1  A:            Didn't he sit next to you?
  2                (0.6)
  3  W:     →      No (.) he sat across from me.
```

An alternative and more subtle method involves what Drew (1992) has termed *implicit rejection*. This mode of resistance is distinguished by (1) the absence of "no" in the response, and (2) the presence a version of events that contrasts with but does not necessarily contradict the attorney's version. These implicit rejections are in Raymond's (2003) terms nonconforming responses, for they decline to comply with the yes/no imperative built into the previous question, and they embody a subtle challenge to the specific terms of the question. The following are some illustrative instances of implicit rejection.

```
(4)  [Drew 1992: implicit rejections]
     A:            An' you went to a: uh (0.9) uh you went to a ba:r?
                   (in) ((city)) (0.6) Is that correct?
                   (1.0)
     W:            It's a clu:b.

     A:            It's where uh (.) uh (0.3) gi:rls and fellas meet.
                   Isn't it?
                   (0.9)
     W:            People go: there.

     A:            An' during that eve:ning (0.6) uh: didn't Mister
                   ((name)) come over (to) sit with you.
                   (0.8)
     W:            Sat at our table.
```

```
A:        Well (yuh) had some uh (.) uh fairly lengthy
          conversations? with the defendant uh: didn' you
          (0.7) on that evening u' February fourteenth?
          (1.0)
W:        (Well) we were all talkin'?

A:        Well you kne:w at that ti:me, that the defendant was
          in:terested in you (.) didn' you?
          (1.3)
W:        He: asked me how I'(d) bin: (un) (1.1) j- just stuff like
          that?
```

In each of these exchanges, the plaintiff avoids saying "no" – or "yes" for that matter – and the alternative versions that she offers do not intrinsically contradict the attorney's version of events. Both versions ("bar" versus "club", "where girls and fellows meet" versus "people go there", "sit with you" versus "sat at our table", etc.) could be correct ways of characterizing the same state of affairs.

The lack of both explicit negation and intrinsic contradiction poses a puzzle as to how these responses are heard to be competing with the attorney's version of events. Part of the explanation hinges on the absence of a confirmatory "yes" in a sequential context where that was the preferred response, together with a discriminably different characterization, both of which are interpretive resources suggesting a competitive understanding of her responses.

But more enters into the interpretive process here, involving what Drew, following Sacks (1992), calls *the maximal property of descriptions*. Since this property is best understood by way of illustration, consider the descriptions embedded in commonplace social invitations such as *Come over for dinner*, *Join us for drinks*, *Come and have lunch*, *Stop by for coffee*. Each invitation contains a brief and necessarily partial characterization of the event, one couched in terms of refreshments to be served. These singular details stand on behalf of the entire social event, and despite their brevity and "incompleteness" they are meant to be informative about that event in ways that will be useful to both inviters and recipients as they make their plans. Given this, each description is heard to be *the most that can be said about the event* on the salient dimension of refreshments. For instance, an invitation to *dinner* may be understood to include *drinks*, but not the reverse, and the same can be said of an invitation to *lunch* as opposed to *coffee*. These alternative characterizations – *dinner/ drinks*, *lunch/ coffee* – while not intrinsically contradictory when considered in the abstract, are nonetheless heard as incompatible when situated in the environment of an invitation by virtue of the maximal property of descriptions.

This same property enters into the plaintiff's implicit rejections. Here the locally salient dimension is the level of intimacy between the parties, at times particularized in terms of what the plaintiff could be expected to have known about the defendant's "interest" in her. The plaintiff's descriptions are hearably competitive because each is offered as the most that can be said about the scene on the intimacy/interest dimension, and hence downgraded relative to the attorney's prior version. Without negating or contradicting what was said previously, such descriptions nonetheless tacitly undermine the attorney's portrayal of events and the defensive case it embodies.

This practice is remarkably effective. Despite the attorney's greater experience in the courtroom, and his command of a formidable line of questioning, the witness throws down a succession of roadblocks and effectively resists being steamrolled. Because of its utility, the practice of implicit rejection is exploited far beyond the confines of this particular trial. The same type of practice appears in the following excerpt from a civil deposition for a sexual harassment lawsuit against President Bill Clinton. The prosecuting attorney, seeking to show that Clinton did favors for Kathleen Willey to keep her quiet about an alleged sexual incident, asks Clinton about Willey's appointment to a desirable position. In the process, he characterizes the appointment ("you appointed Kathleen Willey" in line 1) in a way that portrays Clinton as directly responsible.

```
(5)  [Clinton Deposition, Paula Jones Case]
  1  A:     Now, you appointed Kathleen Willey to travel to
  2         Copenhagen to serve on the official delegation of the
  3         United States of America at a world summit for social
  4         development, true?
  5  W:     She went as a White House appointee....
```

In response, Clinton neither negates nor contradicts that characterization; he reformulates it ("She went as a White House appointee" in line 5) in a way that confirms the appointment while omitting reference to his own involvement. He thereby implies that he was uninvolved without explicitly committing himself to that proposition, thus neatly undercutting the incriminating case that the attorney was seeking to build.

Resisting Material Evidence

Just as witnesses have resources with which to resist and undercut "evidence" invoked in adversarial lines of questioning, they also have the capacity to resist material forms of evidence presented in the courtroom. This is amply demonstrated by Charles Goodwin's (1994) study of the police brutality trial conducted in the wake of the infamous Rodney King beating.

This was a trial where material evidence, in the form of a videotape, played a central role. When four Los Angeles Police Department officers apprehended Rodney King, an African-American motorist, following a traffic violation and a high-speed chase, an amateur videographer happened to capture the officers beating King with metal batons. The videotape was broadcast frequently on local and national TV news programs, and served as the primary evidence against the officers. Many who saw the tape assumed the officers would be found guilty of excessive force. In the words of the chief prosecutor: "What more could you ask for? You have the videotape that shows objectively, without bias, impartially, what happened that night. . . . It can't be rebutted" (quoted in Goodwin 1994: 615). Nevertheless, the officers were acquitted of all charges in the criminal trial (although for one of the charges the jury could not agree on a verdict). That outcome sparked outrage and several days of rioting in Los Angeles culminating in more than 50 deaths and billions of dollars in property damages.

Given the videotape, most observers could not understand how the jury could fail to convict. Numerous factors presumably played a role in this outcome, including the fact that the trial was moved to Simi Valley, a suburb that was home to many police officers but few people of color. However, acquittal was by no means preordained by these circumstances, for any predisposition to acquit still requires an accountable basis (as we'll see in the next chapter). Goodwin argues that such a basis emerged inside the courtroom. Defense attorneys, working with expert witnesses, provided the jury with a way to interpret what they saw on the videotape as a professional and proper exercise of force. And language practices played a crucial role in this process of reinterpretation.

The defense argued that events on the videotape could only be properly understood by considering them in the context of routine policework. This context included standard procedures for apprehending uncooperative suspects, which boil down to two professional norms: (1) if the suspect is being aggressive, escalation of force is justified, whereas (2) if the suspect is cooperating, de-escalation is warranted. These norms in turn imply a coding scheme for categorizing police behavior in one of three basic ways: (1) escalating force, (2) de-escalating force, or (3) evaluating the situation. At the trial, defense attorneys and their expert witnesses applied this scheme to events on the tape as it played in slow motion.

Goodwin argues that this coding scheme does not merely describe police behavior; it functions as a guide for perception, with consequences that tend to exonerate the police. First and foremost, the coding scheme *partitions the beating into discrete phases*. As one of the expert witnesses put it:

(6) [Goodwin 1994: 617]
```
    W:      There were, ten distinct (1.0) uses of force,
            rather than one single use of force....
            In each of those, uses of force there was
            an escalation and a de-escalation, (0.8)
            an assessment period, (1.5)
            and then an escalation and a de-escalation again. (0.7)
            And another assessment period.
```

Thus, what might initially appear to be a single undifferentiated course of action is rendered as a series of discrete episodes, with each episode having its own internal sequence of behaviors.

This partitioning, in turn, has the consequence of *portraying the police conduct as controlled and methodical*. The police are depicted as proceeding carefully, step by step, by reference to what the suspect is doing.

(7) [Goodwin 1994: 617]
```
    A:      Four oh five, oh one.
            We see a blow being delivered.=
            =Is that correct.
    W:      That's correct.  The force has again been escalated
            (0.3) to the level it had been previously, (0.4)
            and the de-escalation has ceased.
              .
              .
              .
    A:      And at- at this point which is, for the record
            four thirteen twenty nine, (0.4)
            we see a blow being struck and thus the end of
            the period of, de-escalation?  Is that correct Captain.
    W:      That's correct.  Force has now been elevated to the
            previous level, (0.6) after this period of de-escalation.
```

Thus, one of the defense attorneys noted that his objective was to show the jury that "what looks like uncontrolled uh brutality and random violence is indeed a very disciplined and controlled effort to take Mr. King into custody" (quoted in Goodwin 1994: 617).

A further consequence of the use of this coding scheme is that *it casts the officers' blows as responsive* to what King was doing. Thus, each set of blows is portrayed as the second move in a sequence of actions initiated by King. This is consistent with the defense's oft-repeated argument that "Rodney King and Rodney King alone was in control of the situation."

Finally, all of this *focuses attention on King's behavior*, which is closely monitored for what might be prompting each successive episode of blows. Although he does comparatively little over the course of the beating, while the police are more visibly active, the coding scheme tends to foreground his image as the one who is exercising the primary interactional initiative.

How, then, was King's behavior categorized? The categories applied to King were just as elementary: his behavior was coded as either (1) cooperative/nonaggressive, or (2) uncooperative/aggressive. Interestingly, both the prosecution and the defense used this same coding scheme for the plaintiff; where they differed was in how these categories should be mapped onto King's behavior. The prosecution conceded that King was initially "uncooperative" when, at the very beginning of the tape, he can be seen running toward the police. This would make use of force justified at that point. But prosecutors argued that once King had been knocked down and was lying on the asphalt, he was no longer "uncooperative" and police had no right to continue to use force.

The defense argued, to the contrary, that even on the ground King continued to aggressively resist the police. This posed a problem for the defense, because at first glance it looks as if King does very little while most of the blows are being administered. However, the slightest movements by King were scrutinized and portrayed as aggressively resistant by expert witnesses for defense.

Language practices were central here as well. At one point, prosecutors played a segment of the video and proposed that King was in fact cooperatively moving into a position appropriate for handcuffs, and one officer can be seen reaching for his handcuffs at that juncture. However, the defense witness – a police sergeant – disagreed, arguing by reference to the videotape that King was still being aggressive.

```
(8)  [Goodwin 1994: 619]
 1  A:          So uh would you, again consider this to be: a
 2               nonaggressive, movement by Mr. King?
 3  W:          At this time no I wouldn't.
 4               (1.1)
 5  A:          It is aggressive.
 6  W:      →   Yes. It's starting to be. (0.9) This foot is lying flat.
 7          →   There's starting to be a bend. in uh (0.6) this leg (0.4)
 8               in his butt (0.4) The buttocks area has
 9          →   started to rise. (0.7) which would put us
10          →   at the beginning of our spectrum again.
```

The sergeant bolsters his aggressiveness claim by characterizing King's behavior as a whole not simply as aggressive, but as "starting to be" aggressive (line 6). Subsequently, each reference to a specific movement by King is prefaced with something analogous to *starting to* (arrowed). These formulations are the linguistic equivalent of a magnifying glass, enlarging King's behaviors by situating them within an impending trajectory of action. Within this discursive framework, tiny movements are recast as the visible tip of an impending iceberg of aggression that would have materialized had it not been for the next application of force by the police. And by implication, such force is portrayed as justified.

In sum, an interlocking matrix of language practices, operating on the recorded actions of both the plaintiff and the defendants, effectively neutralized the central piece of incriminating material evidence in this trial.

Conclusion

The studies synthesized in this chapter converge in support of the idea that interaction in the courtroom is far from epiphenomenal, that the facts don't speak for themselves, and that even material evidence is not self-explicating. For any given case, what the facts are and what their import might be depends crucially on how they are invoked and formulated inside the courtroom. These studies also converge with experimental research (Loftus 1979) in demonstrating that ways of formulating the facts are at the same time ways of seeing, frameworks for perceiving and interpreting the events in question. And the outcome of the King trial suggests that such practices can materially affect juries and their verdicts.

So while they may seem fleeting and ephemeral, language practices in the courtroom are in fact powerful and consequential. Just as such practices mediate the impact of the environing social context on interaction (as we've seen with respect to medical questioning in chapter 10), so do they mediate the impact of the worldly realities to which language refers. And since the legal system is perennially concerned with the question of "what really happened", an understanding of how that system works will be forever incomplete until language practices in interaction are given their full measure.

For Further Reading

The most ambitious conversation analytic study of trial examinations, encompassing phenomena ranging from the turn-taking system to the management of shared attention to the dynamics of cross-examination, remains Atkinson and Drew's pioneering *Order in Court* (1979). Drew (1992) and Ehrlich and Sidnell (2006) provide more focused analyses of practices of cross-examination, and C. Goodwin (1994) offers a provocative investigation of the pragmatics of perception in the Rodney King trial (and other occupational contexts). The theme of language practices as a vehicle for the exercise of power in the courtroom is taken up by Matoesian (1993) and O'Barr (1982). Conley and O'Barr (1998) provide a useful overview of research on language, interaction, and the courtroom.

13

Jury Deliberations

The jury deliberation phase of the courtroom trial has long been something of a mystery. Unlike the public and thoroughly accessible character of trial examinations, jury deliberations are conducted behind closed doors and are thus largely inaccessible not only to social scientists but also to legal scholars, journalists, and the public at large. Even trial lawyers themselves have little direct knowledge of the final and consequential deliberation phase, since lawyers are rarely chosen to serve on jury panels. Sources of information about deliberation practices tend to be decidedly indirect – after-the-fact interviews with jurors, simulated or "mock" deliberations, and literary dramatizations in films like *Twelve Angry Men*. The jury room has thus been a virtual black box, one that takes in trial information and somehow produces a verdict through processes hidden from direct scrutiny.

Following the recording of one jury deliberation for an episode of the PBS documentary television series *Frontline* (Levin & Hertzberg 1986), however, the black box of the jury room began to reveal its secrets. This prominent criminal case, in conjunction with an additional civil case analyzed by sociologists John Manzo and Douglas Maynard (Manzo 1993, 1994, 1996, Maynard & Manzo 1993), and a more recent sample of 50 deliberations analyzed by attorney Shari Diamond and her colleagues (Diamond, Vidmar, Rose, et al. 2003, Diamond, Seidman, & Rose 2005, Diamond, Rose, & Murphy 2006, Tatalovich 2007), shed new and revealing light on the inner workings of deliberation.

The picture that is emerging is one that challenges popular images of juries in action. Juries are alternately praised as a keystone of justice and democracy, and condemned as irrational, prejudiced, and prone to manipulation. Observation of actual juries at work suggests a more nuanced assessment. On the one hand, much like the witnesses examined in the previous chapter, jurors are not rigidly limited by either the objective facts or the letter of the law, which they reason about and articulate in varying and resourceful ways. But jurors are not arbitrary or capricious either; they treat themselves as accountable to the facts and the law, as well as to broader ideals of fairness and justice, as they work toward a verdict.

General Features of Jury Deliberations

Tasks and objectives

The primary objective of deliberation is, of course, to reach a verdict on the case. The required level of consensus varies somewhat across different legal systems and jurisdictions. In the US, where juries are relatively prevalent, most criminal courts require unanimity while most civil courts allow for less than unanimous supermajority verdicts (Jonakait 2006). Even this distinction varies from state to state, with some states allowing non-unanimous verdicts even in criminal cases, and others requiring unanimous verdicts even in civil cases. Granting such variation, juries in general are oriented to the goal of achieving the broadest possible consensus on a verdict.

Of course, this is not the only consideration informing deliberation. If it were, then jurors could simply agree to flip a coin and be done with it! The verdict should also be defensible within the distinctive framework of accountability in which jurors participate. Juries are a key component of the justice system in many democratic societies, and as such they are bound by various procedural rules and institutionalized values. While the precise mandate on juries varies in different legal systems and jurisdictions, juries are generally obliged to render their decisions by considering only such matters as (1) the facts of the case and (2) the law that applies, with the aim of achieving a just outcome. These general constraints are often particularized in the form of a concrete set of instructions provided to the jury. What actually determines a given verdict cannot be known definitively, but what is critical is that jurors conduct themselves so as to be seen as acting judiciously, without prejudice, and with due regard for factual and legal reality (Garfinkel 1967: ch. 4).

Activity structure

The overarching objective of achieving an accountably just verdict shapes the activities of jurors, although in a rather less structured way than we have seen in the forms of institutional talk examined in previous chapters. At the level of turn taking, jury deliberations do not generally adhere to a predetermined format for the ordering of contributions. There may be periods within a given deliberation when a turn-taking format is temporarily engaged, as when jurors initially "go around the table" to present their respective views of the case without interruption (Manzo 1996). But these are locally occasioned islands of formatted turn taking within a sea of more freewheeling and "conversational" speech exchange.

Deliberations also lack an overarching architecture of activity phases. There are, of course, a variety of recurrent activities in this environment, including the "going around the table" noted above, re-enacting or animating events from the case, telling narratives of personal experience (Manzo 1993), taking straw votes, and so on. But with the exception of the opening and closing phases, these component activities unfold in no particular or predetermined order.

The course of activities is, however, guided asymmetrically by the elected jury foreperson. The foreperson's role is not unlike that of a meeting chairperson or discussion facilitator (Manzo 1996), involving both the right and the responsibility to keep the discussion on track and guide it toward a resolution. Hence, it is the foreperson who most often takes the initiative in nominating certain key activities to be pursued (Tatalovich 2007), as when this foreperson (J1) suggests that they begin by going "around the table" (lines 1–8). After two other jurors assent to this suggestion (lines 10, 12), the foreman solicits the first contribution (line 13).

```
(1)  [Frontline jury: Manzo 1996: 112]
 1  J1:    If I make a suggestion? rather than- I know that
 2         juries uh um >like Mr. ( ) mentioned<, like to take a
 3         vote right off the bat and. .hh I think if we do::
 4         that we'll probly end up discussing it anyhow so
 5         let's:: just. go around the table and discuss the case?
 6         and your: .hh views? and uh after:: everybody's said
 7         their piece uh (0.5) we cacn uh. take a vote on uh
 8         what we think. if::: that's agreeable to everybody?
 9         (1.8)
10  J12:   uh huh
11         (2.5)
12  J2:    sounds good=
13  J1:    =so. ((turns and smiles to J2)) you wanna start?
14  J2:    mm okay? .hh I found the three:: points. that the
15         prosecutor. hadda prove? he proved ...
```

Similarly, later in the same deliberation, the suggestion of a formal vote with paper ballots is advanced by the foreperson.

```
(2)  [Frontline jury: 12]
 1  J1:    Why don't we:: uh tear off a little piece of paper.
 2         write down a decision one way or another think about
 3         it for a few minutes and write down whether you think
 4         he's guilty or not guilty::.
```

Even this structural feature of deliberations – the guidance of the process by the jury foreperson – is somewhat loose and variable. While forepersons are marginally more active and influential than other jurors, they do not by any means control either the process or its outcome (Tatalovich 2007). Moreover, while the existence of a foreperson is often institutionally mandated – part of the judge's instructions to the jury – the foreperson's capacity to exercise leadership is an ongoing achievement contingent on the collaboration of other jurors (see excerpt (1), lines 10, 12) (Manzo 1996). Correspondingly, this role exhibits variation both within and across deliberations. Such variability suggests that each jury develops its own somewhat distinctive "local culture" of deliberation, a development that is probably facilitated by the thoroughly private and off-the-record character of these encounters.

Practical reasoning and accountability in the pursuit of a verdict

The substance of deliberation involves a search for the broadest possible consensus on a defensible and hence *accountably just* verdict. This may entail reasoning about and articulating factual realities and legal codes, the judge's instructions, and broader ideals such as fairness, equity, and justice. It may also entail reflexive or self-referential discussion of the jury itself – its aims and purposes, and the rules and procedures it should be observing (Maynard & Manzo 1993).

Of particular sensitivity is the process of bringing initially divergent jurors into alignment with the emerging consensus (Maynard & Manzo 1993: 187–90). Since jurors are often in disagreement when the deliberation begins, some must eventually back down from their positions in order for a verdict to be achieved. The process of juror conversion poses a potential threat to the legitimacy of the verdict, insofar as converting jurors may be seen as "flip-flopping" arbitrarily, or for the sake of mere convenience, or in response to undue pressure from the majority. Accordingly, juror conversion is a locus of intense interactive work geared to preserving the manifest legitimacy of the process and its outcome.

A Case Study: Background on the *Frontline* Case

These characteristics of jury deliberation are exemplified in the *Frontline* case. Our analysis of this case is informed by the pioneering research of John Manzo and Douglas Maynard (Manzo 1993, 1994, 1996, Maynard & Manzo 1993), together with our own examination of the documentary recording and a nearly complete transcript of the two-and-a-half-hour deliberation. Because we focus on forms of practical reasoning and accountability, our analysis here (as compared with previous chapters) is conducted at a relatively coarse level of granularity.

First, some background on the case. The defendant, an ex-convict pseudonymized as "Larry Rex", was charged with violating the terms of his parole by being in possession of a gun. He had purchased the gun to fulfill the requirements of a detective school correspondence course, and the purchase came to light when he inquired about registering the gun.

In rendering a verdict, the jury was instructed by the judge to determine three points of fact: (1) whether the defendant was on parole when the alleged violation occurred, (2) whether the defendant had been in possession of a gun, and (3) whether the defendant *knew* he had been in possession of a gun.

The prosecutor argued that the state had proven its case on the three points beyond a reasonable doubt. He further argued that the jury was obliged to use these points as exclusive criteria for finding the defendant guilty as charged.

The defense attorney also admitted that the state had proven the basic points of fact, although he was more explicit in conceding the first two points than the third point. Despite these incriminating facts, he argued that the defendant was being "nailed on a technicality". He informed the jurors that they were empowered to go beyond the letter of the law, and urged them to find the defendant not guilty.

To encourage an acquittal, the defense exposed a variety of extenuating circumstances bearing on the defendant's intentions, knowledge, and capacity to grasp the ramifications of his actions. (1) The defendant had purchased the gun to fulfill the requirements of a detective school course that he hoped would enable him to secure gainful employment. (2) The police only learned about the handgun when the defendant inquired about registering it, and upon request he went home to retrieve the gun, returned to the police department, and was then arrested. (3) The defendant has borderline mental retardation and is virtually unable to read.

Accountability for Pro-Conviction versus Pro-Acquittal Jurors

Based on the initial "round table" presentation of views, two broad groups of jurors began to emerge. They differed not only in the positions they staked out, but also in the clarity of those positions and the rationales offered to support them (Maynard & Manzo 1993: 178–82).

For those initially favoring a guilty verdict (2 out of 12 at this juncture), the case was straightforward. The prosecution had proven the three points of fact – regarding the defendant's parolee status, gun possession, and knowledge of the latter – beyond a reasonable doubt. The pro-conviction jurors were clear in asserting these facts as criterial for a guilty verdict, and they were also clear in asserting their readiness to support such a verdict. Juror 1, for instance, lays out this position straightforwardly and characterizes himself as following "the letter of the law" (lines 5–6).

(3) [*Frontline* jury: Manzo 1996: 114]
```
 1   J1:     ...our instructions. were to decide >whether beyond
 2           a reasonable doubt he is guilty of this crime.<
 3           I think (.) >those three elements have been met
 4           and that yes he is guilty of this crime....
 5           ...So I think uh: (.) I have to follow? the letter
 6           of the law.
```

These jurors are also unequivocal in rejecting the extenuating circumstances – which have to do with the defendant's subjective knowledge and intentions – as out of bounds and hence beyond the scope of what the jury can properly consider. Juror 4 characterizes such considerations as "the sympathetic point of view" (line 4) and matters that are "not for us to reason over" (line 6).

(4) [*Frontline* jury Manzo 1996: 113]
```
 1   J4:     .hh I feel that the: plaintiff- the city has found
 2           him. uh. guilty >beyond a reasonable doubt< to the
 3           three points that we are (.) to discuss. .uh
 4           the sympathetic point of view would be what his
 5           intent was or what he did not intend to do and
 6           that's not (.) for us to to reason over >Ours are
 7           the three main points< which we have to >find
 8           beyond a reasonable doubt.< and I feel
 9           that we did....
```

The clarity of the pro-conviction position and its supporting rationale stands in contrast to the equivocality of the remaining jurors, who make up the majority of the jury panel (10 out of 12 at this juncture). Although reluctant to endorse a guilty verdict, these jurors generally present themselves as unsure of how they will vote. Correspondingly, while validating the extenuating circumstances as something that should be taken into account, they express uncertainty as to whether such circumstances are sufficient to justify an acquittal given the three basic incriminating facts. Juror 2 is typical of this group. He first concedes the three points of fact as proven (lines 1–5), and then alludes favorably to extenuating circumstances ("because of the record of the defendant" in lines 6–7). He concludes that he is reluctant to vote guilty (lines 8–9), but he sees the merits of both sides and remains undecided (lines 10–13).

(5)   [*Frontline* jury: Manzo 1996: 112]
```
 1  J2:    .hh I found the three:: points. that the prosecutor.
 2          hadda prove? he proved .hh that the defendant did
 3          possess a gun >the defendant knew he possessed a gun<
 4          .hh and that uh: the defendant knew he was (.) a
 5          convicted felon at the time he uh: possessed a gun.
 6          .hh however uh::. because of this case and because
 7          of uhm: (1.6) because of the:: record of the defendant
 8          uh I'd have a re- I 'd have a real tough time .h uh
 9          voting him guilty on this: a:nduh:- I haven't made
10          up my mind yet .hhh but I see both sides of- both
11          sides of uhm: both the cases BOTH of the cases as
12          they've been laid out. and uh: righ'now I haven't made
13          up my mind on uh >how I'm goin' ta vote.
```

Similarly, Juror 3 concedes the three factual points as "technically" indicating guilt (lines 1–2), and then invokes the extenuating circumstances as something that should properly be considered as well (lines 3–7), before concluding that she remains uncertain as to her final vote (lines 8–9).

(6)   [*Frontline* jury: Manzo 1996: 112]
```
 1  J3:    >Okay I feel that the defendant is< guilty. uh. on
 2          all three accusations technically. (.) but I guess
 3          I feel that we should also take into consideration
 4          the fact that. .h he do::es have a reading disability.
 5          as well as maybe some other disabilities >I'm not
 6          trying to play on your sympathies or anything but.
 7          .h it is something that I have to consider tch and
 8          right now I haven't (.) determined whether I should
 9          name the defendant guilty or innocent.
```

There is, in short, an asymmetry between the pro-conviction and pro-acquittal positions at this early phase of the deliberation. The pro-conviction position is endorsed unequivocally and is straightforwardly accountable by reference to three fact-based criteria. This type of rationale for a verdict, which excludes consideration of extenuating circumstances bearing on broader ideals of fairness or justice, may be termed a *letter-of-the-law* or *hardline approach* (Maynard & Manzo 1993). On the other hand, the pro-acquittal position is endorsed only with a great deal of tentativeness and equivocation. Moreover, while recognizing extenuating circumstances, the underlying rationale for this position is less clearly articulated and remains comparatively underdeveloped at this stage of the discussion.

The Crystallization of Rationales for Acquittal

The jury eventually comes to agree unanimously on a not-guilty verdict. The crystallization and spread of this position is intertwined with the emergence of various supporting rationales

of which two are most consequential (Maynard & Manzo 1993: 182–7). Both of these rationales arise from extenuating circumstances, but they take very different forms.

One rationale supplements fact-based criteria with a broader concern with achieving a just
outcome. This rationale, which may be termed a *justice-inclusive approach*, involves a shift
in the terms of accountability, away from relatively specific procedures for determining
guilt and toward the procedures' substantive purpose or objective. The type of argument
involved here is a recurrent element in practical reasoning about norms and rules of social
behavior. As a general principle, departures from a rule can be justified, and may even be
seen as reasonably compliant, if they achieve the purpose for which the rule was intended
(Zimmerman 1970).

Elements of this rationale appeared as early as the initial "round table" presentation of
views, although at that point it was advanced only in a somewhat vague and cautious way.
Juror 12 introduces this rationale in the form of a question, which she characterizes as a
"philosophical argument" about whether the jury is "obligated to follow the letter of the law"
(lines 2–3) or is instead "obligated to use our special level of conscience" (lines 4–5). Justice
is not yet directly invoked as an explicit goal, but it is alluded to indirectly by reference to
the correction of "an injustice that has been done to him" (lines 7–8).

(7)   [*Frontline* Jury: 4]
```
 1   J12:        ...We have a very philosophical argument on our hands.
 2                In terms of are we obligated as a jury to follow the
 3                letter of the law and find him guilty
 4                or are we obligated as a jury to use our special
 5                level of conscience uh as the defense lawyer said,
 6                otherwise it >you know< could be decided by computer,
 7                um:: and acquit him because of perhaps an injustice
 8                that as been done to him...
 9                ...So do we rise above that somehow is there a place
10                for us to then say uh even though he meets the law
11                you know we cannot in good conscience find him guilty?
```

She concludes her opening statement by posing another question, asking "do we rise above
that somehow, is there is a place for us" to go beyond the letter of the law because "we
cannot in good conscience find him guilty" (lines 9–11).

Later in the deliberation, the justice-inclusive argument is articulated more clearly and
asserted more forcefully. After one of the hardline jurors (Juror 1) characterizes the others
as "afraid of doing an injustice" and proposes that the jury's limited role is "to decide the
law, not to be the judge", Juror 6 strongly disagrees. He argues for a more expansive role,
asserting "we're here to do a justice to someone" (line 5). For the most part, this more expansive role is framed as encompassing consideration of the three fact-based criteria as well,
although at one point the justice goal is said to supersede such criteria: "I don't care <u>what</u>
the law says, <u>has</u> justice been done?" (lines 7–8).

(8)   [*Frontline* Jury: Maynard and Manzo 1993: 183]
```
 1   J6:        ...I think we have more capabilities than to say
 2                one two three, these are met on a very simple level,
 3                cut and dried guilty. I don't think that we as jurors,
 4                that is necessarily our role. We are here to do more
```

```
5              than that....we're here to do a justice to someone
6              a:nd my point is the way I'm trying to decide in my
7              own mind, has justice been done here. I don't care
8              what the law says, has justice been done?
```

Still later, yet another juror (Juror 5) asserts the validity of a "larger frame" that encompasses substantive justice considerations.

```
(9)  [Frontline Jury: 14]
 1  J5:       ...I'm having a lot of trouble with that larger frame
 2             too. I'm starting to ask some of these bigger questions
 3             about where is justice, who is being served even why
 4             was this case brought.
```

Certain rhetorical devices are mobilized in support of this more expansive mode of reasoning, most notably the use of a *computer metaphor* to characterize and undermine the hardline approach. For instance, in example (7) above, Juror 12 proposes that such an approach "could be decided by computer" (line 6). It is partly on this basis that she suggests that the jury "rise above that somehow" and use its "special level of conscience" to correct an injustice. Some time later, Juror 6 uses the same metaphor (arrowed), albeit more emphatically, to similar ends.

```
(10)  [Frontline Jury: 7]
 1  J6:    →    ...One other comment I am not a computer, and I
 2             will not accept everything that I'm told or just
 3             because I'm told that it's true. I can't do that
 4             as a thinking breathing human being. .hh And so I'm
 5             I'm on- other things come into play here for me.
 6             I'll tell ya that just to jell me that- just to tell
 7             me that he's been convicted on these three counts,
 8             that's obvious. We're not arguing that we all know
 9             that. Why y- there's more to it than just that
10             there has to be. There has to be more of a purpose
11        →    than just to say yes he is. Bring in the computer....
```

The second rationale for acquittal is very different in that it operates *within* the conceptual space of the hardline approach, rather than as a supplement or alternative to it. This may be termed a *knowledge-focused rationale*, for it uses extenuating circumstances to cast doubt on whether the fact-based criteria, in particular the criterion referencing the defendant's knowledge (*he knew he possessed a gun*), had indeed been proven. One of the earliest steps in this direction was taken by Juror 5, who presents himself as wanting "to think by the facts" and "be a good juror like everyone else" (lines 1–2) before proceeding to problematize the defendant's subjective knowledge of the gun possession (lines 3–6).

```
(11)  [Frontline Jury: 6]
 1  J5:       I wanna try ta think by the facts too 'n I'd like to
 2             be a good juror like everyone else. Um .hh the law as
 3             I recall it says ((clears throat)) you have you have
 4             to kno:w that you have a gun. Now you and I listen to
```

```
5            that sentence and we go right over that word know.
6            Stop....
7            ((discusses defendant's limited intelligence))
```

He then goes on (in talk not shown) to elaborate extensively on the defendant's low IQ and limited capacity for understanding. Some time later, Juror 12 raises similar issues and frames them as relevant to those who "feel we need to follow the letter of the law" (lines 1–2).

```
(12)  [Frontline jury: 8]
  1  J12:        ...I wonder if we could find some room in the law
  2               for those of us who feel we need to follow the letter
  3               of the law that perhaps he didn't in the full sense
  4               of the word know he was a felon and didn't in the
  5               full sense of the word know that he possessed a
  6               firearm. He did show a lot of confusion on that
  7               witness stand....
```

Perhaps, she suggests, the defendant "didn't in the full sense of the word know that he possessed a firearm" (lines 4–6).

At first, this knowledge-focused rationale is supported by reference to his low intelligence level (e.g., example 11, line 7) and confusion on the witness stand (e.g., example 12, lines 6–7). Later on, an additional and perhaps more creative supporting element is introduced. Because the defendant purchased the gun to fulfill the requirements of a detective-school correspondence course, it is proposed that he was merely following instructions and understood the purchased item as a course requirement and a status symbol more than a gun per se. Juror 5 begins to develop this line of argument by situating the gun purchase within a larger course of action that began with the defendant's desire to better himself (lines 2–6), his encounter with the magazine advertising the detective school (lines 1, 6–7), and his realization that one of the course requirements is to have a gun (lines 9–11).

```
(13)  [Frontline Jury: 19–20]
  1  J5:         The origin of this was the fatal magazine article and
  2               I I can see:: this man who is: in in some part of his
  3               mind he's thinking I wanna be useful. I wanna be
  4               productive I wanna have a social role I wanna be a
  5               contributing person I wanna do the right thing .hh
  6               dammit I wanna BE somebody. And all of a sudden
  7               detective and that becomes something that, I am a
  8               detective I can be somebody. Okay so what does he do.
  9               He sets out in a, what are the conditions or
 10               qualifications or requirements for becoming a
 11               detective, lo and behold one of 'em is having a gun.
 12               So in this particular case gun means qualification
 13               for becoming a detective...
```

Juror 5 concludes that for the defendant "gun means qualification for becoming a detective" (lines 12–13). Building on this line of reasoning, Juror 5 later points out that the defendant chose a stylish antique model, suggesting that he was "purchasing a visual image, not what you and I are gonna do with gun" (lines 10–11).

(14) [*Frontline* Jury: 21–2]

```
 1  J5:   ...what Larry was buy:ing was: an outline or
 2         you know a visual image because he goes for a the
 3         antique gun. Why because it looks cool. This
 4         thing looks neat. Hey it's you know it's it's like
 5         [a
 6  J9:    [It's sharp=
 7  J5:    =Sorry?
 8  J9:    SHARP.
 9  J5:    He said it was sharp....It corroborates the
10         notion that he's he's purchasing a visual image,
11         not what you and I are gonna do with gun.
```

Certain rhetorical devices are mobilized in support of the knowledge-focused rationale, most notably the use of narratives designed to animate the defendant's subjective point of view. In example (13) above, for instance, the juror recounts the defendant's course of action in the form of a present-tense narrative told mostly in the first person, with the juror taking the role of the defendant: "He's thinking, I wanna be useful. I wanna be productive, I wanna have a social role . . . Dammit I wanna <u>be</u> somebody." (lines 3–6). He thereby invites his fellow jurors to put themselves into the defendant's shoes, and to contextualize the gun purchase and the meaning of the gun itself in light of the defendant's practical purposes and good intentions.

The second rationale for acquittal thus comes to combine a variety of contextual details – the defendant's limited intelligence, aspirations, prior course of action prompted by a magazine advertisement, specific gun purchased, etc. – in support of the idea that from his point of view the "gun" was in essence a course requirement and a status symbol rather than a firearm. This knowledge-focused rationale casts doubt on a core criterion for conviction, suggesting that "he did not in the full sense of the word *know*" that he possessed a firearm.

Converting Jurors and Achieving an Accountable "Not Guilty" Verdict

Between the justice-inclusive and knowledge-focused rationales for acquittal, the latter proved to be of greater utility in bringing opposing jurors into alignment with the majority. Jurors' "true" motives for changing their positions are not definitively knowable, but it is noteworthy that both of the initially pro-conviction jurors (Jurors 1 and 4) portrayed themselves as persuaded by the knowledge-focused argument. This is understandable, given that (as noted earlier) this argument operates *within* the conceptual space of the hardline approach. This rationale thus provided jurors with a face-saving means of accounting for the reversal. They could present themselves as backing down from their *conclusion* while holding fast to the same *method of reasoning* they had been using all along.

But apart from the specific rationale involved, considerable effort is expended to portray both jurors as having been rationally persuaded rather than unduly pressured into changing their verdicts.

Juror 1's conversion is relatively straightforward. After a ballot vote reveals that the pro-acquittal majority increased from 10 to 11, Juror 1 steps forward to offer a lengthy explanation for what is portrayed as a considered change of heart in light of the new knowledge-based arguments. It particular, he claims to have been persuaded by the idea that, for the defendant, the gun was understood as "a piece of this course" (lines 6–7), and that he was "simply following instructions" (line 9).

```
(15)  [Frontline Jury: Maynard and Manzo 1993: 186]
  1   J1:    I now I've changed my mind. I uh I have somethin' to
  2          say and an' I kinda uhm, what you said 'n, 'n my few
  3          comments I made and I- it's started to make me think.
  4          And uh I believe that what you said, y'know uh taking
  5          into account his mental ability and everything...
  6          It says that he had ta know that he possessed a gun.
  7          He mighta knew he possessed a piece of this course.
  8          Uh and an' when you brought that up it made me think.
  9          And maybe he just was simply following instructions,
 10          had no uh relationship like you or I or anybody else
 11          does in this room, between a gun and bang bang....
```

Moreover, as he winds down his account, Juror 1 distinguishes his reasoning from the justice-inclusive argument, asserting that his decision is motivated not by the goal of achieving justice but because of reasonable doubt on a key question of fact.

```
(16)  [Frontline Jury: Maynard and Manzo 1993: 186]
  1   J1:    ...I'm not sure acquitting him is doing him a justice,
  2          uh I I I personally don't think it is, but I can see your
  3          point and I can see a reason for somewhat of a doubt,
  4          however minor it may be.
```

Thus, while backing down from his belief in the defendant's guilt, he presents himself as faithful to his original mode of reasoning about the case.

For Juror 4, in contrast, the conversion process is lengthy and contentious. This juror holds to his pro-conviction position much longer. When he finally offers to change his vote, he initially presents this as an expedient move (lines 1–3) that was pressured by the majority (lines 4–6), and asserts with manifest emotion that "I will never feel right about it" (line 4).

```
(17)  [Frontline Jury: 32]
  1   J4:    ...I will not hold out ta hold up eleven people that
  2          are very strong in their feelings. I would I will change
  3          and vote along with you to give a unanimous vote but
  4          I will never. feel right about it. I feel it was uh
  5          pushed by the uh jury on uh psychological and uh other
  6          feelings that I do not agree with....
```

Juror 4 thus offers to join in a unanimous verdict, but in a way that threatens the essential legitimacy of that verdict.

This move triggers extensive remedial work aimed at getting Juror 4 to articulate a legitimate rationale for his reversal (Maynard & Manzo 1993: 187–9). When one juror proposes that they "vote right now" to secure a unanimous verdict (lines 1, 3), several others promptly reject the proposal (lines 2, 4, 5), and Juror 5 praises Juror 4's dedication to "getting it right" and to "the integrity of the judicial process" (lines 9–13).

```
(18)  [Frontline Jury: 32-3]
 1  J9:    (        ) we could vote right now.
 2  J5:    No?
 3  J9:    We could vote right [now]
 4  J5:                        [no ]
 5  J10:   No. We're not ready yet. Ye: I don't [I don't think
 6  J9:                                         [Oh y'all tryin'
 7          to make 'im feel better okay fine I'll wait
 8          [(I'll wait right here
 9  J5:    [(Now wait a minute this is important to him.) because uh::
10          I have an enormous amount of respect for: uh y::our sense
11          of the importance of the law, your sense of the importance
12          of getting it right, and your dedication to the integrity
13          of the judicial process....
```

Then in an effort to persuade Juror 4 to affirmatively embrace a not guilty verdict, various jurors step forward to reconstruct their own reasoning processes, "testifying" (in data not shown; see Maynard & Manzo 1993) as to how they arrived at such a verdict. Juror 4 remains unmoved, however. And when he is asked whether he still believes that the defendant *knew* he possessed a gun, he reaffirms his commitment to that key factual criterion. The deliberation thus appears to have reached an impasse.

But then Juror 2 hits upon an argument that successfully breaks the impasse. He stretches and expands the knowledge consideration to encompass *two* criterial points of fact – not only the gun possession, but also the defendant's parolee status – while also problematizing the defendant's capacity to grasp the legal ramifications that follow from understanding "those two things at the same time" (lines 6–9). Although all of this is packaged in the form of a question ("Do you think he was able . . ."), this question is far from neutral (cf. chapter 10); it advances a knowledge-based theory of innocence that J4 is invited to accept.

```
(19)  [Frontline Jury: 35]
 1  J2:    ...Do you think that he was, that he was able to
 2          understand, that he was a keep these two, that he was
 3          able to keep these two thoughts 'n link 'em together
 4          at the same time when he bought the firearm, that he
 5          was a convicted felon, and that he was not supposed
 6          to own a firearm, Do you think he was able, do you
 7          think he had the mental capacity .h to: understand
 8          the ramifications of that, and to hold those and to
 9          understand those two things at the same time?
10  J4:    I think he knows that he was a felon, an I think he
11          knew that he bought the firearm. The possibility of
12          the two together would be the weakest point for me.
13  J2:    Okay, an I think- and I think that is for everyone-
14          is uh one of basic problems everyone's having.
```

In response, Juror 4 reaffirms his belief that the defendant knew both of these separate facts, but he also concedes that "the two together would be the weakest point for me" (lines 10–12).

By this argument, Juror 4 provides for the accountability of a reversal while conceding even less ground than did Juror 1. He retains his commitment to a hardline approach based on three factual criteria, as well as to his belief that the facts have each been proven. It is only in the conjunction of these facts as simultaneously knowable by the defendant – his capacity to grasp the gun purchase *in light of* his parolee status – that he claims to have found a basis for doubt. Shortly after this exchange, the final vote is taken yielding a unanimous verdict of not guilty.

In a fitting coda, Juror 4's singular basis for doubt is subsequently treated as if it were shared by all jurors on the panel (lines 13–14). This move does more than simply minimize cleavages and assuage hard feelings. Just as prior remarks provide for the legitimacy of each juror's individual decision, this remark retrospectively constructs a unified basis and a "legitimate history" (Garfinkel 1967: 114) for the collective verdict.

Conclusion

There is a striking resemblance between the modes of reasoning exhibited by the jurors in the *Frontline* case, and the well-known distinction between formal and substantive justice found in philosophical and social scientific discussions from Aristotle to Max Weber, as well as Weber's more general discussion of the ideal-typical modes of rationality governing social action. Those jurors who took a hardline approach (including its knowledge-focused variant) portrayed themselves as adhering to a formally rational process governed by established procedural rules for deciding guilt or innocence. Correspondingly, those who took a justice-inclusive approach portrayed themselves as engaging in a substantively rational process geared to achieving an outcome consistent with justice as an ultimate value. It is clear that formal and substantive justice and rationality are not merely theoretical concepts employed by professional analysts; they are endogenous "vocabularies of motive" (Mills 1940) that jurors themselves use to articulate their reasons for deciding a case. Correspondingly, the deployment of this vocabulary over the course of a deliberation is integral to achieving an accountably proper and publicly defensible verdict.

Although both vocabularies were employed, they were not equally weighted. Consistently with Weber's historical argument, the vocabulary of formal justice was privileged in the judge's instructions to the jury, which outlined the three fact-based criteria that jurors were to use. (The defense attorney had asked the judge to inform the jury that they also had the power to nullify the law and follow their conscience, but the judge rejected that request.) Correspondingly, in a variety of ways the formal justice vocabulary was also privileged within the deliberation process itself. (1) The formal vocabulary of the hardline approach was clearly articulated and forcefully expressed from the beginning of the deliberation; the substantive vocabulary of the justice-inclusive approach was articulated more cautiously and took time to develop. (2) The formal vocabulary was used both by jurors favoring conviction and those favoring acquittal; the substantive vocabulary was used only by jurors favoring acquittal, and only by a subset of those jurors. (3) The formal vocabulary was apt to be the exclusive rationale offered by those jurors taking a hardline approach; the substantive vocabulary was apt to be used in tandem with the formal vocabulary by those jurors taking a justice-inclusive approach.

Finally, this case reveals the interplay of agency and constraint in courtroom discourse at the critical final stage of the trial process. Jurors are highly resourceful and at times creative in invoking, contextualizing, and formulating aspects of the legal framework that they are duty-bound to uphold. Viewed from within the domain of interaction, the entire conceptual armature of the justice system – factual realities, legal codes, the judge's instructions, the justice ideal, and so on – may be understood as an elaborate discursive toolkit. It furnishes an array of resources that jurors use to pursue courses of action, rather than facts and rules that they rigidly follow (cf. Holstein 1983). This way of thinking casts jurors as knowledgeable agents in the deliberation process, but it also suggests that they exercise agency within identifiable limits. They remain closely attentive to the parameters of the legal system, and they act in ways that will be accountable in terms that are integral to that system and consistent with its governing procedures and ideals.

For Further Reading

While research on simulated or mock juries is commonplace, studies of actual jury deliberations are few and far between. The pioneering observational research was conducted by John Manzo and Douglas Maynard. Using data from the *Frontline* documentary case plus an additional civil case, Manzo has examined various key aspects of the deliberation process, including turn taking and position taking during the opening phase (Manzo 1996), and jurors' use of practical reasoning (Manzo 1994) and personal experience (1993) in the course of deliberation. In a collaborative paper focusing on the overall trajectory of the *Frontline* case, Maynard and Manzo (1993) draw out the larger theoretical implications for the sociology of justice. The PBS *Frontline* documentary, entitled "Inside the Jury Room", was produced by Alan M. Levin and Stephen J. Hertzberg and originally aired on April 8, 1986.

More recent observational research, while not conversation analytic in approach, is nonetheless revealing of the deliberation process. A research team led by attorney Shari Diamond has recorded 50 civil court deliberations in the state of Arizona. Since Arizona was the first state in the US to permit jurors to discuss evidence among themselves during breaks in the trial, one of the first papers to emerge from the project (Diamond et al. 2003) focuses on the impact of such discussions on subsequent deliberation. Diamond, Rose, and Murphy (2006) examine the impact of a non-unanimous verdict rule – Arizona requires only a 6/8 majority in civil trials – on the deliberation process and the treatment of holdout jurors. Diamond and Rose (2005) examine the quality of deliberation in complex cases. Tatalovich (2007) provides a useful summary of the Arizona jury project and its findings.

14

Informal Modes of Dispute Resolution

The formal trial by jury has a special cultural significance as a symbol for the administration of justice in many contemporary societies, but as a method of dispute resolution it is far from typical. The vast majority of conflicts and disputes are resolved through a variety of less formal but nonetheless institutionalized processes. Criminal cases are often resolved through plea-bargaining negotiations between attorneys for the accused and the state. Civil disputes are often resolved without the aid of attorneys at all, as in small claims court or in mediation sessions involving the disputants themselves.

Across all of these institutionalized forms, talk-in-interaction remains the primary medium through which disputes are (or are not) effectively brought to a resolution. And as with formal trials, the specific practices implicated in this process can materially affect the developing trajectory of disputes as well as the form of their resolution.

Background on Dispute Resolution Proceedings

Informal modes of dispute resolution are many and varied, but they share certain common features that distinguish them from trials. The following general observations are derived from studies of plea bargaining (Maynard 1984), small claims court (Atkinson 1992), and mediation (Garcia 1991).

Less constrained forms of turn taking

Unlike trial examinations, where turn taking is tightly constrained to relatively simple questions and unelaborated answers (see chapter 12), other modes of dispute resolution are in varying degrees less constrained. The British small claims court studied by Atkinson (1992) is conducted largely through questions and answers, but the boundaries of permissible conduct are more fuzzy and permeable than in formal trials. Disputants may extend their responses beyond the agenda set by the previous question without fear of sanction, and judges may acknowledge such talk (e.g. *yes, okay*) prior to asking the next question. In the mediation sessions studied by Garcia (1991), turn-taking constraints vary significantly depending on the phase of the session (see below), with an initial phase of uninterrupted story telling following by a discussion phase led by the mediator's questions. Even more freewheeling and essentially "conversational" turn-taking practices characterize the plea-bargaining sessions examined by Maynard (1984).

Phases of activity

Apart from relatively brief opening and closing phases, both plea-bargaining and mediation sessions are primarily organized around two main phases of activity geared to distinct tasks. The first main phase, which may be termed *story telling*, is officially aimed at establishing the basic facts of the case and the divergent interpretations of those facts by parties on each side. The second main phase, *negotiation*, is geared toward bringing the sides together and achieving consensus on a resolution. Although the first phase may be dispensed with in plea bargaining, yielding a direct move into negotiation that constitutes the case as relatively "routine" (Maynard 1984: 104–7), both phases are recurrent and commonplace. Thus, unlike jury trials where these tasks are situationally segregated and discharged by different participants (attorneys elicit divergent accounts from witnesses, whereas juries subsequently decide on an outcome), the essence of plea bargaining and mediation is that both of these tasks are discharged primarily by the disputants or their agents, often within a single session.

Participant roles

The participants fall into two basic categories: (1) the disputants, who may be either the principals (as is typical in small claims court and in mediation) or their agents (as with attorneys in plea bargaining), and (2) a formally neutral third party, who may be either an arbitrator responsible for fashioning a resolution (e.g., the judge in small claims court), or a facilitator who may offer varying levels of assistance to the disputants as they work toward a resolution for themselves (e.g., the judge in plea bargaining; the mediator in mediation sessions). In plea bargaining, the presence of a third party/judge is optional.

While the third party is superficially similar to the judge in a jury trial, this party can play a rather more substantive role here. The trial judge draws on legal expertise to formulate the procedural ground rules and adjudicate procedural disputes. But in other dispute resolution proceedings, the third party's influence can range from actually determining the outcome (e.g., small claims court) to aiding the disputants as they move toward a resolution (e.g., plea bargaining, mediation). For this reason, the role of mediators, arbitrators, and judges in these contexts has been both controversial and of considerable analytic interest. Notwithstanding a professional ethos emphasizing impartiality and – especially in the case of mediation – the empowerment of disputants in the resolution of their own conflicts, both of these characteristics have been subject to critical scrutiny (e.g., Greatbatch & Dingwall 1989, Garcia 1995, 2000, Jacobs 2002, Lee 2005, Heisterkamp 2006).

The Disputants: Description and Story
Telling as Implicit Negotiation

With that as background, we focus on plea bargaining and mediation for the remainder of this chapter, beginning with the first main phase of story telling. Although explicit negotiation and bargaining over outcomes does not occur until the next phase, this objective thoroughly infuses the story-telling phase as well. Descriptions of what happened, and who was involved, are by no means limited by the objective facts of the situation. The disputants retain considerable agency (1) to select which features of the scene to describe, and (2) to formulate those features in particular ways. Both of these decisions are rendered with an eye toward subsequent negotiations, and such descriptions are heard and understood for their negotiational import (Maynard 1984: 119–38). They may even be produced and understood in light of how the story will hypothetically play before a jury, should the current effort at dispute resolution break down (Maynard 1984: 69–75).

To illustrate this general phenomenon – the implicit negotiations that infuse ostensibly "descriptive" story telling – consider plea-bargaining sessions and in particular the case of Frank Bryan, a man charged with disorderly conduct and resisting arrest after the police were called to his house to intervene in a domestic dispute. Following his arrest, the prosecuting and defense attorneys meet with the judge to discuss the case and see if they can agree on a settlement that would avert the need for a trial.[1]

Formulating persons

Implicit negotiation permeates the discussion of this case from the very beginning. The judge, consistent with his role as facilitator, opens the discussion (at line 1) first by marking this as one in a series of cases ("And now that brings us to"), and then by referencing the particular case via the defendant's name ("Frank Bryan"). He subsequently attempts to put a face to the name by asking if he is "the poor chap sitting out there all by himself" (line 3). (In the ensuing transcripts, Jdg=judge, Pro=prosecuting attorney, and Def=defense attorney.)

```
(1)   [Plea Bargaining: Frank Bryan case (Maynard 1984)]
 1  Jdg:    A:n now that brings us to Frank Bryan.
 2  ( ):    ˙hhh[h hhhh
 3  Jdg:       [Is he the poor chap sitting out there all by h[imself,
 4  Def:                                                      [Ye:ah
 5          he's the sweet man with the nice smile, (0.5) a:nd this is
 6          a six forty seven ef ((disorderly conduct)) an' a one forty
 7          eight ((resisting arrest)).
```

The defense attorney confirms that this is indeed Mr. Bryan (lines 4–5), although he does so in a way that is considerably more elaborate than mere confirmation would require. His initial "yeah" would have been sufficient for confirmation, but he continues without pause to append a person description that modulates the previous one embedded the judge's question: "he's the sweet man with the nice smile." The tactical import of this descriptive formulation is striking. Not only does it cast the defendant in a decidedly positive light, but it specifically targets his good-natured disposition and moral character. The defense attorney thus exploits this brief confirmatory action, an action that would otherwise have been wholly extraneous to the ensuing discussion, to begin to portray his client in terms that are distinctly incongruous with the official charges (disorderly conduct, resisting arrest). And he manages to work this in at the very first opportunity, right after the judge has identified the case and before the discussion itself has officially begun.

The tactical import of this initial description (as well as a similarly supportive version offered later in the defense's story; see example (5) below), is registered by the prosecuting attorney. Although he does not counter either version then and there, some time later he notes that the defendant has a prior conviction for the very same two charges (lines 1–3). The similarity of the prior arrest to the current one is highlighted by the prosecutor ("interestingly enough") just before the parallel charges are delivered, suggesting a pattern of improper behavior with decidedly negative characterological implications. That this was indeed intended to undermine the defense attorney's earlier favorable portrayal becomes apparent when, following the defense's objection to this new detail (lines 4–5), the prosecutor justifies it by unpacking its implications: "it's not this happy go lucky chap's first encounter with" the police (lines 6–8).

```
(2)  [Plea Bargaining: Frank Bryan case (Maynard 1984)]
  1  Pro:   He has ub a: one prior. (0.3) conviction in this jurisdiction
  2         with thee uhm (0.8) sheriff's office, of of interestingly
  3         enough. o:f striking a public officer and of disturbing peace.
  4  Def:   Will you knock it off. ((disgusted tone)) (0.5) You wanna make
  5         a federal case out of this¿
  6  Pro:   N:o, [I I just] think [that that i]t's it's not uh this uh=
  7  Def:        [ 'h h h ]        [ h  h  m   ]
  8  Pro:   =happy go lucky chap's uh first (1.0) encounter with uh um (1.8)
  9  Def:   [Statistic]ly if ya got black skin:. you ar (0.2) you ar (.)=
 10  Pro:   [(         )]
 11  Def:   =hhighly likely to contact the police. I think
 12         uh:substantially more likely than if you're white.
 13         Now come on.<Whadda want from 'im.
 14         (0.6)
 15  Def:   He's got a prior.
 16         (1.8)
 17  Jdg:   Well we know he spent ten ho:urs...
```

The defense attorney then moves to shore up his client's moral character by reframing the pattern of arrests as a product of racial bias by the police (lines 9–12). To this end, he formulates a general statistical regularity, referring in the process not to *police arrests* but to the more bland and innocuous *police contacts*. All of this serves, in effect, to normalize such contacts/arrests for anyone who (like his client) happens to have "black skin".

The effort at normalization continues when the defense attorney offers, as the upshot of the statistical generalization, the hearably dismissive "Now come on. What do you want from him? He's got a prior" (lines 13–15). The final assertion ("He's got a prior") draws on the same language that the prosecutor had originally used to introduce the matter of the prior conviction (cf. line 1), while also altering that language in a way that works to detoxify it. Unlike the prosecutor's elaborated and case-specific version (which indicates both the location of the prior conviction and the specific charges), the defense's version is noteworthy for its brief, entirely generic, and professionally idiomatic character ("He's got a prior"). Descriptive formulations couched in nonspecific terms can, at least in principle, refer to a wide range of cases, and when rendered in idiomatic shorthand they may evoke that broader applicability. In the present context, offered as the case-specific upshot of a statistical generalization, the formulation refers to the specific case at hand while simultaneously suggesting a penumbra of similar cases (i.e., all the individuals who've "got a prior"). In so doing, it helps to render the pattern of arrests being referred to as something run-of-the-mill and routine.

Formulating events

Just as personal attributes are selected and formulated with an eye toward their negotiational import, so are attributes and features of events. Consider how the defense attorney begins his account of the events that led to his client's arrest.

```
(3)   [Plea Bargaining: Frank Bryan case (Maynard 1984)]
  1  Jdg:     Now on Frank Bryan?
  2           (2.0)
  3  Def:     ·hh ((lips parting)) Did he actually strike an officer¿
  4           (2.0)
  5  Pro:     Hmm:,
  6           (1.0)
  7  Def:     ·hh See this tu- i- he's comes he's drunk. and he comes home
  8           to his own house at wh-whe- where e'd have a fight with 'is
  9           family,...
```

Following the judge's prompt (line 1), the defense does not immediately launch into his chronological story of what happened; the story is deferred until line 7. He begins instead with a question that jumps forward in time to a later detail contained in the police report (line 3). The wording of this question, by virtue of the negative polarity item "actually", invites a *no*-type answer (see chapter 10), and thus expresses a skeptical stance toward the detail being referred to in the question ("strike an officer"). This happens to be a key detail, one that is central to the more serious of the two charges, resisting arrest. By raising this non-chronological and hearably "skeptical" question, the defense attorney has managed to cast a bit of doubt on a central element of the case against his client before the chronological story telling has even begun. Perhaps not surprisingly, the prosecutor provides an equivocal neither-yes-nor-no response without elaboration (line 5), thereby aligning neither with nor against the skeptical viewpoint advanced by the question.

As for the subsequent story itself, it too is thoroughly infused with implicit negotiation. Consider the first part of the story (below), where the defense attorney begins recounting what transpired when his client came home drunk and got into a fight with his family. Many elements of this initial account are designedly exculpatory, but here we focus on a remark that seems to cast doubt on the reality of a fight having occurred at all (lines 4–5: "*apparently* having such a fight", emphasis added). In addition to conveying skepticism, this formulation is introduced by means of self-repair, so that it also aborts and replaces a prior formulation-in-progress (lines 3–4, "he's . . . in his own front yard with his . . .") that would have placed the defendant in close proximity to other family members with whom he is fighting.

```
(4)  [Plea Bargaining: Frank Bryan case (Maynard 1984)]
 1  Def:   'hh See this tu- i- he's comes he's drunk. and he comes
 2         home to his own house at wh-whe- where e'd have a fight
 3         with 'is family, 'hhh an' he's out in front of 'is in
 4         'is own front yard with 'is (0.2) 'parently: havin' such
 5         a fight er[: least]
 6  Pro:            [His mu-] his mother having called the police.
 7  Def:   M(h)oth(h)er h(h)aving c(h)alled thu(h) c(h)ops, 'hhh
 8         i- it's a fa:mily thing....
```

This is what prompts the prosecutor, who had been silent throughout the unfolding story, to interject and buttress the fight's reality (line 6). He does so by pointing out its real consequence: the defendant's mother called the police, and is by implication an eyewitness to the fight that motivated her to call. But while this observation is substantively competitive with the defense's prior remark, it is framed as if it were cooperative. Notice that the prosecutor avoids any turn-initial marker of disagreement or disalignment (e.g., *well*, *but*), and he packages his observation within a grammatically incomplete unit of talk (specifically, a dependent clause). This renders the observation, not as a disagreement or challenge, but as an increment to the defense attorney's developing story. This is a rather subversive maneuver. Even as the prosecutor acts to undermine an element of the defense's story, he presents himself as a collaborative co-teller of that story.

The prosecutor's implicitly oppositional intervention is responded to in kind. The defense attorney confirms the prosecutor's increment to his story (line 7), although he does so in a way that detoxifies it and substantially undermines its force. Rather than affirming with an agreement token (e.g., *yeah*, *right*), he confirms it by repeating it, thus taking ownership of it (Heritage & Raymond 2005). The repeat, however, has two consequential modifications: (1) the lexical choice of "police" is replaced with the more informal "cops", and (2) laughter is introduced throughout. Both the informal register and the interspersed laughter have the effect of downgrading the gravity or seriousness of the observation at hand (cf. Jefferson 1984). So here again, an exchange regarding a specific factual detail, an exchange that is on the surface non-argumentative, is suffused with tacit negotiation and jockeying for advantage.

Combining forces

A critical point in the story is the arrival of the police and the defendant's response, the latter being the central basis for the charge of resisting arrest (lines 5–9 below). At this consequential juncture, the defense attorney mobilizes a variety of person-descriptive and event-descriptive resources that portray his client's behavior in the most favorable light that the police record will allow.

```
(5)  [Plea Bargaining: Frank Bryan case (Maynard 1984)]
 1  Def:   M(h)oth(h)er h(h)aving c(h)alled thu(h) c(h)ops, 'hhh i-
 2         it's a fa:mily thing.<He's screamin' an' an' ish then
 3         sayin' fuck. an' all that kinda stuff....
 4         ((side sequence omitted))
 5         And he's drunk. And this is I mean the same i- a very
```

```
6          happy go lucky good natured guy, as you can tell for
7          sitteen out in the courtroom, 'hh £an' when the °police    -
8          come onto his own home, his ca(h)stle (h)he dec(h)ides
9          (h)he ai(h)n't go(h)in'° w(h)ithout makin' some trouble.
```

First, just before recounting the police arrival, he steps back from the chronological narrative of events to *re-describe his client's good moral character* (lines 5–7). That is, he halts the action-driven progression of the story to comment on his client's drunken state as transitory and out of character with his essential nature, that of a "happy go lucky good natured guy". (The self-repair in line 5 ("the same i-"), which operates on and in effect deletes "the same [guy]", may be in the service of this characterological portrayal.) This portrayal harkens back to the defense's initial description of his client's sweet disposition (example (1) above), which is now re-invoked in somewhat different terms at a critical juncture in the narrative.

When the defense then resumes the chronological narrative and recounts the arrival of the police ("and when the police come onto his own home, his castle", lines 7–8), he does so specifically *from the vantage point of his client*. His situated, perspectival language ("his own home, his castle") portrays what the arrival ostensibly looked and felt like to his client at the time. Furthermore, the choice of the phrase "his castle" evokes the old adage *a man's home is his castle*, and the associated legal concept known as the *Castle Doctrine* which holds that one's place of residence is a special arena in which one enjoys certain legal protections and immunities for the exercise of self-defense (Delaney 2005; see also Maynard 1984: 50–1). The defense attorney has thus chosen a phrase that, in both general parlance and specialized legal discourse, provides an implicit justification for his client's subsequent behavior.

Finally, as the defense then describes his client's decision to be less than cooperative with the police ("he decides he ain't goin' without makin' some trouble", lines 8–9) *he intersperses laughter throughout*. (The laughter actually begins a bit earlier, on the key phrase "his castle", and indeed the entire sentence describing the police arrival is delivered with an escalating jocular tone that erupts into hearable laughter at this point.) Thus, as in example (4) above, laughter is localized within the description of an event that stands out for its incriminating character. And here again, such artfully placed laughter serves to downgrade the gravity or seriousness of the event thus reported. As a fitting capstone to this implicitly but pervasively exculpatory component of the story, the specific formulation chosen to characterize his client's problematic behavior ("makin' some trouble") is euphemistic, informal, and light-hearted.

The "Neutral" Third Party: Facilitation in Action

We turn now to examine the role of the third party in mediation and plea-bargaining contexts, who may assist the disputants as they work toward a resolution of their conflict. These third parties are not precisely comparable – as noted earlier, the judge's presence and involvement in plea bargaining are optional, while mediators are essential to mediation – but when they are present their contributions nonetheless have common features. Both professional mediators and judges in plea bargaining are obligated by their professional role to remain impartial. Accordingly, they tend to avoid overtly advocating for specific compromises or solutions, and generally restrict themselves to a range of non-assertive and hence formally neutral actions: opening the discussion, soliciting stories from the disputants, summarizing their expressed views, and asking questions (Garcia 1991, Jacobs 2002, Lee 2005, Heisterkamp 2006; see also Atkinson 1992).[2] The avoidance of overt advocacy is especially critical given the culture of mediation and the emphasis (noted earlier) on empowering disputants to resolve conflicts for themselves. Given this constraint, how then do judges and mediators manage to facilitate compromise and dispute resolution?

Passive facilitation

To some extent facilitation results not from anything that mediators or judges actively do, but from the unique position that they occupy within these triadic interactions. As Garcia (1991) has demonstrated for the case of mediation, specialized turn-taking arrangements place the disputants in the position of responding to the mediator's initiating actions (e.g., answering questions, responding to story invitations), so they generally address their remarks to the mediator rather than to other disputants. For instance, here one disputant is building toward accusing the other of vandalizing her car. Not only is her initial story (lines 1–6) already known to the disputants and hence plainly intended for the mediator, but as she articulates the accusation itself (lines 10–13) she is gazing toward the mediator and refers to the target of her accusation in the third person ("Jane", line 13). (Com=complainant; Res=respondent; Med=mediator)

```
(6)  [Garcia 1991: 828–9]
  1  Com:      My car was vandali:zed!, hh (0.3) Early in the
  2             mo::rning, (.) I came ba:ck I was away (0.2) for the
  3             night (.) I came back, and there was paint:, (0.6) on
  4             the interior? (0.7) uh latex paint, (1.5) garbag:e.
  5             (0.8) powdered milk. (0.4) I've got pictures of that=
  6             if- (0.3) you'd like to see it.
  7             (0.4)
  8  Med:      um=hmh.
  9             (0.2)
 10  Com:      What that looked like. (2.1) A:::nd: the only
 11             conceivable person: (0.3) that=it=could=do:: (0.4)
 12             that would be responsible whether she did=it=or not
 13      →     herse:lf, (.) would be Jane!,...
 14  Res:      ((Shakes head as her name is mentioned, but does not
 15             speak or gaze at complainant.))
```

Beyond the specific environment of accusations, disputants generally address their remarks to the mediator rather than to each other, so that third-person references to co-disputants are commonplace.

```
(7)  [Garcia 1991: 829]
  1  Com:      The-first: (0.3) kno:wledge I had of
  2      →     her dislike, uh::m (0.2) .h uhm aggravation with me,
  3      →     one time she:: (0.9) I was co:ming: (0.2) from the car,
  4             with my child who=was about two at the ti:me? (0.6)
  5      →     And her dau:ghter came up to me and said uh:m (0.8)
```

```
6              get her out of the wa:y or something and
7         →    she said. (1.1) .h you=know?, She=just (.) hu::rled
8              a lot=of accusa:tions....
```

This framework of participation has numerous consequences that inhibit the escalation of conflict, in turn providing conditions favorable to compromise and dispute resolution. Within this framework, complaints, accusations, denials, disagreements, and the like are intrinsically indirect and mitigated. To the extent that they are intended to oppose co-disputants' earlier actions, they are temporally and pragmatically disjoined from their targets, packaged as "answers to questions", and directed toward the mediator. These features disrupt and defuse the usual pattern of attack and counterattack that is characteristic of argumentation in ordinary conversation.

All of this, in turn, promotes other forms of mitigation (Garcia 1991), including even the suppression of anger. Consider this excerpt from a mediation session concerning a divorced couple's custody dispute. The ex-husband (Com) is attacking his ex-wife for dating, and, consistent with the mediation participation framework his attack is at first mediator-addressed and hence indirect ("She's gone to Mexico", line 1). However, in the course of the attack, he momentarily moves away from the mediation framework and begins attacking her directly ("and LA with your boyfriends too", lines 1–2), and with that redirection comes a rise in the overt expression of anger ("So don't give me that", line 2)

```
(8)  [Garcia 1991: 826]
 1  Com:     She's gone to Mexico, and to Arizona, and LA with
 2           your boyfriends too? (0.2) So don't give me tha:t?
 3           (0.3)
 4  Med:     Um hm=
 5  Com:     =Okay? (.) Tit is for TAT here.
 6           .h Uh::m, .hh (0.2) I do not agree with, (0.5)
 7           three DA:ys? (0.3) a week ...
```

At this point the mediator intervenes and receipts the attack with an acknowledgement token (line 4). This intervention, which recasts the prior talk as if it were directed toward the mediator, can be understood as a subtle effort to re-establish the mediator-directed pattern of address. Notice that this effort is eventually successful. Although the ex-husband momentarily continues to address his ex-wife directly and with anger ("Tit is for TAT here", line 5), shortly thereafter (lines 6–7) he redirects his talk to the mediator, and as he does so the anger begins to dissipate (Garcia 1991: 826).

What is the scope of this triadic participation framework, wherein the disputants' conflictual actions are elicited by and directed toward a third party? In the relatively formal mediation sessions studied by Garcia, this framework is pervasively engaged and normatively sanctionable. Mediation is not a unitary phenomenon, however (Conley & O'Barr 1998: 40), and in less formal variants, as well as in plea-bargaining sessions, this participation framework may emerge only sporadically and episodically. Farther afield, it can also be found in many other forms of institutional talk that involve deliberation and debate, but are not geared toward achieving a consensual outcome. News interviews are a case in point – a parallel participation framework conditions expressions of disagreement between interviewees (Greatbatch 1992, Clayman & Heritage 2002a: ch. 8; cf. chapter 15 of this book). More generally, aspects of this framework are encoded in rules of parliamentary procedure, which specify that deliberative remarks be addressed to the meeting chairperson. The maintenance of civility and decorum may be a tacit rationale underlying this procedure and its implementation in a wide range of deliberative assemblies: club gatherings, business meetings, committee meetings, legislative debates, and so on.

The utility of this participation framework was registered, at least in a general way, more than a century ago by sociologist Georg Simmel ([1908] 1950) in his writings on small groups. Simmel observed that the addition of a third person to what had previously been a dyadic relationship can change relational dynamics in ways that are favorable to the resolution of conflict, particularly if the third person remains impartial. How does this work? It's not, Simmel argued, merely because mediating third parties have the moral authority to appeal to good will on all sides. Instead, their presence alters expressions of conflict between the other two parties, draining them of their "subjective passion" because "each party to the conflict . . . [is] forced to put the issue in more objective terms than it would if it confronted the other without mediation" (Simmel [1908] 1950: 149). A primary mechanism underlying this happy outcome, while never clearly explicated in Simmel's theoretical writings, is the distinctive participation framework that conditions the placement, design, and social meaning of conflictual actions.

Active facilitation: exerting pressure for concessions

Formally neutral third parties can also actively facilitate conflict resolution through a variety of techniques and procedures during the negotiation phase. They can elicit resolution proposals from the disputants with varying degrees of specificity (Garcia 1997). Once divergent solutions are on the table, they can steer the discussion toward a particular solution, while remaining formally "neutral", by asking questions that invite consideration of that solution over its alternatives (Greatbatch & Dingwall 1989). They can also exert more direct pressure on the disputants to make the concessions necessary to achieve a resolution (Garcia 1995, Lee 2005). Here we consider a key practice, used by both professional mediators and judges in plea bargaining, through which pressure for concessions is exerted.

The practice, which we call transformative relaying, involves modifying and re-presenting one disputant's concessionary position so as to invite a responsive concession from the other disputant. The following illustration (discussed in Lee 2005: 49–50) comes from the plea-bargaining case discussed earlier involving Frank Bryan, the man charged with disorderly conduct and resisting arrest. Here the judge (arrowed) characterizes the prosecuting attorney's position as being willing to "dismiss the one four eight" (the resisting arrest charge), and by implication retain the disorderly conduct charge.

```
(9)  [Plea Bargaining: Frank Bryan case (Maynard 1984)]
((148 is resisting arrest; 647f is disorderly conduct))
  1  Jdg:   →  Well he's gonna dismiss the one four eight,
  2  Def:      Okay,=
  3  Jdg:      ='n you'd plea to the six four seven ef=
  4  Def:      =Ye[ah
  5  Jdg:         ['n what would you realistically
  6             (0.8)
  7  Def:      Well what are you asking for.<>Lemme I mean I always
  8             usually go along with whatever Jerry says.<
```

This characterization is noteworthy for the way in which it *highlights and personalizes the concession* embodied in the prosecutor's position. In this respect, it differs from how the prosecutor had formulated his own position just a few moments earlier.

(10)   [Plea Bargaining: Frank Bryan case (Maynard 1984)]
       Pro: ...I don't know that the substantial interests of justice
                     require anythin' more than a plea to sex forty seven ef,

Notice that the prosecutor originally formulated his position by reference to the charge he was continuing to pursue (647f, disorderly conduct), rather than the charge he was giving up. His concession of the resisting arrest charge was thus implicit rather than explicit. Furthermore, this position was depersonalized in the sense that "the substantial interests of justice" was grammatically framed as the "agent" of the position. By contrast, the judge's re-presentation (in example (9)) inverts all of this, focusing on the charge conceded rather than the charge retained, and overtly attributing the concession to the prosecutor. In this particular case, since a compromise on charges had already been implicitly achieved in previous discussion, this practice and its sequelae (lines 2–5) render the compromise explicit and invites the defense to negotiate on the sentence to be imposed.

Transformative relaying also appears in mediation sessions. As Garcia (1995) has demonstrated, when mediators re-present disputants' positions, they do not merely repeat them in a literal fashion. One pattern of transformation involves highlighting and personalizing the concessionary dimension. The following example is from a mediation session involving a divorced couple clashing over visitation arrangements. The husband was supposed to have the children staying at his home on Thursdays and Fridays, but he indicates a willingness to accept alternating visits of Thursday/Friday one week and Friday the next week. He presents this arrangement as a ratification of what had already become the status quo in recent weeks as a result of the wife's preferences (lines 1–4). He goes on to characterize this arrangement as "compromising a little bit" (line 6), and it is noteworthy that the agent of the compromise remains unstated and implicit.

(11)   [Mediation Session: visitation arrangements (Garcia 1995)]
       1   Husb: The twins said well what happened to Thursdays they,
       2   you know they specifically brought it up to me and
       3   I said well, it looks like Mom wants to spend more
       4   time with you two. So if you know you want to do
       5   Thursday, Friday one week, and then just a Friday
       6   the next week, that's compromising a little bit...

When the mediator re-presents this position a few minutes later, she upgrades its concessionary character by explicitly attributing it to the husband and by characterizing him as "relinquishing" (rather than compromising) two days of visitation (arrowed). Her assertion that "he used the word" is thus a rather stark exaggeration.

(12)   [Mediation Session: visitation arrangements (Garcia 1995)]
       1   Med: And then what I hear, is the last month or so, it's
       2   been every other Thursday, and then that next week
       3   it's uh been the Friday, and you're not willing
       4   Wife: Uh=

```
 5  Med:    →  =to he's willing to relinquish! He used the word. Uh
 6             one of those Fridays.
 7  Husb:      No=
 8  Med:       =Instead of making it cons[iste]nt I MEAN THURSDAYS!
 9  Husb:                               [No  ]
10  Husb:      Thursdays ri:ght.
```

A few minutes later, visitation is again under discussion, and the mediator re-presents the husband's offer once more (arrowed), this time characterizing him as "giving up" something.

```
(13)  [Mediation Session: visitation arrangements (Garcia 1995)]
 1  Med:    →  And he is willing to give up two of those Thursdays.
 2  Wife:      I know.
 3  Med:       Number one I heard it to make it consistent for the
 4             children, and that that would please you!
 5  Wife:      I'll just I'll do it, just to meet him halfway,...
```

When the mediator elaborates on the proposed arrangement as in the interest of both the children and the wife herself (lines 3–4), the wife finally accepts it (line 5). Her acceptance is formulated ("just to meet him halfway") in a way that both registers the husband's concession, and casts her own revised position as a responsive compromise.

This practice – relaying a position from one disputant to another, and in the process highlighting and personalizing its concessionary dimension – transforms what might otherwise be heard as a mere *position report* into an *offer* that clearly invites a response (cf. Garcia 1997). But not just any old response is being invited through this practice. The personalization of the offer, which portrays the prior disputant as having taken the lead in conceding at least some contested ground, engages the norm of reciprocity to exert specific pressure for a reciprocal concession. Beyond exerting pressure, this practice also frames the social meaning of the response, prospectively casting it as a "responsive compromise" rather than a "unilateral concession". All of these features converge to encourage the production of concessionary responses and, ultimately, dispute resolution.

Conclusion

This tour of informal dispute resolution proceedings suggests that the inherent flexibility of ordinary language is implicated in the production of both social division and social solidarity. As we noted at the beginning, such flexibility encompasses the capacity to shine the linguistic spotlight on certain features of reality rather than others, as well as to add shades of color and texture to those features by formulating them in particular socially meaningful and resonant ways. On the one hand, disputants can exploit these flexibilities to heighten their differences, generating and deepening divergent interpretations of the circumstances at issue. On the other hand, judges and mediators can exploit these same flexibilities to bring the disputants closer together, finessing differences and intensifying concessions in pursuit of compromise and a consensual outcome.

The latter practices, in conjunction with the triadic participation framework, combine to make both plea bargaining and mediation remarkably successful as means of resolving disputes and thereby avoiding formal trials. Whether this is a good thing is, however, a matter of some controversy (Conley & O'Barr 1998: 46–9). On the plus side of the ledger, both mediation and plea bargaining are less expensive and much speedier than litigation. Mediation in particular is quite popular with disputants, perhaps because their direct involvement gives them a sense of control and efficacy, and also because it eschews the adversarial approach of the courtroom in favor of one emphasizing civility and compromise. But an ethos of compromise does tend to presume that both parties are essentially equal in moral standing, resources, and power, and that a just outcome lies "somewhere in the middle" (Fineman 1991). To the extent that the realities of the disputants' lives fall short of this ideal, the formal neutrality of judges and mediators may be far from neutral in its consequences, and the harmonious surface of these proceedings may conceal, and help to reproduce, rather deep-seated societal inequalities.

For Further Reading

Among informal dispute-resolution proceedings, plea bargaining and mediation have received the most attention, although insightful inroads into small claims court (Atkinson 1992) have also been made. In the plea-bargaining area, Maynard (1984) presents a wide-ranging analysis encompassing the practices of person description as well as explicit bargaining sequences (see also Maynard 1988). Maynard also develops the theoretical implications of his interactional analysis, including a trenchant critique of efforts to model sentencing decisions on the basis of decontextualized defendant attributes. Lee (2005) offers a more focused analysis of how judges facilitate the plea-bargaining process.

In the mediation area, Garcia (1991) did pioneering work on the distinctive turn-taking arrangements that shape both the story-telling phase and the negotiation phase, focusing on how the resulting participation framework operates to mitigate conflict. In a complementary analysis, Greatbatch and Dingwall (1997) examine various procedures that disputants use to de-escalate their own arguments. In other work focusing on resolutions and compromises, Garcia has examined the genesis of resolution proposals (1997, 2000), and how mediators paraphrase, elaborate, and otherwise re-present the disputants' positions (1995). The issue of mediator neutrality has received extensive attention. Jacobs (2002) and Heisterkamp (2006) have explored how mediators maintain a posture of formal neutrality, while Greatbatch and Dingwall (1989) examine how mediators, acting within a posture of formal neutrality, can nonetheless steer the discussion in a direction that favors certain solutions over alternatives (see also Cobb & Rifkin 1991 and Garcia, Vise, & Whitaker 2002). (The exercise of agency from within a formally neutral posture is also explored in chapter 16 of this book for the case of journalists in broadcast news interviews.) Finally, Conley and O'Barr (1998) offer an insightful overview of the role of language and interaction in various dispute resolution contexts.

Notes

1   Other aspects of this plea-bargaining session are analyzed in Maynard (1984), and the appendix contains a full transcript of the session.
2   For a related and more detailed discussion of formal neutrality and its maintenance in broadcast news interviews, see chapter 15.

V
News and Political Communication

15

News Interview Turn Taking

The news interview occupies a prominent place in the landscape of broadcast journalism and political communication. Interviewing has long been a basic journalistic tool for gathering story information, but with the rapid expansion of electronic media – the proliferation of broadcast channels, cable networks, and informational websites – it takes on added significance as an economical and lively way of presenting information to the public. Whether live or taped, in studio or via remote satellite links, presented in full or excerpted in soundbites reverberating across YouTube and the blogosphere, the interview is now a common form in which news is packaged for public consumption. As a dynamic, unscripted, and increasingly prevalent alternative to the traditional narrative or story form of news presentation, the news interview is central to the practice of contemporary journalism.

The news interview is distinguished from other interaction-based genres of broadcast talk by a unique constellation of participants, subject matter, and interactional form. Interviewers are typically recognized as professional journalists rather than celebrity entertainers or partisan activists. Interviewees are typically public officials, experts, or others with some connection to current events. The discussion focuses on such events, is relatively formal in character, and progresses primarily through questions and answers. Prototypical news interview programs include *Meet the Press* (US), *Nightline* (US), and *Newsnight* (UK).

In the next three chapters, we examine various aspects of news interview interaction, beginning in this chapter with the basic ground rules governing news interview participation, ground rules that constitute a *turn-taking system* for this form of talk.

Significance of Turn Taking

We begin our tour of the news interview with the system of turn taking because of its utter centrality to this genre of talk.

As with any form of institutional talk organized around a specialized system of speech exchange (such as trial examinations; see chapter 12), the turn-taking system is constitutive of the news interview as a singular form of talk. By acting in accordance with a distinctive method for taking turns, the participants construct their interaction, turn by turn, as something that is recognizable as a news interview and hence distinguishable from other forms of broadcast talk and from ordinary conversation. On this basis anyone – audience members as well as the participants themselves – can see at a glance, or hear in an instant, that a news interview is in progress.

Correspondingly, the turn-taking system has consequences for nearly everything else that happens within a news interview. A system of this sort determines how opportunities to speak arise, and hence how successive turns at talk are produced and allocated to the participants. Correspondingly, it defines the boundaries of permissible conduct within turns at talk. The rules and practices underlying the turn-taking system shape the resources that interviewers and interviewees have to pursue their objectives, and they do so asymmetrically. Just as ancient Roman gladiators fought with trident and net against shield and short sword, contemporary interview participants have contrasting resources for attack and defense: the interviewer's resources for confronting and pinning down the interviewee are met by the latter's capacity for deflection and pointed riposte.

Finally, the rules and practices of news interview turn taking are responsive to various institutional demands that are made of broadcasters and their employing organizations. Two of these are particularly important. The first demand arises from the presence of the broadcast audience. The interaction should be managed as "talk for overhearers", so that audience members do not feel that they are listening in on a purely private conversation, but can feel instead that the talk is being conducted for their benefit. The second demand arises from the interviewer's recognized status as a professional journalist. The interviewer should maintain a formally neutral or "neutralistic" posture, and should not editorialize by expressing their own views or the views of the employing news organization. As we shall see, the rules of turn taking are an institutionalized means of addressing these problems, and hence a primary interface between the internal dynamics of interview talk and its environing context.

The Turn-Taking System in Overview

So what is this system and how does it work? It's helpful to begin by thinking of news interview turn taking in contrast to the turn-taking system that is most familiar and most fundamental, namely that of ordinary conversation.

A hallmark of conversational turn taking is its essentially unscripted character. Conversationalists do not adhere to a predetermined plan or format for taking turns. They don't know in advance what any given speaker will say, how long they will speak, or who will speak next. Thus, the content, length, and order of turns are not fixed in advance, but remain to be determined by the participants themselves as the conversation unfolds. One implication of this "open" arrangement is that, every time a speaker arrives at the end of a grammatical unit (e.g. a sentence), that constitutes a *transition relevance place*, a place where turn transition *may* occur as a different speaker takes the floor (Sacks, Schegloff, & Jefferson 1974).

In a news interview, the management of turn taking is dramatically different. Opportunities to speak are powerfully constrained by the existence of plan or predetermined format for taking turns. This format may be summarized in terms of a very simple rule: the talk should be limited to questions and answers. More specifically, interviewers (henceforth IRs) are obliged to restrict themselves to asking questions, while interviewees (henceforth IEs) should restrict themselves to answering them.

We can get an initial sense of the power of this rule by examining its operation in highly conflictual situations where the IR and IE are embroiled in disagreement. What is striking is that such disagreements tend to be expressed in the form of questions and answers. Consider this excerpt from a British interview with Arthur Scargill, then a candidate for president of the National Union of Mineworkers. Here Scargill is being questioned about his economic views.

```
(1) [UK World at One: 13 March 1979: Arthur Scargill]
 1 AS:   ... it's the press that constantly call me a Marxist when
 2       I do not, (.) and never have (.) er er given that
 3       description of myself. [.hh I-]
 4 IR:                          [But I ]'ve heard you- I've heard
 5       you'd be very happy to: to: er .hhhh er describe youself
 6       as a Marxist. Could it be that with an election in the
 7       offing you're anxious to play down that you're a
 8       Marx[ist]
 9 AS:       [er ] Not at all Mister Da:y.=And I:'m (.) sorry to
10       say I must disagree with you,=you have never heard me
11       describe myself .hhh er as a Ma:rxist.=I have only...
12        : ((4 lines omitted))
13 IR:   Do you ascri:be to Marxist economic philosophy.=
14 AS:   =I would say that there: e:r the: (.) philosophy of Marx
15       as far as the economics of Britain is concerned is one
16       with which I find sympathy,=and would support it.=Yes.
17        (.)
18 IR:   Well that makes you a Marxist doe[sn't it.
19 AS:                                    [NOt necessarily...
```

Across this excerpt, the parties are locking horns over whether Scargill is a Marxist. The IR recurrently asserts, implies, or presupposes that Scargill is a Marxist, while Scargill recurrently denies that characterization. And yet these successive claims and counter-claims are, without exception, packaged in the form of questions and answers. This is most striking in the first complete question–answer exchange (lines 4–11). The IR asserts that Scargill "would be happy" to describe himself as a Marxist, but he does so only as a way of leading up to a subsequent question about whether Scargill's denials are politically motivated. Correspondingly, Scargill in response explicitly disagrees with the IR ("I'm sorry to say I must disagree with you"), but he asserts that disagreement only after he produces a *no*-type response ("Not at all Mr. Day") to the question about his political motivations. Both parties are thus working to articulate their disagreements in and through questions and answers.

Now this analysis, which reduces the turn-taking system to a simple question–answer rule, is broadly correct but somewhat unsatisfying. Couched in such general terms, it is inadequate to distinguish the news interview turn-taking system from other systems that are superficially similar. The system for trial examinations (chapter 12), for instance, is also organized around questions and answers, although these take a very different form in the courtroom context. Plainly the question–answer rule is too general to pin down what is distinctive about news interviews per se, so general in fact that it is banal and obvious.

The unexplicated complexity of actual turn taking, in contrast to the utter simplicity of the question–answer rule, becomes apparent when we think about what is required to follow this rule. What must the parties do in order to ensure that their talk will "come off" as a series of questions and answers? What does the IR have to do to be seen as "asking questions"? Indeed, what counts as an acceptable question in this context? And on the other hand, what does the IE have to do to be seen as "answering"? How are departures from the rule managed and dealt with? The question–answer rule doesn't tell us any of this! It is best understood as a very general summary of what occurs, one that glosses over all of the concerted work that the parties must actually do in order to put that rule into operation in the broadcasting context. Thus, as we'll see, while the question–answer rule may be simple and obvious, the practices and procedures underlying it are complex and often surprising.

Constructing Questions

We can begin to unpack the question–answer rule by focusing on the questioning side of the equation. The obligation to question is, on the one hand, such a pervasive constraint on journalists' conduct that the vast majority of their contributions are indeed limited to questions (Heritage & Roth 1995). But this constraint, while pervasive, is also quite loose in the sense that what stands as an allowable question is rather broad. It includes the full range of interrogative forms (yes/no, wh-, alternative choice, statement plus tag questions) and other practices (B-event statements, rising intonation) that are routinely associated with questioning in other environments.

Permissible questions are also understood to include those that are elaborated with prefatory remarks designed as declarative statements. Such statement prefaces might seem to stretch the boundaries of questioning, but they are allowable on the grounds that they provide the kind of background information that the recipient and the media audience will need in order to understand the import of the question and why it is being asked. Consider this question to an anti-apartheid activist from South Africa, where the question proper (line 3) is preceded by a prefatory statement (lines 1–2).

```
(2)  [US ABC Nightline: 22 July 1985: South Africa]
  1   JRN:     .hh Two- two members of your organization (.)
  2            supposedly arrested today:
  3            D'you feel in some danger when you go back,
```

If left to stand on its own, this question – which raises the prospect of personal danger to the interviewee when he returns to South Africa – might seem puzzling or incomprehensible to many viewers. The prefatory statement establishes a context for this inquiry, thereby clarifying the relevance of a question that might otherwise seem to be coming from out of the blue.

While prefaces are fundamentally occupied with the provision of question-preliminary background information, they represent an important opportunity space that skilled IRs may exploit in strategic ways. Such prefaces can be made to expand like an accordion, and can accommodate information that disputes, challenges, or criticizes the interviewee – all under the guise of leading up to a question. This striking example is from a 1985 interview with the South African ambassador to the US just after the apartheid regime had suspended civil liberties and declared a state of emergency. The question proper does not appear until line 14, as the first 13 lines are devoted to an elaborate attack on the necessity of repressive measures and a call for the end of the apartheid system (lines 1–13).

```
(3)  [Nightline 22 July 1985: 4–5]
 1  IR:          As Peter Sharp said in that piece it is a lot easier
 2               to impose a state of emergency than it is to lift it.
 3          →    .hhh You still have the root cause when you lift it.
 4          →    And black leaders in that country have made it very
 5               clear .hhhh that this kind of situation there's no way
 6               of stopping this kind of situation unless there is an
 7               end to apartheid.
 8          →    It seems to me .hh that by doing this by eh imposing
 9               I guess this kind of repression you- .hh you really set
10               up uh system where you can do nothing it seems to me
11          →    #.hh when you lift it# except to change the system
12               that exists there
13          →    (.) the basic system.
14          →    #.hhh# Is that unfair? er
15  HB:          Uh I- I would think it's unfair what is being said=
16               =uh- because if thuh government is committed...
```

But even here the IR eventually comes to a question of sorts (line 14), asking if that whole critical assessment is "unfair".

As this example shows, the question–answer rule can be implemented in a way that allows for the production of elaborate statement-prefaced questions. Such complex questions have further ramifications for the conduct of IEs, as they require IEs' collaboration in order to be realized. In practice, IEs generally withhold speaking until a recognizable question is actually completed. The arrows in excerpt (3) above indicate points where a prior sentence (or some other turn-constructional unit) has been completed, and where the IR either pauses or moves to another unit of talk. If this were an ordinary conversation, these would all be transition relevance places (Sacks, Schegloff, & Jefferson 1974), points where the IE would have the option to take a turn at talk. The IE, however, passes over all of these opportunities, declining to produce either a substantive response or even a minimal token of acknowledgement (*uh huh, yeah, ok, right, oh, oh really*, etc.). The level of forbearance and self-restraint exhibited here is particularly remarkable given the hostile substance of the unfolding remarks, but this IE is by no means exceptional. IEs generally wait until a recognizable question is completed.

Sometimes the effort at self-control is quite literally visible in the details of nonvocal behavior. In the preceding example, as the preface is unfolding, the IE twice readies himself to begin speaking. The first time this occurs (between the "#" marks in line 11), the IE licks his lips, opens his mouth (possibly to take an in-breath), but then closes his mouth again. The second time (marked in line 14), he opens his mouth (again, with a possible in-breath) but withholds speech until the IR delivers the subsequent question. Each of these gearing-up moves occurs at or near what would be a turn-transition place in ordinary conversation; hence, each launches a *conversationally organized* course of action. The subsequent suppression of the course of action – that is, the withholding of speech – is organized by the IE's timely recovery of his orientation to the more restricted turn-taking system for *news interviews*. Here then the IE visibly inhibits a "conversational" response so as to act in accordance with the news interview framework.

This is all part of the work of following the question–answer rule. For the IE to speak earlier would be doubly inappropriate. Not only would it interfere with the IR's capacity to complete a question, but without a question to respond to, the IE would himself be producing something other than a recognizable answer. By waiting, IEs collaborate in the production of elaborated questions and, more generally, act so as to uphold the question–answer rule.

The capacity to produce elaborate question prefaces is a major source of agency for IRs within the otherwise restrictive turn-taking framework of the news interview. Although such agency rests on the tacit cooperation of the public figure, it remains a key resource for the exercise of vigorous journalism (as we will see in the next chapter). Moreover, such agency is in part what distinguishes *journalistic* questions, and the turn-taking system in which they are embedded, from superficially similar actions and turn-taking arrangements associated with trial examinations (see chapter 12). In some courtroom contexts – e.g., direct examination in the American legal system – prefaced questions are objectionable as "leading the witness", so examination questions tend to be structurally simple and relatively brief (see Atkinson & Drew 1979).

Constructing Answers

Even more commonly than their questioning counterparts, answers tend to be complex and elaborate. Most answers extend across many sentences, even when the prior question was narrowly focused as a yes/no interrogative. For instance, the yes/no question to the Ambassador in the preceding example – "Is that unfair, er?" – yields an initial affirmation (line 15 below) followed by a lengthy discursive elaboration.

```
(4)   [Nightline 22 July 1985: 4–5]
14   IR:          ....hhh Is that unfair? er
15   HB:          Uh I- I would think it's unfair what is being said=
16           →   =uh- because if thuh government is committed=h to:
17               bring- e=to bringing about those refor:ms. .hh uh to
18               start ay dialogue .h then at lea:st (0.2) those people:
19               who: are p- to be part of thuh process_ .h they
20               should participate in it.
21           →   .hh Now what do we have her:e at thuh mo:ment. .h
22           →   Those people who've become thuh victims: .h uh- of
23               thuh violence. .h they are actually thuh people
24               who've come to thuh fo:re,
25           →   (.) many of them .h who say that they want to participate.
26           →   .hh Now- the moment th't they start (.) participating
27               in some kind of:- °uh° political process .h uh: they're
28               bei:ng made out=h to be: an::=uh collaborator.
29           →   .h When that is being said all of a sudden they becom:e
30               uh-theh- theh- uh li- there's uh license out_ .hh to
31               kill them.
32           →   .hh And in order to: to prevent that..h we have taken
33               som:e rather:=harsh measures, (eh-) (were)/(or)
```

```
34                extre̲me measures_
35      →         .h but let me also remi̲nd you. h .h thi̲s is not
36                something uni̲que to South Africa because of our own
37                puh- peculiar political sy̲stem the:re.
38      →         .hh Uh: ihb- ehb- a sta̲te of eme̲rgency, .h
39                uh: ma̲ny countries in thuh western world, democra̲tic
40                countries have been u̲sed to it.
41      →         .hh Uh eh- I'm remi̲nded that earlier 'n thi̲s year:
42                in some of thuh- in a very prominen:t uh western
43                cou̲ntry .h a state of emergency was declared.
44      →         .h So it is kno̲wn in thuh world.
```

And as the arrows marking conversational transition points demonstrate, the IR normally remains silent, withholding a subsequent question as well as any and all acknowledgement and receipt tokens (*uh huh, yeah, ok, right, oh, oh really*, etc.). Much as in the collaborative construction of prefaced questions, IRs enable and in effect collaborate in the production of extended blocks of talk as answers.

Elaborated answers are not merely commonplace in news interviews; they tend to be the norm. Indeed, minimal answers can be disconcerting to the IR and are often a sign of incipient conflict. In this excerpt from an interview with Attorney General Janet Reno, the IR asks whether her recent remarks on the problem of television violence indicate a "dangerous embrace of censorship" (lines 1–9). This yes/no question receives only a simple *no* from Reno (line 10), and when invited to elaborate on the specific programs that might be censored (lines 12–14), Reno again responds with a flat *no* (line 15).

(5)   [US Meet the Press 24 Oct 1993]
```
 1  IR:          ... .hh Madam Attorney General you've testified this
 2               week- u- in front of Congress abou:t .h violence
 3               and television. .hhh And said that if the TV
 4               industry didn't in effect clean itself up,
 5               clean its act up, .hhh there may be government
 6               intervention. Government regulation. (0.4)
 7               Thuh New York Ti:mes in an editorial said that
 8               (.) you embarked on a quote <dangerous embrace
 9               of censorship.> (0.3) Didju?
10  IE:    →     No.
11               (0.2)
12  IR:          .hhhh Wha:t kind of government intervention
13               are you thinking about? Would you ba̲n: programs
14               like NYPD: Law and Order, would you [uh:
15  IE:    →                                         [No.
16               (.)
17  IR:          W- Wh:at are we talking about.
18  IE:          We're talking about (.) a̲sking the media
19               to sto̲p talking (.) about what it promises
20               to do, and do it.
```

Both of these minimal responses are initially met with silence by the IR (lines 11, 16) and hesitation in the onset of the next question (note the extended in-breath in line 12, and the initial cutoff and restart in line 17), suggesting that the IR was caught slightly off-guard. The default expectation thus seems to be that IEs will normally go on to elaborate. Given this norm, unelaborated answers can come across as terse and uncooperative. In this example – which involves an accusatory line of questioning casting Reno as a would-be censor of popular entertainment – Reno's minimal answers resist the agenda that the IR is trying to pursue, and her extraordinary terseness registers a tacit complaint about that agenda.

Here again we have a sharp contrast with turn-taking practices in trial examinations (chapter 12). As with the parameters of questioning, the parameters of answering are much broader in news interviews than in trial examinations, where witnesses can be held to minimal answers and where attempts to elaborate can be sanctioned and stricken from the official record (Atkinson & Drew 1979). And since minimal answers are the norm for witnesses under examination, they carry no overtone of uncooperativeness or incipient conflict. Thus, a superficially similar question–answer turn-taking rule is implemented very differently in the broadcasting context, and the meanings and inferences associated with brief as opposed to elaborated turns are correspondingly transformed.

The fact that news interview answers are elaborated poses a puzzle that IRs recurrently have to solve: how to determine when an answer is complete and another question is due. The IR must parse the unfolding answer, unit by unit, to determine where and when to come forward with the next question. While prefaced questions normally end unambiguously upon the completion of a grammatically marked interrogative, the endings of answers are much more difficult to determine. There are a variety of vocal and nonvocal indicators of possible completeness – e.g., falling intonation, the termination of hand gestures, repetition of specific words from the question (Roth 1996, Schegloff 1998) – but these are decidedly rough and approximate. When IEs end their answers abruptly and without warning, as in the preceding example, this can yield hitches of silence as the IR belatedly gears up for the next question. Conversely, when IEs seek to monopolize the floor by taking breaths in mid-sentence and rushing from one sentence to the next (Bull & Mayer 1988), the IR is virtually condemned to "interrupt" as a condition of asking questions at all. In any case, the resolution of this puzzle is part and parcel of the process by which IRs and IEs jointly construct elaborated answers.

Departures from the Question–Answer Framework

The news interview turn-taking system is not a physical law of nature; it is a normative organization that specifies proper forms of conduct. Like any social norm, it may be departed from and returned to. Interview participants can speak out of turn, breaching the boundaries of allowable questioning and answering. However, such departures provide strong evidence that interview participants regard the question–answer framework as normative. Those who endeavor to depart from that framework treat their own actions as sensitive and problematic, while their recipients treat them as negatively sanctionable.

Both the sensitivity and sanctionability of turn-taking departures are illustrated in this excerpt from Dan Rather's infamous interview with George Bush during the 1988 presidential campaign, an interview that focused on Bush's involvement in the Iran–Contra scandal under the Reagan administration. As Rather launches a complex prefaced question by paraphrasing Bush's previous claims regarding his in-principle opposition to the arms-for-hostages swap, Bush intervenes before the question is completed, first with receipt tokens (lines 3, 5) and then with a more substantively defensive response (beginning at line 7).

```
(6)   [CBS Evening News: 25 Jan 1988: Iran–Contra]
  1   IR:        You said tha' if you had known this was an arms
  2              for hostag[es swap, .hh that you would've=
  3   IE:                   [Yes
  4   IR:        =opposed it. .hhhh You also [said thet-=
  5   IE:                                    [Exactly
  6   IR:        =[that you did NOT KNOW thet y-
  7   IE:         [(m- may- may I-) may I answer that.
  8              (0.4)
  9   IE:        (Th[uh) right ( )-
 10   IR:           [That wasn't a question.=it w[as a]=
 11   IE:                                        [Yes ]=
 12   IR:        =[statement eh-]
 13   IE:        =[it was   a   ] statement [and I'll ]=
 14   IR:                                   [Let me ask]=
 15   IE:        =[answer it. The President   ] created this=
 16   IR:        =[the question if I may first]
 17   IE:        =program, .h has testified er s:tated publicly,
 18              (.) he did not think it was arms fer hostages.
```

Bush acknowledges the violative character of his interjection in two distinct ways. First, before launching the substance of his defense, he asks the IR for permission to speak ("May I answer that" in line 7). Second, within his request for permission, he prospectively characterizes his own action as an "answer", thereby furnishing a veneer of propriety to what is an essentially improper move within the interview framework.

Dan Rather, for his part, first rejects the request by appealing explicitly to the question–answer rule (lines 10–16, "That wasn't a question, it was a statement. Let me ask the question if I may first"). Later on, in talk not shown, as Bush barrels ahead with his response anyway, Rather sanctions him for speaking out of turn ("That wasn't the question, Mister Vice President").

In different ways, then, both parties register the violative character of Bush's attempt to interject before a question has been completed. Furthermore, in defending their respective stances, both make more or less explicit appeals to the normative question–answer framework.

One common type of departure that merits closer attention occurs in panel interviews involving two or more interviewees, and involves two IEs speaking in succession following a question. In this sequence of events – IR → IE1 → IE2 – the second IE is speaking out of turn, responding to the previous IE, and hence engaged in a non-answering type of action. IEs have various methods for registering the sensitive and violative character of such actions. One such method, already seen in the Bush–Rather example above, involves *requesting permission to speak*. Here is an additional example (arrowed):

```
(7)   [MacNeil/Lehrer 4 Dec 1989: Summit meeting]
  1   EB:        ...as long as the two systems exist and we need them for
  2              stability .h we will have no:: .h uh unification.
```

```
3                This is absolutely clear.
4  HK:     →   May I say something,
5  IR:         Yes sir.=
6  HK:     →   =on the subject?
7  IR:         Yes sir.
8  HK:         uh (.) ahem I think it is a big mistake. to equate the
9                NATO alliance and the Warsaw Pact....
```

This IE (HK) twice requests permission to speak out of turn, and the IR subsequently grants the request (lines 5, 7). Only then does the IE continue with his point (lines 8–9).

IEs may also offer something less than a full-fledged request, what has been termed a token request for permission (Greatbatch 1988). Here, the IE produces a request-like utterance ("Can I make a point about that" in line 3), but immediately proceeds to develop a response without actually waiting for the IR's permission.

(8) [Greatbatch 1988: 419–20]
```
1  LL:         ...there was no evidence whatever that stiffer penalties
2                di- diminish crime.=
3  MW:     →   =Can I make a point about that.=.hhh which is that (.)...
```

In other cases, IEs eschew both genuine and token requests for permission, while continuing to acknowledge the question–answer framework in a more subtle way: by addressing their remarks to the IR. In the following example, as PJ responds to her co-IE (Sam Brittan) without waiting for a question, she twice refers to Brittan in the third person (arrowed).

(9) [Greatbatch 1988: 420]
```
1  SB:         The most important thing .hh is that Mister Healey .h
2                should stick to his gu:ns.=
3  PJ:         [You s]ee
4  IR:         [Well I-]
5                (.)
6  PJ:     →   I disagree with- with Sam Brittan on a- in a most (.)
7                fundamental way about this, (.) because (0.2) it may
8         →   well be so.=I mean he would arg- Sam Brittan would
9                argue from a monetarist point of vie:w....
```

Thus, even with no actual question on the table and while substantively countering the previous IE, this IE nonetheless delivers her remarks to the IR and thereby comports herself as if she were answering a question. In television news interviews, this IR-directed pattern of address may also be evident at the nonvocal level, as IEs continue to gaze at the IR and steadfastly avoid gazing at one another even when locked in what is otherwise an unmediated course of disagreement (Clayman & Heritage 2002a: ch. 8).

These examples demonstrate how an orientation to the normative question–answer framework may be sustained even during actions that depart from that framework. Of course, if the participants persist in flouting the framework, it may eventually be abandoned, yielding a phase of "conversational" talk within what is otherwise constructed as a formal interview. Sustained assaults on the question–answer framework occur most frequently in highly conflictual interviews characterized by adversarial confrontation between IRs and IEs (Clayman & Whalen 1988/9, Schegloff 1988/9), or between different IEs (Clayman & Heritage 2002a: ch. 8).

Institutional Functions of the Turn-Taking System

Why do we find this particular turn-taking system in this institutional environment? The arrangement is neither arbitrary nor coincidental; it represents a conventionalized solution to certain basic problems that arise in the context of broadcast journalism.

The first problem arises from the IR's identity as a professional journalist. Like most journalists, broadcast interviewers are supposed to remain objective. This overarching professional norm translates, for interviewers, into an obligation to remain neutral in their dealings with public figures. Interviewers should not allow their own views or the views of their employers or sponsors to enter into the process. Absolute neutrality is, of course, an unattainable ideal, but the turn-taking system provides for the maintenance of a formally neutral or "neutralistic" posture for interviewers in a variety of ways. First, by mandating the activity of questioning, the system restricts interviewers to an action that is accountable as "seeking information" rather than expressing opinions. Indeed, "I was only asking a question" is a recurrent and effective defense against charges of bias. The primary action that interviewers are obliged to perform is thus intrinsically neutralistic. (Additional practices bearing on the neutralism requirement will be explored in the next chapter.)

Furthermore, the particular way the question–answer rule is implemented further contributes to the interviewer's neutralistic posture. As we have seen, interviewers generally avoid making opinionated assertions except as a way of leading up to an eventual question. They also avoid producing acknowledgement tokens (*uh huh*, *yeah*, *oh*, *okay*, *right*, etc.) as interviewees' answers are unfolding. Since most of these tokens could be inferred to indicate support for, or belief in, what the interviewee has just said, their avoidance also serves the ideal of neutralism.

Just as the turn-taking system is responsive to problems arising from the professional context, it is also responsive to problems arising from the broadcasting context, and in particular the presence of an audience. When you listen to an interview, or watch one on television, you don't get the feeling that you're listening in on a private conversation. Instead you somehow feel that the interaction is being conducted for your benefit, even though you are rarely if ever addressed in a direct way. Here again, the turn-taking system lies at the heart of this process, helping to create this sense that the talk is being conducted for a ratified but unaddressed audience of overhearers. The key is the avoidance of acknowledgement and receipt tokens, especially by the interviewer. In ordinary conversation, when you acknowledge something that another person has said, you imply that the remark was produced for you in particular, and you cast yourself as the primary recipient of that remark. So receipting talk proposes a particular definition of the situation, one that is systematically avoided by news interviewers. Interviewers act to elicit talk through their questions, but they refrain from acting as the recipients of such talk. In so doing, they allow the elicited talk to be understood as produced, not for them, but for the audience who is listening in. The turn-taking system is thus intertwined with the essentially public and mass-communicated nature of news interview talk.

Conclusion

The organization of turn taking can be likened to a traffic management system, one that minimizes "collisions" on the highway of interaction. But as this tour of turn taking in the news interview demonstrates, the significance of the turn-taking system extends far beyond the avoidance of overlapping speech to influence the substance of interaction itself. The system defines the boundaries of permissible conduct, and shapes the resources that both interviewers and interviewees can use to pursue their respective agendas. Although it can be summarized in terms of a simple question–answer rule, its implementation organizes an enormous range of interactional conduct. While superficially similar to the turn-taking system for trial examinations (cf. chapter 12), it has distinctive features that are fitted to the particulars of just this context. Indeed, the system can be understood as a methodical solution to various tasks and constraints intrinsic to broadcast journalism. It is, correspondingly, part and parcel of how the participants "do" news interview talk. By adhering to a singular method for taking turns, the participants construct their interaction moment by moment as a particular type of occasion, one that is distinct from ordinary conversation and from other forms of institutional talk. The yellow brick road of the news interview rests in no small part on practices of turn taking.

For Further Reading

The pioneering analysis of the news interview as a speech exchange system organized by a specialized mode of turn taking was conducted by David Greatbatch (1988). Further developments can be found in Heritage and Roth (1995) and Clayman and Heritage (2002a: ch. 4). For the historical development of journalistic interviewing, see Schudson (1994) on the newspaper era, and Clayman and Heritage (2002a: ch. 2) on the era of broadcasting. For a broader sampling of research on interviewing as a mode of journalism, see Ekstrom, Kroon, and Nylund (2006). Finally, news interview research comprises one component within the larger field of broadcast talk, which includes noteworthy studies of radio call-in shows (Hutchby 1996), daytime TV talk shows (Tolson 2001), the discourse of traditional broadcast news programs (Montgomery 2007), and trans-genre studies of the participation of ordinary people (Thornborrow 1997, 2001). Important edited collections and special journal issues spanning the field of broadcast talk include Scannell (1991), Thornborrow and van Leeuwen (2001), and Montgomery and Thornborrow (2010). Various attempts to synthesize this emerging field may be found in Clayman (2004), Hutchby (2006), and Tolson (2006), while Myers (2004) develops the implications for expressions of public opinion.

16

Question Design in the News Interview and Beyond

An implication of the previous chapter is that questions lie at the heart of the news interview. But describing a journalist's action as a "question" glosses over an immense range of variation in how questions are designed and the significance of these designs, both for the public figures who must respond to them and for the institution of journalism more generally. In this chapter we focus on variations in question design in two major arenas where questions can be of considerable political significance: formal news interviews and presidential news conferences.

Two Norms of Journalism: Objectivity and Adversarialness

Journalistic questioning in broadcast news is shaped by two broad professional norms, *objectivity* and *adversarialness*.

First, journalists should be objective and unbiased, disinterested even, in the reporting of the news. As we saw in the last chapter, this norm translates into a procedural method: interviewers should avoid unvarnished assertions in favor of asking questions. As we will suggest in a moment, strict objectivity in news questioning is effectively impossible to achieve. But the procedural focus on asking questions at least assures an accountable basis for objectivity, since questioning interviewees is antithetical to overtly agreeing or disagreeing with them. As long as interviewers stick to asking questions, they have addressed this norm and behaved in what we have called a formally neutral or "neutralistic" fashion.

The norm of objectivity stands in tension with a second, equally important, norm of journalism: the norm that journalists should work to be appropriately adversarial. They should actively challenge their sources, rather than being mouthpieces or stooges for them. The norm of adversarialness is one that pushes interviewers to prevent the interview from becoming a kind of platform or soapbox from which political leaders can get away with their own spin on events. The interviewer is responsible for making sure that those views are subject to scrutiny and challenge. Interviewers serve as watchdogs, asking the questions that, as they put it, the public wants answers to: their job is to question public figures on behalf of the "public" (Clayman 2002). Thus interviewers will design their questions to challenge, or even to expose contradictions or impeach public figures.

These two norms are, of course in tension with one another. This tension is managed when journalists develop questions that are penetrating and hard-hitting without sacrificing the questioning role which is their shield against charges of unfairness and bias. Here, we can analogize between interviewing and sumo wrestling, where the struggle takes place within a circular ring and stepping out of bounds leads to penalties. In the news interview, the interaction between interviewer and interviewee must take place within the bounds of the "neutralistic circle". When this happens, adversarial questioning is "safe" because it is defensible as appropriate journalistic questioning. Significant rewards await those who can bring off this balancing act by maximizing adversarialness within the bounds of legitimacy represented by the neutralistic circle. Many famous journalists – Mike Wallace, Dan Rather, and Sam Donaldson in the US, and Robin Day, David Frost, and Jeremy Paxman in the UK – began their careers by courting controversy as highly adversarial questioners, while at the same time avoiding sanctions from disgruntled interviewees, nervous employers, and powerful members of the news audience.

Within the broadcast interview, the operation of these norms resides within what we have called "the interview contract" (Clayman and Heritage 2002a). Journalists need access to public figures for their livelihood, while public figures need journalists to promote their careers by supplying what Margaret Thatcher once referred to as "the oxygen of publicity". Within this framework, interviewees need to be interesting – boring or uncooperative interviewees don't get a second invitation – but interviewers who cross the boundary from adversarial to aggressive can be boycotted.

Dimensions of Adversarialness

As noted earlier, we distinguish between "neutrality" and "neutralism", because strict neutrality (or impartiality or freedom from bias) in questioning is impossible, and for a number of reasons. By definition, questions are substantively focused and they set constraints on respondents' next actions in a number of ways. To see how this is so, it will be helpful to revisit the features of question design that we reviewed in chapter 10 on medical questioning. There we described a number of dimensions of question design, three of which are important for this discussion and are presented in table 16.1.

Table 16.1 Dimensions of questioning and answering

Interviewer questions	*Interviewee responses*
set agendas: (i) topical agendas (ii) action agendas	conform / do not conform with (i) topical agendas (ii) action agendas
embody presuppositions	confirm / disconfirm presuppositions
incorporate preferences	align / disalign with preferences

Source: Clayman and Heritage 2002a

Questions may establish topics for response that interviewees would prefer not to address, and may invoke action agendas – a type of response (for example, "yes" or "no") – that an interviewee would much prefer to avoid (see chapter 17). "Have you been stealing from public funds?" would be such a question! The interviewee can respond with "No" but the accusation is out there nonetheless. Worse, questions may be designed with presuppositions that interviewees would rather not deal with: "When did you start stealing from public funds?" would be such a case. And questions may also embody preferences that favor a particular and undesirable answer: "Isn't it true that you've been stealing from public funds?" Alternatively, of course questions can be designed to favor the interviewee's stated position. In Britain, a Conservative Party politician was once asked: "The Conservative Party has been labeled the party of warmongers. Is there one jot of truth in that?" – an overwhelmingly, and transparently, favorable question to his point of view. In sum, all three of these main features of news interview questioning make it impossible to design a purely "neutral" question (Harris 1986).

Agenda setting

Questions set agendas for response and respondents are accountable in terms of these agendas. This is clear in the following case in which British Labour politician Roy Hattersley is asked a yes/no (or "polar") question about a colleague's victory in an election for office within the party. He initially responds in terms of both the topic and action agendas set. However, at line 12, he shifts to a closely related topic. At this point, he acknowledges that he is shifting topic, and justifies the shift in terms of an earlier ("your original") interviewer question:

(1)   [BBC TV: Panorama: 28 January 1981]
IR: David Dimbleby, IE: Roy Hattersley

```
 1  IR:        Roy Hattersley .hhh is it right to interpret this as a move
 2              back .hh to the right.=This er victory by such a narrow
 3              marg[in of Denis Healey.]
 4  IE:             [ .h h h h     N o  ] I don't believe it i:s. in some
 5              ways I wish I could say that. .hhhh But I don't believe it
 6              i:s. I believe it's a mo:ve back .hhh to the broad based
 7              tolerant representative Labour Part(h)y, .hhh the Labour
 8              Party in which Neil Kinnock and I: who disagree on a
 9              number of policy issue:s .hh can argue about them .hh without
10              accusing each other of treachery:, .hhh without suggesting
11              that one or the other of us is playing into the Tories' ha:nds.
12        →     .hhh And let me say something about the next year because
13              that was your original question. .hhh I think Tony Benn would
14              be personally extremely foo:lish to sta:nd for the deputy
15              leadership again? ...
```

In this case, the interviewee clearly orients to his accountability to respond to the question's agenda. However, as we saw in chapter 2, if respondents fail to orient to a question's agenda, they can be held to account by the questioner. It is just this sanction that is applied to Conservative ex-British Prime Minister Edward Heath, who is asked a simple yes/no question about whether he "quite likes" his arch-rival Harold Wilson. Heath's response (beginning at line 3) is a clear attempt to evade the question's agenda:

(2)   [Omnibus Interview]
IR: David Frost, IE: Edward Heath
```
 1  IR:           Do you quite li:ke him?
 2                (.)
 3  IE:           .hhh .h .h We:ll I th- I think in politics you see: i- it's
 4                not a ques:tion of going about (.) li:king people or not, hh
 5                It's a question of dealing with people, °°h .h°° a:n::d u::h
 6                (.) I've always been able to deal perfectly well with Mister
 7                Wilson,=as indeed: uh- he has with me,
 8                (0.4)
 9  IR:    →      <But do you like> him?
10                (0.1)
11  IE:           .hhhh Well agai:n it's not a question of uh (.) li:kes or
12                disli:kes. I::t's a question of wor:king together:: with
13                other people who are in politics,
14                (0.6)
15  IR:    →      But do y'like him.
16                (0.4)
17  IE:           .hhh (.) That'll have to remain t'be see:n won't it.
```

At lines 9 and 15, the interviewer reissues his original question, marking it as reissued with the word "but". In this way he sanctions Heath for not responding in its terms, and renews his effort to have Heath respond. A similar yes/no question agenda, though dealing with a somewhat more subtle form of evasion, is the following. Here Republican leader Bob Dole is asked whether Paul Volcker should be reappointed as Chairman of the Federal Reserve:

(3)   [US ABC This Week: March 1986: Fed Chair]
IR: Sam Donaldson, IE: Sen. Bob Dole
```
 1  IR:           Talking about money, what about Paul Volcker,
 2                whose term is up next year? Would you like to
 3                see him reappointed to the Fed?
 4  IE:           I, I think he's been very effective.
 5  IR:    →      Well, would you like to see him reappointed?
```

Dole's response to the question (line 4) lies within the question's topical parameters – the merits of Federal Reserve Chairman Paul Volcker; but Dole evades the question's action agenda – the desirability of reappointing him. In this context, the IR has license to pursue a response, which is what he proceeds to do (line 5).

More subtle agenda-setting work may be done by question prefaces. In the following sequence British Prime Minister Margaret Thatcher, a noted opponent of British membership of the European Union's "exchange rate mechanism" referred to in line 1, is asked about her current views. The question preface contrasts Thatcher's standard (and studiedly vague) answer ("we will join when the time is right") with the response of critics who are said to assert that "that means never".

(4)   [UK BBC TV Newsnight 1989]
```
 1  IR:           Now turning to the exchange rate mechanism you:
 2                have consistently said or the government has said
 3                .hh that you will joi:n when the ti:me is right
```

```
4                but people are saying: .hh that that means never.
5                Could you defi:ne the ki:nd of conditions when
6                you think we would go in.
7  IE:      →    Uh no I would not say it means never. For the policy...
```

The net effect of this preface is to block Thatcher from using her stock ("when the time is right") answer, and indeed she begins by rebutting the critics' claim that it means "never".

We will have much more to say about the agenda-setting role of questions in chapter 17.

Presupposition

Like questions in medicine, questions in news interviews are laden with presuppositions that strongly influence the terms from which responses are constructed. For example, in (5) the interviewer's question asks a Republican lobbyist for an explanation of why health industry lobbyists have begun a campaign against the ill-fated Clinton health care proposals "early". This question clearly presupposes the "fact" of the early start, perhaps with the implication that they are jumping the gun and campaigning before the proposals are even complete:

(5) [US PBS MacNeil/Lehrer: 21 October 1993; Health Care]
IR: Margaret Warner, IE: Lobbyist Elizabeth Jenckes
```
1  IR:       =Mizz Jenckes, let me start with you. Ah: y:ou've
2            started all (of) this I think, thuh health industry
3            association.>Health insurance association. .hhh
4            Why:: so early in this debate when there's not gonna
5            be:: a vote on it ih- f'r maybe a year?
6  IE:  →    Margaret (.) health care reform is well under way. ....
```

In this context, the first thing the interviewee does is to dispute this presupposition when she says (at line 6): "Margaret (.) health care reform is well under way. ...."

In (6), from the same interview, another question – this time to a Democratic lobbyist – incorporates a questionable presupposition. Here the presupposition is that public support for health care reform has dropped – at (lines 2–4): "=How do you explain: that (.) public support for thuh President's plan has dropped off rather sharply since he announced it a month ago?="

(6) [US MacNeil/Lehrer 21 October 1993 (Simplified)]
IR: Margaret Warner, IE: Mandy Grunwald
```
1  IR:       (Let me- Let me (just) ask Mandy Grunwald one other question.=
2            =How do you explain: that (.) public support for thuh President's
3            plan has dropped off rather sharply since he announced it
4            a month ago?=
5  IE:  →    =We haven't seen those sharp drops, at all. In fact
6            we'v[e seen
7  IR:           [So your internal p[olling doesn't
8  IE:                              [Our- our internal polling=
9            =has seen sustain:ed ah: support for thuh plan
```

And, like her Republican counterpart in (5), Democratic lobbyist Mandy Grunwald in (6) is also quick to dispute this presupposition.

While yes/no or polar questions are less encrusted with presuppositions than their wh-question counterparts, they can be inferentially loaded nonetheless. In (7) Democratic pollster James Carville is asked if then-Governor Clinton's character should be off-limits. In suggesting a moratorium on attacks, the question clearly implies that Clinton's character is flawed, something which Carville vigorously rebuts:

```
(7)  [US ABC Nightline 15 October 1992 (On the 1992 US Presidential campaign)]
  1  IR:         =.hhh Mister Carville: should Governor Clinton's
  2              character now be off: limits somehow?
  3  IE:    →    Well I don't know anything about his character
  4              being off limits thuh man has magnificent
  5              character...
```

Each one of these disputed claims has clear implications for the array of issues set in motion by the interviewer's question. In each case the interviewee recognizes the underlying presuppositions to be disadvantageous, and swiftly moves to neutralize it.

Question preferences

Polarity in yes/no questions is unavoidable. Such questions, by their very nature, tend to be tilted so as to favor a "Yes" or a "No" response. As we saw in chapter 10, declarative questions with (or without) tags are strongly tilted towards responses that are aligned to the declarative, as in (8) and (9):

```
(8)   UK BBC Radio World at One: Mar. 3 1979: Miners' Election
IR: Robin Day, IE: Arthur Scargill
  1  IR:         =Do you ascri:be to Marxist economic philosophy.=
  2  IE:         =I would say that there: er: the: (.) philosophy
  3              of Marx as far as the economics of Britain is
  4              concerned is one with which I find sympathy.=and
  5              would support it.=Yes.
  6              (.)
  7  IR:    →    Well that makes you a Marxist doe[sn't it.]
  8  IE:                                          [Not= nece]ssarily
  9              makes me a Marxist in the descriptive sense, ...
```

```
(9)  [BBC TV Newsnight: 14 October 1981]
  1  IR:         But do you accept that Sir Geoffrey this afternoon said
  2              he wasn't going to change.
  3              (0.2)
  4  IE:         I:: accept that ye:s.
  5  IR:    →    But you think he's totally wrong.
  6  IE:         Yes.
```

And, as in the medical data, polarity items such as "any" and "at all" can tilt a question so as to favor a "No" response:

(10)　[UK BBC Radio Today: Bosnia Camps]
IR: John Humphrys, IE: Ian Smedley

```
1   IR:        .hhh People have u::sed thuh phrase concentration camps:
2              and thuh Bosnians themselves have used that phrase.
3              Do you believe there's any justification for that at all?
4   IE:        .hh I think in thuh case of some of thuh larger camps ...
```

In (10), where the question is asked of a worker for an aid organization with an operation in Bosnia at the height of its ethnic cleansing, the question's format is cautious in tilting somewhat away from the suggestion that the Serbs were running "concentration camps".

Question prefaces can also tilt questions, often by mobilizing support for the side of an issue to which the interviewee is opposed, thus creating a hostile environment for response:

(11)　[US CBS 60 Minutes] ((Topic is whether US troops could have been exposed to Seron gas during the Gulf War, causing Gulf War syndrome))
IR: Ed Bradley, IE: US Defense Secretary John Deutch

```
1   IR:        Secretary Deutch you say there is no evidence.
2              .hh You've got ca:ses where: khh theh- Czechs: say: that
3              they ↑foun:d seron.
4              You say they didn't, th:ey say: (.) that they did. .hh You
5              have soldiers say:ing: that they experienced burning
6              sensations after explosions in the air. That they became
7              nauseous, that they got .hh headaches.
8              .hh You have two hundred fifty gallons of chemical agents
9              that were found in:si:de Kuwait.
10             .hh You had scuds that had seron in the warheads.
11             (1.0)
12  IR:        If that's not evidence what is it.
```

Here the question preface piles up an impressive array of disinterested witnesses who claim that Seron gas was deployed in the first Gulf War (1991). This is something that Secretary Deutch is reluctant to admit, as it would leave the US military exposed to a heavy burden of veterans' health care claims.

Finally, and most powerful of all, negative interrogative questions (beginning with elements like "Isn't it . . ." or "Don't you . . .") are powerfully tilted towards "Yes" responses (Heritage 2002b). The tilt is so strong that interviewees recurrently respond to them, not as questions that are safely within the "circle of neutralism", but as assertions of opinion. Consider the following question to President Bill Clinton in the aftermath of the 1996 presidential election:

(12)　[Presidential Press Conference: 7 March 1997]

```
1   IR:        W'l Mister President in your zea:l (.) for funds during
2       →      the last campaign .hh didn't you put the Vice President (.)
3              an' Maggie and all the others in your (0.4) administration
4              top side .hh in a very vulnerable position, hh
5              (0.5)
6   IR:   →    I disagree with that.hh u- How are we vulnerable because ...
```

Of course Bill Clinton would be quite unlikely to agree with the point of view expressed here, and so would the US State Department official in the next case, who is asked to agree that the US approach to South Africa's apartheid policy is a failure – something that no State Department official could possibly do.

```
(13)   [PBS MacNeil/Lehrer: 22 July 1985]
  1   IR:   →   But isn't this (.) d- declaration of thuh state of
  2               emergency:: ( ) an admission that the eh South African
  3               gover'ment's policies have not worked, an' in fact that
  4               the um- United States ( ) administration's policy of
  5               constructive engagement ( ) has not worked.
  6   IE:   →   I do not agree with you .hhhh that the approach we
  7               have taken (.) toward south africa is- a- is an
  8               incorrect approach.
```

In both of these examples, the interviewee responds by stating that he does not "agree" with the interviewer, thus suggesting that the interviewer has "asserted a position" rather than "asked a question".

Defensible Questioning

Thus far we have considered features of question design that, in the various ways they cause difficulties for interviewees, are demonstrably adversarial in terms of agenda setting, presuppositions or preferences. These questions are not neutral. They are substantively aggressive and exert pressure on interviewees' responses. At the same time, as adversarial as they are, they are for the most part packaged as neutralistic questions. In addition, some of these questions contain additional defensive elements that go beyond their questioning character per se. In this section we examine two main kinds of defenses: (1) justifying the question, and (2) footing shifts in which adversarial statements are attributed to others.

Justifications

Question prefaces quite often contain materials that deal with the news audience's version of our "Why that now?" question. In a question like (14), the news audience is in effect given the background to the question, a background that justifies it being asked of this interviewee – anti-apartheid activist Allan Boesack:

```
(14)
  1   IR:       .hh Two- two members of your organization (.) supposedly
  2               arrested today:
  3               d'you feel in some danger when you go back
```

Defensive prefaces are often designed to neutralize interviewer accountability for hostile questions. For example, in (15) a hostile question about the interviewee's line of work (dog psychiatry), suggesting that it is "a bunch o' poppycock", is framed by a preface that depicts this point of view as one that many audience members would hold.

```
(15)  [NBC Dateline: 16 Dec. 1997: Dog Psychiatry]
 1  IE:         Goo:d boy:.
 2  IR:    →   A lotta people would hear: (.) about your profession.
 3  IE:         Ye:s.=
 4  IR:    →   =and say that's a bunch o'poppycock.
 5  IE:         Ye:s,
 6              (0.2)
 7  IR:         And you say:?
 8              (.)
 9  IE:         I say they're entitled to their opinion.
```

The effect of this preface is to accomplish a "footing shift" (Goffman 1979, Clayman 1992) that neutralizes any responsibility the interviewer might have for presenting this opinion.

This kind of preface can also justify a question to a particular individual (Roth 1998) by describing the person's experiences or circumstances. In (16) the "Why that now?" question hangs heavily in the air. The topic is a challenge to the party leadership of the then Prime Minister, Mrs. Thatcher, who was then only a year into her premiership but was pursuing unpopular economic policies. Such a challenge, if successful, would have resulted in the challenger becoming Prime Minister. However, the interviewee is a relatively junior politician who, at that time, was being pushed forward for a protest vote against Thatcher's leadership. The moment was one of extreme delicacy for the interviewer and the interviewee:

```
(16)   (UK BBC TV Nationwide 15 October 1980)
 1  IR:       Mister Rippon I must ask you,=your name has come up as you
 2            know in connection with the possibility of standing against
 3            Mrs Thatcher for the .hh leadership. er: (.) Are you likely
 4            to be a candidate [to challenge Mrs Thatcher.=
 5  GR:                         [.hhh Well
 6  GR:       =I du- I think it's very unlikely.=But I- I- I think what
 7            has happened .hhh is that er it's a reflection of the anxiety
 8            part of the pressure quite spontaneous pressure to urge her
 9            to .hhh er change her .hh attitude er uhm direction of policy
10            before it is too late.
```

In this instance the interviewer begins the question almost apologetically with "I must ask you" and then accounts for the question (lines 1–3) by saying that the interviewee's "name has come up as you know" in connection with a leadership contest. Here the justification helps the news audience understand why the question is being asked, but also defends it against possible objections from the interviewee.

An apparently defensive process of justification can have an adversarial dimension as well. In the following question to Phil Gramm, who was at the time a candidate for the Republican presidential nomination, an elaborate account of President Clinton's view of a book is used as bait to see if Gramm will be drawn into a discussion of his avoidance of the draft during the Vietnam War:

```
(17)  [Face The Nation 04/16/95 Senator Phil Gramm (Texas, R)]
 1  IR:        I just wanta get to thuh politics of this McNamara book. .hh
 2       a→   Ah President Clinton avoided thuh draft,
 3       b→   and he seemed to suggest that this book in some way:: ah
```

```
4                    vindicates that draft avoidance and almost removes Vietnam
5                    as a political issue now and forever more.
6         c→         .hh You avoided thuh draft, .h
7         d→         do you feel .h that this ih- this book is gonna help inoculate
8                    you from say Bob Dole, who has this war record, in your own
9                    competition?
10  IE:              I don't think so. I don't- I don't think I need vindication,
11                   (0.3) and I don't think books vindicate you.
```

The preface draws a strong parallel between Clinton and Gramm (arrows a and c), which is not a parallel that the Republican senator would have relished, while still managing a fully fledged justification of the question's relevance for Gramm's situation in a race with war veteran Bob Dole for the nomination.

Footing: speaking on behalf of a third party

A second way of managing an adversarial posture while remaining within the safety of the neutralistic circle is to attribute statements which are hostile to the interviewee's position to third parties – a maneuver which, following Goffman (1979), we refer to as a "footing shift". A number of such shifts have already appeared in the data of this chapter. In (4) for example the interviewer contradicts Margaret Thatcher's public statements with an (unnamed) third-party attributed claim that "people are saying that that means never." In this way, the interviewer can challenge Margaret Thatcher's public position and narrow her options for response while remaining clearly within the safe haven of neutralism.

Footing shifts of this kind can emerge within individual sentences to qualify dangerously assertive phrases. Here the interviewer qualifies his use of the words "negative approach" by attributing them to a political rival of the interviewee.

```
(18)   UK BBCTV Newsnight: May 1989: European Social Policies
IR: Peter Snow, IE: John Redwood
 1   IR:           ...Michael Heseltine said tonight in a speech
 2                 and you know his views about Europe and ah he
 3                 may not say so but he's clearly opposed to the
 4                 (.) .h rather strong line that you and Missus
 5                 Thatcher ta:ke on this. .hhh      He said (.) we can
 6                 (0.2) choose for either to influence the
 7                 community's (.) form as a leading partner (0.3)
 8                 or to be subjected to it by others more
 9                 determined than ourselves. Isn't it a fact that
10                 the rather negative approach you seem to take,
11        →        (.) uh and I:'d and and I'm using words
12        →        characterized by .hh Mister Heselti:ne Mister
13        →        Heath and o[thers .hhh uh is in fact damaging=
14   IE:                      [mm
15   IR:           =(0.3) your chances of contributin[g to the=
16   IE:                                             [no
17   IR:           =future of the community.
18   IE:           What I've been saying tonight is not negative at
19                 all ...
```

Here the footing shift is hardly surprising. The interviewer is using the strongly assertive "isn't it" format for his question, and has already referred to the interviewee's approach as "negative". At this point he seems to become aware that his question is hearably opinionated, and he goes back and "fixes" it by referring to the interviewee's rival (Michael Heseltine) as the author of these words. Another case of repairing a question to fix this kind of a problem is the following:

```
(19)  US PBS NewsHour: 10 Jun. 1985: Nuclear Weapons
IR: Robert MacNeil, IE: Kenneth Adelman
 1  IR:           How d'you sum up the me:ssage. that this
 2                decision is sending to the Soviets?
 3  IE:           .hhh Well as I started- to say:: it is ay- one
 4                of: warning and opportunity. The warning is (.)
 5                you'd better comply: to arms control::
 6                agreements if arms control is going to have any
 7                chance of succeeding in the future. Unilateral
 8                compliance by the United States just not in the
 9                works ...
10                ((Four lines omitted))
11  IR:     →     But isn't this- uh::: critics uh on the
12                conservative side of the political argument
13                have argued that this is:. abiding by the
14                treaty is:. unilateral (.) observance. (.)
15                uh:: or compliance. (.) by the United States.
```

In this case, the interviewer also repairs his question in the interest of avoiding any taint of personal assertion in the suggestion that the kind of US treaty compliance being implemented by the Reagan administration is "unilateral".

This form of neutralistic maneuver is normally validated (or at least not undermined) by interviewees (Clayman 1992). The following case is representative of those in which interviewees accept the third-party attributions that interviewers make. Here the context is South Africa during the apartheid period. Reverend Boesak, an anti-apartheid activist, is asked about a claim by the South African ambassador to the US. The ambassador argued that negotiations with anti-apartheid leaders were impossible because they did not want to be branded as "collaborators" by fellow activists:

```
(20)  US ABC Nightline: 22 Jul 1985: South Africa
IR: Charles Gibson, IE: Rev. Allan Boesak
 1  IR:           Reverend Boesak lemme a- pick up a point uh
 2          1→    the Ambassador made. What- what assurances can
 3                you give u:s .hh that (.) talks between
 4                moderates in that country will take pla:ce when
 5                it see:ms that any black leader who is willing
 6          1→    to talk to the government is branded as the
 7          1→    Ambassador said a collaborator and is then
 8                punished.=
 9  IE:     2→    =Eh theh- the- the Ambassador has it wrong.
10                It's not the people who want to talk with
11                the government that are branded collaborators
```

```
12              it is: those people .hh who are given powers
13              by the government that they use in an oppressive
14              fashion .hh within the township that are branded
15              collaborators....
```

Here the interviewer specifically attributes the expression "collaborator" to the South African ambassador, thus distancing himself from the claim that persons who negotiate with the South African government would be treated as such within the anti-apartheid movement. In response, Boesak – himself a freedom fighter against South Africa's apartheid regime – explicitly accepts the attribution.

Maximizing Adversarialness

As we have seen, within the limits of neutralistic questions, it is still possible to formulate highly adversarial questions. However, two additional practices – forks and contrasts – can be used to crank up the heat on interviewees.

In the first of these, the fork, the interviewee is presented with two highly unpalatable alternatives and asked to choose between them. In the following case, the interviewee is Texaco Chairman, Peter Bijur. The occasion is the settlement of a long-running class action lawsuit between Texaco and its African-American employees who alleged racially discriminatory hiring and promotion policies at Texaco. The case was settled following the emergence of a tape recording of middle managers that was strongly suggestive of discrimination. Following the settlement Texaco's stock, which had been sliding because of investor anxieties about the lawsuit, rose by about ten percent. NBC news anchor Tom Brokaw opened the interview as follows:

(21) NBC Nightly News 15 November 1996]
IR: Tom Brokaw, IE: Peter Bijur
```
 1   IR:        .hhhh Thuh ma::n in thuh cross hairs f'r Texaco: joins
 2              us no:w. He:'s chairman and C E O: Peter Biju:r, .h Mister
 3              Bijur what's pro:- what prompted this settlement. .hh
 4              Thuh fact that you concluded your company was in fact
 5              discrimina:ting¿ or thuh prospects of: (.) more economic
 6              losses.
 7   IE:        T:o:m it was that we wanted to be f:air: to ah all of
 8              the employees involved, we're a: wonderful: gr:oup of
 9              people and family in this company, en we wanta be
10              equitable with everybody.
```

At line 3, Brokaw asks "what prompted this settlement" and then offers two alternative motivations: the company was in fact discriminating, or the lawsuit was causing economic losses. Needless to say, neither of these is the kind of explanation that the chairman of a major US corporation would like to assent to. Bijur avoids responding to either of these options, substituting a third option that casts his company in a more favorable light.

In a similar maneuver, then-Republican Senate Leader Bob Dole is presented with two third-party attributed accounts, and then asked to choose between them. In effect Dole, a

Republican leader with a Republican President in the White House, is asked whether he or
his President is to blame for the fact that "programs are in trouble."

(22) [Meet the Press: December 1985]
```
 1  IR:          Senator (0.5) uh President Reagan's elected thirteen months
 2               ago: an enormous landslide.
 3               (0.8)
 4  IR:          It is s::aid that his programs are in trouble, though he seems
 5               to be terribly popular with the American people.
 6               (0.6)
 7  IR:          It is said by some people at thuh White House we could get
 8               those programs through:: if only we ha:d perhaps more: .hh
 9               uhffective leadership up on thuh hill an' I [suppose]
10  (IE):                                                  [hhhheh ]
11  IR:          indirec'ly that might ( ) relate t'you as well:.
12               ( )
13  IR:          Uh whaddyou think thuh problem is rilly.
14        F→     Is it (0.2) thuhleadership as it might be claimed up on thuh hill,
15        F→     er is it thuh programs themselves.
```

Here Dole is invited to decide whether he personally should accept the blame for failed
legislative programs, or whether he should sell out his own President instead.

The second procedure involves establishing contrasts or inconsistencies in the behavior
or record of the interviewee. The contrast may be between different statements the interviewee has made, or between words and deeds, or between a standard of conduct that the
interviewee endorses and his or her actual conduct. It is this last type of contrast which is
illustrated in the following case which involves a famous interview between CBS news anchor
Dan Rather and then-Vice President Bush (senior) who at the time was a candidate for the
Republican nomination. Here the issue is Bush's involvement in the Iran–Contra scandal,
which included secret arms supplies to right wing Nicaraguan insurgents. The preface to
the question establishes a parallel between two situations in which one person (President
Reagan) did the right thing and the other (Vice-President Bush) did the wrong thing.

(23) [CBS Evening News 1/25/88 Bush–Rather]
```
 1  IR:          Mister Vice President, thank you for being with us tonigh:t,
 2        a→     .hh Donald Gregg still serves as your trusted advisor,
 3        a→     He was deeply involved in running arms to the contras, 'n 'e
 4        a→     didn't inform you.
 5        b→     .hhh Now when President Reagan's (0.3) trusted advisor:
 6        b→     Admiral Poindexter: (0.5) failed to inform him::, (0.7)
 7        b→     thuh President (0.4) fired 'im.
 8               (0.5)
 9  IR:   q→     Why is Mister Gregg still:: (0.2) inside thuh White House
10        q→     'n still a trusted advisor.
11  IE:          Because I have confidence in him, .hh 'n because this matter
12               Dan:, as you well know:, ...
```

The question preface establishes a parallel between President Reagan's conduct and Vice-
President Bush's conduct in connection with the scandal, and then asks Bush to account for
the contrast. The contrast is a pointed one for Bush. Reagan – the role model in this example
– is after all the one that Bush wishes to succeed as President. Yet Reagan is established as
the standard of behavior against which Bush has fallen short.

Slipping Outside the Neutralistic Circle

Almost all of the questions we have presented so far have remained within the safety of the neutralistic circle. However, not all questions will necessarily occupy this charmed sphere. Consider the following interview between Sam Donaldson and Richard Darman who was President Bush Sr.'s budget director. Darman had the task of cleaning up a regulation fiasco in which many US savings and loan organizations went bankrupt, creating large-scale taxpayer liabilities:

```
(24)  [ABC This Week October 1989: Darman]
   1  IR:    →  Isn't it a fact, Mr. Darman, that the taxpayers will
   2               pay more in interest than if they just paid it out of
   3               general revenues?
   4  IE:        No, not necessarily. That's a technical argument—
   5  IR:        It's not a— may I, sir? It's not a technical argument.
   6         →  Isn't it a fact?
   7  IE:        No, it's definitely not a fact. Because first of all,
   8               twenty billion of the fifty billion is being handled in
   9         →  just the way you want — through treasury financing. The
  10               remaining—
  11  IR:    →  I'm just asking you a question. I'm not expressing my
  12         →  personal views.
  13  IE:        I understand.
```

In this fascinating exchange, Donaldson begins with a highly assertive negative interrogative question about taxpayer liabilities ("Isn't it a fact that . . ."). When Darman disagrees, Donaldson interrupts to contradict Darman (line 5), before reframing his assertion as a further negative interrogative ("Isn't it a fact?") at line 6. Subsequently Darman's response incorporates the remark that "fifty billion is being handled in just the way you want", thus clearly attributing a personal position to Donaldson. Donaldson's response is to retreat to the safety of the neutralistic circle: "I'm just asking you a question. I'm not expressing my personal views." This retreat is accepted (line 13).

However, there are questions that can never be neutralistic and can never really be unsaid, or escaped from. These are accusatory questions, whose prototypical form is "How could you X." These questions carry the implication that there is no acceptable explanation for the action or statement under discussion, and hence that the interviewee is guilty of some form of misconduct. In a heated section of his interview with then-Vice-President Bush Sr., CBS news anchor Dan Rather became involved in the following exchange:

```
(25)  [CBS Evening News February 1887]
   1  IR:        =.hhh Can you explain how- (.) you were supposed tuh be the-
   2               eh- you are:. you're an anti terrorist expert. .hhh we- (0.2)
   3               Iran was officially a terrorist state. .hh you went
   4               a[round telling eh::- eh- ehr-       ]
   5  IE:         [I've already explained that Dan, I] wanted those
   6               [hostages-    I    wanted   Mister    Buckley  ] outta there.
   7  IR:        [( ) Mist' Vice President (thuh question is)]
   8  IR:        But-
```

```
9                    (0.3)
10  IE:              [before 'e was killed. ]  [which he (          ) ]=
11  IR:      →       [You've- you've made us hyp]oc[rites in thuh face o' thuh world.]=
12  IR:      →       =How couldja [gr- how couldja-] (.) sign on to such a policy.
13  IE:                          [(That was ba:d) ]
14  IR:              .hh[h And thuh question is, what does that tell us]=
15  IE:                 [Well (half-)     thuh    same    reason     ]=
16  IR:              =[about your record.]
17  IE:              =[thuh President si]gned on to it. (0.2) Thuh same reason thuh
18                   President signed on to it. .hh When a CIA agent is being tortured
19                   tuh death, .h maybe ya err on the side of a human life.
```

At lines 11 and 12, Rather asserts that Bush has made the US "hypocrites in the face of the world" and continues with the accusatory "how couldja sign on to such a policy." Belatedly realizing his error, Rather attempts to continue with "and the question is what does that tell us about your record." – a legitimate question.

But it was too late. Although this was one incident in a highly contentious interview, it was probably the worst. CBS switchboards were jammed with calls protesting Rather's conduct, and his career at CBS subsequently began a long decline.

Journalistic Questioning in Historical Context

In both the United Kingdom and the United States, journalists' questions have changed substantially over time, becoming less deferential and more aggressive over the past half-century (Clayman & Heritage 2002a: ch. 2, 2002b, Clayman, Elliott, Heritage, & McDonald 2006). This historic development entails a shift in the balance (noted earlier) from neutralism toward adversarialness, but it encompasses various other aspects of question design. To illustrate the magnitude of this transformation, consider how the issue of the federal budget was put before two US presidents separated by almost three decades – Dwight Eisenhower and Ronald Reagan.

```
(26)  [Eisenhower 27 Oct 1954: 9]
1   JRN:     Mr. President, you spoke in a speech the other night of
2            the continued reduction of government spending and tax cuts
3            to the limit that the national security will permit.
4            Can you say anything more definite at this time about
5            the prospects of future tax cuts?


(27)  [Reagan 16 June 1981: 14]
1   JRN:     Mr. President, for months you said you wouldn't modify
2            your tax cut plan, and then you did. And when the
3            business community vociferously complained, you changed
4            your plan again.
5            I just wondered whether Congress and other special
6            interest groups might get the message that if they
7            yelled and screamed loud enough, you might modify
8            your tax cut plan again?
```

Although both questions concern budgetary matters and tax cuts, the question to Eisenhower is in various ways more deferential. Its agenda is essentially benign: indeed, it is framed as having been occasioned by Eisenhower's own previous remarks, and it contains nothing that disagrees with, challenges, or opposes his views. It is also non-assertive: it displays minimal expectations about what type of answer would be correct or preferable, and is formally neutral in that respect. And it is cautiously indirect: it exerts relatively little pressure on the president to provide an answer, and even allows for the possibility ("*Can you* say anything . . ." in line 4) that the president may be unable to answer.

Reagan's question is, by contrast, more aggressive. This question is similarly occasioned by the president's previous remarks (lines 1–4), but here the journalist details damaging contradictions between the president's words and his actual deeds, contradictions that portray the president as weak and beholden to special interests. This prefatory material thus sets an agenda for the question that is fundamentally adversarial. Moreover, the adversarial preface then becomes a foundation for the question that follows (lines 4–7), which assumes that the preface is true and draws out the implications for the president's general susceptibility to pressure from special interests. And far from being neutral, the preface assertively favors a *yes* answer, thereby exerting pressure on the president to align with the adversarial viewpoint that the question embodies.

Quantitative research demonstrates that these two questions are fairly representative of the Eisenhower and Reagan eras (Clayman & Heritage 2002b). Indeed, across five decades of US presidential news conferences, White House journalists have grown significantly more adversarial in a variety of ways (Clayman, Elliott, Heritage, & McDonald 2006). To a limited extent, this transformation has affected the basic repertoire of practices available to journalists. Certain extremely deferential practices (e.g., indirect questions on the order of "Would you care to talk about X") have fallen out of use and have essentially disappeared. Other extremely aggressive practices (e.g., coercive negative interrogatives and accusatory *how could you*-type questions), once virtually nonexistent, have become recurrent if not commonplace. For the most part, however, this transformation has affected the relative frequency of questioning practices. Journalists are increasingly likely to exercise initiative via more elaborated (prefaced and compound) forms; the substantive content of their questions has grown increasingly adversarial; and they have exerted greater pressure on the president to address such content via increasingly direct and assertive design forms. Similar trends have been observed qualitatively in both American and British news interviews (Clayman & Heritage 2002a: ch. 2).

Notwithstanding the cross-national scope of this transformation, the process by which it has occurred has been very different in the United Kingdom as compared with the United States. In the UK, a robust tradition of government regulation of broadcasting, coupled with the absence of competition prior to 1958, combined to foster a highly deferential style of questioning in BBC interviews of the 1950s. When the BBC monopoly was replaced by a duopoly in 1958, the resulting competition fueled a sudden and dramatic rise in adversarial questioning. In America, where government regulation of broadcasting has been comparatively minimal and competitive pressures have been present from the outset, adversarial questioning appears to have grown more gradually from a higher baseline.

However, trends in US presidential news conferences have been more volatile, with identifiable phases of relative deference/aggressiveness in question design (Clayman, Elliott, Heritage, & McDonald 2006). The deferential era of the 1950s and 1960s was followed by a marked rise in aggressiveness that extended through the 1970s and into the early 1980s.

This suggests that a series of historical events and conditions prompted journalists to exercise their watchdog role much more vigorously in the latter period. The most proximate factor is the declining journalistic trust in the president that followed the Vietnam War and the Watergate affair (Cannon 1977: 289–92, Broder 1987: 167–8). Lou Cannon of the Washington Post cites these events as having a transformative impact on how reporters view administrative officials: "An attitude of basic trust that was tinged with skepticism was replaced with an attitude of suspicion in which trust occasionally intervened" (Cannon 1977: 291). As David Broder (1987: 167) has observed, even meetings with the president's press secretary were affected: "the style of questioning at White House briefings became, after Watergate, almost more prosecutorial than inquisitive." This shift toward more vigorous questioning was not short-lived; it endured across several administrations and is indicative of a basic "paradigm shift" in the norms of the White House press corps (Clayman, Elliott, Heritage, and Beckett, forthcoming).

A second and perhaps less obvious contributing factor has to do with practical economic conditions. The 1970s and early 1980s were also a period of time when the long post-World War II economic expansion came to an end. Since aggressive questioning of the president is directly associated with both unemployment and interest rates (Clayman, Heritage, Elliott, & McDonald 2007), the persistent stagflation of the era was also a contributing factor in the trend toward rising aggressiveness.

Economic factors may also explain, at least in part, why the trend toward increasingly vigorous questioning subsequently reversed itself. As economic conditions steadily improved following the recession of the early 1980s, aggressive questioning was on the decline from Reagan's second term through the Bush administration. Moreover, during this same period US journalism came under increasing criticism for being excessively negative and overly concerned with strategy and scandal, and for fostering public apathy and cynicism. This would in turn stimulate a reform movement within journalism, the so-called "civic journalism" or "public journalism" movement. The latter development didn't get off the ground until the middle of Bush's term in office (Fallows 1996: 247–54), but it could have further contributed to trends already in progress, trends that show journalists to be reining in their aggressiveness during this period.

Such restraint would not last forever. Aggressiveness was again on the rise over the course of the Clinton administration (1993–2000), with some dimensions of aggressiveness growing to unprecedented levels. It seems clear that question design, in its various manifestations, offers a running index of president–press relations, and more generally an index of the evolving and at times contentious relationship between journalism and the state.

Conclusion

In this chapter, we have tried to convey some of the variety of question designs and strategies that inhabit the news interview context. Choices within this variety define different styles of interviewer, of interview, of news organization, and even of historical period in news interview broadcasting. Changes in the broad pattern of questioning of public figures can develop with great rapidity in response to economic and other trends, but also in response to singular events like Watergate, changes in the regulatory environment such as the scrapping of the "Fairness Doctrine" by the US Federal Communications Commission (Epstein

1973, Clayman & Heritage 2002a), and changes in the institutional context of broadcasting such as the breaking of the BBC monopoly (Clayman & Heritage 2002a).

Fundamental and rapid changes in interactional practice like this rarely, if ever, happen in the realm of ordinary interaction. The speed of their development in news reminds us that news talk is a special and institutionally restricted form of discourse that resides within a political, economic and regulatory environment. Within this context, what is treated as fair questioning and what as foul can also change rapidly. The parameters of the permissible can expand, and they can also contract. Yesterday's "fairness" can seem quaint, tomorrow's may appear shocking. Of all the institutions we examine in this book, the news interview is the most nakedly exposed to raw processes of social change.

For Further Reading

Our previous book on the news interview (Clayman & Heritage 2002a: chs. 5 and 6) contains a more elaborate analysis of forms of question design and their bearing on the journalistic norms of neutralism and adversarialness. Of these two issues, adversarialness has received the greatest share of attention by other scholars (Harris 1986, Adkins 1992, Roth 1998, Emmertsen 2007, Rendle-Short 2007). Historical trends in the prevalence of aggressive questioning have been examined qualitatively in the broadcast news interview (Jones 1992, Clayman & Heritage 2002a: ch. 2) and quantitatively in the case of US presidential news conferences (Clayman & Heritage 2002b, Clayman, Elliott, Heritage, & McDonald 2006). News conferences have also been subject to multivariate analysis of the social factors that explain variations in aggressive questioning (Clayman, Heritage, Elliott, & McDonald 2007). Finally, recent work has begun to examine how styles of questioning vary depending on whether the interviewee is a public figure, expert, or ordinary person (Roth 2002, Montgomery 2007: ch. 7), suggesting that while the news interview remains a recognizable and coherent genre of broadcast talk, it may also be decomposed into a variety of analyzable subgenres.

17

Answers and Evasions

When Albert Gore was Bill Clinton's vice-presidential running mate in 1992, Gore's position on abortion became the focus of controversy. As a congressman, Gore had opposed federal funding for most abortions, but now he was expressing support for it as part of Clinton's health care reform plan. In an aggressive interview conducted by Sam Donaldson, Gore received a barrage of tough questions exposing this apparent contradiction. He was momentarily rescued by a commercial break, at which point he was urged by his media advisor to sidestep questions of this sort: "Don't be afraid to turn their questions. If they ask you about [abortion], just say . . . 'I want to talk today about the new direction that Governor Clinton and I want to take the country'" (quoted in Springer 1995). Politicians and other public figures are often evasive under questioning from members of the news media (Harris 1991, Bull 1994). The impetus to sidestep or resist a line of questioning is understandable given the relatively adversarial character of contemporary interviewing practices documented in the previous chapter. Since interviewers are often drawn to questions that are unflattering or oppositional, interviewees may have to be less than forthcoming if they wish to save face and stay on message (cf. Bull 2003).

However, evasiveness has a downside. As we saw in chapter 3, answering questions is treated as a basic moral obligation not only for public figures in journalistic interviews but for interactional participants more generally. And while interactants generally expect one another to be properly responsive to the questions they receive, the responsiveness of politicians is perhaps more closely scrutinized, so that attempts to resist, sidestep, or evade can be costly. Interviewers themselves monitor for evasiveness, responding to such maneuvers with probing follow-up questions and negative sanctions (Greatbatch 1986). Journalistic monitoring can also extend beyond the occasion of the interview itself, as when moments of evasiveness are singled out and replayed – in the form of quotations and soundbites – in subsequent news stories (Clayman 1990). Even when journalists allow evasive maneuvers to pass without comment, there may still be consequences for the broadcast audience and for public opinion. Insofar as a resistant response is noticed by audience members, they will seek to account for the breach of conduct via inferences that are apt to be unflattering. They may infer that the interviewee has some ulterior motive for avoiding the question, such as something unsavory to hide. American citizens may have a constitutionally protected right to remain silent in the face of police questioning, so that silence cannot be treated as incriminating in courts of law;

but public figures have no such protection in the court of public opinion constituted by the journalistic interview.

In a nutshell, then, interviewees face a dilemma. There are various pressures, both from journalists and from the audience, from within the interview and in subsequent media coverage, to answer straightforwardly. But when the question is adversarial, there are cross-cutting pressures to take precisely the opposite course of action. For those contemplating a resistant response, the problem is how to reap the benefits while also minimizing the potential costs.

This chapter provides an overview of the dynamics of answering and resisting questions in broadcast news interviews. Our emphasis will be on the basic forms that resistance can take, and the various practices through which interviewees manage this attractive but risky course of action.

Conceptual Preliminaries

Evasiveness is an elusive phenomenon. The concept is, in the first instance, a familiar part of interactants' ordinary language for characterizing and sanctioning conduct, but it is also deployed by social scientists in technical analyses of such conduct. From whose perspective is evasiveness to be assessed?

One approach treats the *analyst's perspective* as primary. The boundary between "answering" and "evading" is something that the analyst determines *a priori* and uses as a benchmark by which to assess particular responses. This approach can generate informative results (e.g., Harris 1991, Bull 1994, 2003), but it becomes problematic when the analyst's assessment diverges from that of the participants themselves. It is, after all, the participants' own understandings of their conduct that are consequential for the way the interaction actually develops. In light of these considerations, and consistent with the conversation analytic approach, here the *participants' perspective* is treated as primary. Thus, every effort is made to ground analyses in the understandings of interviewers and interviewees as these become manifest in the interaction itself.

This ideal can be difficult to achieve in practice. One problem is that the participants may not agree on the import of a particular response. What an interviewer treats as improperly evasive, the interviewee may treat as an essentially valid way of dealing with a difficult or flawed question. Indeed, the very terms used to characterize responses can become problematic. "Evasion" connotes moral impropriety and may be seen as embodying a partial and contestable perspective on the action under analysis.

A more fundamental difficulty is the fact that participants' understandings are not always transparent, and sometimes this is by design. Consider that when an interviewee sidesteps a question, he or she may strive to conceal that fact in an effort to avoid various negative consequences. Correspondingly, even if the interviewer recognizes that the question has been sidestepped, he or she may decide to let it pass in the interest of moving the interview along. It is thus possible for an act of evasion to be fully apparent to both parties, and yet for neither party to register that fact in any demonstrable way.

Accordingly, well-grounded analytic judgments must draw not only on resources internal to the particular instance under examination, but also on more general patterns of conduct. To maintain analytic clarity, we will adhere to the following terminological convention. The term "evasion" will be reserved for actions that are treated as inadequately responsive by the participants. Other terms – e.g., resistant response, agenda shift – will be used more broadly to encompass responses that appear to be less than fully responsive, but are not necessarily treated as inadequate by the participants on that occasion.

We further distinguish between two dimensions of resistance. The *negative* dimension is manifest in the degree to which the interviewee's response falls short of an adequate answer to the question. Blanket refusals to answer, as well as answers that are partial or incomplete, embody resistance in its negative aspect. The *positive* dimension is manifest in the degree to which the response moves beyond the parameters of the question, producing actions or addressing topics that were not specifically called for. Given the restrictive turn-taking system examined in chapter 15, even responses that fully address the agenda of the question and then shift away (as in the examples to be discussed below), can become problematic in the news interview context.

Overt Resistance

There are two general approaches to undertaking a resistant course of action. One approach is to be up front and explicit about what is taking place. The strategy of resisting a question *overtly* has, from the interviewee's point of view, an obvious disadvantage: it renders the resistance conspicuous and hence more likely to be noticed by the interviewer and the media audience. However, this disadvantage is offset by an equally important advantage: having chosen to own up to the resistance, the interviewee can take steps to minimize the damage that it might otherwise cause. Three forms of damage control may be distinguished, each of which reduces the potential costs in identifiable ways.

Deference to the interviewer

IEs often preface their resistant responses with remarks that display some degree of *deference to the IR*. Perhaps the greatest deference is conveyed when the IE actually *requests permission* to shift the agenda. As we saw in chapter 15, such requests are used more generally by IEs when departing from the turn-taking system. Their association with resistant responses in particular is exemplified in the following excerpt. Here a China expert first answers a question about whether recent civil unrest will strengthen the position of reform-oriented officials in that country (lines 4–13), and then goes on to talk about various other matters (lines 16–25), including the generational shift in Chinese leadership and problems of corruption. However, he does not raise these other matters without first requesting (arrow 1) and receiving (arrow 2) permission from the IR to do so.

```
(1)  [UK: Newsnight: Civil Unrest in China]
 1  IR:      Well what do you think do you think this strengthen:s
 2            (1.0) a great deal: the hand of Zhao Ze Young and the
 3            reformers, the radicals.
 4  DH:      I think that (0.2) Jao Ze Young just as he was
 5            responsible for bringing (.) China out of the turbulence
 6            which followed the .hhh uh resignation of Hu Yao Bung as
 7            General Secretary in=uh January nineteen eighty seven.
```

```
 8                    .hhh just as he (.) brought China out of that turbulence
 9                    he will bring Chi:na out of this turbulence .hhh and I
10                    think his stature has already been increased (.) by
11                    recent events (.) .h and ah (.) I'll go out on a limb
12                    and say: I think it's likely to be increased further
13                    .hh by future events
14          1→       but I would like to make two very quick points.=
15   IR:    2→       =Very quickly if you would.
16   DH:             There's a genera:tional thing he:re. .hhh U:um (0.4) ih
17                    Dung Zhao Peng is going to be ei:ghty fi:ve on the twenty
18                    second of August this yea:r. .hh he joi:ned the
19                    communist pa:rty (0.3) .h in nineteen twenty fou:r. .hh
20                    When Mister Baldwin had become Prime Minister for the
21                    first time in this coun:try:. Just. .hhh (0.3) Secondly
22                    (0.3) corruption. .hh A lot of (.) what is: (.) ca:lled
23                    corruption .hh is in fact the by:produ:ct (0.1) of a
24                    system of multiple pricing .hhh which I think is going to
25                    have to be rela:xed.
```

A similar request appeared in a debate interview concerning health care reform. The IE – a health insurance industry executive who opposes President Clinton's health care reform plan – is asked whether anti-reform TV ads disclose the fact that they were paid for by the insurance industry (lines 1–4 below). She answers this question in the affirmative (lines 5–8), but she then goes on (arrow 1) to ask the IR for permission to comment on an issue raised earlier in the program by a reform proponent ("Ron"). When the IR grants permission (arrow 2), she proceeds to address this other issue (which has to do with whether the so-called "Coalition for Health Insurance Choices" is actually an association of insurance companies masquerading as a grass roots public interest group).

```
(2)   [US 21 October 1993 MacNeil/Lehrer: Health Care Ad War]
 1   IR:             .hhh Well Miss Jenckes he raises an interesting question.=
 2                    Again just as a matter of stra:tegy your ad doesn't
 3                    say:: that it's sponsored by the heal:th (.)
 4                    in[surance    companies]
 5   LJ:                [Margaret that's abs]olutely incorrect. .hh Our a:ds
 6                    (.) whether they're on TV, .h our print a-advertisements,
 7                    that appear in newspapers .hh even radio spots indicate
 8                    that we have paid for it.=
 9          1→       Let me may- just make one
10                    comm[ent in [terms of wha[t Ron: says.
11   IR:                  [.hhh  [wh-          [ih-
12   IR:    2→       Al[l right.]
13   LJ:                [.h h h  ] Of course. any coalition, I don't care
14                    whether it's Save: the Whal:es .hh I mean Common Cause
15                    you always start with like minded people. But whether
16                    you're an agent or a broker, .hh you have legitimate
17                    health care concerns yourself....
```

Requests for permission openly acknowledge that a shift of the agenda is in the works. Here the IE specifically indicates (lines 9–10) that she wishes to respond, not to the IR's question, but to a point made earlier by another IE. At the same time, however, such requests defer to the IR as the one who is properly in charge of the discussion agenda.

The IE may also offer a *token request for permission* to shift the agenda, which (as we saw in chapter 15) resembles an actual request but is not treated as requiring a response from the IR. Thus, in a discussion of newly proposed legislation to restrict access to abortion, an anti-abortion advocate answers a legalistic question about the wording of legislation, but she then goes on to argue that current law is too permissive. She prefaces this agenda shift with a request-like object: "can I also point out . . ." (arrowed).

```
(3)  [UK Afternoon Plus: Abortion]
 1   IR:        Jill Knight may I ask you how far that's going to be put
 2              into practice and [what- who: is going to deci:de what=
 3   JK:                           [°Ye::s°
 4   IR:        =i[s serious and what [is a substantial-
 5   JK:          [°Ye:s°            [.hh uh
 6   JK:        Well of course the doctor:: and u::h thuh-
 7              [in other a:reas wh(h)ere medical- th'medical profession=
 8   ():        [(                    )
 9   JK:        =is practiced .hhh doctors've been quite capable of
10              deciding what's serious. (.) and what substantial means,
11      →       .hhh And can I also point out, .hh that u::h
12              Professor Huntingford whom you had on .hh your
13              program in December:: .hh supporting the abortion act
14              .hhh u::h eh said (.) really (.) again quite recently
15              there's no do(h)ubt abo(h)ut it=we have got abortion on
16              ^request, .hhh and this is what parliament did NOT ask for...
```

Notice that the IR makes no attempt to either grant or refuse permission, and the IE does not seem to expect a response. Indeed, she actively discourages a response by building her token request as an incomplete clausal unit ("can I also point out that . . .") which projects further talk to come. Because they provide so little opportunity for response, token requests are somewhat less deferential than their full-fledged counterparts. Nevertheless, they do show the IE to be going through the motions of seeking permission, thereby continuing to at least acknowledge the principle that it is the IR who normally sets the agenda.

Whether they are "genuine" or "pro forma", requests for permission openly acknowledge the fact that an agenda shift is being contemplated. At the same time, these practices alleviate one of the main risks associated with such an action, namely the risk of being caught by a difficult and perhaps embarrassing follow-up question. By deferring to the IR as having primary rights to set the discussion agenda, and in some instances actually obtaining the IR's consent to shift away, requests for permission reduce the likelihood that the shift will be probed or negatively sanctioned.

Minimizing the divergence

A second form of damage control involves downplaying the agenda shift by portraying it as a minor digression from the agenda established by the question. Requests for permission often contain *minimizing characterizations*, such as reference to a "very quick" or "just one" comment.

(4) [UK Newsnight: Civil Unrest in China]
```
     DH:           But I would like to make two very quick points
```

(5) [US 21 Oct 1993 MacNeil/Lehrer: Health Care Ad War]
```
     LJ:           Let me may- just make one comment in terms of what Ron says
```

In addition to temporal and numerical minimizers, the inclusion of the adverb "just" further downgrades what is about to be said, as in the preceding example and again in the following:

(6) [UK Today: Child Support]
```
     RH:           Can I say just to (set) the context ...
```

In each of these ways, the divergence is cast as a slight digression from the framework of the question. And since this practice is most often embedded within requests for permission, this encourages a granting of the request.

Justifying the resistance

IEs may also strive to *defend and justify* their efforts to divert the discussion. Justifications may be embedded within requests for permission. For example, in a discussion of the 1992 vice-presidential debate, a Republican strategist first responds to a question about the performance of Ross Perot's vice-presidential candidate, Admiral Stockdale, but he then shifts the agenda (lines 14–16) to defend George Bush's flip-flop on abortion.

(7) [US 13 Oct 1992 Nightline: Presidential Debate]
```
  1  IR:           .hhhh Uh Bill Kristol, does: Stockdale's performance
  2                tonigh:t take some of the air:: (.) out of the the
  3                Pe[rot balloo]n:: just as it was getting bl:own up again.
  4  WK:             [p H H Hhhh]
  5                (0.6)
  6  WK:           Uh:: I'm not sure about that Chris. I think the: ah:
  7                two things were remember- we'll remember about Admirable
  8                Stock- Admiral Stockdale tonight ah: are his: very strong
  9                denunciation of Al Gore:'s extreme environmentalism .hh
 10                and his statement about the important of cah- 'portance
 11                of character. .h to leadership. Both of those statements
 12                will: (reboun:d) to the benefit of President Bush.
 13                .hh Ah and on that last point
 14        →       if I could just speak to Molly's point: uh before the break,
 15                uhm President Bush changed his mind about abortion an:d
 16                said so. . . .
```

The shift is prefaced with a token request for permission (arrowed) containing an implicit justification. By asking to address "Molly's point before the break" (Molly being the IE's Democratic adversary on the panel), the IE justifies the shift on the grounds of fairness and partisan balance. In addition, referencing the impending commercial break further justifies the maneuver by explaining why it is being launched at this particular juncture.

Justifications can also appear outside of permission requests, where they tend to be more explicit and elaborate (arrowed below). Here the IR asks whether corporate mergers are creating monopolies (lines 1–5), and the IE briefly addresses this issue (lines 7–10), but he then raises other concerns about mergers. Before doing so, however, he justifies the shift (arrowed) on the basis that it will concern a key but as yet unaddressed problem with mergers.

```
(8)  [US 5 June 1985 Nightline: Corporate Mergers]
 1   IR:        .hhhh Senator Metzenbaum take me back to the- to that
 2              difference: that uh Mister Forbes made a moment ago,
 3              between monopolies and what we have today:, which it
 4              seems in- in some instances is moving .hh at least (0.2)
 5              gr:adually in the direction of a monopoly. is it not?
 6              (0.3)
 7   HM:        Well I think thet some mergers (.) don't have any element
 8              of monopoly in them at a:ll. .hh (.) Uh for example General
 9              Motors buying Hughes Aircraft (I'm-) not at all certain
10              that there's any monopoly (.) issues there. (0.5)
11      →       On the other hand I think the real concern tha h:asn't
12      →       been addressed (.) previously (.) in this program (0.7)
13              HAS to do with the fact that...
14              ((parenthetical comment omitted))
15              ...when you have a major merger of this kind, (0.2) of the
16              KINd that we've been talking about on this program, (.hh)
17              you haff to worry A does it eliminate (.) competition
18              and therefore what does it do to the consumers, .h uh
19              secondly you have to be concerned as to the impact (.)
20              on the shareholders, (0.4) and third but certainly not
21              least of the three, (.) is the impact upon the community...
```

What about the substance of justifications? In general, the rationales offered for resistant responses tend, not surprisingly, to exclude naked self-interest as a motivating factor. Within that general framework, rationales are quite different depending on whether they address the positive or negative dimension of resistance. Regarding positive resistance, rationales focus on the merits of the alternative line of discussion, and these tend to fall into either of two basic categories. One argument, common in panel interviews involving partisan IEs, is based on the principle of fairness and the need to respond to points raised by opposing IEs. Excerpt (7) above typifies this rationale, but other examples are commonplace:

```
(9)  [US 3 Feb 1992 MacNeil/Lehrer: Haitian Refugee Repatriation]
   BA:     Ahm: let me just respond to a few things that (.)
           Congressman Rangel said...
```

```
(10)  [US 21 Oct 1993 MacNeil/Lehrer: Health Care Ad War]
   LJ:     Let me may- just make one comment in terms of what
           Ron: says
```

Alternatively, unsolicited material may be justified on the basis that it has a significant bearing on the overarching subject at hand. This type of rationale is illustrated in excerpt (8) above, and other examples include the following:

(11) [UK Today: Child Support]
```
   RH:          Can I say just to (set) the context ...
```

(12) [US 5 May 1996 This Week: Gas Tax Repeal]
```
   RR:          But I think there's really a- a mu:ch b:igger (0.4)
                this is part of a much bigger picture ...
```

Regarding the negative dimension of resistance – that is, the refusal to address the agenda of the question – common justifications include the claim that the inquired-about information is not available (excerpt (13) below), or too complex to convey in a limited amount of time (excerpt (14)).

(13) [US 22 July 1985 NewsHour: South Africa]
```
 1  IR:          Who are these people.
 2               (0.7)
 3  HB:      →   I do not know.=
 4  IR:          =You don't know the naych- I don't mean their names
 5               obviously but I mean what kind of peopl:e are falling-
 6               [are falling- (0.4) into the category uh those=
 7  HB:          [I would ha-
 8  IR:          =thetch- need to be arrested.
```

(14) [US: 6 June 1985: Nightline: Nuclear Waste]
```
 1  IR:          Continuing our conversation now with Doctor Rosalyn Yalow.
 2               Doctor Yalow uh- ehh lemme put it in very simple terms.
 3               If it's doable, if it is: easily disposable, why don't we.
 4               (1.0)
 5  RY:      →   Well frankly I cannot- (.) answer all these scientific
 6               questions in one minute given to me....
```

Refusals to answer may also be justified on the grounds that the question is faulty or inappropriate. Here a question to Senate majority leader Bob Dole about how a federal budget impasse will be resolved is cast as premature (arrowed) given the early stage of negotiations.

(15) [US 8 Dec 1985 Meet the Press: Bob Dole]
```
 1  IR:          You can't have it both ways either.=>On this program<
 2               you have said that you don't think, .hhh that you'll
 3               eliminate thirty to fifty programs, [an'] Senator Packwood=
 4  BD:                                            [( )]
 5  IR:          =says ya have to, .hh Number two you say you
 6               hope you will not have a tax increase, [.hhhh And]=
 7  BD:                                                [But I do.]
 8  IR:          =number- and number three you say ya h:ope you can
 9               have a:l [m o s t] three percent on: .hhh on: on=
10  ():              [(    )]
11  IR:          =defe:nse, .hh And yet you hafta cut fifty billion next
12               year. Now which o'those three is gonna give Senator,
13               (0.4)
14  BD:      →   I think that's going to happen sometime next year when
15           →   those of us:: uh in- leadership positions=set=down
```

```
16         →  with the President and make the hard choice. I don't
17         →  think I'd make it today: .hhhhh ih=in December of 1985.
```

And in a more aggressive variant of this practice, questions can be attacked outright as improper and hence unworthy of an answer. When a Serbian spokesperson is asked if recent prisoners of war are being beaten (lines 1–2), the spokesperson suggests that the line of questioning is unnecessarily provocative and biased (lines 5–10).

(16) [US 15 July 1995 NPR All Things Considered: Serbia]
```
 1  IR:     Are they being beaten? Or will you be: are you treating
 2          them (u-) humanely according to inter[national conventions.
 3  IE:                                           [hhh!
 4          (.)
 5  IE:     Well I mean your line of questioning really suggests that
 6          we are the most awful creatures on earth. That we a:re
 7          beating the prisoners, raping women, and so on and so forth.
 8          .hh Please I think I have been very: uh: uh correct in my
 9          answers, an' I would expect you to: .hh be more correct in
10          your line of question=because it's extremely provocative....
```

One type of refusal account merits special attention, namely the refusal to answer *as a matter of general policy*. IEs may assert, in effect, that they never answer questions of that sort. When asked if he intends to run for the presidency of the mineworkers' union (lines 1–2), Arthur Scargill refuses to say, pointing out that he's been similarly unresponsive to "every other pressman over the past forty-eight hours" (lines 3–5).

(17) [UK 13 March 1979 World at One: National Union of Mineworkers]
```
 1  IR:     M:ister Scargill will you run for the presidency of the National
 2          Union of Mineworkers.
 3  AS:     .hhh er Mister Day: I must give you the same answer that I've
 4          been giving every other pressman over the past forty-eight
 5          hours. .hhh If and when Mister Gormley officially (.) hands in
 6          his resignation and that's by no means certain .hhhh er during:
 7          this year or at any time during the next three years .hh then I
 8          will give (.) serious consideration to the matter...
```

Treasury Secretary Robert Rubin does something very similar when asked about the direction of future interest rates. He characterizes his refusal as part of a three-and-a-half-year-old policy of not commenting on the trajectory of financial markets (lines 2–4).

(18) [US 5 May 1996 ABC This Week With David Brinkley: Robert Rubin]
```
 1  IR:     But which way are they going now?=
 2  RR:     =>For three and a half years.< .hhh Sa:m. I have had for
 3          three and a half years a policy of >not commenting on
 4          what markets are gonna do....
```

As a form of damage control, the general-policy account has distinct attractions. By emphasizing that there is a principled rationale underlying the refusal, this type of account *depersonalizes* the refusal as something other than an act of defiance against the IR per se.

Furthermore, insofar as this practice implies that any further questions of this sort will prove fruitless, it also *finalizes* the refusal, inhibiting follow-up questions and strongly bidding to close down the entire line of inquiry.

In whatever form they may take, justificatory accounts have damage-control ramifications for the media audience. Recall that acts of resistance are apt to be viewed negatively by many audience members, whose first inclination is to infer that an ulterior motive lies behind the resistance. Accordingly, justifications may serve to counteract those inferences by offering a legitimate reason for the decision to sidestep the question.

Covert Resistance

Overt resistance has its counterpart in the practice of resisting a question *covertly*, that is without acknowledging that anything out of the ordinary is taking place. The obvious attraction of a covert approach is the prospect that the maneuver may escape the notice of the IR and audience members. On the other hand, if the maneuver *is* noticed, it can be particularly costly for the IE. Those who sidestep questions while pretending to answer them risk being seen as devious and manipulative, and this is over and above the negative inferences generated by the resistance itself. Furthermore, such inferences cannot be forestalled by justificatory accounts because the covert nature of the maneuver precludes any explicit remedial effort. IEs can, however, take other measures aimed at concealing the maneuver and hence reducing the likelihood of it coming to light.

Furnishing the veneer of an "answer"

Certain practices are commonly associated with answers and help to make them recognizable as such. Such practices can be used subversively, to provide a kind of surface camouflage for maneuvers that are in essence resistant.

Consider the practice of incorporating specific words or phrases from the question within the response. A straightforward example occurred in an interview with Arthur Scargill when he was a potential candidate for the presidency of Britain's National Union of Mineworkers. In a question seeking to distinguish candidates on the left, the IR (in lines 1–2) asks Scargill to explain "the difference between your Marxism and Mr. McGarhey's Communism". Because Scargill launches his response (line 3) with a repeat of a key phrase from the question – "*The difference* is . . ." – he appears to be moving straightforwardly to answer the question.

```
(19)  [UK 13 March 1979 World at One: Striking Mineworkers]
  1  IR:    →   .hhh er What's the difference between your Marxism and
  2             Mister McGarhey's Communism.
  3  AS:    ⇒   er The difference is that it's the press that constantly
  4             call me Ma:rxist when I do not, (.) and never have (.)
  5             er er given that description of myself....
```

But appearances can be deceiving; Scargill uses the phrase to mean something quite different from what it meant in the prior question. "The difference" originally referred to a distinction between two candidates and their ideologies. In the response, "the difference" refers to a distinction between two interpretations – the press's and Scargill's – of Scargill's own particular ideology. The shift in the meaning and reference of this key phrase is part and parcel of a more encompassing shift in the discussion agenda. Scargill addresses not the question per se but a hostile presupposition embedded within it, that he is in fact a Marxist. To be sure, this is a relatively mild divergence: Scargill does not change the subject so much as propose that the question is inappropriate. Nevertheless, he does not answer the question in the way in which it was framed, and yet he presents himself as being dutifully responsive. By repeating a key phrase from the question ("What's the difference . . ." → "The difference is . . ."), he packages his response as if it were filling the information gap targeted by the question.

The next example, which combines subversive word repeats with allied practices, is about a proposal to make abortions more difficult to obtain by shortening the time period during which they would be legal. The IR asks an anti-abortion activist about her level of "concern" about the legislation (line 13). This key word – *concern* – also figures in the question preface (single arrows), which makes repeated reference to widespread public "concern" about the proposed restrictions.

```
(20)  [UK Afternoon Plus: Abortion]
 1  IR:          .hhh (Oh) can we now take up then the main issues of
 2               that bill which r- (.) remain substantially the
 3               same. (.) and indeed (.) have caused great deal of
 4        →      concern. (0.4) But first you'll note .hhh is the
 5               clause about (.) time limits h in which h abortions
 6               can be .h legally=
 7  (JK):        =*(yes)*=
 8  IR:          =ha:d. And the time limit h (.) according to the
 9               bill has now dropped .h from twenty eight weeks .h
10               (.) to twenty wee[ks.
11  (JK):                         [Yes.=
12  IR:     →    =Now< a lot of people are very concerned about this.
13          →    [.hh How concerned are you.
14  (JK):        [*yeh*
15  JK:          .hhh Uh: (.) I think this is right. I think that um:
16               .hh again one's had a lot of e:uh conflicting
17               evidence on this but .hh what has come ou::t h an'
18       ⇒       I think that .h the public have been concerned about
19               this. .hhh is that there have been th'most
20               distressing cases. .hhh of (.) live (.) kicking
21               babies who have been destroyed. .hh I've had nurses
22               come to me in great distress (0.2) about this .hh and
23               uh there was undoubtedly (0.1) throughout the whole
24       ⇒       (ambit) of public opinion .hh very great concern .h
25               on this whole question....
```

In her initial response, the IE appears to be moving to answer the question straightforwardly. Her first remark ("I think this is right") refers back to the IR's prior talk, and seems to be expressing some form of agreement. And when she begins to elaborate, she twice uses that same key word, "concern" (double arrows). However, the meaning of this word has been dramatically transformed. In the question it referred to *concern about the more restrictive time frame for legally obtaining abortions*, whereas in the response it refers to *concern about late-term abortions themselves*. It is this latter concern that the response elaborates.

It is useful to entertain a thought experiment contrasting this covert example with an overt mode of resistance. The IE could in principle have said something like "I'm not the least bit concerned about a shorter time frame; what worries me is the destruction of live and kicking babies!" But that more directly adversarial response would make her vulnerable to being seen as insensitive to the plight of those seeking abortion services. Her actual course of action obscures such implications. She presents herself as if she were straightforwardly answering and agreeably expressing "concern", while surreptitiously veering away from the question in the way in which it has been framed. The cover for this maneuver is provided by the back-referencing confirmation and the word repeat, the latter serving as a kind of pivot between the question's agenda and the decidedly different direction pursued in response.

Operating on the question

Agenda shifts can be obscured in other ways. Rather than adjust the surface form of the response to fit the question, one can adjust the question to fit the intended response. This practice, which we term *operating on the question*, involves characterizing, paraphrasing, or otherwise reformulating the question as a prelude to "answering" it.

To illustrate, consider this excerpt from a 1988 interview with US Senator and presidential candidate Gary Hart. The interview was prompted by media reports implicating Hart in an extramarital affair. At one point he is asked specifically if he had such an affair with the woman in question, Donna Rice (arrow 1 below). Before answering, Hart reformulates the question (starting at arrow 2), broadening it to encompass his marital fidelity over 29 years, a span that includes periods of public separation. Upon completing this reformulation he provides an "answer" (arrow 3), an admission of infidelity, but one whose parameters have been set not by the original question but by the reformulated version.

```
(21)  [US Nightline: The Best of Nightline]
  1   IR:          Uh- (0.5) I told you::. (0.4) some days ago when we
  2                spo:ke, and I told our audience this evening that I
  3                would ask you both questions. I will ask you the
  4                first now: just before we tak a brea:k because I
  5                think I know what your answer's gonna be.=
  6        1→      =Did you have an affair with Miss Rice?
  7   GH:  2→      .... .hhhh Mister Koppel (1.1) if the question: (.) is
  8                in the twenty nine y:ear:s of my marriage, including
  9                two public separations have I been absolutely and
 10                totally faithful: to my wife .hhh
 11       3→       I regret to say the answer is no:....
```

The advantages of such a transformation should be obvious. It "steers the question" in a more desirable direction, enabling Hart to appear "forthcoming" and to render an admission that is far less damaging than the one the interviewer was seeking.

In this particular example, Hart seems to acknowledge the fact that the question has been significantly modified. Notice that his reformulation is offered tentatively within an *if-clause*

("Mister Koppel, if the question is . . ."). This case is thus comparatively overt in the way in which it shifts the agenda.

Other question reformulations are asserted straightforwardly, as if they were faithfully preserving the essence of the original question. In a 1988 question to vice-presidential candidate Dan Quayle, a journalist enumerates several prominent Republicans who had been highly critical of Bush's decision to choose Quayle as his running mate (4–16); the journalist then asks Quayle why he hasn't made "a more substantial impression" on his own Republican colleagues (16–19). Quayle begins his response (arrowed) by reformulating the question in terms of his general qualifications for the presidency.

```
(22)  [US 5 Oct 1988 Bentsen–Quayle Debate]
  1   JRN:          hhhh Senator you have been criticized as we all
  2                 know:: for your decision to stay out of the Vietnam
  3                 war::, (0.3) for your poor academic record, .hhhhhh
  4                 but mo:re troubling to so::me are some o'thuh
  5                 comments that've been made by people in your own
  6                 party. tch .hhh Just last week former Secretary
  7                 of State Hai::g. .hh said that your pi:ck. (0.2)
  8                 was thuh dumbest call George Bush could've
  9                 ma[:de.
 10   AUD:            [h-h-hhxhxhx[hxxXXXXXXXXXXXX=          ]
 11   JRN:                        [Your leader in the Senate]
 12   AUD:          =XXXXXXXXXXXXXXXXXXX[XXXXXXXxxxxxxx (5.8)       ]
 13   JRN:                             [Your leader in the Senate] Bob
 14                 Do:le said that a better qualified person could have
 15                 been chosen. .hhh Other republicans have been far
 16                 more critical in private. .hhhh Why d'you think
 17                 that you have not made a more substantial
 18                 impression on some of these people who have been able
 19                 to observe you up clo:se.
 20                 (1.5)
 21   DQ:    →      .hhhhhh The question goe::s (1.0) to whether
 22                 I'm qualified (1.1) to be vice president, (0.8)
 23                 .hhh and in the case of a:: (.) tragedy whether
 24                 I'm qualified to be president. (0.6) .hhhh (0.7)
 25                 Qualifications for:: (0.2) the office of vice
 26                 president 'r president (1.0) are not age alo:ne.
 27                 (1.5) you must look at accomplishments: (1.0)
 28                 and you must look at experience....
```

This is a substantial transformation. On one level, it moves from matters of public record in colleagues' impressions of Quayle – which may be difficult to deny – to a renewed assessment of his qualifications. There is also a change in the presuppositional loading of the question. The original question is presuppositionally negative: it presupposes that Quayle did not in fact make a good impression and asks why this was so. In contrast, the reformulated version is presuppositionally neutral ("whether I'm qualified"), and thus facilitates a more upbeat response. Despite the magnitude of this transformation, the reformulated version is asserted affirmatively and without qualification ("The question goes to . . ."), as if capturing the question in its essence.

To appreciate the significance of this practice for managing an agenda shift, consider what the preceding exchange would look like without it:

(23) [Invented]
```
    JRN:        ...Why do you think that you have not made a more
                substantial impression on some of these people who
                have been able to observe you up close?
    DQ:         Qualifications for the office of vice president or
                president are not age alone. You must look at
                accomplishments and you must look at experience.
```

When the response is made to follow the question without any preparatory work, it is manifestly disjunctive. Against this backdrop, the importance of the reformulation is that it affiliates the matter-to-be-pursued with the matter-that-was-inquired-about, thereby minimizing the discrepancy between the two. Put differently, the reformulation provides a version of the question that the subsequent response can be seen as "answering".

A Case Study in Resistance and Pursuit

The preceding exchange occurred during the 1988 US presidential campaign, when the two main vice-presidential candidates squared off in a nationally televised debate. In a format similar to a small news conference, the candidates answered questions from a panel of four journalists. Opportunities to follow up and pursue evasive answers were more limited than in ordinary news interviews, because the journalists took turns in a prearranged order and were restricted to one question at a time. Nevertheless, acts of both resistance and pursuit were very much in play.

An extended tug of war developed around the issue of presidential succession. It began when Dan Quayle, George Bush's youthful running mate, was asked what he would do if the President died or became incapacitated. The purpose of this plan-of-action question was to test Quayle's readiness for assuming the presidency in an emergency. Quayle sidestepped this issue when it was first raised, prompting several follow-up questions and rounds of resistance and pursuit.

The first journalist to raise this question – Brit Hume, then of ABC News – noted the apprehensions people may feel about Quayle being "a heartbeat away from the presidency" (lines 1–4). He then asks Quayle to describe, in the event of his sudden succession to power, "the first steps that you'd take and why" (lines 5–10).

(24) [US 5 Oct 1988 Bentsen–Quayle Debate]
```
1   JRN:    Senator I wan- I wanna take you back if I can
2           to the question Judy as:- asked you about some
3           o'the apprehensions people may feel about your
4           being a heartbeat away from the presidency. .hhhh
5           And let us assume if we can for the sake of this
6           question that you become vice president- an:d the
7           president is incapacitated for one reason or
8           another and you hafta take the reins of power.
```

```
 9              .hhhh When that moment ca::me, w- what would be
10              thuh first steps that you'd take (0.2) and why::.
11              (3.2)
12  DQ:         .hh First I'd- first I'd say a prayer (1.1) tch for
13              myself (2.3) and for thuh country I'm about to
14              lead, (2.4) And then I would (1.1) assemble his
15              (1.1) people and talk (0.8) .hhh
16       →      And I think this question keeps going ba:ck to: (1.0)
17       →      the qualifications and what kind of (1.1) of vice
18              president 'n (0.7) in this hypothetical situation
19              (1.0) if I had to assume:: (0.8) thuh responsibilities
20              of: (0.3) president what I would be. (1.0) .hhh
21              And as I have said (1.2) tch age alo:ne. (0.3) .hh
22              although I can tell you h.h after the experience of:
23              these last few weeks 'n thuh campaign I've added
24              ten years to my a[ge,
25  AUD:                        [x-x-x-x-x-x[-x (1.7)
26                                          [Age alone. (1.0)
27              is not (0.2) the only (0.5) qualification. .hhhh
28              You've got to look at ex:perience. (.) And you've
29              got to look at accomplishments.....
```

Quayle makes an initial stab at answering the question (lines 12–15), but it is rather half-hearted and insubstantial, noting only that he would "say a prayer" and call a meeting of advisors. He then proceeds to reformulate the question (starting at the arrows), veering away from the issue of his emergency plan for assuming the presidency, and toward the more general issue of his qualifications for high office. He then goes on to discuss his qualifications (lines 21–9), downplaying age in favor of experience and accomplishments.

Although this shift is managed covertly and is obscured by the use of a question reformulation, Brit Hume sees through the camouflage. After a full round of questioning from the other panelists, Hume regains the floor and pointedly pursues the question (line 6 below). He carefully justifies his pursuit by calling attention to the inadequacy of Quayle's previous response, summarizing it in a way that highlights its feebleness ("You said you'd say a prayer, and you said something about a meeting" in lines 4–5), before pressing Quayle to elaborate (line 6). Notice how some in the audience begin to laugh at this point (line 8), displaying appreciation of Hume's stance in pursuit of an answer.

(25) [US 5 Oct 1988 Bentsen–Quayle Debate]
```
 1  JRN:        Senator I wanna take you back to the question
 2              that I asked you earlier about what would happen
 3              if you were to: take over in an emergency and
 4              what you would do first and why:: .hhhh You said you'd
 5              say a prayer:: and you said something about a meeting,
 6              (.) What would you do next.
 7              (.)
 8  AUD:        h-hhhhhhhhhhhhhhhhhhhhhhhhhhhhhhhhh[hh-h-
 9  DQ:                                           [I don't believe that
10              it's (0.6) proper for me:: to: .hh get into the specifics:
11              (0.5) of a hypothetical (.) situation like tha:t (1.2)
12              The situation is: (0.8) that if (0.8) I was called upon
```

```
13              (0.7) to ser:ve (0.7) as the president (0.4) of this country,
14              or the responsibilities of the president of this country,
15              (1.0) would I be capable and qualified (0.2) to do that.
16              (0.5) .hh and I've tried (0.4) to list the qualifications.
17              (1.0) of twel:ve year:s in the United States Congress....
```

But that answer remains elusive. Quayle again sidesteps the question, although his approach here is rather different. Given that his prior covert maneuver has been exposed, Quayle now chooses a more overt mode of resistance. He explicitly justifies his failure to provide a more substantial answer by characterizing the question as hypothetical and suggesting that it would be improper to answer in specifics (lines 9–11). He then proceeds to shift the agenda (lines 12–15) in precisely the same direction as before – away from his plan of action and toward his general qualifications. Thus, while Quayle's resistance is now overt and on record, it is also justified and accounted for.

Unfortunately for Quayle, justificatory accounts do not necessarily bring a line of questioning to a halt, since any account can be contested. The very next questioner on the panel – Tom Brokaw of NBC News – does just that, relinquishing whatever question he'd planned to asked in order to pursue the succession question yet again. Much like Hume before him, Brokaw first justifies his pursuit. After registering the sensitivity of yet another pursuit ("I don't mean to beat this drum until it has no more sound left in it" in lines 1–2 below), he takes issue with Quayle's account for not answering, pointing out that "it is Sir after all the reason that we're here tonight . . ." (lines 4–5). He concludes, not with an interrogatively formatted question, but with a pointed assertion (lines 12–16) that "surely you must have some plan in mind" for emergency succession since it has happened to "so many vice-presidents" in recent years. By rejecting Quayle's account for not answering and by pressing the issue more forcefully, Brokaw increases the pressure for a genuine response.

```
(26)  [US 5 Oct 1988 Bentsen–Quayle Debate]
  1   JRN:      Senator Quayle I don't mean to beat this drum
  2             until it has no more sound left in it but to
  3             follow up on Brit Hume's question w:hen you said
  4             that it was a hypothetical situation, .hhhh it is
  5             Sir after: all: the reason that we're here tonight.
  6             .hh[h because you are=
  7   DQ:          [Mhm
  8   JRN:      =[running [not just for vice president,]
  9   AUD:       [x x     [x-x-x-xxxxxx=                ]
 10             =xxxxxxxxxxxxxxxxxxxxxx[xx-x-x-x-x (4.4)  ]
 11   JRN:                            [And if you cite the] experience
 12             that you had in Congress, (0.2) surely you must have
 13             some plan in mind about what you would do: if it fell
 14             to you to become >president of the United States<
 15             as it ha:s to so many vice presidents .hh just in
 16             the last twenty five years er so.
 17             (0.3)
 18   DQ:       tch .hhh Lemme try to answer the question one more
 19             ti:me. I think this is the fourth ti:me,
 20             (1.0) [that I have had this question, .h [and I think=
 21   JRN:            [(this is-)                        [Third time
```

```
22  DQ:            =that- .hh three times, (0.8) that I have had this
23                 question, and I'll try to answer it again for you.
24                 (0.3) as clearly as I can. (0.7) .hh Because
25         1→      the question you're asking. (1.3) is what (.)
26                 kind (.) of qualifications .hhhhhh does Dan Quayle
27                 have to be president. (1.0) tch
28         2→      What kind of qualifications do I have
29         3→      and what would I do: (1.0) in this kind of a situation.
30                 (0.4) what would I do in this situation, .hh I would (1.9)
31                 make sure. (2.1) that the people in the cabinet, ( )
32                 'n the people 'n the advisors to the President, ( ) are
33                 called in, ( ) an I'll talk to 'em, ( ) an I'll work
34                 with 'em....
```

Quayle, after commenting on the number of times he's had this question (lines 19–22), promises to attempt an answer (lines 23–4). He then does something which is very puzzling on its face. He launches into yet another question reformulation (arrow 1) that begins to reframe the issue once again as a matter of qualifications. However, in the course of this reformulation, he backtracks a bit (arrow 2), and then returns to the original subject of inquiry (arrow 3) – his plan of action for taking charge in an emergency, which he subsequently elaborates (lines 30–4). Why does Quayle start to veer away from the agenda of the question, only to return to it so quickly?

The solution to this puzzle lies at the nonvocal level. After Quayle launches into his reformulation (at line 3 below) and completes the focal word "qualifications" (line 4), Brokaw begins shaking his head (line 6) and he continues to do so until the reformulation reaches a first possible completion point. In this way, Brokaw nonvocally rejects Quayle's bid to shift the agenda.

```
(27)  [US 5 Oct 1988 Bentsen–Quayle Debate]
 1  DQ:       ...and I'll try to answer it again for you.
 2            (0.3) as clearly as I can. (0.7) .hh Because
 3            the question you're asking. (1.3) is what (.)
 4            kind (.) of qualifications
 5            .hh[hhhh does Dan Quayle have to be president. (0.5)] (0.5)
 6  JRN:         [ (( H e a d s h a k i n g ))                    ]
 7  DQ:       tch What kind of qualifications do I have
 8            and what would I do: (1.0) in this kind of a situa [tion. (0.4)]
 9  JRN:                                                         [((Nodding))]
10  DQ:       And what would I do in this situation, .hh I would (1.9)
11            make sure. (2.1) that the people in the cabinet, (0.9)
12            'n the people 'n the advisors to the President, (.) are
13            called in, (0.2) an I'll talk to 'em...
```

This rejection is consequential; Quayle subsequently abandons the incipient agenda shift and returns to the original agenda (lines 7–8). Brokaw nods approvingly (line 9), and Quayle proceeds to elaborate on his emergency plan. Thus, while Quayle initially steers the question in a different direction, Brokaw steers him right back.

In the aftermath of this debate, Quayle was widely perceived to have "lost", and extensive media commentary focused on the shortcomings of his performance. A common criticism was that he came across as overly "rehearsed" or "programmed" in his remarks. This widespread impression may be rooted, at least in part, in patterns of response such as those analyzed here. He repeatedly returns to the same basic theme – qualifications and experience – as a favored response to various kinds of questions (see also excerpt (22) above). Moreover, he repeatedly uses the same basic practice – which we have termed operating on the question – to fit that favored response to the question at hand. This recurrent mode of resistance was first managed covertly, but it was subsequently exposed by persistent follow-up questions from the panel of journalists, at which point it became transparently manipulative. Here, then, patterns of response within the event are congruent with and may help explain subsequent reactions and assessments by media commentators and members of the audience.

Conclusion

In this age of political cynicism coupled with anxiety about the decline of civility in public life, it is tempting to assume that virtual anomie now characterizes the domain of public discourse. Politicians, in such a world, would no longer be bound by traditional norms and could thus ignore with impunity the questions they receive in journalistic interviews. The practices examined in this chapter, taken together, reveal a more complex state of affairs. While it is true that resistant and evasive responses are commonplace, these are managed with considerable care. When resistance is done overtly, interviewees take steps to control the damage that may be caused thereby. When it is done covertly, there are corresponding efforts to conceal the resistance, or at least render it less conspicuous. Both sets of practices represent ways of reducing the negative consequences that can follow from the breach of conduct embodied in an act of evasion, and they demonstrate that such an act continues to be regarded *as* a breach by those involved. These practices are only explicable by reference to a norm of answering that remains in force.

On the other hand, this norm is recurrently danced around and tested by interviewees seeking to gain some wiggle room within the restrictive interview framework. The practices examined in this chapter are the primary means by which skilled politicians, facing adversarial questioning from equally skilled broadcast journalists, struggle to save face and stay on message.

For Further Reading

The study of answers is less fully developed than the study of questions in news interviews, but the theme of evasiveness has received its share of attention. Specific forms of resistance and evasiveness have been delineated (Greatbatch 1986, Clayman & Heritage 2002a: ch. 7), and there have been various attempts to develop a quantifiable system for the analysis of resistant or evasive responses (Harris 1991, Bull 2003). Using such a system, Bull (2003) has evaluated various politicians' interactional styles, and developed a more general theory of evasiveness.

18

Interaction en Masse: Audiences and Speeches

In our final substantive chapter, we shift direction to a very different form of institutional interaction: political speeches. At first sight, political speeches are a far cry from ordinary conversation, from doctor–patient interaction, or even from presidential press conferences. These interactions are largely unscripted, and all of them involve the mutual responsiveness and give and take that is the hallmark of spontaneous interaction. Speeches are frequently scripted and, like lectures, they are monologues. Someone once defined a lecture as "the transmission of the lecturer's notes to the students' notebooks, passing through the minds of neither". And anyone who has had the misfortune to experience this kind of non-communication may wonder if monologues delivered to audiences ever really involve social interaction at all.

A few moments' thought can dispel these doubts – even for lecturers. The British philosopher A. J. Ayer (1977) once described his difficulties in holding an audience's attention when an eye injury forced him to wear dark glasses. And a considerable body of research has shown that eye contact with audience members is essential for effective public speaking (Atkinson 2005). A speaker who is looking at the audience will quickly notice other signs of interaction: audience members are looking back, smiling, nodding, and perhaps writing things down. Additionally there are also more audible forms of response: laughter, clapping and cheering, booing and jeering. In these responsive behaviors, audience members cease to behave as individuals and start to act as a collective entity, so that it is possible to think of speaker–audience interaction as akin to two-party interaction in which one party is the speaker and the audience forms a second, collectively respondent party.

In the context of speeches, the audience has always had a make or break role. In ancient Greece, the earliest form of public opinion polling involved judges who, unable to see or hear the speakers' orations, judged the popularity of speeches by the volume of applause they elicited (Duncan 1984). Two and a half thousand years later, the effectiveness and popularity of a speech is still judged by the applause which greets it. An effective and popular speech at a political convention can launch a political career. In 2004, the young Barack Obama, then a state senator in Illinois, gave a speech to the Democratic National Convention on the theme of "e pluribus unum" (out of many, one). Designed to criticize the "wedge politics" of the 2004 Republican campaign engineered by Karl Rove, in which different religious, ethnic, and lifestyle groups were played off against one another, the speech contained the following passage:

(1)   [Obama: 2004 Democratic National Convention]
```
1  Obama:  Yet even as we speak, there are those who are preparing to
2          divide us, the spin masters the negative ad peddlers who
3          embrace the politics of anything goes.
4          Well, I say to them tonight,
5          there is not a liberal America and a conservative America,
6          there is the United States of America.
```

This segment received a tumultuous reception at the convention and it was frequently replayed on subsequent primetime news shows. The speech made Obama's reputation as a speaker who was in touch with Democratic convictions. He went on to be elected to the United States Senate, and subsequently to the presidency. Obama was not alone. Senator Hubert Humphrey's career was similarly launched by a 1948 convention speech in which he urged Democrats to work for the extension of human rights in the American South. And a highly successful 1984 convention speech by New York politician Mario Cuomo aroused speculation that he would run for his party's nomination for over a decade.

Audience responses to speeches – most prominently clapping and booing – are displays of approval or disapproval of, affiliation with or disaffiliation from, what the speaker has just said. Speeches that are applauded frequently in the aggregate are perceived to be popular, and so are the speakers who make those speeches. These perceptions of popularity are important not just to launch a career, but also to remain effective in office. Perceivedly popular office holders may find it easier to recruit allies, raise money, and negotiate with others. They may also find that opponents may temper their attacks on them. For all these reasons, audiences matter for politicians, and, though perhaps to a lesser extent, for everyone who is engaged in speaking to the public en masse: professors, presenters at business meetings, lecturers in not-for-profit organizations, and so on. But how do the dynamics of speaker–audience interaction actually work?

In the early 1980s, research by Max Atkinson began to open up this issue. Atkinson was idly watching a TV awards show when he realized that audiences applauded award winners for roughly the same amount of time: eight seconds. If applause lasted longer than this norm it was hearably strong, and if less it was hearably weak and lukewarm. He then made a crucial observation: applause is structured by the sentence(s) that lead up to it. In the following instance, an award is announced for best supporting actor in a movie:

(2)   [Atkinson 1984a: 382 (simplified transcript)]
```
1   Ann:  The best supporting actor (0.7) the nominations are:e (0.5)
2         Robert Duva:ll (0.4) for Apocalypse:: Now: (0.8) Denholm
3         Elliott hh(0.4) for Saint Jack (0.8) John Hurt (0.8) for Alien
4         (0.8) Christopher Walken (1.0) for The Deer Hunter.
5         (1.8)
6   Ann:  The winner is::
7         (0.8)
8   Ann:  Robert Duva:[:ll (0.5) for Apocalypse Now:]=
9   Aud:             [x-xxxxxxxxxxxxxxxxxxxxxxxxxxx]=
10        =XXXXXXXXXXXXXXXXXXXXXXXXXXXXXXXXXXXXXXXXXX
          |------------(8.0)------------------------|
```

Atkinson observed that, after the listing of nominees (lines 1–4), the name of the winner is prepared for at line 6 so that the audience can anticipate its appearance, and the name is the last thing to be said (line 8). The announcer also delays the appearance of the name for nearly a second (line 7), giving the audience additional time to anticipate the announcement and prepare to respond. In short, the point at which the name will be announced is *projectable*.

The value of projectability vividly emerged in other examples from the same awards program. In (3), the announcement of the winner is buried in the sentence and cannot easily be anticipated by the audience. The winner was not applauded when he was named (line 5):

```
(3)  [Atkinson 1984a: 383 (simplified transcript)]
  1  Ann:        .hhh an' the Academy: .hh honors the makers of these
  2               programs .hhh with three (.) Rediffusion Star awards (.)
  3               The Flame of Knowledge award for best schools program (.)
  4               went to Richard Hamford .h for "How We Used to Live".
  5       →     (1.4)
  6               The [Har:lequin: Award |--------(2.5)--------|
  7  Aud:            [x — xx — xxx — xx — xx — xxxxxxxxxxxxxxxx
  8  Ann:        [(°Sorry°) |-------(5.0)-------|
  9  Aud:        [XXXXXXXXXXXXXXXXXXXXXXXXXXXXXXX
```

While the unfortunate winner may have thought he was the least popular man in the room, in fact the delayed and feeble applause which greeted his win was the announcer's fault. He failed to project the point at which he would announce the winner's name, and thus failed to create a slot for the audience to begin applauding. The announcer even seemed to recognize his fault when he said "sorry" at line 8.

The Problem of Response Coordination

Why do audiences need this kind of careful signposting of the "slot" in which they can applaud? The short answer is that applause is done in concert with many other people who must somehow coordinate their actions with everybody else. The need for coordination arises from the benefits and costs of applauding. The benefits are pretty straightforward. The first benefit is *expressive*: audience members can show their support for what the speaker is saying. This has intrinsic value in its own right. Second, there are the *instrumental* benefits of making the recipient appear popular to others, whether in the same location or remotely listening in via television. This instrumental payoff is important for competitive opera claques who cheer for their favorite star, and in political conventions and debates where it may be used to drown out others who are responding differently.

If there were only benefits to applauding, we might expect audience members to respond every time they hear something they agree with. But in fact these benefits also have some potential costs associated with them. The most important of these is the possibility that no other audience members will join in and that persons will find themselves clapping alone. Atkinson (1984b) found a considerable body of evidence that responding in isolation is costly and undesirable. Many people report feelings of acute discomfort or embarrassment in this situation. Most people, as social psychologists from Asch (1951) onwards have explored, experience social isolation as uncomfortable and something to be avoided. In the context of speeches, applause usually starts as a "burst" well within a second of the speaker arriving at the end

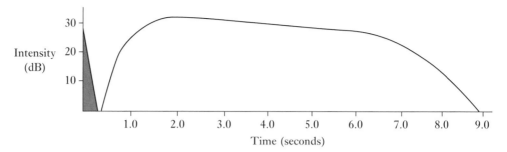

Figure 18.1 Electronic reading of applause intensity and duration for a well-applauded passage. The shaded area shows the talk, the white area the applause. Source: Atkinson 1984a: 373

of a sentence (Atkinson 1984a). These bursts normally last around eight seconds, rapidly increasing in volume and then gradually fading (see figure 18.1). Applause starting with isolated responders rarely builds to the same volume or lasts for eight seconds. Instead, it is weak and peters out quickly. In sum, audience members prefer to express opinions that are in agreement with others, and avoid expressing opinions that seem to be unpopular. The expressive and instrumental benefits of applause are offset by the potential risk of social isolation.

Applauding a speech is an example of what Thomas Schelling (1960), one of the founders of game theory, called games of pure coordination. In these games, everybody benefits if they can coordinate their actions, but they lose if they cannot. To explore this process, Schelling asked his students where they would go in New York City if they had to meet a friend but had not arranged where to meet in advance and could not communicate. A majority said that they would go to Grand Central Station, to the information booth at noon (Schelling 1963: 55). Responding to a speech imposes a similar coordination problem: where in the forest of words and sentences can some hundreds of people meet up to express their support and avoid the costs of social isolation?

Schelling argued that solutions to this problem had the characteristics of "prominence and conspicuousness" (Schelling 1963: 57). Grand Central Station in NYC is a prominent landmark and, of all the times of the day, so is noon. Although he was unaware of Schelling's research at the time, Atkinson (1984a, b) came to the same conclusion. He argued that applaudable statements were normally made prominent by being emphasized through language, rhythm, stress, intonation, and gesture. But this kind of emphasis alone was not enough. Applaudable statements also needed to be projectable. Audience members must be able to see up ahead when applause might be attempted. Atkinson argued that this is because it takes time for an audience member to physically prepare to clap: raise their hands, pull them apart and bring them together. At the same time if applause is delayed or has a ragged start, it may not build up and the early starters will find themselves clapping alone. Everyone has to start at the same time for a burst to begin and social isolation to be avoided. This can only be achieved by creating slots for applause that audience members can anticipate and prepare for. The more obvious the slot is, the more preparation can happen and, through a self-fulfilling prophecy, the audience members will find that their independent decisions have been coordinated and that they are clapping in unison. Projecting the naming of an award winner fulfills this criterion in an awards show, but how does the process work in political speeches?

Formats for Inviting Applause

Atkinson argued that a number of age-old rhetorical formats satisfy the criteria he outlined. We will review some of the main formats here (see Heritage & Greatbatch 1986, Atkinson 2005 for a more detailed review).

Contrasts

The contrast (or antithesis) is a rhetorical device known since the time of Aristotle (Cooper 1932). In its most basic form, a negative statement is counterbalanced by a positive one, as in this example from the then British Prime Minister, James Callaghan:

```
(4)  [Atkinson 1984a: 391 (simplified transcript)]
 1  Pol:        I can say to you Mister Chairman (0.5) that in this
 2        A→   election I don't intend (0.8) to make the most ↓promises
 3             (0.8)
 4  Pol:  B→   I intend that the next Labour government (.) shall ↑KEE:P
 5             (.)
 6  Pol:        the most promises=
 7  Aud:        =[°hear hear°
 8  Aud:        =[x-X-XXXXXXXXXXXXXXXXXXXXXXXXXXXXXXXXXX
                ((edited cut at 6.0 secs))
```

In this case, the negative form of the contrast (what Callaghan is not going to do) is placed first (A→), and the speaker allows nearly a second of silence to elapse before moving on to the positive side (B→). In this second part, which relies on a contrast between making and keeping promises, the word "keep" (line 4) is heavily emphasized, and Callaghan allows a brief silence to intervene between this word and his completion of the sentence. This gives the audience additional time to gear up for response, and to anticipate that other audience members will be doing the same. The emphatic nature of this point is established by contrasting what he will not do (make numerous empty promises), with what he will do – keep his promises. In these ways, Callaghan's point is both strongly emphasized and made clearly projectable.

In (4) the contrast was used to make a boast on behalf of the speaker's own side, but of course contrasts can be deployed against opponents. In (5) then-Georgia Governor Zell Miller uses a contrast to attack Ross Perot, who was a third-party candidate in the 1992 US presidential election, running on a platform of change, fiscal responsibility and an end to "gridlock" in Washington:

```
(5)  [Georgia Governor Zell Miller, 1992 Democratic Convention]
 1  Pol:        He says he's an outsi::der who will shake up the
 2             system in Washington. (0.4) But as far back as 1974
 3             he was lobbying Congress for tax breaks, (0.4) He tri:ed
 4             to turn fifty five thou:sand dollars in contributions
 5             into a special (.) fifteen mill::ion dollar tax
 6             loopho:le that was pa- tailor ma:de. (.) for him.
```

```
 7                    (1.8) ((light cheering))
 8                    Sounds to me like (1.0)
 9          A→        instead o'shakin' the system (0.2) u:p
10                    (0.9)
11          B→        Mister Perot's been shakin' it dow:n.
12   Aud:             xxxXXXXXXXXXXXXXXXXXXXXXXXXXXXXXXXXXXXXXXXXX...
```

Miller's initial framing of this contrast is to report Perot's claim to be an "outsider". He then describes decidedly "insider" lobbying tactics designed to create tax breaks for Perot's corporation. Finally he sums up his view of Perot in the form of a contrast between Perot's claim to be "shaking the system up", with its connotations of reform, and the reality of Perot's "shaking it down" by engineering tax loopholes, with their connotations of sleaze and corruption. The contrast itself is signaled with "instead" and very clearly marked by the pause at line 10. Moreover the word "u:p" is emphasized by raised volume and a brief pause (line 9). The contrast is of course a play on words in which the meaning of the phrase is entirely changed by the substitution of "down" for "up". Finally, the audience has plenty of time to anticipate when applause will be due, and this is perhaps particularly necessary in the arena-sized convention centers holding up to 5000 people in which US party political conventions take place.

The contrast is the most common and diverse weapon in the speaker's armory. In a large-scale study of 476 speeches at annual political conventions in Britain, Heritage and Greatbatch (1986) found that the contrast accounted for nearly 25 percent of all applause events. Within certain limits it is a diverse format. Essentially, contrasts involve greater emphasis on the idea embodied in the second half. In (4), Callaghan was asserting the virtue of his intentions, not the vice of (unnamed) opponents who make promises but do not keep them. In (5). Miller's contrast is framed, with the attack part of the contrast coming second, to tear down Ross Perot's reputation as a reforming outsider. Within these limits there are numbers of subspecies.

Table 18.1   Types of contrast

Type	*Examples*
Contradictions: "not this but that"	Advice is judged by results, not by intentions. (Cicero)
	The house we hope to build is not for my generation but for yours. (Ronald Reagan)
Comparisons: "more this than that"	I count him braver who overcomes his desires than him who overcomes his enemies. (Aristotle)
	The man who reads nothing at all is better educated than the man who reads nothing but newspapers. (Thomas Jefferson)
Opposites: "black or white"	Glory is fleeting, but obscurity is forever. (Napoleon)
	Injustice anywhere is a threat to justice everywhere. (Martin Luther King, Jr)
Phrase reversals	Ask not what your country can do for you; ask what you can do for your country. (John F. Kennedy)
	We didn't land on Plymouth Rock, Plymouth Rock landed on us. (Malcolm X)

Source: Atkinson 2005: 183–90

Contrasts are also strongly associated with audience response. In Heritage and Greatbatch's study they were four times more likely to be applauded than non-formatted sentences and, in the case of senior politicians who tend to be listened to more attentively, 35–45 percent of all contrasts were applauded (Heritage & Greatbatch 1986: 142).

Lists

Lists also show the kind of emphasis and projectability necessary to permit audiences to react. The fundamental point about lists is that they tend to comprise three parts, both in speeches and in ordinary conversation (Atkinson 1984a, Jefferson 1990). In ordinary conversation, lists are often associated with emphasis. In (6) Carol is at pains to tell her co-interactant that she had called and got through, while in (7) May wants to claim that becoming a clairvoyant is something you can develop:

```
(6)  [Jefferson 1990: 64]
  1  Carol:    Did this phone ring? I dialed twice and it n-
  2            rang'n rang'n rang
```

```
(7)  [Jefferson 1990: 64]
  1  May:      I think if you exercise it an' work at it and
  2            studied it you do become clairvoyant.
```

The focus on threes in ordinary conversation is strong enough that, lacking a third item, speakers will complete the list with what Jefferson (1990) calls a generalized list completer:

```
(8)  [Jefferson 1990: 66]
  1  Ernie:    I said no I know his name is something else.
  2        →   Teddy'r Tom'r somethin.
```

```
(9)  [Jefferson 1990: 67]
  1  Rudd:     Oh they come from Jamaica en, South Africa'n,
  2        →   all over the place,
```

Moreover, recipients will wait for a speaker to produce the third item of a list, and regularly start to respond on a completed third item even though a speaker may seek to continue the list (Heritage & Greatbatch 1986, Jefferson 1990). In a word, three-ness is a basic norm for lists.

Three-part lists are also frequent in speeches, where they combine emphasis (by repetition) and the projectability that arises from the norm of response on the third item. Thus in (10) a list of three negatives is used to attack the British Liberal Democratic party by the then Prime Minister, Margaret Thatcher:

```
(10)  [Heritage and Greatbatch 1986: 126]
  1  Pol:       At a ti:me of growing dan↓ger (0.7) for all:
  2             who cherish and believe in ↓freedom (0.8) this
  3             party of the soft centre is
  4       1→    no shiel:d
  5             (0.2)
```

```
6           2→  no refu:ge
7               (.)
8           3→  and no answer.
9   Aud:        Applause (8.2 seconds)
```

And in (11) a similar list by Republican presidential nominee Bob Dole attracts a similar reaction, including the beginnings of anticipatory applause at the third item of the list (line 12):

(11) [Bob Dole: 1996 Republican National Convention]
```
1   Pol:        (I) can tell you that every family_ (0.6) wage earner,
2               (0.5) and small business in America can do better.
3               (0.4)
4               If only we have thuh right policies in Washington DC.
5               (0.5)
6               And make no mistake about it.
7               (1.5)
8               My economic program i:s thuh right policy
9           1→  for America
10          2→  'n for thuh future an'
11          3→  [for thuh next century.]
12  Aud:        [ ( x  x  x  x  x  x ) ] x XXXXXXXXXXX...
```

Like contrasts, lists come in multiple forms (see table 18.2). Lists are more effective in mobilizing audience response when there is a brief delay before the final item (as in (10) above), or when the final item is longer than the other three (as in (11)). In both instances, each individual audience member has a little more time to gear up to applause, and a stronger sense of the likelihood that others will do the same. Lists are fairly frequently used and frequently effective. Heritage and Greatbatch found that they were associated with about

Table 18.2 Types of list

Type	*Examples*
Three identical words	There are three things that make for a successful speech: first delivery, second delivery and third delivery (Cicero)
	I shall fight, fight and fight again to save the party I love (Hugh Gaitskell)
Three different words	*Veni, vidi, vici* [I came, I saw, I conquered] (Julius Caesar)
	No way, no how, no McCain (Hillary Clinton)
Three phrases	Government of the people, by the people, for the people (Abraham Lincoln)
	I stand before you today the representative of a family in grief, in a country in mourning before a world in shock. (Lord Spencer, funeral oration for Princess Diana)
Three sentences	Dogs look up to us. Cats look down on us. Pigs treat us as equals. (Winston Churchill)

Source: Atkinson 2005: 194–7

6.5 percent of all applause events at the British conventions and were twice as likely to be applauded as unformatted statements (Heritage & Greatbatch 1986: 142).

Puzzle-solution

A third important format that embodies emphasis and projectability is the puzzle-solution format. In this format, the speaker arouses the interest of the audience by first establishing a problem or puzzle. By then delivering the point as the solution to the puzzle, the speaker emphasizes the point while also providing the audience with advance warning that an applaudable point is coming, thus inviting applause at the first possible point at which the solution emerges. Puzzle-solutions offer opportunities to combine humor with a political message, and generate laughter as well as applause. In (12) Liberal Democrat leader David Steel launches an attack on Margaret Thatcher through an extended medical analogy. Towards the end, he sets up a puzzle by referencing a warning on prescription medication labels that everyone has seen but no one can easily call to mind. The warning, clearly, expresses his criticism of the economic "medicine" that Thatcher was inflicting on the British economy:

```
(12)  (Liberals: Tape 7: Leader's Address: ST)
 1  Pol:      Margaret Thatcher has portrayed herself (0.5) as the
 2            ↑nation's ↓nurse (0.5) administering: (0.2) nasty:
 3            but necessary medicine to us >in the belief that
 4            what↑ever< (.) short term pain we may suffer in the
 5            long run it's going to do us good.
 6            (0.7)
 7            And I'm surpris:ed that as a qualified chemist (0.2)
 8     P→     she seems to have forgotten (.) the wa:rning on
 9            every bottle,
10            (0.2)
11     S→     Caution (.) it is dangerous to exceed [the sta [ted dose:.
12  Aud:                                            [Laughter[......
13  Aud:                                                     [Applause
                                                             (13.0 secs)
```

As Steel articulates the familiar warning, audience members first begin to laugh and then to applaud a statement that attacks Thatcher's severe anti-inflation policies as "exceeding the stated dose" while embedding within it a reference to the fact that she has a chemistry degree. As pharmacies are called "chemists" in Britain, the elements in the puzzle and its solution are perfectly integrated.

Although they are less frequent than lists, puzzle-solutions have higher success rates (Heritage & Greatbatch 1986: 142). Moreover, they readily combine with the other two formats so far described. It is to these combinations that we now turn.

Combinations

All of the formats described so far are frequently combined to enhance emphasis and projectability. Combinations can unite puzzles with contrasts. In the following case, two British

Conservative leaders are compared; both are present in the hall where this statement is made and are known to be implacably hostile to one another:

```
(13)  [Heritage and Greatbatch 1986: 130]
 1  Pol:              You know Mister Chairman er Margaret Thatcher an
 2         P→         Ted Heath (0.4) both have great vision.
 3                    (0.7)
 4        ┌(a)→       The difference i:s that Margaret Thatcher (0.2) has
 5        │           a vision that one day Britain will be great aga:in,
 6    S→  │           (0.4)
 7        └(b)→       and Ted Heath has a vision (0.2) that one day Ted
 8                    Heath will be great again.=
 9  Aud:              =xxXXXXXXXXXXXXXXXXXXXXXXXXXXXXXXXXXXXXXXX (19.4 secs)
```

In this case the puzzle takes the form of a riddle: what could arch-enemies Margaret Thatcher and Ted Heath possibly have in common? The solution takes the form of a blistering assault on Ted Heath's character and integrity.

Contrasts and lists are also very frequently found in combination. In the next case, an initial statement of duty is contrasted with its irresponsible alternative. The latter is presented through a three-part list:

```
(14)  (Conservatives: Tape 6: Employment: Norman Tebbit: ST)
 1  Pol:                And I have a duty (.) a duty that falls upon
 2                      all responsible politic↓ians
 3                      (.)
 4        A→           to lead others to f:fi- to face reality.
 5                      (0.4)
 6                      Not a duty to feed the people a diet of
 7              ┌1→     compromising pap
 8        B→    │       (0.2)
 9              │2→     pie in the sky:
10              └3→     and false hopes.
11  Aud:                Applause (10.7 seconds)
```

Contrasts and lists can combine in a number of ways. One is as lists of contrasts, as in John F. Kennedy's inaugural speech:

```
(15)  [John F. Kennedy: Inaugural Address 1961]
We observe today not a victory of party but a celebration of freedom,
symbolizing an end as well as a beginning
signifying renewal as well as change
```

Another is where the third item in a list contrasts with the previous two, as in George H. W. Bush's "read my lips" pledge not to raise taxes. Here he portrays his reaction to congressional demands for tax raises:

```
(16)  [George H. W. Bush Republican National Convention 1988]
The congress will push me to raise taxes and I'll say "No",
and they'll push and I'll say "No",
```

```
And they'll push again and I'll say to them
"Read my lips, no new taxes."
```

Here the first two items portray a steadfast Bush resisting congressional demands, while the final contrastive item depicts a president who is now exasperated and believes that the repeated congressional demands are a sign of deafness.

Some of the most complex and memorable combinations are those in which each item of a list contrasts with the item before it, as in the following:

[17] [Abraham Lincoln]
```
You can fool some of the people all of the time,
and all of the people some of the time,
but you cannot fool all of the people all of the time.
```

[18] [Winston Churchill]
```
This is not the end.
It is not even the beginning of the end.
But it is perhaps the end of the beginning.
```

[19] [Ronald Reagan]
```
Recession is when your neighbor loses his job.
Depression is when you lose yours.
And recovery is when Jimmy Carter loses his.
```

Contrasts, lists, and puzzle-solutions can combine in many permutations and can be extremely complex. They are comparatively frequent and effective. Heritage and Greatbatch (1986) found that combinations accounted for approximately 10 percent of all applause events in the British party conventions they studied, and were up to five times more likely to be associated with applause than unformatted political claims.

The combination of contrasts and lists may help to shed light on the significance of the number three in lists of all sorts. Three-ness is a staple of jokes the world over, as the format "there was an Englishman, an Irishman, and a Welshman . . ." attests. Moreover, many children's stories have a tripartite format. The Three Little Pigs, the Three Billy Goats Gruff, Goldilocks and the Three Bears all involve circumstances in which two actions turn out wrong, while the third turns out right. However, if the first two items in a structure can always establish a pattern that a third departs from, then three items constitute an irreducible minimum to establish the undeviating continuation of a pattern. In either case, contrast or continuation, three is the minimum number for a list.

Rescuing Duds

Of course, not every contrast or list has the desired effect. Errors of construction or execution can cause any one of these rhetorical formats to fail. However, even then all is not lost. Even moderately skilled politicians can re-invite audience response by re-completing the previous point, thus giving audiences a second chance to applaud. In the following case there is a subtle failure in the construction of a three-part list. Although technically well built and

delivered emphatically, the speaker's point is made as if it is his policy, rather than that of
Party leader Thatcher, that is at issue:

```
(20)  (Conservatives: Tape 6: Employment: Norman Tebbit: ST)
 1  Tebbit:              I am not willing to throw away the prospects
 2                       of lasting re covery (.) in an orgy of
 3                 1→    self indulgence,
 4                 2→    false sentimentality
 5                 3→    and self justification.
 6                       (.)
 7      Pursuit →        And no one in this [government is.
 8  Audience:                              [Applause (11.6 seconds)
```

The pursuit rectifies this problem by making the point a matter of general government responsibility, rather than the speaker's personal decision, whereupon the audience, presented with
a second chance, duly applauds. However, some damage was done. At line 7 of this datum, TV
cameras cut from the speaker to Margaret Thatcher, who is seen biting her lip and apparently vexed.

Generating Applause: The Three-stage Rocket

So far we have considered the rhetorical language in which political points must be made if
they are to reliably attract applause. We have also briefly mentioned the ways in which aspects
of the delivery of the point matters: delay and extension of final components, volume and
intonation shifts, rhythmic patterns and eye gaze are involved in the micro-management of
the audience's expectations towards the moment when applause is due.

However, we should also recall that each one of these applause lines is itself embedded
in an argument structure that occupies a much longer time structure than the mid-level rhetorical format, or the micro-level of the gesture or sound shift. To recall this, it is useful to
return to Barack Obama's "E pluribus unum" speech, with which we started this chapter.

At the time of this speech Obama was a rising political star who used his speech to express
his own and his generation's opposition to the wedge politics practiced by the Republican
party under the tutelage of Karl Rove. His speech was framed by a description of his mixed-
race heritage and his faith in America as a land of rights and opportunity for persons of all
races. It also stressed the commonality of experience and ordinary life for American citizens
regardless of race, and argued that this is the basis of the connections between all
Americans. Just before the passage which we focused on, Obama said this:

```
(21)  [Barack Obama: 2004 Democratic National Convention]
 1  Obama:  John Kerry believes in America. And he knows it's not enough for
 2          just some of us to prosper. For alongside our famous individualism,
 3          there's another ingredient in the American saga.
 4          A belief that we are connected as one people.
 5
 6          If there's a child on the south side of Chicago who can't read,
 7          that matters to me, even if it's not my child.
 8          If there's a senior citizen somewhere who can't pay for her
 9          prescription and has to choose between medicine and the rent,
```

```
10            that makes my life poorer, even if it's not my grandmother.
11            If there's an Arab American family being rounded up without
12            benefit of an attorney or due process, that threatens my civil
13            liberties.
14
15            It's that fundamental belief — I am my brother's keeper, I am
16   Obama:   my sister's keeper — that makes this country work. It's what
17            allows us to pursue our individual dreams, yet still come together
18            as a single American family. "E pluribus unum." Out of many, one.
```

Obama gives three examples of caring for others (lines 6–13) and then summarizes them with an adaptation from scripture, "I am my brother's keeper" (line 14). He then launches his critique of wedge politics. The initial climax of that rejection is built from his portrayal of a threat to the fundamental commitment of all Americans to a single American family (line 18), regardless of race or creed. Obama portrays this threat as emanating from (Republican) political operatives – the spin doctors, the negative ad peddlers who embrace the politics of anything goes:

(22)   [Obama: 2004 Democratic National Convention]
```
1   Obama:  Yet even as we speak, there are those who are preparing to
2           divide us, the spin masters and negative ad peddlers who
3           embrace the politics of anything goes.
```

It is at this point that Obama rejects these operatives and their works with the declaration "Well, I say to them tonight" and then with the assertion of the essential unity of all Americans, which is packaged as a classic contrast between a country divided into Democratic and Republican America and the "United States of America":

(23)   [Obama: 2004 Democratic National Convention]
```
4           Well, I say to them tonight,
5           there's not a liberal America and a conservative America,
6           there's the United States (.) of America.
```

By the time Obama has paused slightly before the last two words of his contrast, those last two words have become so overwhelmingly predictable that the whole audience can safely launch into applause ahead of the contrast's actual completion, and they did so.

We use this example to stress that structuring an audience's expectations towards a particular slot for applause involves three main levels of action (Heritage & Greatbatch 1986). First there is the argument structure in which positions are staked out – often against those of opponents. Second, and within that structure, there is a level at which particular points are made and are rhetorically structured to build towards a specific slot. Finally, there is a micro-structural level of intonation, rhythm, timing, and gesture which guides the audience towards an exact opening in the talk where response can be initiated. Great speakers link all three of these levels into a seamless structure of argumentation.

Responding to Speeches: Form versus Content

In their 1986 study, Heritage and Greatbatch found that fully two thirds of all applause was evoked by seven basic rhetorical formats which were, in the aggregate, between three and four times more likely to elicit applause than unformatted messages. Such a finding raises the issue of whether audience response is primarily a matter of formatting. Doesn't it matter what the speaker is asserting? Doesn't content count?

A few moments' reflection will lead to the conclusion that the "form versus content" issue is a false contrast. Content obviously does matter. When people applaud, they are affiliating with assertions that they approve of. Although those audiences responded two thirds of the time to formatted assertions, they applauded a third of the time to unformatted assertions, and in those cases they must have been responding to the content! Different types of content matter too. It has been known since Aristotle that audiences prefer refutation to advocacy (Cooper 1932: 235). Party political audiences tend to be more sure of what they are against than of what they are for. They tend to be more united in their response to attacks on others – the "red meat" of party conventions – than they are in response to policy advocacy. This shows up in their rates of applause to the two types of content. Audiences applaud attacks with a higher overall frequency, and at a higher rate, than they do advocacy (Heritage & Greatbatch 1986: 121).

However, the much greater success rate of formatted statements in getting applause also suggests that just agreeing with a statement, although a necessary condition for response, is not a sufficient one. Heritage and Greatbatch investigated this in two different ways. First they looked at very unbalanced debates in which the audience was clearly biased in favor of a popular majority position. In these debates, where the costs of applauding a popular assertion would be reduced for the average audience member by the likelihood that almost everyone would agree with it, one might expect content to hold sway and formatting to matter less. However, unformatted assertions were not significantly more likely to be applauded than in other, more balanced debates (Heritage & Greatbatch 1986: 147). Indeed, audiences who are strongly committed to a partisan position may find its expression in unformatted assertions to be lukewarm and insufficiently committed. Heritage and Greatbatch also looked at how formatting impacts the likelihood that given types of political assertions will be applauded. Formatting doubled the success rate of attacks on others. But it increased the success rate of advocacy statements by a factor of three to five. In a context where advocacy has a more uphill struggle for audience acknowledgement, formatting is clearly more valuable in contributing to its applaudability.

In sum, both form and content matter. Content is a necessary condition for applaudability, but not always a sufficient one. Form enhances applaudability by lowering the perceived risks of applauding to the point at which individual audience members feel able to express their support for positions that they believe in. In the broadest sense, the rhetorical formats serve the converging interests of speakers and their audiences. Speakers want immediate, substantial, and hearably enthusiastic bursts of applause in response to their assertions. Audience members want to show their support for speakers while minimizing the risk that they will be clapping alone. This is, indeed, a "game of pure coordination".

The Long Half-Lives of Contrasts and Lists

As you will have seen in tables 18.1 and 18.2, some contrasts and lists have lived on for hundreds and sometimes thousands of years. There is a simple reason for this: they were remembered and written down. This happened 250 years ago when Dr. Johnson insulted anglers by describing their sport as an activity involving a "stick and a string, with a worm at one end and a fool at the other". And when the British nineteenth-century prime minister Benjamin Disraeli insulted his arch-rival William Gladstone by suggesting that a "misfortune" would be if Gladstone fell in the Thames, while a "calamity" would be if someone dragged him out again. Even a brief glance at books from a university library will show that the underlined passages often include contrasts and lists. Contrasts and lists tend to be memorable and repeatable.

As an illustration of this process, consider a passage from the Vice-Presidential Debate in the US Presidential Election of 1988. The Republican contender, Dan Quayle, had been dogged by suggestions that he was inexperienced and not ready for the VP position. Goaded by a questioner, he unwisely committed himself to the claim that he was just as experienced as John F. Kennedy had been when he ran for office. At this point, his opponent, Lloyd Bentsen, was invited to reply and said:

```
(24)
  1  Bentsen:  Senator,
  2            (1.6)
  3            I served with Jack Kennedy,
  4            (0.5)
  5            I knew Jack Kennedy,
  6            (1.1)
  7            Jack Kennedy was a friend o'mi:ne.
  8            (1.3)
  9            Senator you're no Jack Kennedy.
 10  Aud:      Applause (15.8 seconds)
```

This response is built as a contrast, the first part of which is a three-part list credentializing Bentsen's knowledge of Kennedy, while the second flatly denies the parallel that Quayle had been attempting to establish. The audience's reaction was loud and very sustained – double the duration of a normal burst of applause. But more importantly, Bentsen's remark was quotable, forming a self-contained soundbite that could be replayed on television news and quoted in newspaper reports (Clayman 1995). This aspect of the debate was reported in great detail, including the body language of Bentsen and the "stunned" and "stony-faced" reaction of Quayle. During the next several days it came to be treated as the defining moment in the debate: an event that came to stand for everything that had occurred and was replayed as such. The quote was not forgotten. In the ensuing four years "You're no Jack Kennedy" resurfaced 155 times in news, television, and wire service reports (Clayman 1995) and even now, twenty years on, it is still replayed during the election season as an object lesson in political disaster.

Although telling, the Bentsen quote is no isolated incident. Both print and broadcast journalists have an urgent need to compress extensive spoken and written material into representative or epitomizing packages that news audiences will have the patience to attend to. Contrasts and lists solve this compression problem, and Atkinson's research (1984b, 1986, 2005) has repeatedly shown that contrasts and lists form the staples of the television and newspaper soundbites that emerge in news coverage of speeches and press conferences.

How do soundbites, and quotations more generally, survive beyond today's news? As Atkinson (1984b) suggests, the element of contrast, ideally in combination with a list, is

effectively essential for long-term survival. The final phrase of President Lincoln's
Gettysburg Address (1863) embodies a three-part list with contrasting prepositions:

```
(25)  [Gettysburg Address]
 1  Lincoln:   and that government of the people,
 2             by the people,
 3             for the people,
 4             shall not perish from the earth.
```

Churchill's remarks in the British House of Commons following the repulse of Germany's
1940 aerial attack in the Battle of Britain was similarly a list embodying a contrast:

```
(26)  [House of Commons, 1940)
   Churchill:  Never in the field of human conflict has
               so much been owed
               by so many
               to so few
```

And Neil Armstrong's first words after stepping down from the landing craft onto the moon
also embodied a contrast:

```
(27)  [Moon Broadcast 1969]
   Armstrong:  That's one small step for man.
               One giant leap for mankind.
```

Finally, as undergraduate students' markings in textbooks suggest, big theoretical, philosophical, and theological ideas are most easily sustained through the condensation of ideas
that contrasts and lists permit. Table 18.3 illustrates some of these cases. The survival of
ideas, whether emergent from evanescent spoken words or from relatively enduring printed
texts, has largely depended on the same kind of packaging that mobilizes audience responses
to political speeches. This packaging gives them "prominence and conspicuousness"
(Schelling 1963) and sustains them as memorable, quotable, and ultimately reproducible
elements of human culture.

Table 18.3   Condensed theoretical contrasts and lists

Christian Trinity	Father, Son and Holy Spirit
Primary slogan of French Revolution	Liberty, equality, fraternity
Primary slogan of Nazi Party	Ein Volk, ein Reich, ein Führer
Hegel's theory of history	Thesis, antithesis, synthesis
Freud's theory of the mind	Id, ego, superego
Turgot's three-stage history of social organization	Hunters, shepherds, husbandmen
Durkheim's classification of suicide	Egoistic, altruistic, anomic[1]

[1] Condensed from two contrasting classifications: egoistic–altruistic, anomic–fatalistic. The final category was not
developed by Durkheim and is largely ignored today.

Conclusion

It is instructive to compare applause with booing as a response to political speeches. Of course speakers do not prepare or signpost slots for booing. Conversation analysts have shown that disaffiliative actions tend to be delayed in comparison with affiliative ones (Heritage 1984b, Pomerantz 1984). In keeping with this principle, Clayman (1993b) has shown that while applause tends to be prompt, booing tends to be delayed. He also shows that different mechanisms of collective organization are implicated in booing. A burst of applause must involve a large number of people starting simultaneously. This means that each individual must make a separate independent decision to applaud. Convergence in that decision making, aided by the rhetorical devices we have discussed here, results in the burst. In delayed reactions, Clayman (1993b) shows, audience members' decisions are based on mutual monitoring. Hearing another person boo, hiss, or produce some other expression of disapproval, the next person may decide that the costs of isolation are reduced and that they can go ahead and do the same. Interdependent decision making is the order of the day in a process in which the volume of booing slowly builds in loudness. Booing is unshaped by rhetoric and, by and large, the assertions which prompt it go unremembered.

Finally, while charisma cannot be taught and is in some ways an ineffable speaker quality, charismatic oratory can be a matter of art. Once again Atkinson (1985) leads the way, finding that charismatic speakers like John F. Kennedy and Martin Luther King have systematic ways of enhancing their charismatic appeal. Of course, charismatic speakers use all the practices we have identified in this chapter to get their message across, elicit audience response, and enhance their appeal. However, in contrast to their more everyday counterparts, charismatic speakers continue talking into the applause that results. As a consequence, they appear oblivious to the audience reactions to their words, and ultimately seem overwhelmed by storms of applause that prevent them from continuing. Apparently innocent of any interest in the applause they solicit, yet simultaneously engulfed in it, charismatic oratory presents the leader's success as the natural product of content, personality, and spirit, untainted by calculation.

For Further Reading

Max Atkinson is the major conversation analytic investigator of public speaking and audience reactions. His two books *Our Masters' Voices* (1984) and *Lend Me Your Ears* (2005) give elegant accounts of his analyses. Two additional articles, "Refusing invited applause" (1985), and "The 1983 election and the demise of live oratory" (1986), respectively discuss the question of charisma and the role of public speaking in an age of television soundbites. Atkinson's ideas were given quantitative support in the Heritage and Greatbatch (1986) study referred to earlier, which also contains additional formats. They were applied to Italian by Brodine (1986), and to ordinary public meetings by Llewellyn (2005). Peter Bull (1986) has examined the role of a variety of nonverbal behaviors in the context of political speeches, and the application of the model to comedy (Wells & Bull 2007). Finally, David Greatbatch and Timothy Clark (2005) have applied the whole model to the activities of management gurus and other kinds of motivational speakers.

19

Conclusion

We began this book with Erving Goffman's conception of the interaction order. Recall that, with this fundamental innovation, Goffman asserted the existence of a distinct institutional order that nonetheless pervades all other social institutions. This order is a coherent institution in its own right, composed of a multitude of interactional practices through which social rights and obligations are managed, identities are displayed and affirmed, and both personhood and coherent sense-making are achieved. At the same time, this interactional order is the means by which all other institutional entities are enacted. The interaction order, then, is both an institution in itself and an intrinsic part of other societal institutions.

The analyses in this book have been predicated on that conception. Our specific focus has been on the interface between the interaction order and some of the institutions that it enables. This interface embodies lines of influence that operate in both directions of the interaction–institution interface. We have shown ways in which the practices of the interaction order infuse the workings of institutional domains. These practices constitute an invisible infrastructure giving life to the official structures of institutions, the roles that comprise them, and the identities that are associated with them. The practices can also have practical consequences of enormous significance. Did life-saving help get sent (chapter 7)? Were antibiotics prescribed unnecessarily (chapter 11)? Were Rodney King's attackers exonerated (chapter 12)? Did the political careers of Dan Quayle (chapter 17) and Barack Obama (chapter 18) prosper?

Just as the workings of institutions are influenced by the interaction order, so too the interaction order is influenced by the institutional contexts of its implementation. In fact, as we have argued, the very visibility of institutional activities and the roles and identities associated with them arises through modifications and adjustments to the practices through which ordinary conversational interaction is managed. For instance, the systematically reduced openings and closings of calls to 911 emergency, the confinement of participation to questioning or answering in news interviews and courts, and the virtual elimination of the word *oh* from numerous task-related domains, are cases in point.

In the initial phase of the study of institutional talk, there was a primary focus on what made such talk distinctive by contrast with ordinary conversation. This focus was not surprising. Almost all CA findings to that point had focused on ordinary conversation, and this was a natural point of departure. Subsequently, with a more sustained focus on specific occupational contexts, the issue of their distinctiveness one from another became more prominent. Aided by significant advances in the study of ordinary conversation, it became possible to pinpoint the distinctive contribution of particular interactional practices to institutional tasks with much greater specificity and precision. As a result, the contrast between "ordinary conversation" and "institutional talk" receded as a significant theme preoccupying the field.

At the same time, there has been a growing recognition of the practical utility of CA as a research tool and as a means of intervention in organizational process. CA researchers found that interactional practices were readily recognized as powerful and significant by the participants in the contexts they studied. Simply showing participants recorded data and pointing out the relevance of particular interactional practices, it turned out, could be revelatory for participants, and introduced new potentials for institutional reflexivity and organizational change.

The growing significance of CA as an approach to interactions and institutions has also been accompanied by access to larger resources for their study. The larger and more focused data sets that resulted have strengthened the evidence base that now undergirds conversation analytic findings. The availability of large data sets, in conjunction with the accumulation of findings about basic forms of institutional practice, made it possible to map a much larger topography of conduct implemented in an institutional domain. Correspondingly, it has become possible to describe the frequency of particular interactional practices with greater precision and reliability, and to be more secure of their scope and robustness. Thus studies that had previously been exclusively qualitative and interpretive in character can now be augmented with formal statistical techniques. For example, with a big enough sample it is possible to document the frequency of interactional practices that may be associated with inappropriate prescribing decisions. In a study of this kind, Stivers (2002b) was able to reject the notion that patient requests for drugs are a significant driver of inappropriate prescribing, because these requests were very infrequent in a large data set. At the same time, she documented other frequently used practices which seemed to be treated by physicians as a sign that patients were angling for an antibiotic prescription. Similarly, while political scientists have intuited a growing aggressiveness in presidential news conferences, CA analysis made it possible to document this change as manifested in the distribution of specific questioning practices (Clayman, Elliott, Heritage, & McDonald 2006).

One step beyond distributional analysis is the documentation of systematic associations between interactional practices, dimensions of context, and outcomes. Two main kinds of association have so far emerged as significant themes. The first is the association between particular interactional practices and the outcomes of interaction, such as the patterning of applauses in political speeches, perceptions of patients' medical goals, and appropriate and inappropriate treatment recommendations. In the Stivers study noted above, strong associations were found between particular interactional practices and physician perceptions that patients were lobbying for antibiotics, and also increased prescribing even when that contravened medical guidelines.

The second type of association concerns social context and the implementation of particular practices. The growth of aggressive questioning practices in presidential news conferences has turned out to be tied to a variety of contextual dimensions, varying from elements as proximate as the topical content of the question, to those as distant as the business cycle (Clayman, Heritage, Elliott, & McDonald 2007). In many institutional domains, it seems likely that more diffuse elements of identity such as race, gender, and socioeconomic status will be found to be significant determinants of the deployment of particular social actions, the practices by which they are implemented, and the outcomes they engender (West 1984, Stivers & Majid 2007).

These studies are simply the earliest results of treating the conversational practices of the interaction order as independent and dependent variables in studies of institutions and social process. They are likely not the most important results that we will see, and they are certainly not the last. They inaugurate a new direction in the application of conversation analysis in studies of the social world. Because they build on classical case-by-case conversation analytic techniques, they employ observations that have been rigorously validated as socially meaningful for the participants themselves. Their deployment in quantitative studies permits conversation analytic findings to be augmented by the dimensions of frequency and association. If practices of interaction have the significance and efficacy that the studies described in this book suggest, this development will be an important next step in the analysis of talk in action.

Transcript Symbols

1 Temporal and sequential relationships

A. Overlapping or simultaneous talk is indicated in a variety of ways.

[Separate left square brackets, one above the other on two successive lines with
[utterances by different speakers, indicate a point of overlap onset, whether at the start of an utterance or later.

] Separate right square brackets, one above the other on two successive lines with
] utterances by different speakers, indicate a point at which two overlapping utterances both end or where one ends while the other continues, or simultaneous moments in overlaps which continue.

// In some older transcripts or where graphic arrangement of the transcript requires it, a double slash indicates the point at which a current speaker's utterance is overlapped by the talk of another, which appears on the next line attributed to another speaker. If there is more than one double slash in an utterance, then the second indicates where a second overlap begins, the overlapping talk appearing on the next line attributed to another speaker, etc. In transcripts using the // notation for overlap onset, the end of the overlap may be marked
* by a right bracket (as above) or by an asterisk. So, the following are alternative ways of representing the same event: Bee's "Uh really?" overlaps Ava's talk starting at "a" and ending at the "t" of "tough."

```
Ava:  I 'av [a lotta  t]ough cou:rses.
Bee:        [Uh really?]

Ava:  I 'av // a lotta t*ough cou:rses.
Bee:  Uh really?
```

= B. Equal signs ordinarily come in pairs, one at the end of a line, and another at the start of the next line or one shortly thereafter. They are used to indicate two things:

(1) If the two lines connected by the equal signs are by the same speaker, then there was a single, continuous utterance with no break or pause, which was broken up in order to accommodate the placement of overlapping talk. For example, TG, 02: 18–23:

```
Bee:   In the gy:m? [(hh)
Ava:              [Yea:h. Like grou(h)p therapy.Yuh know
       [half the grou]p thet we had la:s' term wz there en we=
Bee:   [ O h : : : . ]'hh
Ava:   =[jus' playing arou:nd.
Bee:   =['hh
```

Ava's talk is continuous, but room has been made for Bee's overlapping talk (the "Oh").

(2) If the lines connected by two equal signs are by different speakers, then the second followed the first with no discernible silence between them, or was "latched" to it.

(0.5)   C. Numbers in parentheses indicate silence, represented in tenths of a second; what is given here in the left margin indicates 0.5 seconds of silence. Silences may be marked either within an utterance or between utterances, as in the two excerpts below:

```
Bee:   'hhh Uh::, (0.3) I don'know I guess she's aw- she's
       awright she went to thee uh:: hhospital again tihda:y,
Bee:   Tch! .hh So uh I don't kno:w,
                      (0.3)
Bee:   En:=
```

(.)   D. A dot in parentheses indicates a "micropause," hearable but not readily measurable; ordinarily less than 0.2 of a second.

((pause)) E. In some older or less carefully prepared transcripts, untimed silences may be indicated by the word "pause" in double parentheses.

2   Aspects of speech delivery, including aspects of intonation

.   A. The punctuation marks are *not* used grammatically, but to indicate intonation.
          The period indicates a falling, or final, intonation contour, not necessarily the end
?   of a sentence. Similarly, a question mark indicates rising intonation, not neces-
,   sarily a question, and a comma indicates "continuing" intonation, not necessarily
          a clause boundary. In some transcript fragments in your readings you may see a
?,   combined question mark and comma, which indicates a rise stronger than a comma
          but weaker than a question mark. Because this symbol cannot be produced by
¿   the computer, the inverted question mark is used for this purpose. Sometimes
          completely level intonation is indicated by an empty underline at the end of a
—   word, e.g., "word_".
: :   B. Colons are used to indicate the prolongation or stretching of the sound just
          preceding them. The more colons, the longer the stretching. On the other hand,

graphically stretching a word on the page by inserting blank spaces between the letters does *not* necessarily indicate how it was pronounced; it is used to allow alignment with overlapping talk. Thus,

```
Bee:   Tch! (M'n)/(En ) they can't delay much lo:nguh they
       [jus' wannid] uh-'hhh=
Ava:   [ O h  :  . ]
Bee:   =yihknow have anothuh consulta:tion,
Ava:   Ri::ght.
Bee:   En then deci::de.
```

The word "ri::ght" in Ava's second turn, or "deci::de" in Bee's third are more stretched than "oh:" in Ava's first turn, even though "oh:" appears to occupy more space. But "oh" has only one colon, and the others have two; "oh:" has been spaced out so that its brackets will align with the talk in Bee's ("jus' wannid") turn with which it is in overlap.

C. A hyphen after a word or part of a word indicates a cut-off or self-interruption, often done with a glottal or dental stop.

word D. Underlining is used to indicate some form of stress or emphasis, by either increased loudness or higher pitch. The more underlining, the greater the emphasis.

word Therefore, underlining sometimes is placed under the first letter or two of a word, rather than under the letters which are actually raised in pitch or volume.

WOrd Especially loud talk may be indicated by upper case; again, the louder, the more letters in upper case. And in extreme cases, upper case may be underlined.

°   E. The degree sign indicates that the talk following it was markedly quiet
°word° or soft. When there are two degree signs, the talk between them is markedly softer than the talk around it.

F. Combinations of underlining and colons are used to indicate intonation contours, as follows:

If the letter(s) preceding a colon is (are) underlined, then there is an "inflected" *falling* intonation contour (you can hear the pitch turn downward).

If a colon is itself underlined, then there is an inflected *rising* intonation contour (you can hear the pitch turn upward).

So, in

```
Bee:   In the gy:m? [(hh)
Ava:               [Yea:h. Like grou(h)p therapy.Yuh know
       [half the grou]p thet we had la:s' term wz there en we=
Bee:   [ O h  :  :  :  . ]'hh
Ava:   =[jus' playing arou:nd.
Bee:   =['hh
Bee:   Uh-fo[oling around.
Ava:        ['hhh
```

```
Ava:   Eh-yeah so, some a' the guys who were bedder y'know wen'
       off by themselves so it wz two girls against this one guy
       en he's ta:ll.Y'know? ['hh
Bee:                                    [ Mm hm?
```

the "Oh::::." in Bee's second turn has an upward inflection while it is being stretched (even though it ends with falling intonation, as indicated by the period). On the other hand, "ta:ll" at the end of Ava's last turn is inflected downward ("bends downward," so to speak, over and above its "period intonation."

↑   G. The up and down arrows mark sharper rises or falls in pitch than would be
↓   indicated by combinations of colons and underlining, or may mark a whole shift, or resetting, of the pitch register at which the talk is being produced.

> <   H. The combination of "more than" and "less than" symbols indicates that the
< >   talk between them is compressed or rushed. Used in the reverse order, they can indicate that a stretch of talk is markedly slowed or drawn out. The "less than"
<   symbol by itself indicates that the immediately following talk is "jump-started", i.e. sounds like it starts with a rush.

hhh   I. Hearable aspiration is shown where it occurs in the talk by the letter *h* – the more *h*'s, the more aspiration. The aspiration may represent breathing, laughter,
(hh)   etc. If it occurs inside the boundaries of a word, it may be enclosed in parentheses in order to set it apart from the sounds of the word. If the aspiration is an
·hh   inhalation, it is shown with a dot before it (usually a raised dot) or a raised degree symbol.

```
Bee:   [Ba::]sk(h)etb(h)a(h)ll? (h)(°Whe(h)re.)
```

J. Some elements of voice quality are marked in these transcripts. A rasping or "creaky" voice quality is indicated with the "#" sign. Similarly a 'smile voice' –
£   a voice quality which betrays the fact that the speaker is smiling while speaking is normally indicated with the "£" sign.

3 Other markings

(( ))   A. Double parentheses are used to mark the transcriber's descriptions of events, rather than representations of them: ((cough)), ((sniff)), ((telephone rings)), ((footsteps)), ((whispered)), ((pause)), and the like.

(word) B. When all or part of an utterance is in parentheses, or the speaker identification is, this indicates uncertainty on the transcriber's part, but represents a likely possibility.

(   ) Empty parentheses indicate that something is being said, but no hearing (or, in some cases, speaker identification) can be achieved.

(try 1) C. In some transcript excerpts, two parentheses may be printed, one above the
(try 2) other; these represent alternative hearings of the same strip of talk. In some instances this format cannot be printed, and is replaced by putting the alternative hearings in parentheses, separated by a single oblique or slash, as in

```
Bee:   °(Bu::t.)=/°(Goo:d.)=
```

Here, the degree marks show that the utterance is very soft. The transcript remains indeterminate between "Bu::t." and "Goo:d." Each is in parentheses and they are separated by a slash.

The core of this set of notational conventions was first developed by Gail Jefferson. It continues to evolve and to adapt to the work of analysis, the developing skill of transcribers, and changes in technology. Not all symbols have been included here, and some symbols in some data sources are not used systematically or consistently. Other publications may introduce additional conventions, especially for registering body behavior in relation to the talk.

References

Adkins, Barbara 1992. Arguing the point: the management and context of disputatious challenges in radio current affairs interviews. *Australian Journalism Review* 14(2): 37–49.

Albert, E. 1964. "Rhetoric," "logic," and "poetics" in Burundi: culture patterning of speech behavior. *American Anthropologist* 66(6), part 2: 35–54.

Arborelius, E., S. Bremberg, and T. Timpka 1991. What is going on when the general practitioner doesn't grasp the situation? *Family Practice* 8: 3–9.

Arminen, Ilkka 2005. *Institutional Interaction: Studies of Talk at Work*. Aldershot, UK: Ashgate.

Asch, Solomon E. 1951. Effects of group pressure on the modification and distortion of judgments. In H. Guetzkow (ed.), *Groups, Leadership and Men*. Pittsburgh: Carnegie Press, pp. 177–90.

Atkinson, J. Maxwell 1982. Understanding formality: notes on the categorisation and production of "formal" interaction. *British Journal of Sociology* 33: 86–117.

Atkinson, J. Maxwell 1984a. Public speaking and audience responses: some techniques for inviting applause. In J. Maxwell Atkinson and John Heritage (eds.), *Structures of Social Action: Studies in Conversation Analysis*. Cambridge: Cambridge University Press, pp. 370–409.

Atkinson, J. Maxwell 1984b. *Our Masters' Voices: The Language and Body Language of Politics*. London: Methuen.

Atkinson, J. Maxwell 1985. Refusing invited applause: preliminary observations from a case study of charismatic oratory. In Teun van Dijk (ed.), *Handbook of Discourse Analysis. Volume 3: Discourse and Dialogue*. London: Academic Press, pp. 161–81.

Atkinson, J. Maxwell 1986. The 1983 election and the demise of live oratory. In Ivor Crewe and Martin Harrop (eds.), *Political Communications: The General Election Campaign of 1983*. Cambridge: Cambridge University Press, pp. 38–55.

Atkinson, J. Maxwell 1992. Displaying neutrality: formal aspects of informal court proceedings. In Paul Drew and John Heritage (eds.), *Talk at Work*. Cambridge: Cambridge University Press, pp. 199–211.

Atkinson, J. Maxwell 2005. *Lend Me Your Ears*. New York: Oxford University Press.

Atkinson, J. Maxwell and Paul Drew 1979. *Order in Court: The Organisation of Verbal Interaction in Judicial Settings*. London: Macmillan.

Atkinson, J. Maxwell and John Heritage (eds.) 1984. *Structures of Social Action: Studies in Conversation Analysis*. Cambridge: Cambridge University Press.

Ayer, Alfred J. 1977. *Part of My Life*. London: Collins.

Baker, Carolyn, Michael Emmison, and Alan Firth (eds.) 2005. *Calling for Help: Language and Social Interaction in Telephone Helplines*. Amsterdam: Benjamins.

Bales, Robert Freed 1950. *Interaction Process Analysis: A Method for the Study of Small Groups*. Reading, MA: Addison-Wesley.

Balint, Michael 1957. *The Doctor, His Patient, and the Illness*. London: Pitman.

Barnes, Barry 1982. *T. S. Kuhn and Social Science*. London: Macmillan.

Bates, B., L. S. Bickley, and R. A. Hoekelman 1995. *Physical Examination and History Taking*. Philadelphia: Lippincott.

Beach, Wayne A. 1993. Transitional regularities for casual "okay" usages. *Journal of Pragmatics* 19: 325–52.

Beckman, Howard and Richard M. Frankel 1984. The effect of physician behavior on the collection of data. *Annals of Internal Medicine* 101: 692–6.

Bergmann, Jörg R. 1993a. Alarmiertes Verstehen: Kommunikation in Feuerwehrnotrufen. In T. Jung and S. Mueller-Dohm (eds.) *Wirklichkeit im Deutungsprozess: Verstehen und Methoden in den Kultur- und Sozialwissenschaften*. Frankfurt: Suhrkamp, pp. 283–328.

Bergmann, Jörg R. 1993b. *Discreet Indiscretions: The Social Organization of Gossip*. Chicago: Aldine.

Bloor, Michael J. and Gordon Horobin 1975. Conflict and conflict resolution in doctor–patient interactions. In C. Cox and A. Mead (eds.), *A Sociology of Medical Practice*. London: Collier Macmillan, pp. 271–85.

Boden, Deirdre and Don H. Zimmerman (eds.) 1991. *Talk and Social Structure*. Cambridge: Polity Press.

Bolinger, Dwight 1957. *Interrogative Structures of American English*. Tuscaloosa: University of Alabama Press.

Boyd, Elizabeth and John Heritage 2006. Taking the history: questioning during comprehensive history taking. In John Heritage and Douglas Maynard (eds.), *Communication in Medical Care: Interactions between Primary Care Physicians and Patients*. Cambridge: Cambridge University Press, pp. 151–84.

Bredmar, Margareta and Per Linell 1999. Reconfirming normality: the constitution of reassurance in talks between midwives and expectant mothers. In Srikant Sarangi and Celia Roberts (eds.) *Talk, Work and Institutional Order: Discourse in Medical, Mediation and Management Settings*. Berlin: Mouton DeGruyter, pp. 237–70.

Britten, Nicky and Obioha Ukoumunne (1997). The influence of patients' hopes of receiving a prescription on doctors' perceptions and the decision to prescribe: a questionnaire study. *British Medical Journal* 315: 1506–10.

Broder, David S. 1987. *Behind the Front Page: A Candid Look at How the News is Made*. New York: Touchstone.

Brodine, R. 1986. Getting the applause. In R. M. Bollettieri Bosinelli (ed.), *U.S. Presidential Election 1984: An Interdisciplinary Approach to the Analysis of Political Discourse*. Bologna: Pitagora, pp. 171–211.

Brown, Penelope and Stephen C. Levinson 1987. *Politeness: Some Universals in Language Usage*. Cambridge: Cambridge University Press.

Bull, Peter 1986. The use of hand gesture in political speeches: some case studies. *Journal of Language and Social Psychology* 5: 103–18.

Bull, Peter 1994. On identifying questions, replies and non-replies in political interviews. *Journal of Language and Social Psychology* 13(2): 115–31.

Bull, Peter 2003. *The Microanalysis of Political Communication: Claptrap and Ambiguity*. London: Routledge.

Bull, Peter and Katherine Mayer 1988. Interruptions in political interviews: a study of Margaret Thatcher and Neil Kinnock. *Journal of Language and Social Psychology* 7: 35–45.

Button, Graham 1990. On members' time. In B. Conein, M. de Fornel, and L. Quéré (eds.), *Les Formes de la Conversation*, vol.1. Paris: CNET, pp. 161–82.

Byrne, Patrick S. and Barrie E. L. Long 1976. *Doctors Talking to Patients: A Study of the Verbal Behaviours of Doctors in the Consultation*. London: Her Majesty's Stationery Office.

Cannon, Lou 1977. *Reporting: An Inside View*. Sacramento: California Journal Press.

Cantril, Hadley 1940. *The Invasion from Mars: A Study in the Psychology of Panic*. Princeton, NJ: Princeton University Press.

Carmichael, L., H. P. Hogan, and A. A. Walter 1932. An experimental study of the effect of language on the reproduction of visually perceived form. *Journal of Experimental Psychology* 15(1): 73–86.

Cassell, Eric 1985. *Talking with Patients. Volume 2: Clinical Technique*. Cambridge, MA: MIT Press.

Cassell, Eric 1997. *Doctoring: The Nature of Primary Care Medicine*. New York: Oxford University Press.

Chafe, Wallace and Johanna Nichols 1986. *Evidentiality: The Linguistic Coding of Epistemology*. Norwood, NJ: Ablex.

Charon, Rita, Michele J. Greene, and Ronald D. Adelamn 1994. Multi-dimensional interaction analysis: a collaborative approach to the study of medical discourse. *Social Science and Medicine* 39(7): 955–65.

Cherry, Donald K., David A. Woodwell, and Elizabeth Rechtsteiner 2007. National ambulatory medical care survey: 2005 summary. *Advance Data from Vital and Health Statistics* 387 (June 29).

Clayman, Steven E. 1988. Displaying neutrality in television news interviews. *Social Problems* 35(4): 474–92.

Clayman, Steven E. 1989. The production of punctuality: social interaction, temporal organization and social structure. *American Journal of Sociology* 95(3): 659–91.

Clayman, Steven E. 1990. From talk to text: newspaper accounts of reporter–source interactions. *Media, Culture and Society* 12(1): 79–104.

Clayman, Steven E. 1991. News interview openings: aspects of sequential organization. In P. Scannell (ed.), *Broadcast Talk: A Reader*. Newbury Park, CA: Sage, pp. 48–75.

Clayman, Steven E. 1992. Footing in the achievement of neutrality: the case of news interview discourse. In Paul Drew and John Heritage (eds.), *Talk at Work*. Cambridge: Cambridge University Press, pp. 163–98.

Clayman, Steven E. 1993a. Booing: the anatomy of a disaffiliative response. *American Sociological Review* 58: 110–30.

Clayman, Steven E. 1993b. Reformulating the question: a device for answering/not answering questions in news interviews and press conferences. *Text* 13(2): 159–88.

Clayman, Steven E. 1995. Defining moments, presidential debates and the dynamics of quotability. *Journal of Communication* 45(3): 118–46.

Clayman, Steven E. 2001. Answers and evasions. *Language in Society* 30: 403–42.

Clayman, Steven E. 2002. Tribune of the people: maintaining the legitimacy of aggressive journalism. *Media, Culture, and Society* 24: 191–210.

Clayman, Steven E. 2004. Arenas of interaction in the mediated public sphere. *Poetics* 32(1): 73–98.

Clayman, Steven E., Marc N. Elliott, John Heritage, and Megan Beckett, forthcoming. A watershed in White House journalism: explaining the post-1968 rise of aggressive presidential news. *Political Communication*.

Clayman, Steven E., Marc N. Elliott, John Heritage, and Laurie McDonald 2006. Historical trends in questioning presidents 1953–2000. *Presidential Studies Quarterly* 36: 561–83.

Clayman, Steven E. and John Heritage 2002a. *The News Interview: Journalists and Public Figures on the Air*. Cambridge: Cambridge University Press.

Clayman, Steven E. and John Heritage 2002b. Questioning presidents: journalistic deference and adversarialness in the press conferences of Eisenhower and Reagan. *Journal of Communication* 52(4): 749–75.

Clayman, Steven E., John Heritage, Marc N. Elliott, and Laurie McDonald 2007. When does the watchdog bark? Conditions of aggressive questioning in presidential news conferences. *American Sociological Review* 72: 23–41.

Clayman, Steven E. and Jack Whalen 1988/9. When the medium becomes the message: the case of the Rather–Bush encounter. *Research on Language and Social Interaction* 22: 241–72.

Cobb, Sarah and Janet Rifkin 1991. Practice and paradox: deconstructing neutrality in mediation. *Law and Social Inquiry* 16(1): 35–62.

Conley, John M. and William M. O'Barr 1998. *Just Words: Law, Language and Power*. Chicago: University of Chicago Press.

Cooper, L. (ed.) 1932. *The Rhetoric of Aristotle*. New York: Appleton Century Crofts.

Cuff, Edward C. and Wesley Sharrock 1985. Meetings. In T. van Dijk (ed.), *Handbook of Discourse Analysis. Volume 3: Discourse and Dialogue*. New York: Academic: 149–60.

Curl, Traci S. and Paul Drew 2008. Contingency and action: a comparison of two forms of requesting. *Research on Language and Social Interaction* 41(2): 1–25.

Delaney, David 2005. *Territory: A Short Introduction*. Oxford: Blackwell.

Dersley, Ian and Anthony Wootton 2000. Complaint sequences within antagonistic argument. *Research on Language and Social Interaction* 33: 375–406.

Diamond, Shari Seidman and Mary R. Rose 2005. Real juries. *Annual Review of Law and Social Science* 1: 255–84.

Diamond, Shari Seidman, Mary R. Rose, and Beth Murphy 2006. Revisiting the unanimity requirement: the behavior of the non-unanimous civil jury. *Northwestern University Law Review* 100(1): 201–30.

Diamond, Shari Seidman, Neil Vidmar, Mary Rose, Leslie Ellis, and Beth Murphy 2003. Inside the jury room: evaluating juror discussions during trial. *Judicature* 87(2): 54–8.

Dingwall, Robert 1980. Orchestrated encounters: an essay on the comparative analysis of speech exchange systems. *Sociology of Health and Illness* 2: 151–73.

Drew, Paul 1992. Contested evidence in a courtroom cross-examination: the case of a trial for rape. In Paul Drew and John Heritage (eds.), *Talk at Work: Social Interaction in Institutional Settings*. Cambridge: Cambridge University Press, pp. 470–520.

Drew, Paul 1997. "Open" class repair initiators in response to sequential sources of trouble in conversation. *Journal of Pragmatics* 28: 69–101.

Drew, Paul 2006. Mis-alignments in "after-hours" calls to a British GP's practice: a study in telephone medicine. In John Heritage and Douglas Maynard (eds.), *Communication in Medical Care: Interactions between Primary Care Physicians and Patients*. Cambridge: Cambridge University Press, pp. 416–44.

Drew, Paul and John Heritage 1992. Analyzing talk at work: an introduction. In Paul Drew and John Heritage (eds.), *Talk at Work*. Cambridge: Cambridge University Press, pp. 3–65.

Drew, Paul and Marja-Leena Sorjonen 1997. Institutional discourse. In T. van Dijk (ed.), *Discourse Analysis: A Multidisciplinary Introduction*. London: Sage, pp. 92–118.

Drew, Paul and Anthony Wootton 1987. *Erving Goffman: Exploring the Interaction Order*. Cambridge: Polity Press.

Duncan, Otis Dudley 1984. *Notes on Social Measurement: Historical and Critical*. New York: Russell Sage Foundation.

Duranti, Alessandro 1994. *From Grammar to Politics*. Berkeley: University of California Press.

Duranti, Alessandro and Charles Goodwin (eds.) 1992. *Rethinking Context: Language as an Interactive Phenomenon*. Cambridge: Cambridge University Press.

Edwards, Derek (ed.) 2007. *Calling for Help*: special issue of *Research on Language and Social Interaction* 40(1).

Edwards, Derek and Elizabeth Stokoe 2007. Self-help in calls for help with problem neighbors. *Research on Language and Social Interaction* 40(1): 9–32.

Egbert, Maria M. 1997. Schisming: the collaborative transformation from a single conversation to multiple conversations. *Research on Language and Social Interaction* 30(1): 1–52.

Ehrlich, Susan and Jack Sidnell 2006. "I think that's not an assumption you ought to make": challenging presuppositions in inquiry testimony. *Language in Society* 35: 655–76.

Ekstrom, Mats, Asa Kroon, and Mats Nylund 2006. *News from the Interview Society*. Copenhagen: Nordiskt Informationscenter.

Elstein, A. A., L. S. Shulman, and S. A. Sprafka 1978. *Medical Problem Solving: An Analysis of Clinical Reasoning*. Cambridge, MA: Harvard University Press.

Emanuel, Ezekiel J. and Linda L. Emanuel 1992. Four models of the physician–patient relationship. *Journal of the American Medical Association* 267: 2221–7.

Emmertsen, Sophie 1997. Interviewers' challenging questions in British debate interviews. *Journal of Pragmatics* 39: 570–91.

Enfield, N. J. and Stephen C. Levinson (eds.) 2006. *Roots of Human Sociality: Culture, Cognition, and Interaction*. London: Berg.

Enfield, N. J. and Tanya Stivers 2007. *Person Reference in Interaction: Linguistic, Cultural and Social Perspectives*. Cambridge: Cambridge University Press.

Engel, George L. 1977. The need for a new medical model: a challenge for biomedicine. *Science* 196: 129–36.

Epstein, Edward Jay 1973. *News from Nowhere*. New York: Random House.

Epstein, Ronald M., Peter Franks, Kevin Fiscella, Cleveland G. Shields, Sean C. Meldrum, Richard L. Kravitz, and Paul R. Duberstein 2005. Measuring patient-centred communication in patient–physician consultations: theoretical and practical issues. *Social Science and Medicine* 61: 1516–28.

Fallows, James M. 1996. *Breaking the News: How the Media Undermine American Democracy*. New York: Vintage.

Fineman, Martha A. 1991. *The Illusion of Equality: The Rhetoric and Reality of Divorce Reform*. Chicago: University of Chicago Press.

Fisher, Sue and Alexandra Todd (eds.) 1993. *The Social Organization of Doctor–Patient Communication*. Norwood, NJ: Ablex.

Freidson, Eliot 1970. *Profession of Medicine: A Study of the Sociology of Applied Knowledge*. Chicago: University of Chicago Press.

Freidson, Eliot 1986. *Professional Powers: A Study of the Institutionalization of Formal Knowledge*. Chicago: University of Chicago Press.

Frosch, Dominick L., and Robert M. Kaplan 1999. Shared decision making in clinical medicine: Past research and future directions. *American Journal of Preventive Medicine* 27(11): 1139–45.

Garcia, Angela 1991. Dispute resolution without disputing: how the interactional organization of mediation hearings minimizes argumentative talk. *American Sociological Review* 56: 818–35.

Garcia, Angela 1995. The problematics of representation in community mediation hearings: implications for mediation practice. *Journal of Sociology and Social Welfare* 4: 23–46.

Garcia, Angela 1997. Interactional constraints on proposal generation in mediation hearings: a preliminary investigation. *Discourse and Society* 8(2): 219–47.

Garcia, Angela 2000. Negotiating negotiation: the collaborative production of resolution in small claims mediation hearings. *Discourse and Society* 11(3): 315–43.

Garcia, Angela and Penelope Ann Parmer 1999. Misplaced mistrust: the collaborative construction of doubt in 911 emergency calls. *Symbolic Interaction* 22(4): 297–324.

Garcia, Angela, Krist Vise, and Stephen Paul Whitaker 2002. Disputing neutrality: a case study of a bias complaint during mediation. *Conflict Resolution Quarterly* 20(2): 205–30.

Garfinkel, Harold 1963. A conception of, and experiments with, "trust" as a condition of stable concerted actions. In O. J. Harvey (ed.), *Motivation and Social Interaction*. New York: Ronald Press, pp. 187–238.

Garfinkel, Harold 1967. *Studies in Ethnomethodology*. Englewood Cliffs, NJ: Prentice-Hall.

Garfinkel, Harold 2002. *Ethnomethodology's Program: Working out Durkheim's Aphorism*. Lanham, MD: Rowman and Littlefield.

Goffman, Erving 1955. On face work. *Psychiatry* 18: 213–31.

Goffman, Erving 1959. *The Presentation of Self in Everyday Life*. Garden City, NY: Doubleday.

Goffman, Erving 1964. The neglected situation. *American Anthropologist* 66(6), part 2: 133–6.

Goffman, Erving 1967. *Interaction Ritual: Essays in Face to Face Behavior*. Garden City, NY: Doubleday.

Goffman, Erving 1971. *Relations in Public: Microstudies of the Public Order*. New York: Harper and Row.

Goffman, Erving 1979. Footing. *Semiotica* 25: 1–29.

Goffman, Erving 1981. *Forms of Talk*. Philadelphia: University of Pennsylvania Press.

Goffman, Erving 1983a. Felicity's condition. *American Journal of Sociology* 89: 1–53.

Goffman, Erving 1983b. The interaction order. *American Sociological Review* 48: 1–17.

Goffman, Erving 1993. An interview with Erving Goffman, 1980. *Research on Language and Social Interaction* 26(3): 317–48.

Goodwin, Charles 1994. Professional vision. *American Anthropologist* 96(3): 606–33.

Goodwin, Charles 1995. Seeing in depth. *Social Studies of Science* 25: 237–74.

Goodwin, Charles 1996. Transparent vision. In Elinor Ochs, Emanuel Schegloff, and Sandra Thompson (eds.), *Interaction and Grammar*. Cambridge: Cambridge University Press, pp. 370–404.

Goodwin, Charles and John Heritage 1990. Conversation analysis. *Annual Review of Anthropology* 19: 283–307.

Goodwin, Marjorie Harness 1983. Aggravated correction and disagreement in children's conversations. *Journal of Pragmatics* 7: 657–77.

Greatbatch, David L. 1986. Aspects of topical organisation in news interviews: the use of agenda shifting procedures by interviewees. *Media, Culture and Society* 8: 441–55.

Greatbatch, David L. 1988. A turn-taking system for British news interviews. *Language in Society* 17(3): 401–30.

Greatbatch, David L. 1992. On the management of disagreement between news interviewees. In Paul Drew and John Heritage (eds.), *Talk at Work*. Cambridge: Cambridge University Press, pp. 268–301.

Greatbatch, David L. and Timothy Clark 2005. *Management Speak: The Live Oratory of Management Gurus*. London: Routledge.

Greatbatch, David L. and Robert Dingwall 1989. Selective facilitation: preliminary observations on a strategy used by divorce mediators. *Law and Society Review* 23: 613–42.

Greatbatch, David L. and Robert Dingwall 1997. Argumentative talk in divorce mediation sessions. *American Sociological Review* 62: 151–70.

Günthner, Susanne 1996. The prosodic contextualization of moral work: an analysis of reproaches and "why"-formats. In Elizabeth Couper-Kuhlen and Margret Selting (eds.), *Prosody in Conversation: Interactional Studies*. Cambridge: Cambridge University Press, pp. 271–302.

Halkowski, Timothy 2006. Realizing the illness: patients' narratives of symptom discovery. In J. Heritage and D. Maynard (eds.), *Communication in Medical Care: Interactions between Primary Care Physicians and Patients*. Cambridge: Cambridge University Press, pp. 86–114.

Hampton, J. R., M. J. Harrison, J. R. Mitchell, J. S. Prichard, and C. Seymour 1975. Relative contributions of history-taking, physical examination, and laboratory investigation to diagnosis and management of medical outpatients. *British Medical Journal* 2(5969): 486–9.

Harris, Sandra 1986. Interviewers' questions in broadcast interviews. In J. Wilson and B. Crow (eds.), *Belfast Working Papers in Language and Linguistics*, vol. 8. Jordanstown: University of Ulster, pp. 50–85.

Harris, Sandra 1991. Evasive action: how politicians respond to questions in political interviews. In P. Scannell (ed.), *Broadcast Talk*. London: Sage, pp. 76–99.

Heath, Christian 1986. *Body Movement and Speech in Medical Interaction*. Cambridge: Cambridge University Press.

Heath, Christian 1989. Pain talk: the expression of suffering in the medical consultation. *Social Psychology Quarterly* 52(2): 113–25.

Heath, Christian 1992. The delivery and reception of diagnosis and assessment in the general practice consultation. In Paul Drew and John Heritage (eds.), *Talk at Work*. Cambridge: Cambridge University Press, pp. 235–67.

Heath, Christian and Paul Luff 2000. *Technology in Action*. Cambridge: Cambridge University Press.

Heinemann, Trine 2006. "Will you or can't you?" Displaying entitlement in interrogative requests. *Journal of Pragmatics* 38: 1081–1104.

Heisterkamp, Brian L. 2006. Conversational displays of mediator neutrality in a court-based program. *Journal of Pragmatics* 38(12): 2051–64.

Heritage, John 1984a. A change-of-state token and aspects of its sequential placement. In J. Maxwell Atkinson and John Heritage (eds.), *Structures of Social Action*. Cambridge: Cambridge University Press, pp. 299–345.

Heritage, John 1984b. *Garfinkel and Ethnomethodology*. Cambridge: Polity Press.

Heritage, John 1985. Analyzing news interviews: aspects of the production of talk for an overhearing audience. In Teun A. Dijk (ed.), *Handbook of Discourse Analysis*, vol. 3. New York: Academic Press: 95–119.

Heritage, John 1987. Ethnomethodology. In Anthony Giddens and Jonathan Turner (eds.), *Social Theory Today*. Cambridge: Polity Press, pp. 224–72.

Heritage, John 1997. Conversation analysis and institutional talk: analyzing data. In David Silverman (ed.), *Qualitative Analysis: Issues of Theory and Method*. London: Sage, pp. 161–82.

Heritage, John 1998. Oh-prefaced responses to inquiry. *Language in Society* 27(3): 291–334.

Heritage, John 2002a. Ad hoc inquiries: two preferences in the design of "routine" questions in an open context. In Douglas Maynard, Hanneke Houtkoop-Steenstra, Nora Kate Schaeffer, and Hans van der Zouwen (eds.), *Standardization and Tacit Knowledge: Interaction and Practice in the Survey Interview*. New York: Wiley Interscience, pp. 313–33.

Heritage, John 2002b. The limits of questioning: negative interrogatives and hostile question content. *Journal of Pragmatics* 34(10–11): 1427–46.

Heritage, John 2005. Conversation analysis and institutional talk. In Kristine Fitch and Robert Sanders (eds.), *Handbook of Language and Social Interaction*. Mahwah, NJ: Erlbaum, pp. 103–47.

Heritage, John 2008. Conversation analysis as social theory. In Bryan Turner (ed.), *The New Blackwell Companion to Social Theory*. Oxford: Blackwell, pp. 300–20.

Heritage, John 2009. Negotiating the legitimacy of medical problems: a multi-phase concern for patients and physicians. In Dale Brashers and Deana Goldsmith (eds.), *Communicating to Manage Health and Illness*. New York: Routledge, pp. 147–64.

Heritage, John 2010. Questioning in medicine. In Alice F. Freed and Susan Ehrlich (eds.), *"Why do you Ask?" The Function of Questions in Institutional Discourse*. New York: Oxford University Press, pp. 42–68.

Heritage, John, Marc Elliott, Tanya Stivers, Andrea Richardson, and Rita Mangione-Smith 2009. Reducing antibiotics prescribing: the role of online commentary. Unpublished paper, Department of Sociology, UCLA.

Heritage, John and David Greatbatch 1986. Generating applause: a study of rhetoric and response at party political conferences. *American Journal of Sociology* 92(1): 110–57.

Heritage, John and Anna Lindström 1998. Motherhood, medicine and morality: scenes from a medical encounter. *Research on Language and Social Interaction* 31: 397–438.

Heritage, John and Douglas Maynard (eds.) 2006a. *Communication in Medical Care: Interactions between Primary Care Physicians and Patients*. Cambridge: Cambridge University Press.

Heritage, John and Douglas W. Maynard 2006b. Problems and prospects in the study of physician–patient interaction: 30 years of research. *Annual Review of Sociology* 32: 351–74.

Heritage, John and Geoffrey Raymond 2005. The terms of agreement: indexing epistemic authority and subordination in assessment sequences. *Social Psychology Quarterly* 68(1): 15–38.

Heritage, John and Geoffrey Raymond, forthcoming. Navigating epistemic landscapes: acquiescence, agency and resistance in initial elements of responses to polar questions. In J-P. De Ruiter (ed.), *Questions*. Cambridge: Cambridge University Press.

Heritage, John and Jeffrey Robinson 2006a. Accounting for the visit: patients' reasons for seeking medical care. In John Heritage and Douglas Maynard (eds.), *Communication in Medical Care: Interactions between Primary Care Physicians and Patients*. Cambridge: Cambridge University Press, pp. 48–85.

Heritage, John and Jeffrey Robinson 2006b. The structure of patients' presenting concerns: physicians' opening questions. *Health Communication* 19(2): 89–102.

Heritage, John, Jeffrey D. Robinson, Marc Elliott, Megan Beckett, and Michael Wilkes 2007. Reducing patients' unmet concerns: the difference one word can make. *Journal of General Internal Medicine* 22: 1429–33.

Heritage, John and Andrew Roth 1995. Grammar and institution: questions and questioning in the broadcast news interview. *Research on Language and Social Interaction* 28(1): 1–60.

Heritage, John and Sue Sefi 1992. Dilemmas of advice: aspects of the delivery and reception of advice in interactions between health visitors and first time mothers. In Paul Drew and John Heritage (eds.), *Talk at Work*. Cambridge: Cambridge University Press, pp. 359–417.

Heritage, John and Marja-Leena Sorjonen 1994. Constituting and maintaining activities across sequences: *and*-prefacing as a feature of question design. *Language in Society* 23: 1–29.

Heritage, John and Tanya Stivers 1999. Online commentary in acute medical visits: a method of shaping patient expectations. *Social Science and Medicine* 49: 1501–17.

Holstein, James A. 1983. Jurors' use of judges' instructions. *Sociological Methods and Research* 11(4): 501–18.

Houtkoop-Steenstra, Hanneke 2000. *Interaction and the Standardized Survey Interview*. Cambridge: Cambridge University Press.

Hutchby, Ian 1996. *Confrontation Talk: Arguments, Asymmetries and Power on Talk Radio*. New York: Lawrence Erlbaum.

Hutchby, Ian 2006. *Media Talk: Conversation Analysis and the Study of Broadcasting*. New York: Open University Press.

Jacobs, Scott 2002. Maintaining neutrality in dispute mediation: managing disagreement while managing not to disagree. *Journal of Pragmatics* 34(10–11): 1403–26.

Jefferson, Gail 1974. Error correction as an interactional resource. *Language in Society* 2: 181–99.

Jefferson, Gail 1980. On "trouble-premonitory" response to inquiry. *Sociological Inquiry* 50: 153–85.

Jefferson, Gail 1981. The abominable "Ne?": a working paper exploring the phenomenon of post-response pursuit of response. Occasional Paper no. 6. Manchester: University of Manchester, Department of Sociology.

Jefferson, Gail 1984a. On stepwise transition from talk about a trouble to inappropriately next-positioned matters. In J. Maxwell Atkinson and John Heritage (eds.), *Structures of Social Action*. Cambridge: Cambridge University Press, pp. 191–221.

Jefferson, Gail 1984b. On the organization of laughter in talk about troubles. In J. Maxwell Atkinson and John Heritage (eds.), *Structures of Social Action*. Cambridge: Cambridge University Press, pp. 346–69.

Jefferson, Gail 1988. On the sequential organization of troubles-talk in ordinary conversation. *Social Problems* 35(4): 418–41.

Jefferson, Gail 1990. List construction as a task and interactional resource. In George Psathas (ed.), *Interaction Competence*. Lanham, MD: University Press of America, pp. 63–92.

Jefferson, Gail 2004. "At first I thought": a normalizing device for extraordinary events. In Gene Lerner (ed.), *Conversation Analysis: Studies from the First Generation*. Amsterdam: John Benjamins, pp. 131–67.

Jefferson, Gail and John Lee 1981. The rejection of advice: managing the problematic convergence of a "troubles-telling" and a "service encounter". *Journal of Pragmatics* 5: 399–422.

Johnson, D. M. 1945. The phantom anesthetist of Mattoon: a field study of mass hysteria. *Journal of Abnormal and Social Psychology* 40: 175–86.

Jonakait, Randolph N. 2006. *The American Jury System*. New Haven, CT: Yale University Press.

Jones, W. 1992. Broadcasters, politicians and the political interview. In W. Jones and L. Robins (eds.), *Two Decades in British Politics*. Manchester: Manchester University Press, pp. 53–77.

Kassirer, J. P. and G. A. Gorry 1978. Clinical problem solving: a behavioral analysis. *Annals of Internal Medicine* 89: 245–55.

Kendon, Adam 1987. Erving Goffman's contributions to the study of face-to-face interaction. In Paul Drew and Anthony Wootton (eds.), *Erving Goffman: Explorations in the Interaction Order*. Cambridge: Polity Press, pp. 14–40.

Kleinman, Arthur 1988. *The Illness Narratives: Suffering, Healing and the Human Condition*. New York: Basic Books.

Koenig, Christopher J. 2008. The interactional dynamics of treatment counseling in primary care. Unpublished PhD thesis, University of California Los Angeles.

Kollock, Peter, Philip Blumstein, and Pepper Schwartz 1985. Sex and power in interaction: conversational privileges and duties. *American Sociological Review* 50: 24–46.

Korsch, Barbara M. and Vida F. Negrete 1972. Doctor–patient communication. *Scientific American* 227: 66–74.

Kotthoff, Helga 1993. Disagreement and Concession in Disputes: On the Context Sensitivity of Preference Structures. *Language in Society* 22: 193–216.

Kravitz, R. L., Ronald M. Epstein, M. D. Feldman, C. E. Franz, R. Azari, M. S. Wilkes, L. Hinton, and P. Franks 2005. Influence of patients' requests for direct-to-consumer advertised antidepressants: a randomized controlled trial. *Journal of the American Medical Association* 293: 1995–2002.

Kuhn, Thomas 1962. *The Structure of Scientific Revolutions*. Chicago: University of Chicago Press.

Kuhn, Thomas 1977. Second thoughts on paradigms. In Thomas Kuhn (ed.), *The Essential Tension: Selected Studies in Scientific Tradition and Change*. Chicago: University of Chicago Press, pp. 293–319.

Labov, William and David Fanshel 1977. *Therapeutic Discourse: Psychotherapy as Conversation*. New York: Academic Press.

Lee, Seung-Hee 2005. The scales of justice: balancing neutrality and efficiency in plea-bargaining encounters. *Discourse and Society* 16(1): 33–54.

Lee, Yo-An 2007. Third turn position in teacher talk: contingency and the work of teaching. *Journal of Pragmatics* 39: 180–206.

Lee, Yo-An 2008. Yes–no questions in the third-turn position: pedagogical discourse processes. *Discourse Processes* 45(3): 237–62.

Lerner, Gene H. 2003. Selecting next speaker: the context-sensitive operation of a context-free organization. *Language in Society* 32: 177–201.

Levin, Alan M. and Stephen J. Hertzberg 1986. Inside the jury room. *Frontline*, PBS.

Levinson, Stephen C. 1983. *Pragmatics*. Cambridge: Cambridge University Press.

Levinson, Stephen C. 1988. Putting linguistics on a proper footing: explorations in Goffman's concepts of participation. In Paul Drew and Anthony Wootton (eds.), *Erving Goffman: Exploring the Interaction Order*. Boston: Northeastern University Press, pp. 161–227.

Levinson, Stephen C. 1992. Activity types and language. In Paul Drew and John Heritage (eds.), *Talk at Work*. Cambridge: Cambridge University Press, pp. 66–100.

Levinson, Stephen C. 2000. *Presumptive Meanings: The Theory of Generalized Conversational Implicature*. Cambridge, MA: MIT Press.

Light, Donald W. 2000. The medical profession and organizational change: from professional dominance to countervailing power. In Chloe E. Bird, Peter Conrad, and Allen M. Fremont (eds.), *Handbook of Medical Sociology*. Upper Saddle River, NJ: Prentice Hall, pp. 201–16.

Linell, Per and Margareta Bredmar 1996. Reconstructing topical sensitivity: aspects of face-work in talks between midwives and expectant mothers. *Research on Language and Social Interaction* 29(4): 347–79.

Linell, P., L. Gustavsson, and P. Juvonen 1988. Interactional dominance in dyadic communication: a presentation of initiative–response analysis. *Linguistics* 26: 415–42.

Livingston, Eric 1987. *Making Sense of Ethnomethodology*. London: Routledge.

Livingston, Eric 2008. *Ethnographies of Reason*. Burlington, VT: Ashgate.

Llewellyn, Nick 2005. Audience participation in political discourse: a study of public meetings. *Sociology* 39(4): 697–716.

Loftus, Elizabeth 1979. *Eyewitness Testimony*. Cambridge, MA: Harvard University Press.

Mainous, A. G., R. J. Zoorob, M. J. Oler, and D. M. Haynes 1997. Patient knowledge of upper respiratory infections: implications for antibiotic expectations and unnecessary utilization. *Journal of Family Practice* 45(1): 75–83.

Mangione-Smith, Rita, Marc N. Elliott, Tanya Stivers, Laurie L. McDonald, and John Heritage 2006. Ruling out the need for antibiotics: are we sending the right message? *Archives of Pediatric and Adolescent Medicine* 160: 945–52.

Mangione-Smith, Rita, Elizabeth McGlynn, Marc N. Elliott, Paul Krogstad, and Robert H. Brook 1999. The relationship between perceived parental expectations and pediatrician antimicrobial prescribing behavior. *Pediatrics* 103(4): 711–18.

Mangione-Smith, Rita, Tanya Stivers, Marc Elliott, Laurie McDonald, and John Heritage 2003. Online commentary during the physical examination: a communication tool for avoiding inappropriate prescribing? *Social Science and Medicine* 56: 313–20.

Manzo, John F. 1993. Jurors' narratives of personal experience in deliberation talk. *Text* 13(2): 267–90.

Manzo, John F. 1994. "You wouldn't take a seven-year-old and ask him all these questions": jurors' use of practical reasoning in supporting their arguments. *Law and Social Inquiry* 19: 601–26.

Manzo, John F. 1996. Taking turns and taking sides: opening scenes from two jury deliberations. *Social Psychology Quarterly* 59: 107–25.

Marvel, M. Kim, Ronald M. Epstein, Kristine Flowers, and Howard B. Beckman 1999. Soliciting the patient's agenda: have we improved? *Journal of the American Medical Association* 281(3): 283–7.

Matoesian, Gregory 1993. *Reproducing Rape*. Chicago: University of Chicago Press.

Maynard, Douglas W. 1984. *Inside Plea Bargaining: The Language of Negotiation*. New York: Plenum.

Maynard, Douglas W. 1985. How children start arguments. *Language in Society* 14: 1–29.

Maynard, Douglas W. 1988. Narratives and narrative structure in plea bargaining. *Law and Society Review* 22(3): 449–81.

Maynard, Douglas W. 1996. On "realization" in everyday life. *American Sociological Review* 60(1): 109–32.

Maynard, Douglas W. 2003. *Bad News, Good News: Conversational Order in Everyday Talk and Clinical Settings*. Chicago: University of Chicago Press.

Maynard, Douglas W., Hanneke Houtkoop-Steenstra, Nora Kate Schaeffer, and Hans van der Zouwen (eds.), 2002. *Standardization and Tacit Knowledge: Interaction and Practice in the Survey Interview*. New York: Wiley Interscience.

Maynard, Douglas W. and John F. Manzo 1993. On the sociology of justice: theoretical notes from an actual jury deliberation. *Sociological Theory* 11: 171–93.

McHoul, A. 1978. The organization of turns at formal talk in the classroom. *Language in Society* 7: 183–213.

McKinlay, John B. and Lisa D. Marceau 2002. The end of the golden age of doctoring. *International Journal of Health Services* 32(2); 379–416.

McKinley, R.K. and J.F. Middleton 1999. What do patients want from doctors? Content analysis of written patient agendas for the consultation. *British Journal of General Practice* 49: 796–800.

McWhinney, I. 1989. The need for a transformed clinical method. In M. Stewart and D. Roter (eds.), *Communicating with Medical Patients*. Newbury Park, CA: Sage.

Mead, Nicola and Peter Bower 2000. Patient centredness: a conceptual framework and review of the empirical literature. *Social Science and Medicine* 51: 1087–1110.

Meehan, Albert J. 1989. Assessing the "police-worthiness" of citizens' complaints to the police: accountability and the negotiation of "facts". In D. Helm, W. T. Anderson, A. J. Meehan, and A. Rawls (eds.), *The Interactional Order: New Directions in the Study of Social Order*. New York: Irvington, pp. 116–40.

Mehan, Hugh 1979. *Learning Lessons*. Cambridge, MA: Harvard University Press.

Mehan, Hugh 1985. The structure of classroom discourse. In Teun A. Dijk (ed.), *Handbook of Discourse Analysis*, vol. 3. New York: Academic Press, pp. 120–31.

Mills, C. Wright 1940. Situated actions and vocabularies of motive. *American Sociological Review* 5: 904–13.

Mishler, Elliot 1984. *The Discourse of Medicine: Dialectics of Medical Interviews*. Norwood, NJ: Ablex.

Montgomery, Martin 2007. *Discourse of Broadcast News*. London: Routledge.

Montgomery, Martin and Joanna Thornborrow (eds.) 2010. *Foregrounding the Personal in Broadcast News*: special issue of *Discourse and Communication*.

Myers, Greg 2004. *Matters of Opinion: Talking about Public Issues*. Cambridge: Cambridge University Press.

O'Barr, William 1982. *Linguistic Evidence: Language, Power and Strategy in the Courtroom*. New York: Academic Press.

Orth, J. J., W. B. Stiles, L. Scherwitz, D. Hennrikus, and C. Vallbona 1987. Patient exposition and provider explanation in routine interviews and hypertensive patients' blood pressure control. *Health Psychology* 6: 29–42.

Parsons, Talcott 1937. *The Structure of Social Action*. New York: McGraw-Hill.

Parsons, Talcott 1951. *The Social System*. New York: Free Press.

Peräkylä, Anssi 1995. *AIDS Counselling: Institutional Interaction and Clinical Practice*. Cambridge: Cambridge University Press.

Peräkylä, Anssi 1998. Authority and accountability: the delivery of diagnosis in primary health care. *Social Psychology Quarterly* 61(4): 301–20.

Peräkylä, Anssi 2002. Agency and authority: extended responses to diagnostic statements in primary care encounters. *Research on Language and Social Interaction* 35(2): 219–47.

Peräkylä, Anssi 2006. Communicating and responding to diagnosis. In John Heritage and Douglas Maynard (eds.), *Communication in Medical Care: Interactions between Primary Care Physicians and Patients*. Cambridge: Cambridge University Press, pp. 214–47.

Percy, Stephen L. and Eric J. Scott 1985. *Demand Processing and Performance in Public Service Agencies*. Tuscaloosa: University of Alabama Press.

Pomerantz, Anita M. 1984. Agreeing and disagreeing with assessments: some features of preferred / dispreferred turn shapes. In J. Maxwell Atkinson and John Heritage (eds.), *Structures of Social Action: Studies in Conversation Analysis*. Cambridge: Cambridge University Press, pp. 57–101.

Pomerantz, Anita M. 1988. Offering a candidate answer: an information seeking strategy. *Communication Monographs* 55: 360–73.

Pomerantz, Anita M. 2004. Investigating reported absences. In Gene Lerner (ed.), *Conversation Analysis: Studies from the First Generation*. Amsterdam: John Benjamins: 109–29.

Raymond, Geoffrey 2003. Grammar and social organization: yes/no interrogatives and the structure of responding. *American Sociological Review* 68: 939–67.

Raymond, Geoffrey 2010. Grammar and social relations: alternative forms of yes/no-type initiating actions in health visitor interactions. In Alice F. Freed and Susan Ehrlich (eds.), *"Why Do You Ask?" The Function of Questions in Institutional Discourse*. New York: Oxford University Press, pp. 87–107.

Raymond, Geoffrey and Don H. Zimmerman 2007. Rights and responsibilities in calls for help: the case of the Mountain Glade fire. *Research on Language and Social Interaction* 40: 33–61.

Rendle-Short, Johanna 2007. "Catherine, you're wasting your time": address terms within the Australian political interview. *Journal of Pragmatics* 39: 1503–25.

Rist, Ray 1970. Student social class and teacher expectations: the self-fulfilling prophecy in ghetto education. *Harvard Educational Review* 40(3): 411–51.

Robinson, Jeffrey D. 1998. Getting down to business: talk, gaze, and body orientation during openings of doctor–patient consultations. *Human Communication Research* 25(1): 97–123.

Robinson, Jeffrey D. 2003. An interactional structure of medical activities during acute visits and its implications for patients' participation. *Health Communication* 15(1): 27–57.

Robinson, Jeffrey D. 2006. Soliciting patients' presenting concerns. In John Heritage and Douglas Maynard (eds.), *Communication in Medical Care: Interactions between Primary Care Physicians and Patients*. Cambridge: Cambridge University Press, pp. 22–47.

Robinson, Jeffrey D. and John Heritage 2005. The structure of patients' presenting concerns: the completion relevance of current symptoms. *Social Science and Medicine* 61: 481–93.

Robinson, Jeffrey D. and Tanya Stivers 2001. Achieving activity transitions in primary-care encounters: from history taking to physical examination. *Human Communication Research* 27(2): 253–98.

Rosenthal, Robert and Lenore Jacobson 1968. *Pygmalion in the Classroom: Teacher Expectation and Pupils' Intellectual Development*. New York: Holt, Rinehart and Winston.

Rossano, Federico 2005. When it's over is it really over? On the effects of sustained gaze vs. gaze withdrawal at sequence possible completion. Paper presented at the 9th International Pragmatics Conference, Riva del Garda, Italy, July 10–15, 2005.

Rossano, Federico 2009. Gaze as a method of pursuing responses. Paper presented at the 104th annual meeting of the American Sociological Association, San Francisco, August 8–11.

Roter, Debra and Judith Hall 2006. *Doctors Talking with Patients/ Patients Talking with Doctors: Improving Communication in Medical Visits*, 2nd edn. Westport, CT: Praeger.

Roter, Debra and Susan Larson 2002. The Roter Interaction Analysis System (RIAS): utility and flexibility for analysis of medical interactions. *Patient Education and Counseling* 42: 243–51.

Roter, Debra, Moira Stewart, Samuel Putnam, Mack Lipkin, William Stiles, and Thomas S. Inui 1997. The patient–physician relationship: communication patterns of primary care physicians. *Journal of the American Medical Association* 227(4): 350–6.

Roth, Andrew L. 1998. Who makes news: descriptions of television news interviewees' public personae. *Media, Culture and Society* 20(1): 79–107.

Roth, Andrew L. 2002. Social epistemology in broadcast interviews. *Language in Society* 31: 355–81.

Rubinstein, Jonathan 1973. *City Police*. New York: Hill and Wang.

Ruusuvuori, Johanna 2001. Looking means listening: coordinating displays of engagement in doctor–patient interaction. *Social Science and Medicine* 52: 1093–1108.

Sacks, Harvey 1972. On the analyzability of stories by children. In John J. Gumperz and Dell Hymes (eds.), *Directions in Sociolinguistics: The Ethnography of Communication*. New York: Holt, Rinehart and Winston, pp. 325–45.

Sacks, Harvey 1979. Hotrodder: a revolutionary category (edited by Gail Jefferson from a lecture delivered at the University of California, Los Angeles, Spring 1966). In George Psathas (ed.), *Everyday Language: Studies in Ethnomethodology*. New York: Irvington, pp. 7–14.

Sacks, Harvey 1984a. Notes on methodology (edited by Gail Jefferson from various lectures). In J. M. Atkinson and J. Heritage (eds.), *Structures of Social Action*. Cambridge: Cambridge University Press, pp. 21–7.

Sacks, Harvey 1984b. On doing "being ordinary". In J. Maxwell Atkinson and John Heritage (eds.), *Structures of Social Action*. Cambridge: Cambridge University Press, pp. 413–29.

Sacks, Harvey 1987. On the preferences for agreement and contiguity in sequences in conversation. In Graham Button and John R. E. Lee (eds.), *Talk and Social Organisation*. Clevedon, England: Multilingual Matters, pp. 54–69.

Sacks, Harvey 1992 [1964–72]. *Lectures on Conversation*, 2 vols. Oxford: Basil Blackwell.

Sacks, Harvey, Emanuel A. Schegloff, and Gail Jefferson 1974. A simplest systematics for the organization of turn-taking for conversation. *Language* 50: 696–735.

Scannell, Paddy (ed.) 1991. *Broadcast Talk*. London: Sage.

Schegloff, Emanuel A. 1968. Sequencing in conversational openings. *American Anthropologist* 70: 1075–95.

Schegloff, Emanuel A. 1972. Notes on a conversational practice: formulating place. In David Sudnow (ed.), *Studies in Social Interaction*. New York: Free Press, pp. 75–119.

Schegloff, Emanuel A 1979. Identification and recognition in telephone conversation openings. In George Psathas (ed.), *Everyday Language: Studies in Ethnomethodology*. New York: Irvington, pp. 23–78.

Schegloff, Emanuel A. 1982. Discourse as an interactional achievement: some uses of "uh huh" and other things that come between sentences. In D. Tannen (ed.), *Georgetown University Round Table on Languages and Linguistics 1981: Analyzing Discourse: Text and Talk*. Washington, DC: Georgetown University Press, pp. 71–93.

Schegloff, Emanuel A. 1984. On some questions and ambiguities in conversation. In J. Maxwell Atkinson and John Heritage (eds.), *Structures of Social Action*. Cambridge: Cambridge University Press, pp. 28–52.

Schegloff, Emanuel A. 1986. The routine as achievement. *Human Studies* 9: 111–51.

Schegloff, Emanuel A. 1987. Between macro and micro: contexts and other connections. In J. Alexander, R. Munch, B. Giesen, and N. Smelser (eds.), *The Micro–Macro Link*. Berkeley: University of California Press, pp. 207–34.

Schegloff, Emanuel A. 1988/9. From interview to confrontation: observations on the Bush/Rather encounter. *Research on Language and Social Interaction* 22: 215–40.

Schegloff, Emanuel A. 1990. On the organization of sequences as a source of "coherence" in talk-in-interaction. In B. Dorval (ed.), *Conversational Organization and Its Development*. Norwood, NJ: Ablex, pp. 51–77.

Schegloff, Emanuel A. 1991. Reflections on talk and social structure. In Deirdre Boden and Don H Zimmerman (eds.), *Talk and Social Structure*. Berkeley: University of California Press, pp. 44–70.

Schegloff, Emanuel A. 1992a. Introduction. In G. Jefferson (ed.), *Harvey Sacks: Lectures on Conversation. Volume 1: Fall 1964–Spring 1968*. Oxford: Blackwell, pp. ix–lxii.

Schegloff, Emanuel A. 1992b. On talk and its institutional occasions. In Paul Drew and John Heritage (eds.), *Talk at Work: Social Interaction in Institutional Settings*. Cambridge: Cambridge University Press, pp. 101–34.

Schegloff, Emanuel A. 1992c. Repair after next turn: the last structurally provided for place for the defense of intersubjectivity in conversation. *American Journal of Sociology* 95(5): 1295–1345.

Schegloff, Emanuel A. 1996. Turn organization: one intersection of grammar and interaction. In Elinor Ochs, Sandra Thompson, and Emanuel Schegloff (eds.), *Interaction and Grammar*. Cambridge: Cambridge University Press, pp. 52–133.

Schegloff, Emanuel A. 1998. Word repeats as a practice for ending. Paper presented at the annual meeting of the National Communication Association, New York.

Schegloff, Emanuel A. 1999. Discourse, pragmatics, conversation, analysis. *Discourse Studies* 1(4): 405–35.

Schegloff, Emanuel A. 2000. On granularity. *Annual Review of Sociology* 26: 715–20.

Schegloff, Emanuel A. 2003. On conversation analysis: an interview with Emanuel A. Schegloff. In Carlo Prevignano and Paul J. Thibault (eds.), *Discussing Conversation Analysis: The Work of Emanuel A. Schegloff*. Philadelphia: John Benjamins, pp. 11–56.

Schegloff, Emanuel A. 2006. Interaction: the infrastructure for social institutions, the natural ecological niche for language and the arena in which culture is enacted. In N. J. Enfield and Stephen C. Levinson (eds.), *The Roots of Human Sociality: Culture, Cognition and Interaction*. New York: Berg, pp. 70–96.

Schegloff, Emanuel A. 2007. *Sequence Organization in Interaction: A Primer in Conversation Analysis*, vol. 1. Cambridge: Cambridge University Press.

Schegloff, Emanuel A. and Gene H. Lerner 2009. Beginning to respond: Well-prefaced responses to Wh-questions. *Research on Language and Social Interaction*(42): 91–115.

Schegloff, Emanuel A. and Harvey Sacks 1973. Opening up closings. *Semiotica* 8: 289–327.

Schelling, Thomas 1963. Bargaining, communication, and limited war. In Thomas Schelling (ed.), *The Strategy of Conflict*. New York: Oxford University Press, pp. 53–80.

Schudson, Michael 1994. Question authority: a history of the news interview in American journalism, 1830s–1930s. *Media, Culture and Society* 16: 565–87.

Searle, John R. 1969. *Speech Acts: An Essay in the Philosophy of Language*. Cambridge: Cambridge University Press.

Searle, John R. 1979. *Expression and Meaning: Studies in the Theory of Speech Acts*. Cambridge: Cambridge University Press.

Sharrock, Wesley 1974. On owning knowledge. In R. Turner (ed.), *Ethnomethodology*. Harmondsworth: Penguin, pp. 45–53.

Sharrock, Wesley and Roy Turner 1978. On a conversational environment for equivocality. In James Schenkein (ed.), *Studies in the Organization of Conversational Interaction*. New York: Academic Press, pp. 173–98.

Shorter, Edward 1985. *Bedside Manners: The Troubled History of Doctors and Patients*. New York: Simon and Schuster.

Silverman, David 1987. *Communication and Medical Practice*. London: Sage.

Silverman, Jonathan, Susanne Kurtz, and Juliet Draper 2005. *Skills for Communicating with Patients*, 2nd edn. Oxford: Radcliffe Publishing.

Simmel, Georg [1908] 1950. *The Sociology of Georg Simmel*, trans. Kurt Wolff. Glencoe, IL: Free Press.

Sinclair, J. McH. and R. M. Coulthard 1974. *Towards an Analysis of Discourse*. London: Oxford University Press.

Sorjonen, Marja-Leena, Liisa Raevaara, Markku Haakana, Tuukka Tammi, and Anssi Peräkylä 2006. Lifestyle discussions in medical interviews. In John Heritage and Douglas Maynard (eds.), *Communication in Medical Care: Interaction between Primary Care Physicians and Patients*. Cambridge: Cambridge University Press, pp. 340–78.

Springer, Brian 1995. *Spin*. USA, Art Institute of Chicago.

Starr, Paul 1982. *The Social Transformation of American Medicine*. New York: Basic Books.

Stiles, William B. 1989. Evaluating medical interview process components: null correlations with outcomes may be misleading. *Medical Care* 27(2): 212–20.

Stivers, Tanya 1998. Pre-diagnostic commentary in veterinarian–client interaction. *Research on Language and Social Interaction* 31(2): 241–77.

Stivers, Tanya 2002a. Presenting the problem in pediatric encounters: "symptoms only" versus "candidate diagnosis" presentations. *Health Communication* 14(3): 299–338.

Stivers, Tanya 2002b. Participating in decisions about treatment: overt parent pressure for antibiotic medication in pediatric encounters. *Social Science and Medicine* 54(7): 1111–30.

Stivers, Tanya 2004. "No no no" and other types of multiple sayings in social interaction. *Human Communication Research* 30(2): 260–93.

Stivers, Tanya 2005a. Non-antibiotic treatment recommendations: delivery formats and implications for parent resistance. *Social Science and Medicine* 60(5): 949–64.

Stivers, Tanya 2005b. Parent resistance to physicians' treatment recommendations: one resource for initiating a negotiation of the treatment decision. *Health Communication* 18(1): 41–74.

Stivers, Tanya 2006. Treatment decisions: negotiations between doctors and patients in acute care encounters. In John Heritage and Douglas Maynard (eds.), *Communication in Medical Care: Interactions between Primary Care Physicians and Patients*. Cambridge: Cambridge University Press, pp. 279–312.

Stivers, Tanya 2007a. *Prescribing Under Pressure: Parent–Physician Conversations and Antibiotics*. New York: Oxford University Press.

Stivers, Tanya 2007b. Practicing patienthood: determinants of children's responses to physicians' questions in routine medical encounters. Unpublished manuscript, Max Planck Institute for Psycholinguistics.

Stivers, Tanya, forthcoming. An overview of the question–response system in American English. *Journal of Pragmatics*.

Stivers, Tanya, Nicholas J. Enfield, Penelope Brown, Christina Englert, Makoto Hayashi, Trine Heinemann, Gertie Hoymann, Federico Rossano, Jan Peter De Ruiter, Kyung-Eun Yoon, and Stephen Levinson (2009). Universals and cultural variation in turn-taking in conversation. *Proceedings of the National Academy of Sciences* 106(26): 10587–92.

Stivers, Tanya and John Heritage 2001. Breaking the sequential mold: answering "more than the question" during medical history taking. *Text* 21(1/2): 151–85.

Stivers, Tanya and Asifa Majid 2007. Questioning children: interactional evidence of implicit bias in medical interviews. *Social Psychology Quarterly* 70(4): 424–41.

Stivers, Tanya, Rita Mangione-Smith, Marc N. Elliott, Laurie McDonald, and John Heritage 2003. Why do physicians think parents expect antibiotics? What parents report vs what physicians perceive. *Journal of Family Practice* 52(2): 140–8.

Stoeckle, John D. and J. Andrew Billings 1987. A history of history-taking: the medical interview. *Journal of General Internal Medicine* 2: 119–27.

Suchman, Lucy A. 1987. *Plans and Situated Actions: The Problem of Human Machine Communication*. Cambridge: Cambridge University Press.

Tatalovich, Anne 2007. How Civil Juries Really Decide Cases: Lessons From an Empirical Study of Actual Jury Deliberations. *Researching Law* 18(2): 1–11.

ten Have, Paul 1991. Talk and institution: a reconsideration of the "asymmetry" of doctor–patient interaction. In Deirdre Boden and Don Zimmerman (eds.), *Talk and Social Structure*. Berkeley: University of California Press.

Thornborrow, Joanna 1997. Having their say: the function of stories in talk show discourse. *Text* 17(2): 241–62.

Thornborrow, Joanna 2001. Authenticating talk: building public identities in audience participation broadcasting. *Discourse Studies* 3(4): 459–79.

Thornborrow, Joanna and Theo Van Leeuwen (eds.) 2001. *Authenticity in Media Discourse*: special Issue of *Discourse Studies*.

Todd, Alexandra D. 1989. *Intimate Adversaries: Cultural Conflict between Doctors and Women Patients*. Philadelphia: University of Pennsylvania Press.

Tolson, Andrew 2001. *Television Talk Shows: Discourse, Performance, Spectacle*. Mahwah, NJ: Erlbaum.

Tolson, Andrew 2006. *Media Talk: Spoken Discourse on TV and Radio*. Edinburgh: Edinburgh University Press.

Torode, Brian 1995. Negotiating "advice" in a call to a consumer help line. In Alan Firth (ed.), *The Discourse of Negotiation: Studies of Language in the Workplace*. Oxford: Pergamon, pp. 345–72.

Tracy, Karen 1997. Interactional trouble in emergency service requests: a problem of frames. *Research on Language and Social Interaction* 30: 315–43.

Tracy, Karen and Susan Tracy 1998. Rudeness at 911: reconceptualizing face and face attack. *Human Communication Research* 25: 225–51.

Tracy, Susan 2002. When Questioning Turns to Face Threat: An Interactional Sensitivity in 911 Call Taking. *Western Journal of Communication* 66: 129–157.

Tuckett, D., M. Boulton, C. Olson, and A. Williams 1985. *Meetings between Experts: An Approach to Sharing Ideas in Medical Consultations*. London: Tavistock.

Turner, Patricia 2008. Grammar and epistemics in question construction: After hours calls to an on-call physician. Unpublished paper, Department of Applied Linguistics, UCLA.

Waitzkin, Howard 1985. Information giving in medical care. *Journal of Health and Social Behavior* 26: 81–101.

Waitzkin, Howard 1991. *The Politics of Medical Encounters: How Patients and Doctors Deal with Social Problems*. New Haven, CT: Yale University Press.

Wakin, Michelle and Don H. Zimmerman 1999. Reduction and specialization in emergency and directory assistance calls. *Research on Language and Social Interaction* 32(4): 409–37.

Wells, P. and P. Bull 2007. From politics to comedy – a comparative analysis of affiliative audience responses. *Journal of Language and Social Psychology* 26: 321–42.

West, Candace 1984. *Routine Complications: Troubles with Talk between Doctors and Patients*. Bloomington: Indiana University Press.

West, Candace and Don H. Zimmerman 1983. Small insults: a study of interruptions in cross-sex conversations with unacquainted persons. In B. Thorne, C. Kramarae, and N. Henley (eds.), *Language, Gender and Society*. Rowley, MA: Newbury House, pp. 102–17.

Whalen, Jack 1995. A technology of order production: computer-aided dispatch in public safety communications. In Paul ten Have and George Psathas (eds.), *Situated Order: Studies in the Social Organization of Talk and Embodied Activities*. Washington, DC: University Press of America, pp. 187–230.

Whalen, Jack and Don H. Zimmerman 1998. Observations on the display and management of emotions in naturally occurring activities: the case of "hysteria" in calls to 9–1–1. *Social Psychology Quarterly* 61(2): 141–59.

Whalen, Jack and Don H. Zimmerman 2005. Working a call: multiparty management and interactional infrastructure in calls for help. In Carolyn D. Baker, Michael Emmison, and Alan Firth (eds.), *Calling for Help*. Philadelphia: John Benjamins, pp. 309–46.

Whalen, Jack, Don H. Zimmerman, and Marilyn R. Whalen 1988. When words fail: a single case analysis. *Social Problems* 35(4): 335–62.

Whalen, Marilyn and Don H Zimmerman 1987. Sequential and institutional contexts in calls for help. *Social Psychology Quarterly* 50: 172–85.

Whalen, Marilyn and Don H. Zimmerman 1990. Describing trouble: practical epistemology in citizen calls to the police. *Language in Society* 19: 465–92.

Wilkinson, Sue and Celia Kitzinger 2007. Surprise as an interactional achievement: reaction tokens in conversation. *Social Psychology Quarterly* 69: 150–82.

Wilson, Thomas P. 1991. Social structure and the sequential organization of interaction. In Deirdre Boden and Don H. Zimmerman (eds.), *Talk and Social Structure*. Cambridge: Polity Press, pp. 22–43.

Wolinsky, F. D. and S. R. Wolinsky 1981. Expecting sick-role legitimation and getting it. *Journal of Health and Social Behavior* 22: 229–42.

Zimmerman, Don H. 1970. The practicalities of rule use. In J. Douglas (ed.), *Understanding Everyday Life*. London: Routledge, pp. 221–38.

Zimmerman, Don H. 1984. Talk and its occasion: the case of calling the police. In D. Schiffrin (ed.), *Meaning, Form, and Use in Context: Linguistic Applications*. Georgetown University Round Table on Languages and Linguistics 35. Washington, DC: Georgetown University Press, pp. 210–28.

Zimmerman, Don H. 1992. The interactional organization of calls for emergency assistance. In Paul Drew and John Heritage (eds.), *Talk at Work: Social Interaction in Institutional Settings*. Cambridge: Cambridge University Press, pp. 418–69.

Zimmerman, Don H. 1998. Identity, context, and interaction. In Charles Antaki and Sue Widdicombe (eds.), *Identities in Talk*. London: Sage, pp. 87–106.

Zimmerman, Don H. and Michelle Wakin 1995. "Thank you's" and the management of closings in emergency calls. Presented at the Annual Meeting of the American Sociological Association, Washington, DC.

Zimmerman, Don H. and Candace West 1975. Sex roles, interruptions and silences in conversation. In Barrie Thorne and Nancy Henley (eds.), *Language and Sex: Difference and Dominance*. Rowley, MA: Newbury House, pp. 105–29.

Zola, Irving K. 1973. Pathways to the doctor: from person to patient. *Social Science and Medicine* 7: 677–89.

Index of Names

Adelman, Ronald D. 118
Adkins, Barbara 244
Albert, E. 37
Arborelius, E. 105
Aristotle 198
Arminen, Ilkka 14
Armstrong, Neil 278
Asch, Solomon E. 265
Atkinson, J. Maxwell 13–14, 16, 37, 176–7, 185, 200, 207, 212, 222, 263–7, 269, 277, 279
Ayer, Alfred J. 263
Azari, R. 169

Baker, Carolyn 68
Bales, Robert Freed 8
Balint, Michael 103
Barnes, Barry 154
Bates, B. 135
Beach, Wayne A. 113
Beckett, Megan 143, 152
Beckman, Howard 105–7
Bentsen, Lloyd 277
Bergmann, Jörg 54, 69, 76, 78, 82–3, 86
Bickley, L. S. 135
Bijur, Peter 238
Billings, J. Andrew 135
Bloor, Michael J. 134
Blumstein, Philip 14
Boden, Deirdre 17
Boesak, Allan 234, 237–8
Bolinger, Dwight 142
Boulton, M. 118
Bower, Peter 118, 156
Boyd, Elizabeth 39, 105, 135, 142, 144
Bredmar, Margareta 147

Bremberg, S. 105
Brinkley, David 29
Brittan, Sam 224
Britten, Nicky 166
Broder, David S. 243
Brodine, R. 279
Brokaw, Tom 238, 260–1
Brook, Robert H. 166
Brown, Penelope 14, 23, 143
Bull, Peter 222, 245–6, 262, 279
Bush, George H. W. 222, 239–41, 250, 258–9, 272–3
Button, Graham 17
Byrne, Patrick 40, 103–5, 118, 156–9, 169

Caesar, Julius 270
Callaghan, James 267–8
Cannon, Lou 243
Cantril, Hadley 73
Carmichael, L. 174
Carville, James 232
Cassell, Eric 135–6
Chafe, Wallace 160
Charon, Rita 118
Cherry, Donald K. 122
Churchill, Winston 270, 278
Cicero 270
Clark, Timothy 279
Clayman, Steven E. 17, 29, 35, 38–40, 43, 137, 208, 224–8, 235, 237, 241–5, 262, 277, 279, 281
Clinton, Bill 182, 233, 235–6, 245
Clinton, Hillary 270
Cobb, Sarah 212
Collins, Randall 19

Conley, John M. 185, 208, 212
Cooper, L. 267, 276
Coulthard, R. M. 27
Cuff, Edward C. 37
Cuomo, Mario 264
Curl, Traci S. 82, 121

Darman, Richard 240
Day, Robin 228
Delaney, David 206
Dersley, Ian 98
Deutch, John 233
Diamond, Shari 186, 199
Dingwall, Robert 39, 201, 209, 212
Disraeli, Benjamin 277
Dole, Bob 230, 236, 238–9, 252, 270
Donaldson, Sam 228, 240, 244
Draper, Juliet 105, 133
Drew, Paul 12, 15–17, 19, 35–7, 46, 49–50, 82,
    116, 121, 134, 141, 145–6, 151, 175–7,
    179–81, 185, 222
Duberstein, Paul R. 118
Duncan, Otis Dudley 263
Duranti, Alessandro 21, 32, 37
Durkheim, Émile 278

Edwards, Derek 68, 79
Egbert, Maria M. 176
Ehrlich, Susan 185
Eisenhower, Dwight 241–2
Ekstrom, Mats 226
Elliott, Marc N. 16, 42, 48, 123, 143, 152, 166,
    168, 241–4, 281
Ellis, Leslie 186
Elstein, A. A. 135
Emanuel, Ezekiel J. 118, 155
Emanuel, Linda L. 118, 155
Emmertsen, Sophie 244
Emmison, Michael 68
Enfield, N. J. 23, 49
Engel, George L. 118, 155
Epstein, Edward Jay 243
Epstein, Ronald M. 106–7, 118, 169

Fallows, James M. 243
Fanshel, David 140
Feldman, M. D. 169
Fineman, Martha A. 212
Firth, Alan 68
Fiscella, Kevin 118
Fisher, Sue 49

Flowers, Kristine 106–7
Frankel, Richard M. 105–6
Franks, Peter 118, 169
Franz, C. E. 169
Freidson, Eliot 104, 120–1, 124, 155, 169
French, Peter 33
Freud, Sigmund 278
Frosch, Dominick L. 118
Frost, David 226

Gaitskell, Hugh 270
Garcia, Angela 37–8, 100, 200–1, 207–12
Garfinkel, Harold 2, 8–12, 15, 19, 21, 32, 187,
    198
Gladstone, William 277
Goffman, Erving 2, 7–9, 13–15, 19, 133–4,
    235–6, 280
Goodwin, Charles 7, 21, 32, 50, 182–5
Goodwin, Marjorie Harness 92, 98
Gore, Albert 245
Gorry, G. A. 135
Gramm, Phil 39, 235–6
Greatbatch, David L. 17, 37–9, 201, 208–9, 212,
    224, 226, 245, 262, 267–71, 273, 275–6, 279
Greene, Michele J. 118
Grunwald, Mandy 232
Günthner, Susanne 92
Gustavsson, L. 39

Haakana, Markku 139
Halkowski, Timothy 48–9, 76, 128, 133
Hall, Judith 105, 118, 135, 142
Hampton, J. R. 135
Harris, Sandra 229, 244–6, 262
Harrison, M. R. G. 135
Hart, Gary 256
Hattersley, Roy 229
Haynes, D. M. 123
Heath, Christian 17, 50, 89, 134, 157–9, 161,
    164, 166, 169
Heath, Edward (Ted) 229–30, 236, 272
Hegel, Georg W. F. 278
Heinemann, Trine 142
Heisterkamp, Brian L. 201, 207, 212
Hennrikus, D. 105
Heritage, John 7, 11–12, 14–19, 24–5, 27, 29,
    32, 35, 37–40, 42–4, 46, 48, 50, 97, 104–6,
    109–11, 118, 120–1, 123–4, 134–5, 137, 140,
    142–5, 147–52, 157, 166, 168, 175, 205, 208,
    218, 224–6, 228, 241–4, 262, 267–71, 272,
    273, 275–6, 279, 281

Hertzberg, Stephen J. 186, 199
Heseltine, Michael 237
Hinton, L. 169
Hodgson, Ralph 27
Hoekelman, R. A. 135
Hogan, H. P. 174
Holstein, James A. 199
Horobin, Gordon 134
Houtkoop-Steenstra, Hanneke 50
Hume, Brit 258–60
Humphries, Hubert 264
Hutchby, Ian 226

Inui, Thomas S. 142, 152

Jacobs, Scott 201, 207, 212
Jacobson, Lenore 50
Jefferson, Gail 12, 15–16, 37, 47, 77, 90, 108,
    115, 117, 123, 130, 132–3, 136, 157
Johnson, D. M. 73
Jonakait, Randolph N. 187
Jones, W. 244
Juvonen, P. 39

Kaplan, Robert M. 118
Kassirer, J. P. 135
Kendon, Adam 9, 19
Kennedy, John F. 272, 277, 279
Kennedy, Robert 69
King, Martin Luther 279
King, Rodney 182, 184–5, 280
Kitzinger, Celia 25
Kleinman, Arthur 154
Koenig, Christopher J. 165
Kollock, Peter 14
Korsch, Barbara M. 103, 118
Kotthoff, Helga 98
Kravitz, Richard L. 118, 169
Krogstad, Paul 166
Kroon, Asa 226
Kuhn, Thomas 154
Kurtz, Susanne 105, 133

Labov, William 140
Larson, Susan 118
Lee, John 90
Lee, Seung-Hee 201, 207, 209, 212
Lee, Yo-An 27
Lerner, Gene H. 16, 109
Levin, Alan M. 186, 199
Levinson, Stephen C. 7, 14, 28, 38, 143, 145, 153

Light, Donald W. 155, 169
Lindström, Anna 18
Lincoln, Abraham 270, 278
Linell, Per 39, 147
Lipkin, Mack 142, 152
Livingston, Eric 19
Llewellyn, Nick 279
Loftus, Elizabeth 174, 185
Long, E. L. 40, 103–5, 118, 156–9, 169
Luff, Paul 50

Mainous, A. G. 123
Majid, Asifa 135, 281
Mangione-Smith, Rita 42, 48, 123, 166, 168
Manzo, John F. 186–92, 196–7, 199
Marceau, Lisa 155
Marvel, M. Kim 106–7
Matoesian, Gregory 179, 185
Mayer, Katherine 222
Maynard, Douglas W. 42, 49–50, 92, 98, 118, 132,
    157, 168, 186, 189–92, 196–7, 199–202, 206, 212
McDonald, Laurie 42, 48, 123, 166, 168, 241–4,
    281
McGlynn, Elizabeth 166
McHoul, A 17, 27, 37
McKinlay, John B. 155
McKinley, R. K. 105
McWhinney, I. 105
Mead, Nicola 118, 155–6
Meehan, A. J. 81, 86
Mehan, Hugh 27, 37
Meldrum, Sean C. 118
Middleton, J. F. 105
Miller, Zell 267–8
Mills, C. Wright 198
Mishler, Elliot 49, 105, 118, 137–8, 152, 155
Mitchell, J. R. A. 135
Montgomery, Martin 226, 244
Murphy, Beth 186, 199
Myers, Greg 226

Negrete, Vida F. 103, 118
Nichols, Johanna 160
Nylund, Mats 226

Obama, Barack 50, 263–4, 274–5, 280
O'Barr, William 185, 208, 212
Okoumunne, Obioha 166
Oler, M. J. 123
Olson, C. 118
Orth, J. J. 105

Parmer, Penelope Ann 100
Parsons, Talcott 14, 104, 119–20, 134, 155, 169
Paxman, Jeremy 228
Peräkylä, Anssi 37, 134, 139, 160–3, 166, 168–9
Percy, Stephen L. 69
Perot, Ross 250, 267–8
Pomerantz, Anita M. 16, 45, 150, 279
Prichard, J. S. 135
Putnam, Samuel 142, 152

Quayle, Dan 257–61, 277, 280

Raevarra, Liisa 139
Rather, Dan 222, 228, 239–41
Raymond, Geoffrey 16, 69, 86, 138, 140, 152, 180, 205
Reagan, Ronald 239, 241–2
Rechtsteiner, Elizabeth 122
Rendle-Short, Johanna 244
Reno, Janet 221
Rice, Donna 256
Richardson, Andrea 168
Rifkin, Janet 212
Rist, Ray 50
Roberts, John 50
Robinson, Jeffrey D. 16–17, 40, 42, 104, 106, 109–11, 120, 124, 134, 140, 143, 152, 164
Rose, Mary R. 186, 199
Rosenthal, Robert 49
Rossano, Federico 158
Roter, Debra 105, 118, 135, 142, 152
Roth, Andrew L. 218, 222, 226, 235, 244
Rove, Karl 263, 274
Rubin, Robert 29, 253–5
Rubinstein, Jonathan 72
Ruusuvuori, Johanna 42

Sacks, Harvey 7, 12–16, 19, 23, 37, 40–1, 47, 61, 77, 90, 136, 139, 176, 181, 216, 219
Scannell, Paddy 226
Scargill, Arthur 217, 253
Schaeffer, Nora Kate 50
Schegloff, Emanuel A. 7, 12–19, 22–3, 27, 35, 37, 39, 41, 49, 60–2, 65, 90, 109, 113, 136, 139, 143, 176, 216, 219, 222, 225
Schelling, Thomas 266, 278
Scherwitz, L. 105
Schudson, Michael 226
Schwartz, Pepper 14
Scott, Eric J. 69
Searle, John R. 13–14, 19, 28

Sefi, Sue 18
Seidman, Shari 186
Seymour, C. 135
Sharrock, Wesley 37, 69, 86, 140
Shields, Cleveland G. 118
Shorter, Edward 154–5, 169
Shulman, L. S. 135
Sidnell, Jack 185
Silverman, David 152
Silverman, Jonathan 105, 133
Simmel, Georg 209
Sinclair, J. 27
Sorjonen, Marja-Leena 17, 36, 49–50, 139, 149
Spencer, Lord 270
Sprafka, S. A. 135
Springer, Brian 245
Starr, Paul 154–5, 169
Steel, David 271
Stewart, Moira 142, 152
Stiles, William B. 105, 118, 142, 152
Stivers, Tanya 23, 42, 44, 48–9, 115, 122–3, 134–5, 141, 145–6, 148–9, 151, 159, 164–9, 281
Stoeckle, John D. 135
Stokoe, Elizabeth 79
Suchman, Lucy A. 50

Tammi, Tuukka 139
Tatalovich, Anne 186, 188, 199
ten Have, Paul 17, 36
Thatcher, Margaret 230–1, 235, 236, 269, 271–2, 274
Thornborrow, Joanna 226
Timpka, T. 105
Todd, Alexandra D. 49, 152
Tolson, Andrew 226
Torode, Brian 68
Tracy, Karen 95, 99–100
Tracy, Susan 99–100
Tuckett, D. 118
Turgot 278
Turner, Patricia 86, 141–2
Turner, Roy 69

Vallbona, C. 105
van der Zouwen, Hans 50
Van Leeuwen, Theo 226
Verhoeven, Jef 19
Vidmar, Neil 186
Volcker, Paul 230

Waitzkin, Howard 49, 118, 152, 163
Wakin, Michelle 83, 86
Wallace, Mike 228
Walter, A. A. 174
Weber, Max 198
Wells, P. 279
West, Candace 14, 49, 152, 281
Whalen, Jack 49, 54–6, 59, 68–9, 71, 88–9, 91, 93, 98, 100, 225
Whalen, Marilyn 49, 54, 59, 62–5, 67–9, 71, 73–5, 86, 93, 98, 100
Wilkes, Michael 143, 152, 169
Wilkinson, Sue 25
Willey, Kathleen 182

Williams, A. 118
Wilson, Harold 229
Wilson, Thomas P. 65
Wolinsky, F. D. 134
Wolinsky, S. R. 134
Woodwell, David A. 122
Wootton, Anthony 19, 98

Zimmerman, Don H. 2, 14, 17, 39–40, 49, 54–5, 57–9, 62–9, 71–6, 80, 83, 86, 88–91, 93, 98, 100, 122
Zola, Irving K. 124, 133–4
Zoorob, R. J. 123

Index of Subjects

accountability 10–11
  in emergency calls 69–71
  in jury deliberations 188–91, 195–8
  normative 15
  of physician treatment recommendations
    160–3
acknowledgement tokens 25–7, 64, 113–16, 175,
    219, 221, 225
  and institutional roles 27–32, 64, 113, 175,
    219, 221, 225
  "mm hm" 113
    absence of 29
  "oh" 25–7
    absence of 29–32, 157
  "okay" 113
  "right" 113
adjacency pairs 22–4
answers 22–32, 46–7, 137–45, 150–1, 177–8,
    180–2, 220–2, 245–62
  agenda shifts 248–9, 256–8
  covert resistance 254
  and institutions 27–32
  "oh"-prefaced 25–7, 29–32
  overt resistance 247–54
  refusals 252–4
  "well"-prefaced 109
antibiotics prescribing 166–8
applause 262–79
  as coordinated action 265–6
  formats for inviting 267–73
    combinations 271–3
    contrasts 267–9
    lists 269–71

  puzzle-solution 271
  form vs. content in applaudable
    messages 275–6
  projectability of see projectability
  three stages in generating 274–5
"At first I thought" 108
  see also narrative
authority, medical see medical authority

B-event information 140
breaching experiments 10–11

Castle Doctrine 206
classroom interaction 27–8
context 21–2
  and talk 14–15
continuers 113–14
conversation analysis 7–19
  basic principles of 12–14
  history of 12
  institutional talk 16–17
  ordinary conversation 15–16
  research traditions in 15–17
  use of naturally occurring data in 13
  use of structural analysis in 13–14
conversational practices 15–16

Dallas call 93–9
dispute resolution, informal 200–11
  participant roles 201
  phases of activity in 201
  third party's role in 206–11
doctor–patient interaction see medical interaction

emergency calls 53–100
    actionable problems 60–71
    background 54–6
    call takers 54
        collaboration with dispatchers 54
        response to emotional callers 89–91
        skepticism of 72–4, 84–5, 93–4, 96–9
    caller's accountability 69–71
    caller's epistemic access to problem 73–8,
        96–7
    caller's expressions of concern 80–1
    caller's motivations 72–6
    caller's physical access to problem 75, 96–7
    caller's social involvement 75, 96–7
    computer-aided dispatch 55
    vs. conversational calls 60–2
    emotion 58–9, 87–92
        activity contamination 98–9
        "angry" callers 92
        displays of 88–9
        "hysterical" callers 91
        labeling of 91
        responses to 89–91, 93–9
    failure 58–9, 93–9
    five-phase structure 57–61, 99–100
    gatekeeping considerations 72–82, 85
    genuineness of caller's problem 72–8, 85
    history of 911 service 54
    identification/recognition process 63–4
    as interactional achievement 99–100
    interrogative series 57–8, 73–4, 82, 92, 94,
        96–7
        and emotion 92
        relevance of questions 58–9, 92, 95
        routine vs. investigatory questions 74, 82,
            94
    narratives 76–9
    openings 61–4
        vs. ordinary conversational calls 61–3
        reduction of 62–3
    promises of assistance 57–8, 82–5
        and closings 57
        "thank you" in 57, 82–5
    as public vs. private service 69–72
    relevance of caller's problem 78–82, 85
    requests 57–9, 64–7, 69–70
        descriptions of 65
        explicit 65
        justification of 69–72, 80–1
        narratives 76–9
        problem reports 65

    special patterns of inference 64–7
    "thank you" in 82–5
epistemics 25, 73–8, 96–7, 140–2
ethnomethods 9

face 8
frontline PBS series 186, 198

granularity 109

history taking in medicine *see* medical history
    taking

illness
    conditionally legitimate 120
    unconditionally legitimate 120
institutional talk 16–50
    characteristics of 34–7
    lexical choice 47–9
    objectives of researching 18–19
    vs. ordinary conversation 15–17, 36–49
    sequence organization 43–4
    structural organization 40–3
    turn design 45–7
    turn taking in 37–40
    see also conversation analysis
interaction order 8–9, 280
intersubjectivity 15
Iran–Contra scandal 222

journalism
    adversarialness in 228–9
    objectivity in 227–8
jury deliberations 186–99
    accountability in 188–91, 195–8
    activity structure 187–8
    juror conversions 189, 195–8
    practical reasoning in 188, 190–8
        hardline approach 191–3, 195, 198
        justice-inclusive approach 192, 195–6, 198
        knowledge-focused rationale 193–5, 198
    rationales for acquittal 191–5
    tasks of 187
jury foreperson 187–8
justice, formal vs. substantive 198

King, Rodney, trial of 182–5

legal formalism 173
legal realism 173
legitimation of illness

explicit 121
tacit 121
lexical choice 47–9, 205

maximal property of descriptions 181
mediation 200–1, 206–12
  facilitation, active 209–11
  facilitation, passive 207–9
  participant roles 201
  phases of activity in 201
medical authority 154–69
  and accountability *see* accountability
  changes in 154–5
  patient passivity to 157–60, 164
  physician-centered vs. patient-centered
    156–7
medical diagnosis 154–63
  evidence formulating 160–1
  evidentials 160, 162
  interactional management of 156–63
  and medical authority 156–63, 166–9
  patient resistance to 158–9
  patient response to 157–60, 164
  straight assertions in 160
  verbal design of 161
  see also online commentary
medical history taking 110–12, 115–17, 135–52
  importance of 135
  patient responses to 137–45
  question design in 136–51
    agenda setting 137–9
    checklist question 148–50
    congruent vs. cross-cutting preferences
      143–8
    dimensions of 136
    epistemic stance of 140–2
    lifestyle questions 150–1
    optimization 143–5
    preference organization 142–3
    presuppositions in 139–40
    problem attentiveness 145–7
    recipient design 147–8
    transition from problem presentation
      110–12, 115–17
medical interaction 31–2, 103–70
  origins of research in 103–4
  phases in 104–5
medical problem presentation 105–32
  beginning 109
  candidate diagnosis vs. symptoms only 122–3
  ending 110–12

extended 108–19
  importance of 104–5
  incompleteness in 113–15
  legitimacy of problems 120–32
    conditional vs. unconditional 120–2
  length of 106–7, 109–10
  narratives in 108–10, 112, 115, 128–32
    turning points 130–2
  negotiation of length 110–15
  resistance to ending 111–12
  tense in 111–12
  transition to history taking 110–12, 115–17
  troubles resistance, displays of 123, 131–2
  types of 121–32
    recurrent 124–7
    routine 122–4
    unknown 127–32
medical treatment recommendations 164–8
  and antibiotics *see* antibiotics prescribing
  patient endorsement of 165
  patient resistance to 165–7
  physician accountability for 160–3

narratives 76–9, 108–10, 112, 115–16, 128–32,
    195
  see also medical problem presentation
neutralism 29, 216, 225, 228, 237–8, 240–1
  departures from 240–1
news interviews 215–62
  acknowledgement tokens, absence of 29–30,
    219, 221, 225
  adversarialness 228–34, 238–9
  answers in 220–2, 245–62
    elaborated 220–1
    minimal 221–2
  defensible questioning in 234–8
  historical context of 241–3
  neutralism in *see* neutralism
  question–answer rule 217–18, 220
    departures from 222–5
  questions in 218–20, 227–41
    accusatory 240
    adversarialness of 228–34, 238–9
    agendas 229–31
    contrasts 239
    footing shifts 236–8
    forks 238–9
    justifications 234–6
    prefaces 218–19, 230–4
    preferences 232–4
    presuppositions 231–2

news interviews (*Cont'd*)
   resistance to questions in 221–2, 247–62
      covert 254–8
      dimensions of 247, 252
      overt 247–54
   as talk for overhearers 29, 216
   turn-taking in 215–18
      significance of 215–16
      institutional functions 225
norms *see* accountability; normative

online commentary 168
ordinary conversation 12–16
   primacy of 12–13
   vs. institutional talk *see* institutional talk

physician diagnostic styles 156–7
plea bargaining 200–12
   event formulation 204–5
   facilitation, active 209–11
   facilitation, passive 207–9
   implicit negotiation in 202–6
   judge's role in 206–7, 209–10
   laughter during 205–6
   lexical choice in 205
   participant roles 201
   person formulation 202–4
   phases of activity in 201
problem presentation in medicine *see* medical
      problem presentation
projectability 265–6

question design 22–32, 45–7, 106–7, 135–52,
      175–8, 204, 218–20, 227–41
   action agendas 136–8, 228–30
   agenda setting 137–9, 228–31
   declarative 140–3
   epistemics 25, 140–2
   footing 236–8
   forks and contrasts 238–9
   interrogative 140–3, 220

justifications 234–6
optimization 143–5
polarity 142–3, 204
prefaces 218–19, 230, 234
preference organization 142–5, 232–4
presuppositions 139–40, 231–2
topic agendas 136–8, 228–9
yes/no formulation 138–41, 180, 220, 232–3

receipt tokens *see* acknowledgement tokens
recipient design 136, 147–51
reflexivity 11

shift implicatives 113, 115
sick role 119, 120
speeches, public 263–79
   applause and *see* applause

tic-tac-toe 10–11
transition relevance place 216
trial examinations 173–85
   answers in 177–8, 180–2
      implicit rejection 180–2
      resistance 177–8, 180–5
   general features of 176–8
   language practices in 174, 184
   questioning in 177–8
   receipt tokens, absence of 175, 221
   resisting material evidence 182–5
   Rodney King trial 182–5
   as talk for overhearers 30–1, 175
   turn-taking system 176
turn design *see* institutional talk
turn taking 36–40, 215–26
   as a normative organization 39
   departures 222–5
   see also institutional talk
troubles resistance, displays of *see* medical
      problem presentation

YouTube 215